COMPARATIVE PUBLIC ADMINISTRATION

Dr. Sewa Singh Dahiya
and
Dr. Ravindra Singh

STERLING PUBLISHERS (P) LTD.
Regd. Office: A1/256 Safdarjung Enclave, New Delhi-110029.
CIN: U22110DL1964PTC211907
Phone: +91 82877 98380 /+91 120-6251823
E-mail: mail@sterlingpublishers.in
www.sterlingpublishers.in

Comparative Public Administration
© 2012, Dr. Sewa Singh Dahiya and Dr. Ravindra Singh
ISBN 978 81 207 7752 1
Reprint : 2014, 2021

All rights are reserved. No part of this publication may be reproduced, stored in a retrieval system or transmitted, in any form or by any means, mechanical, photocopying, recording or otherwise, without prior written permission of the original publisher.

Printed and Published by

Sterling Publishers Pvt. Ltd.,
Plot No. 13, Ecotech-III, Greater Noida - 201306, U. P. India

PREFACE

The present work is an attempt to provide a simple understanding of the literature in the field of comparative public administration. It is an endeavour to highlight the context as well as contents of this sub-discipline. This sub-discipline tries to analyse the administrative systems of various countries embedded in different cultures by penetrating into the internal dynamics of their administrative systems. Even though several efforts have been made to generate literature in this field, yet the need of a textbook encompassing the conceptual framework is widely felt. The present work is a modest attempt in this direction. The first five chapters of the book deal with the conceptual framework of the sub-discipline whereas the administrative systems of UK, USA, France, India and Japan are explained in the next five chapters. The book has been written mainly to cater to the academic requirements of the post-graduate and M. Phil students of Public Administration and Political Science disciplines. It will also serve the purpose of candidates appearing for civil services examinations in India and abroad.

Our thanks are due to Prof. S.C. Arora, Prof S.S. Charar and other colleagues from the Department of Public Administration, M.D. University, Rohtak and Prof. Mohinder Singh and Prof. Ajmer Singh from the Department of Public Administration, Kurukshetra University, Kurukshetra, for their help and active encouragement which was a great source of inspiration for getting this book published. We are also thankful to the other scholars who have contributed in this field and from whom we borrowed liberally. We would also like to express our sincere thanks to Mr. S.K. Ghai, Managing Director, Sterling Publishers, who constantly encouraged us to complete this venture. In the end, we want to express our deepest gratitude to our wives and children for their constant support, endurance and encouragement.

The second author expresses his deep sense of gratitude to Professor Mool Chand Sharma, Vice-Chancellor, Central University of Haryana, who through his democratic leadership not only creates ample opportunities for learning in the university but also emphasises on development of scientific temperament. Indeed, the great educationist, educational administrator and legal luminary has been a great source of motivation for the second author who has been immensely benefitted by his scholarly wisdom in numerous ways, which, of course, includes the present work.

We accept the sole responsibility for any errors of fact or interpretation that might have inadvertently crept into this book. We would like to welcome suggestions from the readers towards the improvement of the book.

Authors

CONTENTS

Chapter-1	Introduction	1

- **Post Second World War Phase**
- **Systematic Beginning of Comparative Public Administration**
- **Nature**
- **Scope**
- **Significance**

Chapter-2	Comparative Public Administration: Approaches	17

- **Ecological Approach**
  - Meaning
  - Development
  - Salient Features
  - Appraisal
- **Structural-Functional Approach**
  - Essence
  - Terms Defined
  - Basic Assumptions
  - Salient Features
  - Contribution
  - Critical Evaluation
- **Behavioural Approach**
  - Essence
  - Development
  - Salient Features
  - Contribution
  - Appraisal

Chapter-3	Environment of Administration	33

- **Social Environment**
  - Social Stratification
  - Familial and Kinship Ties
  - Social Ethos and Values
  - Social and Voluntary Associations
  - Societal Ambitiousness
- **Cultural Environment**
  - Issue of Language
  - Regionalism
  - Religion
  - Communication
  - Symbols

- **Economic Environment**
  - Prioritisation Through Planning
  - Level of Economic Development
  - Technology
  - Technical Manpower
  - Resources
- **Political Environment**
  - Nature of State
  - Constitution
  - Political Parties
  - Pressure Groups
  - Public Opinion and Mass Media
  - Coalition Government

Chapter-4 Administrative Features: Developing & Developed   51

A. Developing Countries
- Structural Features
- Functional Features

B. Developed Countries
- Structural Features
- Functional Features

Chapter-5 Contribution of F.W. Riggs & Ferrel Heady in CPA   62

Riggs
Life Sketch
Main Contributions
- Prismatic Model
  - Formalism
    - Heterogeneity
  - *Poly-Communalism and Existence of 'Clects'*
    - *Heterogeneity in Economics: Bazar Canteen Model*
  - *Poly-Normativism and Lack of Consensus*
    - Overlapping
- Sala Model
  - Bureaucratic Recruitment/Nepotism
  - Institutionalized Corruption
  - Influence of Clects
  - Normlessness or Dissensus in Sala
  - Disengagement of Authority and Control
  - Bureaucratic Domination over Political Leadership

Appraisal

Ferrel Heady
- **Life Sketch**
- **Main Contributions**
- **Administration In Less Developed Countries**
  Political Regime Variations
  - Bureaucracy-Prominent Political Regimes
  - *Traditional Elite Systems*

- Personalist Bureaucratic Elite Systems
- Collegial Bureaucratic Elite System
- Pendulum System
- Party Prominent Political Regimes
- Polyarchal Competitive Systems
- Dominant Party Semi-Competitive Systems
- Dominant Party Mobilisation Systems
- Communist Totalitarian Systems •

-- **Common Administrative Patterns**
  - Imitative rather than Indigenous Administrative Patterns
  - Bureaucracy with Unskilled Manpower
  - Non-Achievement Orientation of Bureaucracy
  - Widespread Discrepancy Between Form and Reality
  - Operational Autonomy of Bureaucracy

-- **Administration in More Developed Countries**
  • Shared Political and Administrative Characteristics
  • Variation in the Administrative Systems of Developed Nations

-- **Evaluation**

Chapter-6 Administrative System in Great Britain   88
- Administrative Features
- Political Executive
- Local Government
- Control over Administration

Chapter-7 Administrative System in the USA   144
- Administrative Features
- Political Executive
- Local Government
- Control over Administration

Chapter-8 Administrative System in France   193
- Administrative Features
- Political Executive
- Local Government
- Control over Administration

Chapter-9 Administrative System in India   227
- Administrative Features
- Political Executive
- Local Government
- Control over Administration

Chapter-10 Administrative System in Japan   274
- Administrative Features
- Political Executive
- Local Government
- Control over Administration

1
INTRODUCTION

*C*omparative public administration is the youngest discipline among the family of social sciences. As an academic discipline, it came into existence in the post Second-World War period. Even though literature on public administration in the pre-War period lacked cross-cultural component, it was not devoid of a comparative element. Besides, it provided necessary background for the growth and development of the discipline in the post-War period. Therefore, it would be pertinent to analyse the early literature from that perspective.

Before the passage of the Pendleton Act in 1883, spoils system was prevailing in the US.[1] This Act replaced spoils system for selection to the civil services by merit criterion. The passage of this Act was the result of assassination of President Garfield by one of his disgruntled supporter whom the former failed in providing a job. His assassination was followed by political and administrative turmoil in America. While the relevance of spoils system as a method of recruitment was being debated, Woodrow Wilson published his seminal essay *The Study of Administration*[2] in 1887. In his writing, Wilson floated the idea that certain administrative practices of European countries need be studied and even could be borrowed by the U.S.A., "without adopting their autocratic spirit". He argued that "if I see a murderous fellow sharpening a knife cleverly, I can borrow his way of sharpening the knife without borrowing his probable intention to commit murder with it"[3]. He was interested in gaining more and more knowledge about the administrative systems of European countries and to borrow certain good practices from their administrative systems for incorporating them in the administration of the United States of America. Thus, Woodrow Wilson, the father of public administration, may also be regarded as a pioneer in the field of introducing a comparative element in the study of public administration.

F.W. Taylor launched the scientific management movement in the late nineteenth and early twentieth century. This emerged in response to gross inefficiency and wastage of resources at the time of onset of industrial revolution in Europe and USA. The principles of scientific management were proclaimed to have universal applicability. His philosophy of "one best way" was conceived to be a "scientific methodology of careful observation, measurement and generalization". Taylor's ideas

---

1   Public administration as a discipline of study originated in America and, therefore, it would be pertinent to explore the American literature on public administration in order to trace the comparative element in that literature. Also, early American administrative thought may be traced back to the Jacksonian era but the systematic beginning of the discipline does not go beyond 1887.
2   Wilson, Woodrow, "The Study of Administration", *Political Science Quarterly*, II, 1887, pp. 197-222.
3   *Ibid*

and philosophy culminated in an international movement for scientific management and were even adopted by Lenin in managing Soviet industrial enterprises. Taylor's ideas, viewed from his temporal perspective, were applicable in a cross-national setting for large-scale production. The scientific management in the United States emphasized the concepts of "economy" and "efficiency" in the administrative working and thus popularized the search for universal generalizations on administrative procedure.[4]

White's *Introduction to the Study of Public Administration* and Willoughby's *Principles of Administration,* as also of others during the 1920s and 1930s claimed, that public administration is a science and laid down certain principles (of public administration) having universal applicability. While supporting this claim, L.D. White observed "a principle, considered as tested hypothesis and applied in the light of its appropriate frame of reference, is a useful guide to action in the public administration of Russia as of Great Britain, of Irak as of the United States."[5] Willoughby also pointed out that there are "fundamental principles of general application analogous to those characterizing any science,... and these principles are to be determined and their significance made known, only by the rigid application of scientific method."[6] Other scholars of this period expressed almost identical views and claimed that the principles of public administration have cross-cultural applicability.

Human relations school of thought, pioneered by Follet, Carnage, Rothlisberger, Dickson and Mayo challenged the mechanistic view of organisation and the claim of the earlier scholars regarding the universal applicability of the principles of public administration. This school of thought strongly condemned the idea that human beings are solely motivated by the economic incentives and emphasized that human beings are not merely "cogs" or "glorified tools" to fit into the mechanistic theory of organisation. Elton Mayo and Rothlisberger conducted a series of experiments, popularly known as the "Hawthorne experiments" and on the basis of these experiments proved that human beings are motivated by "non-economic considerations" as well. In the process of these experiments, they also propounded the concept of informal organisation, which was considered to be the precondition for the success of formal organisation.

Though the studies conducted by the human relationists were inter-organisational, they were not cross-cultural because this movement "was a response to the specific needs of an industrial society in a particular period of economic stress."[7] Hence this movement, though contributed to the behavioural movement in public administration, could not contribute much to the field of comparative public administration.

The Roosevelt administration responded to the economic depression of the 1930s by launching the New Deal programme, which expanded the scope of activities of American administration. Through this programme, certain internal changes – both

---

4   Al-Salem, Faisal S.A., *The Ecological Dimensions of Development Administration*, New Delhi: Associated Publishing House, 1977, p. 53.
5   White, L.D., "*The Meaning of Principles of Public Administration*" in Gaus, John M., L.D. White, and Marshall E. Dimock (eds.), *The Frontiers of Public Administration*, Chicago: University of Chicago Press, 1936, p. 7.
6   Willoughby, W.F. as quoted in Arora, R.K., *Comparative Public Administration*, New Delhi: Associated Publishing House, 1996, p. 8.
7   *Ibid*, p. 9.

qualitative and quantitative – in the U.S. administrative system were brought in. This programme was comparative to the extent that it highlighted the "desirability of cross-cultural borrowings and adaptations"[8]. In other words, this programme expressed the desirability of exploring the possibility of borrowing certain administrative practices from other countries.

Thus, it may be concluded that though there existed a comparative element in the traditional literature but it failed in providing a systematic shape to the discipline. It was because the comparisons in that literature were primarily descriptive rather than analytical. These comparisons were "culture bound", limited to the western nations, were non-ecological in perspective and lacked cross-cultural, cross-temporal and cross-national element. Therefore, the traditional literature was "non-comparative" in character[9]. However these studies contributed significantly in promoting the traditional concepts such as authority, control, co-ordination, planning, organization, efficiency, economy etc. thereby preparing a base for the systematic development of comparative public administration.

POST SECOND WORLD WAR PHASE

The post Second World War phase is characterized by an identity crisis in public administration. The claim for universal applicability of the principles of public administration had been belied and the human relations movement also could not provide much direction to the discipline. This rendered the discipline directionless and its scholars were hard pressed to identify certain new trends to give a direction to the discipline. These efforts came from many and varied quarters. Scholars like Edwin Stene, Herbert Simon and Dwight Waldo emphasized the need for more "scientific" explanations in the literature on public administration;[10] others like Robert Dahl, demanded more rigorous cross-cultural comparisons in the study of public administration. He held that traditional literature on public administration was culture-bound, normative, non-ecological, and was primarily descriptive rather than analytic, explanatory and problem oriented and seldom involved cross-cultural and cross-temporal analyses. This literature was restricted to the study of western administrative systems, which represented the same culture. Highlighting the inability of this literature to provide the discipline of public administration the status of a 'science', Robert Dahl emphasized the importance of comparison as a pre-requisite for the development of a science of public administration. [11] This provided much needed direction to the discipline and the scholars got motivated to transcend the national boundaries while conducting research in public administration. Thus, dissatisfaction of the scholars with the parochial nature of traditional literature may be stated as an important reason for the growth of the discipline of comparative public administration during the post-War period.

---

8 Al-Salem, Faisal S.A., *The Ecological Dimensions of Development Administration*, New Delhi: Associated Publishing House, 1977, p. 53.
9 Arora, R.K., *op. cit.*, 1996, p. 10.
10 *Ibid*, p. 9.
11 Dahl emphasized that "as long as the study of public administration is not comparative, claims for a 'science' of public administration sound rather hollow." See Dahl, Robert, "The Science of Public Administration: Three Problems", *Public Administration Review*, VII, 1947, pp. 1-11.

Secondly, during the war period, both sides annexed some of the colonies of the rival forces in the Afro-Asian and Latin American continents. These annexations provided an opportunity to the practitioners of administration to get an exposure to the administrative systems of the annexed countries. They, however, found that the administrative systems of the annexed territories differed a great deal from that of their native system and when they tried the established principles of administration evolved in the western setting, they could not succeed. This evoked an urge among the scholars to study the administrative systems of the countries outside Europe and America.

Thirdly, after the Second World War, several countries of Asia, Africa and Latin America became independent by throwing away the yoke of imperialism. The newly emerged countries were greatly exploited and at the dawn of their independence, they were facing enormous problems like those of poverty, unemployment, hunger, ill-health, illiteracy, agricultural and industrial backwardness, lack of infrastructure, to name a few. Centuries of imperial rule, however, rendered them impoverished to an extent that they were not able to resolve their problems with their internally generated resources. They badly needed technological and financial assistance which the NATO and the Warsaw Pact blocks[12] offered to provide on the condition of diplomatic support in the UN General Assembly. However, the assistance programme failed in realizing the desired objectives and the newly liberated countries, even with this generous technical and financial support could not resolve many of their problems, which evoked a keen interest among the scholars of the funding countries[13] to analyze the administrative systems of these liberated countries with a view to locate the reasons for the failure of these programmes.

Fourthly, in the post war period, a number of agencies came forward to extend financial support to the institutions and scholars engaged in conducting research abroad, particularly in the developing countries. The Ford Foundation and the Agency for International Development were prominent among them. These agencies were interested to know more about the administrative problems of the emerging countries. This gave impetus to research efforts in comparative public administration. With financial assistance from the Ford Foundation, the Comparative Administrative Group (CAG) contributed significantly in the study of administrative system of developing countries. Thus, favourable opportunities existed for those interested in conducting research in the field of comparative public administration during the 1950s and 1960s.

Further, before independence the leadership of the freedom movement of the newly liberated countries promised a 'problem free life' to their countrymen once they gained independence. This immensely increased the expectations of the people of these countries. However, due to poor economic conditions and inexperienced

---

12 North Atlantic Treaty Organisation or NATO is an intergovernmental military alliance based on the North Atlantic Treaty which was signed on April 4, 1949. The WARSAW Pact was a mutual defense treaty between eight communist states of Eastern Europe initiated on the initiative of Soviet Union. It was signed on May 14, 1955 in Warsaw.

13 Since America and the Soviet Union were the leaders of their respective block, the scholars from the two countries were more keen to study the administrative system of the developing countries. However, far greater contribution came from the side of America than from the USSR.

politico-administrative leadership, these countries failed in fulfilling the expectations of their countrymen and came under fire. Consequently, the administrations in the developing countries were compelled to seek guidance from the developed countries of the West to make their administrative system more efficient so that it could fulfill the expectations of the people. Several of these countries even invited administrative experts and scholars for this purpose from the developed countries, particularly from America.[14] This helped promote comparative studies in the field of public administration.

Again, the post Second War phase witnessed the rise of neo-imperialism in which the developed countries of the West, instead of capturing the third world countries politically, showed their interest in capturing them economically and socially. Consequently, research institutes in a greater number were promoted for conducting research on social and economic issues in developing countries and generous financial help was extended to them. This also gave impetus to comparative administrative studies during the post Second World War period.

Systematic Beginning of Comparative Public Administration

The systematic beginning of comparative public administration can be traced to the first Conference on Comparative Public Administration, which was held at Princeton University (USA) in 1952 under the auspices of the Public Administration Clearing House. The Conference appointed, under the Committee on Public Administration, a Sub-Committee on Comparative Public Administration to develop "criteria of relevance" and a design for field studies in foreign countries. In 1953, an ad hoc Sub-Committee on Comparative Administration was constituted by the American Political Science Association (APSA) that continued till the creation of the Comparative Administration Group under the American Society for Public Administration (ASPA).[15]

The Comparative Administration Group (CAG) was setup in 1963 with a membership comprising of academics and practitioners from countries other than the United States. The Ford foundation was the chief funding agency of the CAG. Study of administrative problems of the developing countries was the primary focus of the Ford Foundation and "the CAG was expected to analyse these problems in the context of societal environmental factors found in these countries."[16] The CAG was initially funded for a period of 3 years. However, in 1966 the second grant to the CAG was provided for a period of 5 years. Riggs was its first chairman and held this position for seven years, from 1963-1970. He was succeeded by Richard Gable in 1970. In 1971, the Ford Foundation withdrew its financial support to the CAG, which thereafter managed its resources from other quarters. The CAG was created with the following three-fold objectives

(i) Increasing the volume of research
(ii) Improving teaching material and methods, and

---

14 For instance, the services of the famous American administrative expert Paul H. Appleby were hired by the Indian government to point out the maladies in the Indian administration and to suggest suitable measures for improvement.
15 Arora, R.K. *op. cit.,* 1996, pp. 18-19.
16 Heady, Ferrel., *Public Administration: A Comparative Perspective*, New York:Marcel Dekker, 1991, p. 18.

(iii) Stimulating the formulation and implementation of more effective public policies in the field of development administration.[17]

The CAG framed an elaborate network for carrying out its obligations to stimulate interest in comparative public administration, with special reference to the social, cultural, political, economic problems faced by the administration in developing countries. Special conferences and seminars were scheduled on various topics both in the United States and abroad in order to improve teaching materials and methods. A number of small sub-grants were provided for experimental teaching programmes. the CAG acted as a bridge between the scholars of administration and administrative officials (practitioners) who were interested in the groups' programmes. The CAG was international in scope and conducted and encouraged research in comparative public administration in Asia, Latin America, Africa and Europe. The cross-cultural and cross-national approach was adopted with a view to make theory-building exercise meaningful. The CAG members remained engaged in the business of advising and delivering lectures on varied problems in these emerging nations regarding their administration.

A committee structure was evolved and 11 committees were constituted under the CAG. These committees can be bifurcated into two categories: committees having geographical orientation and committees having subject matter orientation. The committees having geographical orientation included – committees on Asia, Europe, Latin America and Africa while the committees having subject matter orientation included – committees on comparative urban studies, national economic planning, comparative educational administration, comparative legislative studies, international administration, organization theory and systems theory. These committees were not equally active or productive[18]. Most of these committees worked in liaison with international agencies such as the United Nations Organizations, Agency for International Development as well as with various national governments[19].

The CAG made a tremendous contribution to the study of public administration in general and comparative public administration in particular, through the sponsorship of research seminars and conferences abroad and works for the improvement of teaching materials and approaches. The work of the CAG was reflected in its publications in various forms such as newsletters, seminar reports, teaching materials, occasional papers etc. The regular publication of the CAG Newsletter, served as a channel of communication among its members working at far-flung places. The literature produced by the CAG scholars on comparative public administration was enormous and was published in various forms. The Duke University Press published a series of seven volumes in co-operation with the CAG during the period 1969 to 1973. This included several books and research papers on different aspects of comparative public administration and development administration. Sage Publications also issued a quarterly journal on comparative public administration in co-operation with CAG for a period of five years from 1969-1974[20].

---

17 Quah, Jon S.T., *Comparative Public Administration: What and Why?*, in Arora, R.K. (ed.) (1979), *Perspective in Administrative Theory*, New Delhi: Associated Publishing House, p. 14.
18 *Ibid*, p. 19.
19 Arora, R.K., *op. cit.*, 1996, p. 20.
20 Heady, Ferrel, *op. cit.*, 1991, p. 19.

The CAG was rich in its scholarship, prominent among whom were F.W. Riggs, Ferrel Heady, William Siffin, John Montgomery, D. Waldo, Ralph Braibanti, James Heaphey, Fredrick Cleveland, and Frank Sherwood. These scholars contributed significantly and opened new vistas in the field of comparative administration. Their contribution proved helpful in opening the doors of the discipline to the scholars of different disciplines which made the discipline of comparative public administration highly inter-disciplinary.

The main contributor to the CAG was the Ford Foundation, which continued to finance its activities till 1971. However, when in 1971, the Ford Foundation enquired about the direction in which the CAG was going and the progress made by it, the later could not solicit a satisfactory answer whereupon the former decided to terminate the grant for any further duration. The Group faced severe financial crisis but somehow managed to exist with financial support coming from other quarters. But ultimately, it went out of existence in 1973, when it was merged with the International Committee of the American Society for Public Administration to form a new Section on International and Comparative Administration (SICA). SICA continued with the same membership and engaged in almost all the activities started by the CAG i.e. participation in professional meetings, issuance of a newsletter and distribution of occasional papers, but all at a somewhat reduced level.[21]

Besides, the post CAG phase is marked by the creation of several regional institutes for the promotion of comparative public administration. The South-East Asian Development Administration Group (SEADAG) by the Asia Society of New York, the Asian Centre for Development Administration (ACDA) in Kuala Lumpur, Malaysia, by the member governments of the ESCAP countries and the United Nations and the Latin American Development Administration Committee (LADAC) by the former CAG are prominent among them. All these institutes "provided scholars from these regions with further avenues of co-operating among themselves or with other scholars in joint research projects designed to improve both the quality and quantity of public administration research in the developing countries"[22].

At present the Institutes of Public Administration in most of the developing countries, such as the Indian Institute of Public Administration, the Philippines Institute of Public Administration etc., are engaged in conducting researches, seminars and workshops on comparative administration. Besides, the students and scholars of public administration are conducting comparative studies on various aspects in their respective countries adopting cross-cultural, cross national, intra-national, inter-institutional, cross-temporal settings. The literature so produced is enriching the subject matter of comparative public administration.

In 'comparative public administration', the word 'comparative' is a prefix to 'public administration'. Therefore, to understand the meaning of 'comparative public administration', we first need to define public administration. The word 'administration' refers to "management of affairs to achieve certain goal(s)". Taken in this sense, 'public administration' means "management of governmental affairs

---

21 *Ibid*, p. 26.
22 Quah, Jon S.T., *Comparative Public Administration: What and Why?* in Arora, R.K. (ed.) (1979), *op. cit.*, p. 15.

towards the realization of common goal(s)". Thus comparative public administration may mean 'the management of governmental affairs towards the realization of common goal(s) in a comparative perspective'. But this definition does not give a true idea of comparative public administration.

The CAG adopted the following definition of comparative public administration: "the theory of public administration as applied to diverse cultures and national settings" and "the body of factual data, by which it can be expanded and tested."[23] Robert H. Jackson defined comparative public administration as "that facet of the study of public administration which is concerned with making rigorous cross-cultural comparisons of the structures and processes involved in the activity of administering public affairs,"[24] This definition of comparative public administration seems more convincing.

NATURE

Jon S.T. Quah has laid down certain characteristics of comparative public administration. It seems that these characteristics portray the nature of comparative public administration and are, therefore, related below:

1. Recent Origin

Comparative public administration, which is a sub-discipline of public administration, is of recent origin. According to Raphaeli, "Comparative public administration is a new comer to the community of academic instruction and research"[25]. Its origin can be traced to the post-Second World War phase, to the *Princeton University Conference on Administration* held in 1952, to be precise. Thus the sub-discipline is barely 60 years old and may be stated as still an infant. It came into existence as a result of probing into the failures of techno-economic assistance programme of the US to the third world countries.

2. Absence of Dominant Paradigms

In natural and physical sciences, the research efforts are generally guided by the existence of some universally recognized scientific achievements usually termed as paradigms. These paradigms play a significant role in resolving the problems faced by the scientific community. Whenever some paradigm fails in resolving some problem, the existing paradigm is replaced by a new one. This process of replacement is called scientific revolution[26].

Taken in this sense, none of the social sciences can boast of having a paradigm. Even the grandparent discipline of comparative public administration i.e. political science, lacks a paradigm in the sense of what the natural and physical sciences

---

23 Quoted in Heady, Ferrel, *Comparative Public Administration: Concerns and Priorities* in Heady, Ferrel and Stokes, Sybil L. (eds.), 1962, *Papers in Comparative Public Administration*, Ann Arbor, Michigan: Institute of Public Administration, University of Michigan, p. 4.
24 Jackson, Robert H., *An Analysis of Comparative Public Administration Movement* in *Canadian Public Administration*, No. IX (March), 1966, p. 110.
25 Raphaeli, Nimrod, *Comparative Public Administration: An Overview* in Raphaeli, Nimrod (ed.), *Readings in Comparative Public Administration*, Boston: Allyn and Bacon, 1967, p. 1.
26 Kuhn, Thomas S. as quoted in Quah, Jon S.T., *Comparative Public Administration: What and Why?* in Arora, R.K. (ed.), 1979, *op. cit.*, p. 13.

have. However, most of the social sciences claim to have certain paradigms which though have limited applicability. Comparative public administration has not been able to develop some paradigm even in this sense. Thus, there exists a multitude of competing approaches in the field of comparative public administration.

3. Multi-Perspective Character

Comparative public administration is characterized by the existence of a number of perspectives. Several scholars have provided several perspectives, most prominent among whom is the Riggsian classification of these perspectives. He observed three broad trends in the comparative study of public administration. These are

1. From Normative to empirical orientation
2. From ideographic to nomothetic orientation
3. From non-ecological to ecological orientation[27]

Those studies which are "value-laden" are called normative studies whereas "value-free" or data based studies are categorized as empirical studies. Non-ecological studies neglect the environmental setting in which an administrative institution is operating while the ecological studies give due importance to these settings. The terms of second category are peculiarly Riggsian. To him, "ideographic studies" focused on the "unique case – the historical episode or 'case study', the single agency or country, the biography or the 'culture area" whereas nomothetic studies pertain to "generalizations, 'laws', hypotheses that assert regularities of behaviour, correlation with variables"[28]. In other words, ideographic studies are case studies whereas nomothetic studies are generalized ones.

Heady also attempted to classify various perspectives in comparative public administration in the following four categories:

1. Modified Traditional
2. Development Oriented
3. General System Model-Building
4. Middle-Range Theory-Formulation[29]

The modified traditional studies are in continuity with the earlier traditional literature and basically include descriptive comparison of administration in Western countries. The development-oriented studies generally take into consideration the "rapid socio-economic and political change" having emphasis on the "capabilities of the administrative systems to direct socio-economic change in a society". The general system model building studies focus on the whole society and are concerned with the "administrative systems in the overall contexts of their social environment". The focus of the subject matter of studies on middle-range theory is more specific. Besides, these concentrate on more important parts of an administrative system that are sufficiently large in size and scope of functioning[30].

---

27 Riggs, F.W., "Trends in the Comparative Study of Public Administration" in *International Review of Administrative Sciences*, Vol. XXVIII, 1962, pp. 9-15.
28 *Ibid*, p. 11.
29 Heady, Ferrel, *op. cit.*, 1991, p. 13.
30 Arora R,.K. *op. cit.*, 1996, p. 36.

Henderson has highlighted the following three-fold categorization of the perspectives in comparative public administration:
1. The Bureaucratic System Approach
2. The Input-Output System Approach
3. The Component Approach[31]

The bureaucratic system approach may be regarded as a middle-range conceptual construct and thus may be equated with Heady's fourth categorization viz. 'middle-range theory formulation'. Similarly, the second categorization of Henderson viz. input-output approach can be equated with Heady's third category of 'general system model building as it is based on general systems framework. Henderson's component approach includes "all types of partial approaches dealing with administrative procedures, with control and responsibility and with informal behaviour of administrators."[32]

4. Dominance of American Scholarship

Most of the literature produced on comparative public administration until recently is contributed by the American scholars on public administration and in that also particularly by the CAG scholars. Also the financial assistance came from the US government as well as other agencies such as the Ford Foundation. The US provided techno-economic assistance to the newly emerging third world countries of the Asian, African and Latin American continents. The failure of this assistance programme generated an urge in both the American scholars on public administration and the US government.

5. Theory-Building Efforts

There has been considerable emphasis on theory building by the scholars in comparative public administration mainly because theories and models prove helpful in developing a new field of enquiry. Initially, theory-building efforts in comparative public administration focused on general and middle-range theories. The Agraria-Industria and the Fused-Prismatic-Diffracted models of Riggs and the Information-Energy model of John T. Dorsey may be categorized as the general theories in the field whereas the Weberian Ideal Type Bureaucracy is generally regarded as the middle-range theory. Later on, several scholars including Robert Presthus and Subramanian have advocated a shift from the general theory-building to the middle-range and micro level theorization. This has been because of the unduly comprehensive, all-inclusive and abstract character of the general theories.[33]

6. Emphasis on Development Administration

The techno-economic assistance programme of the then two superpowers had twin objectives. First, was to provide technological and economic assistance to the newly emerged nation states so that they might resolve their socio-economic problems that they received in inheritance and thus to help them to develop. But the more

---
31 Henderson, Keith, *Emerging Synthesis in American Public Administration*, Bombay: Asia Publishing House, 1966, pp. 52-58.
32 Arora R.K. *op. cit.*, 1996, pp. 36-37.
33 Quah, Jon S.T., *Comparative Public Administration: What and Why?* in Arora, R.K. (ed.), *op. cit.*, 1979, p. 16.

significant objective was to woo the maximum number of these countries to their respective block. Through this process they wanted to ensure diplomatic support from the assistance recipient countries for all their deeds in the United Nations General Assembly in which, each one of these newly emerged countries had a vote.

The diplomatic objective aside, however, the techno-economic assistance programme definitely tried to help these countries to develop. Through the assistance programme the administrative systems of these countries were assigned the responsibility to take up the task of development thereat. Consequently, the administration in these countries was nomenclatured as Development Administration. But the assistance programme failed in realizing its objective. There arose, therefore, the necessity for analysis. The scholars in the field of public administration, therefore, studied the administrative systems of these countries in a comparative perspective to find out the reasons behind the failure. These scholars found that the administrative systems prevailing in these countries were found to be a total misfit to take up the gigantic task of development thereat. They concentrated their research efforts on the administrative system, of these countries and reached the conclusion that there was a need to build up the capability of their administration to cope with the challenges of development.

Consequently, development administration with both of its facets viz. administration of development and development of administration became a focus of attention of the comparative public administration scholars. In this connection, Quah has rightly observed, "development administration is just one facet, albeit an important facet, of the study of comparative public administrative and should be seen as such. Its importance should not be exaggerated nor underestimated."[34]

SCOPE

It is as quite difficult to describe the scope of comparative public administration, as that of public administration for, the scope of comparative public administration is coterminous with the scope of public administration. This is because whatever one administrative structure does in one environmental setting is comparable with its counterpart in another environmental setting and are thus, comparable.

But now the question arises as to what should be included in the scope of comparative public administration. One may highlight the following broad areas, though the list is, by no means, exhaustive:

1. **Polity:** Irrespective of the nature of State and of the form of government, the polity of a country has always deep imprint on the administrative system. The political leadership, political ideology and the style of functioning of the chief executive are most prominent areas in this connection. Therefore, a comparative analysis of various countries of all the above said areas can be conducted and therefore, constitute an integral part of the scope of comparative public administration.

2. **Social Welfare:** Social welfare covers the problems pertaining to food, housing, health, education, social security, social welfare, employment etc. Various administrative systems devise structures to discharge these functions. The structures performing these functions in diverse environmental settings are comparable and thus fall in the purview of comparative public administration.

---
34 *Ibid,* p. 18.

3. **Economy:** It deals with the activities of various sectors of the economy viz., industry, agriculture, foreign trade and commerce, public enterprises etc. for ensuring a prosperous and stable economy. All the administrative structures involved in discharging these functions across the globe in different environmental settings can be compared with one another.
4. **Education:** Elementary education is regarded as an important obligation of the administration in almost all the countries of the world. To this end, administrative structures are created by it. Therefore, a comparative analysis of these structures working in one cultural setting may be conducted with their counterparts rooted in another cultural setting. Resultantly, such comparisons also constitute a part of the scope of the comparative public administration.
5. **Defense:** The administration is also obliged to take effective measures in the field of defense as well, for, the stability and progress of a country depends upon how much effectively its policies in the field of defense are. These policies include both maintenance of internal order and defending its external boundaries. Therefore, a comparative analysis of the defense strategies adopted by the administrative systems of various countries is an integral part of the scope of comparative public administration.
6. **Management of Financial Affairs:** Analysis of the entire financial managements of two different administrative structures operating in diverse environmental settings also comes in the fold of comparative administrative studies. This includes the realm of taxation, circulation of money, borrowings, debt structure, foreign exchange and the like.
7. **Administrative Efficiency**: Another area that can be compared in the field of public administration pertains to the efficiency of two administrative structures embedded in diverse environmental settings. It may be found out as to which administrative structure is operating in a more efficient manner in comparison with the other. In this field it may also be compared as to which one of the two administrative structures possesses more capability in the sense of realizing the tasks before it.
8. **Environmental Protection:** Environment pollution had already become a major threat for the world towards the close of the previous century. Hence, protection and maintenance of the environment in modern times has been recognized as an important obligation of the administration the world over. Consequently, various steps taken to this end by the different administrative structures operating in diverse environmental settings also fall in the ambit of comparative public administration.
9. **Development of Infrastructure:** The acid test of a country's development and progress is that how efficiently it has developed its infrastructure. Thus the comparative analysis of the different administrative structures related with the construction & maintenance of roads, high-ways, power generation, irrigation, transport and means of communications etc. are engaged in this task in diverse cultural settings can be undertaken and hence, such analyses become part of the scope of comparative public administration.

10. **Local:** Effective, efficient and well-developed local administration is regarded as the sine-qua-non of the political maturity and development of a country. Hence, comparative public administration also takes into its fold those studies of local bodies that are taken up in diverse cultural settings.

The above-described ten fields that constitute the scope of comparative public administration can be studied in different environmental settings. Thus we have to identify the settings in which the comparative studies of different administrative systems could be conducted. However, it need be mentioned that only those studies can be described as comparative that involve a comparative analysis of administrative structures rooted in diverse environmental settings. These settings are highlighted below.

1. INTER-INSTITUTIONAL COMPARISONS

Among the various comparative studies of the administrative systems in different settings that may be taken up, the first may be the one that involves comparisons between two or more institutions working in different environmental contexts. The structure, the functions performed by that structure as well as the processes involved in discharging these functions of different institutions might be compared. For instance, experiences of the Scandinavian countries with the institution of ombudsman may be compared with the British experiences with the institution of Parliamentary Commissioner or Mediator in France. Such comparisons may be intra-national as well.

2. INTRA-NATIONAL COMPARISONS

Intra-national comparative studies involve comparisons of the different administrative structures within a country. However, the structures involved in such comparisons must be embedded in different environmental settings. Thus we may compare the District Administration of Bihar with that of Himachal Pradesh as the two have entirely different socio-cultural setting. We may also compare the municipal administrations of Karachi and Lahore. Comparative studies of the health administrations of the states of Virginia and New Jersey also fall within the purview of such studies. Likewise, the public service commission of some northeastern states may be compared with that of some southern or northern states as these parts of the Indian federation have entirely different social-cultural, economic and religious environments.

3. CROSS-NATIONAL COMPARISONS

Cross-national studies incorporate those studies in which comparisons of administrative structures of two or more nations are undertaken. Since different nations represent entirely different environmental settings, therefore, comparative analysis of structures, functions and processes of administrative systems of different nations will rightly be called comparative administrative studies. Thus for instance the recruitment process for civil services of Japan may well be compared with that of Indonesia or for that matter with that of Australia or Switzerland. Similarly, we may conduct a comparative study of Harvard University with Jawaharlal University or for that matter we may compare the Indian Institute of Public Administration with that of the Philippines.

4. CROSS-CULTURAL COMPARISONS

A nation may represent one or more than one cultural setting. If comparative studies of administrative institutions within one nation (representing single culture) are conducted, then those studies cannot be considered as comparative studies. However, if such a nation represents more than one culture, then these studies will definitely be called comparative studies. These cross-cultural comparisons may be intra-national or inter-national in setting. Such comparative analysis includes studies of different administrative structures that are rooted in different cultural settings. Since the developing and the developed as well as the capitalist and the socialist societies have different sets of cultural settings, their administrative institutions can well be compared. Thus we can compare the administrative systems of China with that of Japan or the US. Similarly, we can compare the administrative system of the former Soviet Union with that of France. Likewise, we may also compare the administrative system of a developing country like that of Indonesia or Thailand or Saudi Arabia with that of some developed countries like Japan or England or America.

5. CROSS-TEMPORAL COMPARISONS

Cross-temporal analyses are those studies that have been conducted at different points of time. Such comparisons may involve the administrative systems of different countries or of the same country. A cross-temporal analysis may be inter-institutional, intra-national, cross-national or cross-cultural. We may, therefore, compare administrative systems of the Mughals with that of the Mauryans. We may also compare the administrative system during the governor-generalship of Lord Cornwallis and Lord Elton Mayo or for that matter with any other governor general. Even the administrative systems of Jawaharlal Nehru and Indira Gandhi can also be compared. The administrative system of Louis XIV can also be compared with the administrative system of Elizabeth I. Likewise, such innumerable comparisons can be conducted.

In addition to these settings, comparative studies can be conducted at three analytical levels – macro level, middle-range and micro level. Earlier, greater emphasis was laid on macro level studies covering the entire administrative systems of two or more countries. In this context, the Agraria-Industria model and the Prismatic Sala Model of Riggs may be cited. However, at present, there has been a shift from macro level to middle range and micro level studies. Thus usually a comparative analysis of some smaller units of two or more administrative systems working in diverse cultural settings is compared. For example, the recruitment system of one country is compared with that of the other.

SIGNIFICANCE

Comparative public administration helps in the growth of the subject of public administration by developing theoretical constructs applicable across the globe. Without undertaking comparative analysis, the theories and models will lack cross-national applicability. Also, comparative studies are significant for both the developed and developing countries. They help in conducting SWOT (Strengths, Weaknesses, Opportunities and Threats) analysis of different administrative structures thereby making the different administrative structures capable of strengthening themselves in the given circumstances. In this way, it proves helpful by creating examples for the students of public administration as well as for the practical administrators. In this regard the views of Ferrel Heady about the significance of the comparative studies are worth quoting: "aside from the demands of scientific enquiry, there are other advantages to be gained from a better understanding of public administration across national boundaries. The increasing interdependence of national and regions of the world makes comprehension of the conduct of administration of much more importance than in the past."[35]

Quah has described the significance of comparative analysis in public administration by dividing it into two parts viz., comparison as a prerequisite for the development of a science of public administration and comparison for more practical reasons. In the first category he has stated that "comparative studies ... in various countries are superior ... because ... [these] deal with more than one case. Moreover, ... it enables scholars to identify the factors responsible for the success or failure of administration in a country; and also to account for the differences in bureaucratic behaviour and bureaucracies in different country"[36]. In the second category, he has highlighted two points viz. "to help students, practicing administrators, specialists and technical assistance experts know and understand more about public administration in other countries" and "to consider the possibility of administrative reform in the form of transplantation of certain administrative institutions and/or practices from other countries"[37].

The significance of the comparative studies in the field of public administration can be highlighted with the help of following main points:

1. Comparative studies in public administration help in widening the horizon of the discipline of public administration by promoting cross-cultural and cross-national studies that were previously limited by cultural bonds and ties.
2. Comparative studies in public administration contribute in formulating theoretical constructs thereby providing scientific base to the discipline.
3. Comparative public administration not only contributes the understanding the characteristics of individual administrative systems operating in diverse cultural settings but also helps in explaining factors responsible for cross-national and cross-cultural similarities and dissimilarities in those administrative systems.
4. It also helps to facilitate explanations in the literature of public administration as it enables scholars to identify the factors responsible for the success or failure of administration of a country. Such explanations are also helpful for practical administrators by creating examples for them.
5. Comparative analysis further contributes in highlighting which of the environmental factors helps in the promotion of administrative effectiveness and which administrative structure functions more successfully in what type of environment. Such analysis will also prove helpful for measuring the administrative capability of different structures as well as promoting their efficiency.

---
35 Heady, Ferrel, *op. cit.*, 1991, p. 5.
36 Quah, Jon S.T., *Comparative Public Administration: What and Why?* in Arora, R.K. (ed.) (1979), *op. cit.*, p. 21.
37 Ibid

6. The comparative studies in public administration also help in comprehending how one particular administrative system reacted to a particular problem or situation thereby creating examples for the rest. For instance, India has a lot to learn from the comparative studies as to how the Israel administration has reacted to the problem of insurgency in that country. Such a study will prove very effective and helpful for containing the problem of extremism in India.
7. Comparative studies further help in finding out how and with what modification, the administrative structure of a particular country can be successfully transplanted in another country given their different cultural settings. Thus institution grafting is another advantage arising out of the comparative studies of public administration.

Since World War-II, the scope of the discipline of public administration has increased tremendously as the comparative perspective has been added to its fold. This perspective incorporates comparative study of the administrative systems that operate in diverse social, economic, political and cultural milieu. Comparative public administration also studies the administration in historical perspective i.e., conducting comparative studies of the administrative systems in diverse temporal settings. It utilizes empirical tools which help in making a comparative analysis of different structures operating in different countries for discharging certain common functions. The unprecedented increase in the number of states, particularly in the developing world with their own unique political and administrative systems has promoted comparative public administration as a broad and significant discipline to examine and analyze the process of development.[38]

---

38 Ali, Ashraf and Mishra, S.N., *Public Administration: A New Paradigm,* New Delhi: Cadplan Publishers and Distributors, 1996, pp. 202-03.

2
COMPARATIVE PUBLIC ADMINISTRATION: APPROACHES

There are a number of approaches to the study of comparative public administration. All these approaches study public administration from different perspectives. Prominent among these are 'Ecological Approach', 'Behavioural Approach' and 'Structural Functional Approach'. These three approaches are immensely helpful in studying public administration comparatively. A systematic and detailed discussion about each one of these approaches is presented in this chapter.

I. ECOLOGICAL APPROACH

Ecological approach is the latest approach to the study of comparative public administration. It became popular in the 1970s, in the field of administration due to the emphasis of the CAG scholars particularly by Prof. Riggs. These scholars and practitioners while studying and analyzing the administrative systems of developing countries, emphasised the need to relate the administrative systems with the environments in which they operate. This emphasis resulted in promoting research regarding the study of administrative systems in developing countries vis-à-vis their environment. Riggs' belief was that the "nature of public administration in any country cannot be understood without grasping the social setting in which it operates"[1]. Hence the reference point of this approach is the administrative systems of developing countries and the main theme of this approach is built around the idea of development administration and social change.

MEANING

The term ecology was coined by combining two Greek words – *Oikos* meaning 'house' or 'dwelling place' and *Logos* meaning 'the study of' – to denote the relationship between the organism and its environment. This term is borrowed from biology. It is the science concerned with the interrelationships and interactions of organisms and their environment[2]. In biology, this term is concerned with the interplay of living organisms and their physical and social environment and how organisms and environment are kept in balance for survival and other important objectives[3]. In other words, ecology studies how organisms and environment influence each other. .

---

1 Arora R.K., *Comparative Public Administrative*, New Delhi: Associated Publishing House, 1996, p. 106.
2 Bews, J.W., *Human Ecology*, London: Oxford University Press, 1935, p. 232.
3 Dimock and Dimock, *Public Administration*, Minsdale: The Druden Press, 1953, p. 46.

Likewise, the administration also has its own environment in which it operates and the two interact with each other i.e., the administration and its environment influence each other. Thus in order to understand the dynamics of the administration, the knowledge of its interactions with environment is inevitable. Hence the approach, which studies the interplay between administration and environment i.e. how the administration influences environment and vice versa, as well as the constant interaction of the two, is termed as ecological approach. So the interrelationship between the administrative structures and their environment (political, social, cultural and economic) is the focal point of this approach. This approach is based on the idea that an administrative system may not act as an independent variable in all circumstances. It acts and reacts under the influence of various sub-systems surrounding it[4].

DEVELOPMENT

The term 'ecology' was introduced in public administration vocabulary primarily through the writings of the late Harvard Professor, John M. Gaus, one of the early pioneers of public administration. He elaborated this approach in a series of famous lectures at the University of Alabama in 1945, which were later compiled and published as *Reflections on Public Administration*. Gaus was mainly concerned with identifying key ecological factors for an understanding of contemporary American public administration, and he explored a list of factors which he found to be particularly useful: people, place, physical technology, social technology, wishes and ideas, catastrophe, and personality.[5] In 1947, Robert A. Dahl in his article *The Science of Public Administration*, pleaded for an ecological approach to the study of public administration. He held that "we are a long way from a science of public administration" and that public administration cannot acquire the status of a science unless "there is a body of comparative studies from which it may be possible to discover principles and generalities that transcend national boundaries and peculiar historical experiences"[6]

The relevance of the study of ecological approach was realised during the U.S. technical assistance programme to the newly emerged nations in the 1950s. In 1952, Roscoe Martin in his article *Technical Assistance: The Problem of Implementation* further emphasized the ecological aspect with regard to the effective implementation of techno–assistance programmes[7]. In fact, the failure of techno-assistance programmes generated the interest of many scholars towards studying the administrative patterns in the developing countries. When the scholars found that the administrative systems of the newly liberated countries are not responding to the general principles of organizations evolved in the western countries, they concentrated their attention

---

4   Basu, Rumki, *Public Administration: Concepts and theories*, New Delhi: Sterling Publishers, 1992, p. 33.
5   Heady, Ferral, *Public Administration: A Comparative Perspective*, New York: Marcel Dekker, INC, 1991, p. 84.
6   Dahl, Robert A., "The Science of Public Administration: Three Problems" in *Public Administration Review*, VII, 1947, p. 11.
7   Martin, Roscoe, "Technical Assistance: The Problem of Implementation" in *Public Administration Review*, No. XII, 1952, p. 266.

towards the effects of social settings on the administrative systems of these countries. Riggs, who was most prominent among these scholars, was "primarily interested in analyzing the interactions between the administrative sub system on the one hand and the political, social, cultural and economic sub systems of the society, on the other"[8]. In fact, the most notable contribution to the literature on this approach has come from F.W. Riggs, who in his scholarly contributions, *The Ecology of Administration* (1961) and *Administration in Developing Countries – The Theory of Prismatic Society* (1964) threw considerable light on this aspect.

SALIENT FEATURES

Following are the main features of this approach

1. Inter-Disciplinary

Ecological approach is inter-disciplinary in character as it takes into consideration a deep understanding of all the environmental forces (political, social, economic and cultural etc.). These forces exert considerable influence on the administrative systems and get influenced by it. So this approach utilizes knowledge from various disciplines to understand the dynamics of environmental forces and their impact on the administrative structures, procedures and goals and vice versa. Riggs highlighted that administration is influenced by its surrounding environment and in order to understand the administrative system of a country, the study of all these ecological forces is must. Hence this knowledge of different ecological forces promotes the inter-disciplinary character of this approach.

2. Complex Subject Matter

The subject matter of this approach is quite complex. The word 'ecology' in itself is very much comprehensive and involves all sorts of environmental forces which overtly or covertly influence the administrative system and get influenced by it. The entire gamut of all these forces, increase the complexity of subject matter of this approach because it is quite difficult to identify all these forces and to understand their influence on the administrative machinery. Riggs resolved this entangle by suggesting that only the forces of primary importance having direct bearing on the administration should be taken into account. Riggs focused his attention on 5 aspects – economic, social, symbolic, communicative and political – that most influence the administration of any country.[9] According to him, these five environmental factors have enormous direct and deep effect on the functioning of public administration in transitional societies[10].

3. Importance of Interactions

Another important feature of this approach is that it gives due importance to the interactions between administrative structures and their environment in which they operate. Interactions are outcome of interplay between the administration and

---

8   Arora, R.K., *op. cit.* 1996, p. 106.
9   Riggs, F.W., *The Ecology of Public Administration*, New York: Asia Publishing House, 1961, p. 4.
10 Naidu, S.P., *Public Administration: Concepts and Theories*, New Delhi: New Age International Publishers, 1996, p. 139.

its environment. The knowledge of these interactions helps in promoting a clear understanding of the administrative system and its environment.

4. Mutual Influences

This approach recognises the importance of mutual influences, i.e., how the administration is modified as a result of the interaction with its environment and vice-versa. This means not only the surrounding environment influences the administration but the administration, also exerts its influence on its environment. The intimate and close interaction between the two, results in promoting mutual modifications and alterations in each other. "Organisations, structures, procedures and goals are largely created and changed as a result of interaction between an organisation and its environment. Thus, if an organisation is to survive, it must adapt itself to the changing needs and conditions of its external environment, which is continuously changing."[11] Arora has observed that "the bureaucratic system is continually interacting with ... the political, economic, and socio-cultural sub systems in a society. It is both a modifying influence upon these systems and a system which is modified by their activity."[12]

5. Frame of Reference is the Overall Environment

Another feature of this approach is that its frame of reference is the overall social environment. The underlying idea of this approach is that it considers the administration as a sub system, which interacts with the other sub systems of the overall environment that surrounds it. This approach takes into account and emphasizes the need to understand the entire environment in which the administrative unit is situated.

APPRAISAL

The ecological approach originated and became popular on account of the study of problems of administration in developing countries. The significant contribution of this approach is that it takes into account the impact of socio-economic forces on the administrative system. "The great merit of this approach lies in the value and relevance of studying people in relation to their environment, taking into consideration their peculiar characteristics and problems. Public co-operation is a vital input for the successful operation of any administrative system. Unless the administration caters to particular public needs, wishes, activities and problems they cannot solicit public co-operation to the extent desired"[13].

This approach gives importance to those environmental forces which exert influence on the administrative system and their mutual interactions and modifications. Earlier, either these forces were not taken into account or were given less importance in the administrative studies. Thus this approach contributed a lot in highlighting those environmental forces which have a serious impact on the administrative system.

Still the problem remains that ecological approach lacks predictability. That's how even after the valuable contribution, in the times of crisis and administrative collapse this approach proved hardly helpful. For instance, this approach could not

---

11 Basu, Rumki, *op. cit.*, 1992, p. 33.
12 Arora, R.K. *op. cit.*, 1996, p. 105.
13 Basu, Rumki, *op. cit.*, 1992, p. 35.

be of much help in resolving or even identifying the crisis and collapse of Marcos' administration in the Philippines and the crisis-ridden situation in Thailand. It needs to be mentioned here that these were the countries selected for the study by ecological scholars for administrative analysis. However despite these basic problems, the contribution of this approach cannot be undermined or minimized in the discipline of comparative public administration.

II. STRUCTURAL FUNCTIONAL APPROACH

Structural functional analysis is new neither in social sciences nor in natural sciences. This approach, as an analytical tool, in social sciences was developed from the works of renowned anthropologist Milinowski and Radcliff Brown in the early years of the 20th Century[14]. Several prominent scholars like Talcott Parsons, R.K. Merton, Marian Levy, Gabriel Almond and David Apter used this approach in the analysis of social phenomenon. Hence this approach emerged as an important mechanism for the analysis of different social processes.

In the field of public administration, it was Dwight Waldo who first suggested this approach in 1955. He pointed out that this analysis might provide some guidance in the construction of "a model of what an administrative system should be like as a general type"[15]. Later, this approach was utilized by Riggs in the development of his *Agraria-Industria typology* in 1957[16]. Riggs also used this approach in developing the *Fused–Prismatic-Diffracted typology* two years later, in 1959. With this approach Riggs studied the administrative systems of different societies from ecological perspective in terms of structures and functions. Besides Riggs, several other scholars of public administration – influenced by its comparative features and "value-neutral" premises – have also been using this approach[17].

ESSENCE OF THE APPROACH

This approach revolves around two key concepts – structures and functions. In simple terms, this approach signifies, the study and analysis of structures and their functions in a system. This approach considers that in every society certain important functions have to be discharged by a number of structures by applying some specific methods. Thus structural-functional approach analyses the functions that are performed in a society, the structures that are responsible to carry out these functions and the methods that are utilized in under-taking the functions[18]. For a proper understanding of the approach, it is obligatory to first understand the terms structures, functions, and structural and functional requisites. Hence these terms are defined below:

---

14 Basu, Rumki, *op. cit.*, 1992, p. 31.
15 Waldo, Dwight, *The study of Public Administrative*, New York: Doubleday and Co., 1955, p. 9.
16 Siffin, W.J. *Towards a Comparative Study of Public Administration*, Indiana University Press, 1977, pp. 23-110.
17 Arora, R.K., *op. cit.*, 1996, p. 108.
18 Parsad, D. Ravindra, Parsad, V.S. and Satyanarayana, P. *Administrative Thinkers*, New Delhi: Sterling Publishers, 1991, p. 236.

STRUCTURE

Structure means "any pattern of behaviour which has become a standard feature of a social system"[19]. Structures are of two types – "Concrete" and "Analytical."[20] Concrete structures are those that are physically separable from others. These are perceptible, discernible and identifiable with human eyes. The Railway board, The Indian Institute of Public Administration, The Prime Minister's Office, government departments, The Planning Commission, The Union Public Service Commission may be cited as examples in Indian context. Analytical structures, on the other hand, are those which are perceptible through our intellect and are not physically separable from others. Such structures are abstract and are derived from realistic relationships. The structures of administrative authority and political power are the most important examples in this regard. Although not concrete, yet they are structures as they become patterns because of being consistently happening.

FUNCTION

Function is an outcome of the interdependence and interaction of two or more structures. In fact, function is a condition of structure i.e. when any structure operates, the result is the function. In other words, when any structure actually goes into action or operation, its output is function. In this context Riggs has aptly remarked "by function we mean any consequences of a structure in-so-far as they affect other structures or the total system of which they are a part ... a function is a pattern of inter-dependence between two or more structures, a relationship between variables."[21] Functions are also of two types – Concrete and Analytical. Concrete functions are those functions that are perceptible to our eyes. In other words, those functions that can be observed as have been performed or as being performed by human eyes are called concrete functions. For instance transportation, electricity and water supply, education and health and the like can be cited as examples of concrete functions. Analytical functions are those that are imperceptible to the human eyes and which pertain to our intellect or mental faculties. Decision making, policy formulation, co-ordination can be cited as examples.

In addition to this main classification, there are two other categories of functions viz. Manifest and Latent Functions. Manifest functions are those that are intended and observable whereas the latent functions are those that have happened automatically as a result of the manifest functions. That means they were not intended. In other words, they are the impact of the manifest functions. For instance, if the administration is constructing a road, it creates some cleanliness in the surrounding environment. In this case, construction of road is the manifest function while the cleanliness of environment is the latent function.

Besides, functions can also be divided as Eufunctions and Dysfunctions. Eufunctions are those which increase the adaptability of the structure and strengthen it. These functions promote stability of the structure. For instance, civic amenities provided by municipal administration. On the other hand, dysfunctions are those

---

19 Riggs, F.W., *Administration in Developing Countries : The Theory of Prismatic Society*, Boston : Houghton Mifflin Co., 1964, p. 20
20 Inkeles, Alex, *What is Sociology*, New Jersey: Prentice Hall, 1964, p. 35.
21 Riggs, F.W. *op. cit.*, 1964, p. 20.

which weaken the structure. For instance, if the municipal administration cares more for cinema halls or for wine and liquor shops etc. at the cost of civic amenities, then such functions are called dysfunctions.

STRUCTURAL AND FUNCTIONAL REQUISITES

In the case of structural-functional analysis, one determines the important structures and then attempts to trace the functions of those structures. In order to maintain a system, it is necessary that the structure should not collapse and the functions must not undergo change, the requisites of structures and that of functions must be fulfilled for the survival of the system. However, identification of structural and functional requisites is the precondition to the structural-functional analysis. This is because if we don't have the structural and functional requisites, the system is bound to collapse. The structural and functional requisites may be clarified as under:

STRUCTURAL REQUISITES

Structural requisites pertain to the techniques, i.e. 'how' to perform certain functions or 'how' to operate the functions. For instance, Food Corporation of India, which is a structure, must have certain structural requisites. Thus for instance, it must have officials, warehouses (godowns), vehicles for transportation, preservatives etc. In the absence of these and other such structural requisites, the Food Corporation of India will not be able to perform the functions assigned to it or expected of it. Resultantly, the structure will collapse. Thus the structural requisites are those which provide answer 'how to perform the functions'.

FUNCTIONAL REQUISITES

Functional requisites are 'conditions' that if a structure is to survive, it has to perform certain functions. Again taking the example of the Food Corporation of India, it may be said that if it has to survive, it must have to perform certain functions. In other words, there are some functional requisites of this structure. Procurement of food grains, construction and maintenance of warehouses, distribution of food grains etc. are all functional requisites of the Food Corporation of India. If these functional requisites are not fulfilled, the structure (Food Corporation of India) will cease to exist.

BASIC ASSUMPTIONS OF THE APPROACH

The structural-functional approach is based on certain assumptions. The more significant among these are:
1. This approach presumes social and circumstantial stability i.e., there will not be any fundamental and drastic changes in the structures and functions of the administrative system under study.
2. This approach also assumes that the causes of all happenings are pre-determined. This is termed as 'teleological assumption' of this approach.[22]

SALIENT FEATURES

Following are the main features of this approach.

---

22 Sharma, R.D., *Advance Public Administration,* New Delhi: H.K. Publishers and Distributors, 1990, p. 76.

1. Value-Free Approach

One of the important characteristics of this approach is its value-neutral character. This approach actually deals with the analysis of structures and functions in a system and in this analysis, it tries to concentrate on the facts or empirical aspect rather than the normative aspect. Resultantly, it gives no importance to values and thus it is a value-free approach.

2. Descriptive and Evaluative Approach

The structural-functional approach is descriptive and evaluative in nature. This approach describes that, in every administrative system there are a number of structures performing various functions. This approach aims at conducting comparative analysis and evaluation of these structures of different administrative systems performing diverse functions.

3. Status Quoist Approach

Structural-functional approach is status quoist as it considers only minor changes instead of holistic changes in the overall system. It does not believe in total transformation of the structures and functions in the system. In this regard, this approach not only considers the social and circumstantial stability but also assumes the stability of structures and functions and considers that this stability is almost permanent. Thus it is a system maintaining approach.

4. Focus on Interactions

This approach envisages that a system consists of sub-systems and these sub-systems are in constant interaction with each other. The outcome of these interactions is a function. Thus it focuses on these interactions among different component parts (sub-systems). It considers public administration and its various structures as a planned dynamic machine that can be studied like a scooter, motor car or cycle and their parts. All these parts perform their functions with co-ordination and interdependence and are called organizational functions.

CONTRIBUTION

The structural-functional approach has significantly contributed to the discipline of public administration and thus has enriched its subject matter considerably. Its contribution to the field can be discussed as under:

1. Widens Horizon of Discipline

The structural-functional approach makes the analysis of the structures and functions of an administrative system convenient. Therefore, the students of public administration are attracted towards using this approach and thus have studied different administrative systems using this approach. Consequently, this has helped in generating sizeable volume of literature on public administration. For instance, basing on this approach, Riggs conducted several studies and developed some models and typologies regarding the administrative systems that have been particularly helpful in understanding the administrative systems of developing countries. Several other scholars have also used this approach in their studies. Thus this approach has contributed significantly in widening the scope of public administration in general and of comparative public administration, in particular.

2. Promotes New Insights

Several scholars of public administration have conducted field level studies in the post Second World War phase. The main focus of these studies has been the developing countries which have peculiar features of administration and therefore, it is quite difficult to make generalizations about their administrative systems. Yet, on the basis of constant and rigorous cross cultural and cross national and inter institutional comparative studies, these scholars have made it possible to develop certain models and theories to understand the administrative systems of developing countries. Besides, the macro level theorization of Riggs, several middle and micro level theories, models and generalizations have become possible. Thus it may be stated that new heights have been reached in the field of the discipline in the last five decades. However, it needs to be mentioned that several of these studies have been based on the structural-functional approach. The contribution of the approach in the direction of providing new directions, opening new vistas in the field of the discipline of public administration, therefore, can hardly be undermined.

3. Develops Critical Outlook

The structural and functional approach analyses the structures and functions of an administrative system (in a comparative perspective). In other words, this approach not only helps in studying the interactions of different structures in a system but also evaluates their outcomes. On the basis of such an analysis, it becomes possible to know which of the structures are performing the functions in an efficient and effective manner. The contribution of this approach lies in the fact that it helps in developing a critical outlook towards the structures and the functions.

4. Highlights Vital Points of Difference between Developed and Developing Countries

Besides undertaking a comparative analysis of the structures and functions of the same administrative system, the structural-functional approach attempts an analysis of the administrative structures of different countries performing identical functions. This approach contributes significantly in proving the vital points of difference between the administrative culture and processes of developing and developed societies[23]. In other words, the approach helps in highlighting the points of differences and similarities in the administrative systems of the developed and the developing countries. Such a comparison is extremely helpful for the developing countries as they might bring necessary structural and functional changes in their administrative systems in tune with those of the developed countries. This exercise is also of immense help to the scholars in the field of public administration who will concentrate their research efforts in the desired direction.

CRITICISM

This approach is not free from criticisms and a number of serious charges are leveled against this approach, which can be discussed as under:

---

23 Basu, Rumki, *op. cit.*, 1992, p. 32.

1. Ambiguous Terminology

The first criticism of this approach is that its concepts are ambiguous. They are not stable; rather they change according to the conditions and circumstances. In other words, there is no precision, clarity and stability in the structures and functions of a system, which are the basic concepts of this approach. We find that structures, at times, become functions and functions become structures and this is particularly so in the case of third world countries. In this regard Marian Levy is correct in highlighting that the concepts of structure and function "...fall into a peculiar set of concepts. Classification of a referent as a function or a structure depends in part on the point of view from which the phenomenon concerned is discussed. What is a function from one point of view is a structure from another"[24].

2. Hollow Assumption of Social and Circumstantial Stability

Further, this approach has made the presumption of social and circumstantial stability. It is a basic or rather the central assumption of this approach. But it is a hollow one because society is always changing and transforming. In that also though some minor changes are acceptable to this approach but the basic and fundamental changes, which alter nature as well as the structures of the whole system, are not acceptable. However, the possibility of drastic and fundamental changes cannot be ruled out in any society, let alone the developing countries. This assumption has been the major source of criticism of this approach right from the very beginning.

3. Teleological Assumption

Again, this approach assumes that the causes of all happenings are pre-determined and thus based on the 'teleological assumption'. But this is also an erroneous assumption because it ignores the fact that under certain circumstances it is possible that the causes may become the impact and the impact may become the cause. For instance, we say that the spread of education is the cause of unemployment. In this case 'spread of education' is the cause and 'unemployment' is the impact. But it is possible under certain circumstances that people get education because they are unemployed. Here 'unemployment' is the cause and 'education' is the impact.

Again, suppose the Department of Health opened a hospital and as a result of that people become healthy. So, here 'hospital' is the cause and 'health' is the impact. Now due to sound health, they are in a position to earn more and their income increases. Here 'health' is the cause 'increased income' is the impact. With this increased income, their capacity to pay increases, thus making 'increased income' the cause and 'increased capacity to pay' the impact. On account of the 'increased capacity to pay', demand of goods increases and thus production increases. Thus here 'increased capacity to pay' become the cause and the 'increased production' becomes the impact. So, this is a chain process which never ends thus proving that causes and impacts of happenings are never predetermined, rather they change.

4. Neglects the Historical Perspective of the System

This approach considers administration as a system and analyses its structures and functions. But the moment, we talk of studying the administrative system we

---

24 Marian Levy as quoted in Sharma R.D., *Advanced Public administration, Vol.1*, New Delhi: H.K. Publishers & Distributors, 1990, pp. 76-77.

must take into consideration the social and historical circumstances in which the administrative system and its component parts evolved. This is because unless we know its (administrative system) evolution and the other linkages, it is difficult to understand the administrative system. But this approach does not give any weight to this aspect.

Sharma, while criticizing this approach, observed "structural-functional analysis, in the most general sense, is short of confusion of terminology, *misness* of stability assumptions, teleology and scientific analysis in general"[25]. However, despite these weaknesses and drawbacks, the contribution of this approach in the field of public administrative especially in studying the structures and functions of different administrative systems in comparative perspective cannot be underestimated.

III. BEHAVIOURAL APPROACH

Modern behavioural movement emerged in the late 1930s and early 1940s. Such intellectual and social movements do not appear suddenly. So this movement is also an outcome of the long historical developments in social sciences. Its roots may be traced to 'positivism' and 'neo-positivism' in the early part of this century. It emerged as a protest against traditional, historical, normative and largely descriptive approaches to social sciences. It is an effort to build a unified theory through the study of human behaviour under the name of "behavioural sciences". The behavioural sciences school became popular after the Second World War. This period witnessed the flourshing of behavioural sciences[26].

In public administration, behaviouralism as a separate line of study started in the 1930s with the human relations movement and was later developed by Chester Barnard and Simon. This approach views the administrative system as a pattern of behaviour that depends on a network of human relations[27]. The behavioural approach is termed as "a modern approach because of the new trend towards the action or behaviour of individuals rather than the traditional framework"[28]. This approach in public administration emphasises on conducting and promoting scientific research and developing systematic theory building. Using this approach, the scholars of public administration conducted several cross-national, cross-cultural, cross-temporal and inter-institutional studies of administrative behaviour. Thus it proved helpful in promoting knowledge of public administration in the comparative contexts[29] and hence it is one of those approaches that played a significant role in the development of comparative public administration.

ESSENCE OF BEHAVIOURAL APPROACH

The essence of this approach lies in studying the human behaviour in a scientific way. Thus it is mainly concerned with the scientific study of human behaviour in diverse cultural settings. Human behaviour is the focal point of this approach around which

---

25 Sharma, R.D., *op. cit.*, 1990, p. 76.
26 *Ibid*, p. 86.
27 Naidu, S.P., *Public Administration: Concepts and Theories*, New Delhi: New Age International Publishers, 1996, p. 50.
28 Sharma, R.D., *op. cit.*, 1990, p. 86.
29 Basu, Rumki, *Public Administration: Concepts and Theories*, New Delhi: Sterling Publishers, 1992, p. 28.

it revolves. In public administration, it stresses on the impact of human behaviour on administration and analyses how the human behaviour affects the working of administration in different cultural contexts. This approach highlights that, in order to understand the administrative system it is essential to have a scientific analysis of the behaviour of administrative officials. Rather than focusing on rules and regulations, this approach emphasizes scientific study of individual and group behaviour in an organizational setting.

DEVELOPMENT

The genesis of behaviouralism in public administration can be traced to the human relations movement of the 1930s. By conducting a series of experiments and thereby highlighting the importance of human dynamics in administration, Elton Mayo contributed significantly to the development of this approach. Earlier, the writings of M.P. Follet inspired new thinking in the discipline and in a way her writings can be regarded as a precursor to the human relations movement. Inspired by her thinking, a team of researchers headed by Elton Mayo from Harvard Business School conducted Hawthorne experiments at the Hawthorne Plant of Western Electric Company. The findings of the Hawthorne experiments gave a serious jolt to the scientific management movement and classical thinking.

The human relation movement was further strengthened by the writings of Chester Barnard in the late 1930s. He worked in various capacities with the New Jersey Telephone Company and had rich administrative experiences as an administrator and manager. He made an attempt to set forth an all embracing theory of organization. He defined "organizations as co-operative and essentially dynamic systems, which are engaged in a process of continual readjustment to their physical, biological and social environments."[30] The theoretical framework he setup was quite complex and not completely successful, but his work contained many new mind-opening insights. His new insights resulted in challenging the various aspects of classical theory and contributed in the development of this approach.

Simon was the next contributor to this approach in the field of public administration. He provided a sound basis to this approach and became the prime user of this approach. He wrote an article *Proverbs of Administration* in which he shattered the classicists' claim of universality of the principles of public administration, which he called as mere "proverbs". He was of the opinion that the principles developed by the classicists were not properly evolved and were applicable only in contextual settings. In 1947, he wrote a famous book entitled *Administrative Behaviour* in which he advocated behavioural research in administration. While highlighting "administrative behaviour" Simon observed that it is "a part of the behavioural sciences and the study of public administration should involve the study of individual and collective human behaviour in administrative situations"[31]. His main ideas of 'bounded rationality' and 'administrative man' were based on the study of human behaviour. However, since the early 1950s, sociologists and psychologists (while working in their respective fields) contributed significantly to the development of behaviouralism in public administration. Abraham Maslow, Douglas McGregor,

---

30   Sharma, R.D., *op. cit.*, 1990, p. 87.
31   Basu, Rumki, *op. cit.*, 1992, p. 27.

Rensis Likert and Chris Argyris, are some of the foremost behavioural scientists who used this approach in their respective fields. However, the contributions of these scholars have considerably enriched the subject matter of public administration and the development of behavioural approach in this discipline.

SALIENT FEATURES

Following are the main salient features of this approach –

1. ANALYTICAL APPROACH

One of the important characteristic of Behavioural approach is that it is an analytical approach. This approach emerged as a protest against the traditional outlook towards administrative problems. This approach "was a 'new' way of analysing administrative situations. It was a rejection of the traditional, historical, legalistic, juridical, normative, philosophical ways of looking at administration problems"[32]. It does not believe in idealism; rather believes in analysis of behaviour in different administrative settings. This approach analyses the behaviour of the administrative functionaries scientifically. Through comparative studies of the different administrative systems, it analyses the effectiveness of the behaviour of administrative functionaries in different settings. In this way it analyses which of the administrative system would lead to better goal-realization. Thus this approach does not concentrate on "how the administrative functionaries should behave" rather it merely explains "how they behave?" Hence the literature of this approach is descriptive as well as analytical rather than prescriptive, "with the studies on motivation being an exception"[33].

2. INTERDISCIPLINARY CHARACTER

Behavioural approach is highly interdisciplinary in nature as it draws heavily from different social sciences especially from sociology and psychology for analysing administration behaviour in different contexts. Simon explains behaviouralism in public administration as "interdisciplinary" in character and makes considerable use of propositions drawn from other social sciences and of empirical data on administrative behaviour to test such prepositions in organisational contexts[34].

3. SCIENTIFIC APPROACH

Another important characteristic of this approach is that it is scientific in nature as it is essentially concerned with studying human behaviour in a scientific way. In this enquiry, this approach takes into consideration the mathematical models that impart a scientific status to this approach. In this connection, Arora states that this approach, to a great extent, "is concerned with quantification, mathematization and formal theory construction"[35]. This approach lays emphasis on empiricism and drawing realistic judgements. In this way it aims at replacing value judgements by empirical data and facts.

---

32 Sharma, R.D., *op. cit.*, 1990, p. 87.
33 Arora, R.K., *op. cit.*, 1996, p. 15.
34 Herbert Simon as quoted in Arora, R.K., 1996, p. 15.
35 Basu, Rumki, *op. cit.*, 1992, p. 15.

4. COMPLEX SUBJECT MATTER

Behavioural approach studies behaviour of human beings in different administrative settings. However, behaviour in itself is a very complex and complicated phenomenon. Hence the subject matter of the approach becomes very complex. Besides, being interdisciplinary in nature, this approach draws heavily not only from social sciences but even from physical sciences. This further adds to the complexity of its subject matter.

5. EMPIRICAL APPROACH

The behavioural approach is concerned with scientific analysis of human behaviour. However, human behaviour is not a phenomenon that can be tested in a closed room. It has to be tested in the field. This approach emphasizes on conducting "empirical study based on rigorous methods such as field observation, controlled field experiments, and laboratory studies of organisations – like groups"[36]. Thus if we wish to study the behaviour of the officials of the Delhi police, we cannot conduct this study in laboratories; rather we shall have to go in the field to gather the relevant information about the behaviour of the police functionaries.

6. LONG RANGE VENTURE

Another important feature of this approach is that it is a long-range venture, as almost all the studies conducted in connection with the behavioural aspect are an outcome or product of long periods of consistent observations of the situation.

CONTRIBUTION OF THE APPROACH

The contribution of behavioural approach in administration studies can be discussed as under –

1. PROMOTES SCIENTIFIC RESEARCH

This approach has motivated greater scientific research in the field of public administration. It is also considered as a leap (a vigorous jump) in the direction of systematic theory construction, which is an outcome of a series of field studies and laboratory experiments. For instance, a number of Indian scholars such as Pai Panandikar, Kuldeep Mathur, Ramashray Roy, Shanti Kothari, and C.P. Bhambhari[37] have made use of this approach for conducting scientific research studies. Thus this approach proved helpful in promoting scientific research enquiries in the discipline of public administration.

2. PROMOTES INTER–CULTURAL STUDIES

This approach lays emphasis on conducting studies about the behaviour of the administrative systems embedded in different cultural settings. This is because the study of the behaviour of two or more administrative systems rooted in the same cultural setting will not much deviate from one another. Therefore, if we conduct

---

36 Arora, R.K., *op. cit.*, 1996, p. 15.
37 Pai Panandikar has made an empirical analysis of values and behaviours of India's developmental administrators; Roy and Kothari have made an empirical study of relationship between politicians and administrators of a UP district, Kuldeep Mathur has studied the background, approaches and values of Sub-divisional Development officers of UP and Rajasthan and C.P. Bhambhari has studied the behavioural patterns of IAS officers.

comparative studies of two or more administrative systems with the same cultural settings, it will not lead us anywhere nor will it contribute to the literature of the discipline much. In this way this approach plays a significant role in promoting inter-cultural or cross-cultural studies.

However, in the field of comparative public administration, very few such studies have been conducted. More so whatever number of such studies have been conducted are the endeavour of the western scholars. In this connection, cross-cultural and empirical studies conducted by scholars like Robert Presthus, and Michael Crozier[38] may be cited as examples.

3. WIDENED HORIZON OF THE DISCIPLINE

Behavioural approach is inter-disciplinary. Thus it relies heavily on the subject matter, tools, concepts and findings borrowed from other diverse disciplines like sociology, psychology, mathematics, political science etc. This inter-disciplinary character of the approach has, consequently widened the horizon of the study of public administration in general and comparative public administration in particular. The interdisciplinary focus in comparative administration helps in broadening the vision of the students and researchers of public administration and made the subject more interesting. Commenting on the inter-disciplinary orientation of the approach Arora has remarked "behaviouralism itself has acted as an umbrella under which comparative public administration has found several models of interaction, not only with public administration but also with other disciplines"[39].

APPRAISAL

Behavioural approach has contributed significantly to the field of public administration as also in other social sciences. Yet this approach is not without defects. It is generally criticized on the following grounds:

1. SCIENTIFICISM -- A HOLLOW CLAIM

The behavioural approach claimed to be a scientific approach. However, critics deny this claim on the ground that its basic concept is human behaviour, which is, besides being complex, not quantifiable. The study of human attitude, values, norms, perceptions and sentiments in a scientific way is very difficult. They cannot be measured in quantifiable terms because no yardstick can be developed for this purpose. Further, comparison of behaviour of two or more administrative systems in diverse cultural settings is still more difficult.

2. IGNORANCE OF THE CIRCUMSTANCES

Another ground on which this approach is criticized is that it emphasizes only on the study of behaviour of the functionaries of an administrative system but it ignores the circumstances or the situation in which they are working. Thus it gives no importance to the circumstances that affect behaviour of the administrative functionaries and shape or reshape it.

---

38 Robert Presthus, "Behaviour and Bureaucracy in Many Cultures" in *Public Administration Review*, Vol. XIX (1959), pp.25-35; Michael Crozier, *The Bureaucratic Phenomenon*, Chicago: University of Chicago Press, 1964.
39 Arora, R.K., *op. cit.*, 1996, p. 16.

3. PROBLEM OF OBSERVATION

Being empirical in nature, this approach is data based. However, the main tool of data collection is the method of observation, which is not a reliable tool of data collection. But it is difficult to determine the accuracy of the data collected through this method. Resultantly, the data in behaviouralism is not highly dependable.

4. PROBLEM OF CHANGE

Another problem or weakness of this approach is that, with the passage of time, the changes in the behaviour of the administrative functionaries also take place. Moreover, even a single functionary is more likely to react differently to the same circumstances at different points of time.

3
ENVIRONMENT OF ADMINISTRATION*

While studying the administrative systems of the developing countries of the Afro-Asian and Latin American continents during most part of the 1960s and early 1970s, Riggs and other CAG scholars observed that like human and other living organisms, organizations also have an environment. The administrative organizations do not work in isolation, they are affected intimately by the environment that environs them. These scholars also observed that the process of influencing is not uni-directional but a two directional process. Thus, not only the environment affects the administrative organizations but the former also gets influenced by the latter and therefore, this process of mutual influence is given the name of 'interaction'. It needs, however, to be noted that in contrast to the natural environment, the environment that surrounds organizations consists of social, cultural, economic and political and the like rather than the biological forces. A brief view of the interaction of these components of the environment (of administration) with the administration is discussed below:

SOCIAL ENVIORNMENT

A society is a group of people who are sufficiently organized to create conditions necessary to live together with a common identification. It is a network or web of social interrelationships, social interactions and patterned behaviors. Every society has a number of social institutions, traditions, values and belief systems. Some of these are inherited while others are developed. Even in a single society, these institutions, traditions, values and beliefs are characterized by diversity on account of caste, creed, colour, region, religion, language, dialect and the like. All these factors, taken together, constitute the social environment. The social environment interacts with the administrative system and influences the administration as well as influenced by it. Highlighting the influence of social forces on public administration, Riggs remarked, "… Such matters also affect the system of public administration"[1]. He has further observed that the social environment of a community, based on its institutions, associational patterns, class or caste relationships, historical legacy, traditions, religion, value–systems, beliefs and ideals, ethos, etc., deeply influence its public administration"[2]. The social environment of public administration can be explained with the help of following points:

---

1 Riggs, F.W., *The Ecology of Public Administration*, New Delhi: Asia Publishing House, 1961, p. 14.
2 *Ibid*

* Environment of Administration has already been published in the Journal of Constitutional and Parliamentary Studies (ICPS), New Delhi Vol 39 No. 1-4, 2005, pp. 131-161.

SOCIAL STRATIFICATION

Stratification is an important characteristic of every society and they are usually stratified on the basis of class. In contrast, however, the Indian society is stratified on caste basis. The stratified society may be an open or a closed society. In an open society, the mobility between the classes/castes is permitted and recognized whereas a closed society is characterized by the absence of such mobility.[3] Developed and developing countries are the ideal examples of an open and a closed society respectively. Thus, for instance, the Indian society with its rigid caste system can well be categorized as a close society. The caste system based on birth created divisions in the society and caused socio-economic inequalities. This caste-ridden character of the Indian social system causes conflicts and tensions in the society, which, many a time, cause social crisis. This is ultimately reflected at the administrative level as well. All the administrative functionaries (belonging to different castes) working at various tiers of administrative ladder show caste loyalties, which hinders unbiased administrative working. Keeping in view the inegalitarian social system, the Indian constitution provided for preferential treatment to scheduled castes, scheduled tribes and other backward classes in public services. Paradoxically, this preferential treatment system designed to bring equality in the society is also a cause of internal tension in the public organizations. It leads to the formation of informal groups among public servants on caste lines and this, to an extent, adversely affects the efficiency of the public organizations.

FAMILIAL AND KINSHIP TIES

Family is an important social unit and the bonds of familial and kinship ties are very strong particularly in Asian societies like Japan, China and India. Traditionally, joint family system was prevailing in India and it played an important role as a social and economic institution. The social norms expect the subordination of individual interests to that of family interests. In modern times, due to various socio-economic reasons, the joint family system is gradually giving way to the nuclear family system. But still, the emotional ties of extended family continue to dominate the social life. The patriarchal structure and operation of family affected the administrative system numerously. It promoted paternalistic and authoritarian behavioural orientations of administrators who may regard it as their natural obligation to help their family members and relatives by "exploiting" their administrative positions. This even promotes corrupt practices in the administrative functioning. "A family does not aggregate specific functional interests. It cannot press for the adoption of a policy universally applicable to everyone. Instead, it seeks to promote the particular interests of its family members – an elevation in status, appointment as an official, enlargement of the number of clients, or a favourable judgment in a dispute."[4] Many studies have pointed out the existence of familial and kinship orientation among the administrative officials. For instance in Nigeria, "the impact of the extended family is of importance, and nepotism is a larger problem than political patronage.... (therefore) politicians and civil servants alike are under extreme and constant pressure to support or give

---

3   *Ibid*, p. 24.
4   F.W. Riggs, *op. cit.*, p. 65.

assistance to a circle of relatives"[5]. What has been said about Nigeria also stands true about most of the other developing countries.

The administrative problems (nepotism, favouritism and corruption etc.) generated due to the familial and kinship ties are a direct fall out of the problem of formalism, which is a characteristic of the developing countries. In these countries, what is theoretically prescribed is usually not effectively practised. In these countries, though the administration is stated to be functioning in accordance with the rule of law, yet in practice, almost all the decisions of the administrative functionaries are affected by the familial and kinship ties.

SOCIAL ETHOS AND VALUES

The values and norms cherished by the society also play a dominant role in influencing administrative behavior. These social ethos are cultivated in that society for its betterment and to regulate the behavior of its members. Thus the administration will also cherish the values developed by the society and vice-versa. For instance, development orientation is a social value. If the society cherishes this value i.e., if the society at large is development oriented, then this value will be reflected at the level of the administration as well. If on the other hand, the society will lack developmental perspective, the administration is bound to show such a neglect of the developmental orientation. In this context R.B. Puri has remarked "The administrator's responsiveness can hardly be considered in isolation from his social back-ground, values, and attitudes which have a tremendous influence on his decision-making and the kind of people in society with whom he identified himself"[6].

For instance, lack of integrity widely prevails in Indian society and this social vice is widely prevalent. It is reflected at almost all levels of the Indian administration as an important feature (problem). According to Transparancy International, "the common citizen pays bribe totaling Rs 21,068 crores every year for availing himself of one or more of the public services."[7] Due to unethical practices like scams and fraudulent allotments, the total loss to the public exchequer is estimated to be 4 lakh crores.[8] As per the survey of 2010 of Transparency International, India is ranked ... "at 87 among 178 nations and its Corruption Perception Index score has come down to 3.3 from 3.4 in 2009 and 3.5 in 2007."[9] Further, in a statement filed before the High Court, the Jharkhand Government, "conceded that 37 percent of the bureaucracy" is corrupt in the state.[10] However, Jharkhand is not an exception and the position of bureaucracy in other states is equally lamentable. For the wrongful appointment of Mr. P.J. Thomas as the Central Vigilance Commissioner (CVC), the responsibility itself was accepted by the Prime Minister, Man Mohan Singh and his government. This societal vice is also rampant at the political level and this is evident by the fact

---

5 The Times of India, New Delhi; May 28, 1989 p.16. Also *Encyclopedia of General knowledge* by Dr.B.L. Sadana; New Delhi: New Light Publishers, 1989, p. V15.
6 Puri, R.B., *Understanding India Bureaucratic Behaviour* in Puri, K.K (ed.) (1985), *Public Administration: Indian Spectrum*, p. 103.
7 Prakash Singh, "Blessed are the Corrupt" in the Tribune, Chandigarh, August 7, 2005, p. 12.
8 The Tribune (editorial), New Delhi, March 10, 2011, p. 11.
9 *Ibid*
10 Prakash Singh, *op. cit.*, p. 12.

that the Central Bureau of Investigation (CBI) even during the present millennium has registered several cases of disproportionate assets against a number of political leaders. It is well accepted by government in its Approach Paper of the Eleventh Five Year plan (2007-12) which mentioned clearly that, "corruption is seen endemic in all spheres and this problem needs to be addressed immediately"[11].

This vice has deep roots in the Indian social system so much so that even the judiciary is not free from it. The immoral acts of justice V. Ramaswami [12], who worked as the chief justice of the Punjab and Haryana High Court at Chandigarh from 1987-89 can be cited as an example in this regard. The recent impeachment proceedings against Justice Soumitra Sen in the Parliament and his consequent resignation as a Judge of the Kolkata High Court, is a matter of the same. "Justice Sen has been charged with misappropriating money and misrepresenting facts about the misuse of money."[13] This phenomenon is also common among the judiciary at the subordinate level where, "Corruption, Nepotism, misconduct and mal-administration are the order of the day." The following two recent cases may be cited in this regard. In the first case the Chief Judicial Magistrate of Jhajjar (in Haryana) was placed under suspension by the Punjab and Haryana High Court, "for his questionable role during his earlier stint at Sonipat (in Haryana)." While in the second case, the Additional District and Session Judge of Ludhiana (Punjab) was deprived of all judicial work till his retirement, with an order of the same honourable High Court.[14] In the light of the above, the demand of Mr Anna Hazare and his team from the government to pass the Jan Lok Pal Bill in the Parliament seems to be justified.

SOCIAL AND VOLUNTARY ASSOCIATIONS

Every society is characterized by a number of social and voluntary associations such as trade unions, religious or professional bodies, social groups, residents' welfare associations etc. Associations play a significant role in aggregating and articulating the interests of a large number of people and give effective expression to their demands. Thus they act as the vehicle through which differing interests are mediated from the citizens to the government.[15] These associations have a specific purpose or a set of goals to be realized. These associations serve two purposes. On the one hand, they play a significant role in articulating the demands of their members and exerting considerable pressure on public authorities to get their interests fulfilled. Resultantly, they come in direct contact with the administrative functionaries. They

11　The Tribune (editorial), New Delhi, March 10, 2011, p. 11.
12　Justice V. RamaSwami was found involved in "several acts of omission and commission". An Enquiry Committee constituted to look into the charges leveled against him observed that Justice Ramaswami indulged in "...gross misuse of office, purposeful and persistence negligence in the discharge of duties, intentional and habitual extravagance at the cost of public exchequer, moral turpitude by using public funds for private purpose in diverse ways and reckless disregard of statutory rules and bring dispute to the high judicial office and dihonour to the institution of judiciary and undermine the faith and confidence which the people repose in the administration of justice." For details, refer, C.K Jain, "Justice Rama Sawmi Case" in *Journal of Constitutional and Parliamentary Studies*, Vol.XXXVII, No1-4, January – December 2002, p. 461.
13　The Tribune (Editorial), New Delhi, August 20, 2011, p. 2.
14　The Tribune (Editorial), Chandigarh, August 22, 2005.
15　F.W. Riggs, *op. cit.*, p. 19.

also provide relevant information as well as feedback to the administration thereby helping it in the formulation of policies. The administration is also benefited from the co-operation extended by these associations at the level of policy implementation. Thus it is a two way process of interaction between the administration and the social associations in which, both influence each other.

In this regard, Riggs has aptly remarked that the consequences of the linkage with associations are of paramount significance. On the one side a system of persistent pressure "...keeps the administrator alert and responsive, providing him with information and making him even conscious of the audience which stands ready to condemn or reward. Conversely associations provide the administrator with a weapon of incalculable power to assist him in the implementation of government programmes."[16] In this way these social and voluntary associations apart from fundamentally shaping the conduct of administration, also contributes in multiplying its effectiveness". It is to be noted that, the greater the number of such associations in a society, the more the administration would be benefited and the more would it be responsive to the public.

SOCIETAL AMBITIOUSNESS

Level of societal ambitiousness is another key element of the social environment, which influences the public administration heavily and gets influenced by it. A society in which the people have a high level of ambitiousness, people will be more demanding. They will be progressive and forward-looking. Closely related to societal ambitiousness is social consciousness. If the people are more ambitious, than there will be an urge on their part to know about their surroundings, rights and duties as well the rights and duties of the administration. This makes the people forward looking, with clarity of vision and broader perspective.

This will have a direct bearing on the administration. They will expect greater efficiency, efficacy as well as responsiveness from the administration. Resultantly, the administration will be more vigilant. Simultaneously, the administration will also be greatly benefited by the higher level of societal ambitiousness because people with higher social ambitiousness will extend all possible help to and will co-operate generously with the administrative functionaries in discharging their administrative obligations. On the other hand, if the level of societal ambitiousness is low i.e., the people are less demanding and less careful about their rights and the obligations of the administration, the administration will adopt a non-responsive and non-reactive posture. The administration will also be less efficient as well as less effective in that case.

Conversely, if the administration is more ambitious, it will promote the ambitiousness among the people. It will generate awareness about their rights and duties as well as those of itself. It will, through the mechanism of public relations department, raise the societal consciousness and their ambitiousness of the people.

CULTURAL ENVIRONMENT

Culture refers to the 'way of life' developed by a society. It includes the entire gamut of modes of expression and communication as well as the system of values and

---

16 *Ibid*, p. 17.

beliefs that regulate social behaviour. Values refer to expression of preferences i.e. ideas of good or bad, desirable or undesirable. Culture determines what is desirable conduct or behaviour for the members of the society. Rumki Basu defined culture as the "entire sum total of beliefs and social behaviour"[17] that governs the society. She has further observed that the "culture of a country finds expression through the medium of language and art, philosophy and religion, education and science, films and newspapers, radio and television, social habits and customs, political institutions and economic organization."[18]. Thus the culture of a society is the storehouse of various mediums and symbols which are usually unwritten and helps in communicating messages in the shortest possible time.

Hence culture is the complex whole and comprises knowledge, belief, art, morals, law, custom and any other capabilities and habits acquired by man as a member of society. It is an outcome of long processes of evolution and thus is reflected in the social, economic, political and administrative institutions of a nation. Culture contributes greatly to the development or otherwise of a society. Thus culture may help in advancement or progress and it may also hinder the path of societal development. In the earlier case, it may be regarded as 'progressive' while in the later case it may be considered as 'retrogressive'.

Therefore culture of a society plays a significant role in influencing its administrative system as it is reflected in its institutions, its processes and structures and affects them to a large extent. The various cultural factors exert their constant influence to a large extent directly on the working of administration. A brief account of these cultural factors is as under:

ISSUE OF LANGUAGES

Diversity of Languages is an important cultural aspect in a society that exerts its influence on the administrative working. Language is a medium of expressing and exchanging views and ideas. It may be stated to be a vehicle through which one communicates one's ideas, views etc. to others. "Obviously language is the main vehicle of assimilation for, if everyone speaks the same language, they can receive the messages sent by the elite, and they in turn can communicate more readily with the elite".[19] However, it is generally observed that those societies in which more than one language is used (multilingual societies), the groups of people using different languages are at loggerheads with one another. Language, being a cultural phenomenon becomes a very sensitive issue on many occasions. Linguistic disputes and riots have at times threatened national unity and solidarity.

Each one of the groups considers their respective language superior to those of the others and this cause social tension. This tension is also reflected at the administrative level. Firstly, the administrative functionaries are also the part of the society and therefore, they give more weight to the language which they use/speak. This brings biasness in their official functioning. Secondly, there remains a communication gap between different administrative functionaries using different

---

17 Rumki Basu, *Public Administration: Concepts and Theories*, Sterling publishers Pvt. Ltd. 1992, p. 133.
18 *Ibid*, p. 133-134.
19 Riggs, F.W., *op. cit.*, p. 36.

languages. The message given by one administrative functionary may not be communicated to the other functionary due to language problems or barriers thereby creating the problem of lack of co-ordination. Moreover, administrative functionaries belonging to different language groups form informal groups and this is reflected in their administrative functioning and decision making. Simultaneously, the people belonging to one language group would not be ready to co-ordinate with the administrative functionaries belonging to the other language group. All this creates unnecessary tension, confusion and suspicion among the administrative functionaries thereby affecting the efficiency of the administration adversely. Formation of groups on linguistic lines i.e., linguistic ties affect the administration in another form also. It promotes the problem of favouritism and nepotism on lingual considerations.

For instance, India is a multi-lingual country. The Indian constitution has given recognition to as many as 22 languages. Besides, there are several other languages, which though have not been given constitutional status, but are equally rich. Along with this there are a number of dialects in each of the language. All this makes the culture of India highly diverse in so far as the language is concerned. In the absence of an all India language as a unifying force, the formation of linguistic states has taken the country towards narrow, sectionalism, provincialism and parochialism, endangering national integration. Hence, instead of giving strength to the culture, this multi-lingual character is creating social tensions and thus causing serious problems for the administration.

REGIONALISM

Regionalism is another crucial cultural aspect, which exerts a serious influence on the administration working. Regional diversities may promote regional feelings not only on the part of common people but also on the part of administrative functionaries belonging to different regions. Such regional feelings lead to develop narrow perspective and vision of the administrative personnel working at various rungs of administration. The administrative personnel may show more commitment and loyalty to regional interests and give more priority to these interests at the cost of national interests i.e., the broader national interests become subservient to the parochial regional interests. These fissiparous forces may emerge as a serious threat to administrative unity. They may not only promote national disintegration rather becomes a hindrance in the path of administration. It becomes a serious problem to promote administrative uniformity through out the country and to realize the broad national goals. The issue of Sutlej-Yamuna Link (SYL) canal may be cited in this regard. This is a regional issue between the two states of Haryana and Punjab. Haryana has been advocating the completion of this canal while Punjab is adamant not to let the water flow in that canal. Without going into the details of the rationality of arguments given in their respective favour, it may be stated that this issue, besides, creating animosity among the people of the two states, is constantly plaguing their administration.

Similarly, another regional problem having almost similar repercussions is that of Cauvery river water dispute among Tamil Nadu, Andhra Pradesh, Karnataka and the union territory of Pondicherry. The issue of neglect of the southern parts (now Jharkhand State) of Bihar at the cost of the northern parts created serious administrative problems in Bihar and ultimately culminated in the creation of the Jharkhand state after a long drawn conflict between the people of southern Bihar and the Bihar administration. These and several other such regional issues have been constantly plaguing the administration, trying to exert pressure on the administration and trying to pull the administration in their own directions.

RELIGION

Religion is another important aspect of the cultural environment of the administration. It plays an important role in social engineering or social fusion. It is a faith or belief, which binds the people together, besides directing their behaviour in the desired direction. It is also a controlling and regulating factor in the society. Thus religion is an important vehicle of assimilation. "To the extent that the whole population shares the same religious faith, they can be readily assimilated, whereas differences in basic belief tend to separate a population in separate communities. If religious creeds vary in population, assimilation requires that they be reduced to a secondary social role."[20] Though all the religions have the same objective viz. to direct and regulate the behaviour of the people to avoid social disorder yet each one does it in its own way. In other words, it may be said that different religions preach different ways of regulating human conduct. This does not mean that different religions have contradictory viewpoints, rather, if seen in a deeper perspective, support each other. However, generally, people adopt a parochial viewpoint and regard their own religion superior in comparison to that which others follow. This results in the creation of religious disharmony and even religious intolerance. Consequently, if a country has people following one religion, it will be marked by religious harmony thereby smoothening the path of the administration. If on the other hand, a country is multi-religious, it is likely to be marred by problem of religious disharmony. These religious conflicts are reflected at the level of the administration because, firstly, the administrative functionaries, belonging to different religious communities, will show their commitments and loyalties towards their respective religions. Secondly, the administration will have to face the problem of religious intolerance at the societal level that will create hazards in the process of smooth functioning of the administration. The religious problems compel the administration to deviate from its priority of development to solving the problem of religious conflicts.

The long drawn issue of the Babri-Masjid at Ayodhya in India may be cited in this connection. It even resulted in the culmination of the heinous crime committed at the Godhra railway station in Gujarat on 27th February, 2002 early in the morning.[21] But the story did not end here. This incident was followed by the communal riots in Gujarat in which several innocent people were killed while several others have been rendered homeless during the riots that continued in the state for about a month. The merciless killing (by burning to death) of the religious missionary Staines, who ran a leprosy home at Baripada, and his two sons Philip and Timothy, by a mob that set ablaze the station wagon in which they were asleep, at Manoharpur in Keonjhar district of Madhya Pradesh in, 1999, is still another incident of religious intolerance.[22]

---

20 *Ibid*
21 The Times of India, New Delhi, February 28, 2002, p. 1.
22 The Tribune, Chandigarh, May 20, 2005, p. 1.

Recently, after the 7th July, 2005, terrorist attacks in London (popularly known as, the 7/7 incident), the 'subsequent attacks on mosques and gurudawaras in England by the British people in anger, narrates the story of religious fundamentalism. However, the Sikhs and the Muslims who made Britain their dwelling place, have no concern with the Islamic terrorists. This was the replica of what happened in USA after the 11th September, 2001 terrorist attacks on World Trade Centre incident (popularly known as the 9/11 attacks)[23].

SYMBOLS

Communication is a significant force or element in the context of cultural environment that has direct link with the administration and influences it considerably. Symbols are the vehicles or the channels for communication. Mainly there are two types of channels for transmission of experiences viz. horizontal and vertical transmissions. In horizontal transmission, the experiences of one segment of society are transmitted to another segment of that society at the same time. Vertical transmission is that in which the experiences of one generation are transmitted to the next generation. Such type of communication is mainly available in Oriental Societies (Asiatic Societies). These experiences are collected by these societies though not in the form of written reports but even than they are transmitted. In fact, every society tries to communicate its tiny experience from one generation to another. The mode of transmission of these experiences is through mediums and symbols. So mediums and symbols are the significant ways of communication, having a direct impact on administration and thus influence it. Through these mediums and symbols, the ruler and the ruled gradually come to think alike on major issues. Thus they help in promoting administrative communication which contributes to raising the level of administrative efficiency.

Through symbols, views and ideas are transmitted without actual conversation and that also in a relatively very short period. They constitute a 'standardized' form of communication – standardization in terms of universal applicability or regional applicability. Usually, the symbols having regional applicability are those developed and used by the local people. On the other hand, generally, symbols having universal applicability are those created by the State. Through such symbols, "the ruler and the ruled gradually come to think alike on major issues, the structure and goals of government, the basis of legitimacy etc"[24] For example, the traffic police in every country uses a number of symbols through which the required message is communicated to the vehicle drivers in an extremely short time period. Besides, every society develops certain symbols of its own from which it draws certain messages. For instance, in Indian society, a *pagari* (turban) is a symbol of respect. Therefore, a person who has been publicly offered a *pagari* will be honoured by the people and accordingly the administration will also be influenced by this factor. Even if such a person commits some crime the police officials, would not, in the first instance, dare to arrest him. The same happens to the white *khadi kurta payjama* which is regarded to be a symbol of political power. Thus a person wearing it will be taken to be political leader and given the more weight by the administration in comparison to a common person.

---

23 *Ibid*, July 12, 2005, p. 10.
24 *Ibid*

On the other hand, administration influences the behaviour of the society by the use of certain symbols. For instance, a vehicle having installed 'red-lights' atop it, is regarded to be a symbol of authority. Consequently, the person traveling in these vehicles are looked at with respect and honour. Similarly, khaki (the police uniform) is a symbol of fear and hatred (because of the colonial legacy attached to it). Thus a person wearing khaki will be looked at with terror and dislike. Likewise, in every country several such symbols are part of the culture. All these symbols not only influence the behaviour of the members of the society, as well as that of the administrative functionaries. The Administrative functionaries get the necessary message from these symbols and carry out their administrative obligations accordingly.

ECONOMIC ENVIRONMENT

Economy is another sub-system that is in constant interaction with the public administration. The economic system is one of the sub systems of a larger system, society. Its significance can be understood from the fact that Marx builds up his political superstructure upon the foundations of the economic structure[25]. The economy of a country deeply influences the form, structure and nature of activities of public administration. Simultaneously, public administration also directs, shapes and influences the economy. In fact, economy is the basis of all administrative activity. In economy, it is essential to study its various aspects, which influence the administration viz. economy as a system of production, the technology used, the instruments utilized, the level of technology and the entire system of exchange. "The economy could not survive without the administrative system and the system is determined in many respects by the requirements of the economy. Moreover, the administrative system could not survive were it not for the productivity of the economy supporting it."[26]

The economic context of public administration can be examined under following heads –

Prioritisation Through Planning

In every country, a large plethora of functions are performed by the administration but there are fewer resources in comparison to the problems faced by it. This is particularly so in the developing countries. In view of this it becomes inevitable for the administration (for the proper and effective utilization of the resources) to adopt planned development. Planning is the process of prioritization i.e., through planning, the administration assesses the existing resources, lays down the list of priorities (of problems) and allocates the resources to them keeping in view their availability. Thus through planning, the administration not only addresses itself to the problems faced by it in a systematic order but also reduces the possibility of wastage of resources. However, the extent to which the administration will be able to resolve the problems through planning depends on the availability of resources. Thus, if the resources are scarce, the administration will not be able to resolve many problems at a particular point of time.

---

25 Gurdev Sumra, *Public Administration: A Pragmatic Approach,* New Delhi: Atma Ram and Sons, 1993, p. 81.
26 Riggs, *op. cit.,* p. 12.

LEVEL OF ECONOMIC DEVELOPMENT

Economic development of a country is a yardstick to measure its level of overall development. If the economy of a country is more developed, the country will also be more developed and, therefore, there will be fewer problems for the administration of that country. Moreover, the level of the problems that the administration will be addressing will also be high. Such an administration will, for instance, not be engaged in resolving the problem of fulfillment of the basic needs of the people, rather the administration will trying to provide better housing, clean environment and better civic amenities including sanitation to its citizens.

If the level of economic development in a country is low, the administration will be plagued by serious problems. The economy will be facing the problem of low productivity and insufficient surplus generation due to which the administration will not be able to pay as much salary as their counterparts in those countries which are economically developed. Due to low salaries, the officials are not able to fulfill their basic requirements, which create two possibilities. Firstly, the efficient administrative functionaries will quit the job and will either join the private sector or will leave the country for higher gains. Secondly, they may develop the tendency to earn money through unfair means, which promotes administrative corruption. In either case, the efficiency of the administration will be adversely affected. This will also result in low morale, low administrative capability and ultimately in low level of goal-realization. Given this situation, the formulation and implementation of better and sound policies towards economic development would be seriously hindered.

TECHNOLOGY

The technology used in the production of goods and services also influences the administrative system of a country directly. Technology influences the administration in two ways. Firstly, it increases administrative efficiency and secondly, it helps in developing new methods of management and organization. Poor and backward technology used in the production will result in low economic output and less efficiency. If the economy has poor and backward technology, then the administration will also use backward technology. This will affect the administrative efficiency adversely. On the other hand, if the level of technology in the economy is higher, then the administration will also be using better technology which will go a long way in improving its efficiency.

For instance, the Delhi Police acquired the Maruti Gypsy car produced by the Suzuki Motor Company of Japan, which also set up a plant at Gurgaon in India, in the early 1980s. It was one of the fastest cars in India at that time. This helped increase the efficiency of Delhi Police as it could then chase and apprehend the culprits more rapidly.

TECHNICAL MANPOWER

The technological advancement in the economy will be of no use if there is paucity of technical manpower not only to use and maintain that technology, but for constant research and development on that technology. In the want of technical manpower, the technological advancement will be short lived, as the life span of technology is very short in modern times. The administration has a great role to play in the development of technical manpower required by the economy. It is the administration that has to establish technical institutes for the development of trained manpower. Moreover, the administration also has a considerable role to play in the establishment of institutes to cater to the research and development needs in various fields of the economy. However, the administration will not be able to perform this function if it is poor in resources i.e., the economy is unable to spare enough resources for this purpose. Hence, the administration and economy are interdependent in so far as the development of technical manpower is concerned.

Further, if the economy needs some such technical manpower, which is not available in the indigenous market, it may be acquired from other countries. However, the economy is dependent on the administration in so far as this aspect is concerned. It is the administration that frames such rules and laws that allow the economy to hire the services of experts from abroad. Simultaneously, if the economy is not able to pay to the foreign experts, than even the administrative provisions will be futile.

RESOURCES:

Another significant dimension of the interaction of the administration and the economy is the availability of physical resources in the economy. If the economy does not have adequate resources, it will be less developed. This is because economic activity is the process of changing less usable resources into more usable resources. But if the raw material or the less usable resources are lacking, then the economy will not be able convert them into better usable resources. This makes the promotion of economic activity sluggish. However, in the generation of material resources, the role of administration is significant. It is the administration which has to acquire, exploit and plan the material resources.

INFRASTRUCTURE

For the smooth and proper development as well as functioning of the economy, a well-developed infrastructure is required. In the absence of adequate infrastructure, economic activity will be hindered. In fact, infrastructure is a precondition to economic development. It mainly includes, means of transportation and communication, electricity, banking, insurance etc. However, the administration has a key role to play in the development of infrastructure. But again the administration is dependent on the economy for developing the infrastructure. The administration requires finances to create and develop infrastructure that will be made available by the economy. If the economy is unable to generate sufficient surplus, the administration will fail in providing the adequate infrastructure.

Moreover, in the absence of properly developed infrastructure, the internal management of the administration will also be hindered. It will not be able to establish proper co-ordination among different administrative units working at various levels, which increases the possibility of inefficiency and wastage of resources.

POLITICAL ENVIRONMENT

Of the entire gamut of environmental forces of public administration, the impact of political environment is most significant; this is because public administration functions under the direction and control of the polity. Political factors play a crucial role in enhancing or impeding the operational working of administration to a greater extent. In fact, no aspect of public administration can be conceived of without an inevitable political influence. The impact of politics on public administration is at once direct and immediate. The relation between the two is intimate to the point of being inseparable. There is a close, constant and intimate interaction between the two. The whole field of public administration is ingrained in the political environment[27].

In almost every country, the administrative structures, functions, processes, rules and regulations are shaped by the polity of that country. In most of the states the written constitution establishes the whole apparatus of public administration at all levels. Constituent Assemblies and legislative bodies formulate acts, laws and enactments that provide for the establishment and functioning of all structures. Major processes of public administration like planning, policy making, budgeting and the like are basically the important areas of public administration, but at every stage and at every level of these activities, political direction continuously flows to "influence" these processes till they are finally approved by the legislature[28].

Not merely at the formulation level of the planning and policy formulation, but at the level of their execution as well, the public administration operates under political supervision. "No administrator can claim any exclusive authority of his own... All programmes, projects and works are executed by administrators under strict surveillance of a political supervisor"[29].

NATURE OF STATE

The nature of State underwent a drastic change in the second half of the nineteenth century. Prior to that, the State was not expected to look into the personal affairs of the citizens. The state was expected to perform three functions only viz. the collection of revenue, maintenance of internal order and protection of the State from external aggressions. Since the State had limited role to play, that's why the scope of the activities of administration was also very limited. However, with the onset of the industrial revolution, the problem of exploitation of the have-nots by the haves made it mandatory on the part of the State to give up the limited role and to adopt the "garb of a Welfare State". This led to a massive increase in the scope of activities of the administration, which was then expected to work for the welfare of the society. Hence it performed all those functions which were regarded to be necessary for the well-being of the largest number.

During the second decade of the twentieth century, the nature of the State further witnessed a great change. The cruel regime of the Tsar in Russia was overthrown by a group of revolutionaries called the "Bolsheviks" led by Lenin. The Bolsheviks later created the "totalitarian" state (following the ideas of Karl Marx) and laid the foundation of the Soviet State. In this system of governance, the administration was expected to perform all the functions for the survival of the individuals. Private sector was not allowed to operate and all the activities such as commercial, industrial, agricultural, trade, infrastructural, banking etc. were brought under the purview of the administration. Thus the role of administration became holistic. Hence, the nature

---

27 R.D. Sharma, *Advance Public Administration*, New Delhi: H.K. Publishers and Distributors, 1990, p. 98.
28 *Ibid.*
29 *Ibid.*, p. 99.

of the State influences the scope as well as the nature of activities falling under the purview of public administration.

On the contrary, the administration also helps in shaping the nature of the State. The example of India may well be cited in this context. The Indian Constitution aimed at the establishment of a "socialistic pattern of society". However, the administration in India failed in giving shape to this "intention" of the constitution. Therefore, the nature of Indian State has undergone considerable change during the last decade. The State has now decided to give up the earlier character and is emphasizing on "limited State role".

CONSTITUTION

The constitution is an exhaustive document containing the laws, rules and regulations enacted by a duly constituted body governing a country. All democratic countries of the world today have their constitutions and their government and administration work and function according to the provisions of that constitution. The basic structure of the administration of a country is drawn from its constitution. It is the constitution that prescribes the nature of State and the form of government. Also it is laid down in the constitution whether the country will be a federal or unitary in nature. Thus whether the country will have a parliamentary or presidential form of government will be decided by the constitution. Besides, the procedure of appointment and removal of the key functionaries, including the chief executive, are also laid down in the constitution. Thus, different administrative functionaries draw their powers, authority and functions from the constitution.

Not only the structure of administration and the functions of the administrative functionaries are decided upon by the constitution, but even the manners in which those functions are to be discharged by them are provided in the constitution. In other words, the methods or procedures as to how these functionaries have to perform their functions are also highlighted in the constitution. Besides, the rules and regulations in accordance to which these functions are to be performed are governed by the constitution of that country. The constitution also mentions the rights and duties of the citizens of that country. For instance, the Constitution of America as well as that of India, provides for the fundamental rights of their citizens. The constitution also lays down the procedure for restoration of the rights of the citizens in case they are abridged by the administration. In addition to the key administrative functionaries, the constitution, at times, also provides for and elaborates the civil service rules and guidelines regulating their conduct. It may also provide for the rights of the civil servants in a country.

In this way, it is obvious that the administration of a country is guided, directed, governed and controlled by the constitution. On the other hand, the constitution of a country is also influenced by the administration of that country. It is constantly reviewed, amended and reshaped as per the changing needs of the time. In the connection, the Indian Constitution, which has been amended about a hundred times during the last fifty years may be cited as an example. It is even, at times, redrafted or reconstituted as per the experiences of the administration. Thus for instance the Constitution of France had to be redrafted five times during the previous century.

POLITICAL LEADERSHIP

Political leadership also constitutes the environment of the administration in a country. The administration of a country functions under the direct control of the political leadership. In fact, the two work in unison for better administering the country. The political leadership is directly responsible to the sovereign of the country i.e., the people. Hence, they are given the authority to control and direct the administration. The two constitute the executive. The polity being the temporary executive while the administrative being the permanent executive. The main function of the polity is to frame policies while that of the latter is to implement them.

The character of the political leadership influences the administration greatly. A dynamic, progressive, confident and far-sighted leadership directs the administration in the desired direction. The administration under the guidance and direction of such a leadership works efficiently and effectively. It becomes result-oriented, action-oriented, change-oriented as well as responsive to the public needs and demands. On the contrary, weak political leadership fail to provide the required direction to the administration in the absence of which it also becomes inefficient and less-effective as well as less capable. It fails to achieve its objectives. The weak political leadership is unable to exercise effective control over the administration. Consequently, the possibility of misuse of authority by the administrative functionaries increases. In so far as the administration is concerned, it also influences the character of the political leadership. The administration may or may not extend full support and co-operation to the political leadership. By extending full support and co-operation, it may help in the emergence of strong political leadership while by withholding it, the administration may create obstacles.

POLITICAL PARTIES

A political party is a group trying to capture power through legal and authentic means and have an ideological base. It consists of a body of persons who come together for promoting national interests. A political party is, "any group, howsoever loosely organized, seeking to elect government office-holders under a given label."[30] The role of political parties in shaping governmental policy and influencing the working of administrative system can be delineated in terms of their function of interest aggregation of different interest groups. However, this process of interest articulation would differ from country to country depending upon political party system prevailing there at. Thus in a country having the two – party system such as the U.S. and England, both the parties would try to woo the maximum number of streams of interests. However in a multi party system, obviously, the mass base of each of parties reduces considerably and a lesser amount of interest aggregation is possible due to the stiff competition. In case of single party system like in China and the former Soviet Union there hardly arises the question of interest aggregation. In the parliamentary systems, among the different parties the one having majority

---

30 Leon D. Epstein, *Political Parties in Western Democracies*, New York: Praeger, 1967, p. 9.

support, forms the government and is naturally in a position to frame policies. The role of political parties in influencing the administrative system can be discussed under the following three heads:

Party Ideology

Every political party has an ideology, which always has an imprint on the policy it wishes to frame. Whichever party is voted to power, frame the policies and programmes in the light of its ideology. Since the administration is supposed to carry out the policies that the party in power has framed and, therefore, it will have to implement them. These policies and programmes are reframed and modified if some other political party – with different ideology – replaces the earlier party. Again, the administration cannot question this change in the policies; it will be obliged to carry out them in letter and spirit. Even if the administration feels that such alterations will not be appropriated in the light of ground realities, it can only submit its proposal to the government, which the latter is not compelled to follow.

Thus the administration is strongly influenced by the ideology of the political party in power. Also, the ideology of the political parties, especially of that in power, is greatly influenced by the administration. The proposals submitted by the administration, though are not mandatory for the government, have a far-reaching impact on the political party, and they are based on wide field experiences of the administration.

Structural Base

A political party with large and strong structural base, in terms of geographical spread of its units, will be in a position to exert more influence on the working of administration in sharp contrast to those having poor structural base and less geographical spread. For instance, the Forward Block in India, with limited organisational base is less capable to exert influence on the administration. On the other hand, the Congress and the BJP significantly influence the administration owing to their strong organisational base. This is because these parties articulate the greater number of interests, therefore, the administration is obliged to pay heed to what these parties – whether in power or out of power – state.

Similarly, the administration also influences the organisational and mass base of a political party. The administration executes the policies and programmes framed by the party-in-power keeping in view the ideology it pursues. The administration may highlight the weaknesses or the strengths of these policies. In this way the administration gives a clandestine message to the people about the effectiveness of the ideology or otherwise, which the party-in-power is pursuing. This will go a long way in promoting or reducing the structural or mass base of the political party. Obviously, the increase or decrease in the organisational base of the political party (in power) has a direct bearing on that of the other parties.

Party Manifesto

In a country having multi-party system, every political party tries to capture power. To gain power they prepare and present their manifestos containing important issues pertaining to the needs and requirements of the varied sections of the society. The party coming to power is morally bound to fulfill the commitments made before the public through their party manifestos. The party manifesto thus, influences the administrative working as it has to deviate its attention from its earlier programs and policies and switch over to the major issues reflected in the manifesto of the winning party. Hence, the manifesto of a political party effects alterations in the operational working of the administrative system. Conversely, in the light of the experiences of the administration, at times, the party-in-power is obliged to deviate from its manifesto.

PRESSURE GROUPS

A pressure group is an organization with a formal structure whose members share common objectives. They carry out programmes to influence government institutions, officials and public policies. These groups seek the realization of their objectives through exerting pressure on political and administrative functionaries. Pressure groups are instrumental in aggregating and articulating interests in such a way as to help in framing the governmental "policies" which become the foundation for public administration. Without them, "attempts to build modern administrative machinery are like efforts to construct a skyscraper without first having a foundation on which to build".[31] There are various such groups in every country. However, the strength and legitimacy of such groups differs from country to country depending upon whether they are developing or developed, democratic or dictatorial[32].

These groups not only influence the policy making aspects of the government but also have an impact on the working of administration in order to get their interests served. In developing countries, the importance of pressure groups in the realm of politico-administrative interaction can be better understood by the following remarks of Anderson, "In all systems, however, groups perform an interest articulation function; that is, they express demands and present alternatives for policy action. They may also supply public officials with much information, often of a technical sort, concerning the nature and possible consequences of policy proposals"[33].

PUBLIC OPINION AND MASS MEDIA

Public opinion is another important aspect that affects the working of the administration in an effective manner. Democracy is based on the assumption that the government is an affair of the governed and the entire working of the government and the administration should be strictly in accordance with the public opinion freely formed and freely expressed. If the administration is indulging in mal administrative activities viz. arbitrariness, vindictive use of authority, power grabbing, corruption etc., serious public opinion may be generated to overcome the problem generated by the corrupt officials. "Public opinion can sometimes be sufficiently strong to impel government towards particular policies, and perhaps more often it imposes restraints on what the government can do."[34] In this connection, mass media plays a significant role in generating mass opinion regarding the wrong deeds of the administration.

---

31 Riggs, *op. cit.*, p. 52.
32 Rumki Basu, *op. cit.*, p. 285.
33 Anderson, James E., "*Public Policy Making: An Introduction*; Boston: Houghton Mifflin Company, 1990, p. 60.
34 Riggs, *op. cit.*, p. 36.

COALITION GOVERNMENT:

A coalition government also exerts its strong influence on the working of the administration. In a multi-party system sometimes, no political party is in a position to secure requisite majority to form the government. Thus, more than one party, on the basis of their pre-poll or post-poll alliance forms the government. During the last, about a decade and half, India is continuously having coalition governments at the central level and even some of the states are no exception to this phenomenon. In a coalition government, the various coalition partners try to pull the government in different directions. The coalition partners create several compulsions in the smooth working of the government and even threaten to walk out of the coalition in the event of non-acceptance of their demands thereby endangering the very existence of the coalition government. The remaining partners are seldom left with any options but to bow down before them by sidetracking their own ideology. For instance, the present UPA government at the centre has faced an embarrassing situation on the issue of 'tainted' ministers and on some other such issues. Thus, the administration is obliged to modify its policies under the pressures of the coalition partners.

On the other hand, the administration also influences the operation of the coalition governments. In fact, the administration has a great role to play in the smooth functioning of coalition governments. This is done through the informal groups in the administration which have liaisons with the different segments of the coalition government. Further, the administration participates or retards the coalition conflicts keeping in view whether the conflict is in favour or against the interest of the administration.

4
ADMINISTRATIVE FEATURES: DEVELOPING & DEVELOPED COUNTRIES

The administration of every country whether developed or developing has certain peculiar characteristics. These characteristics are the reflections of the functioning of the administration of a country. These features may evolve over a period of time and thus will be evolutionary in nature or they may emerge spontaneously in case of the administrative system coming into existence as an outcome of some revolutions. These characteristics are dependent on a number of factors such as historical background, geographical conditions, socio-cultural milieu and the economic conditions. The administrative features of a country may even witness certain changes over a period of time depending upon the changing ecology of the administration. Some of these are related to the structure of the administration while others may be the outcome of its functioning. The earlier are termed as structural features while the latter are christened as functional features. In the present chapter, the administrative features of both developing and developed countries have been discussed in detail.

A. DEVELOPING COUNTRIES

Emergence of a number of independent countries of Asia, Africa, Latin America and Middle East in the post Second World War phase was the most significant development of the twentieth century. These countries were earlier the colonies of the imperial mights of the West. "The new nations emerged out of the dark experience of imperial exploitation and embarked upon a complex process of social reconstruction. Poverty, illiteracy, diseases and mal-nutrition, low agricultural and industrial productivity together posed a formidable challenge for the governments of the new nations"[1]. To overcome these problems, most of them chose the path of planned development and assigned this task to their administration, which was thus named as Development Administration. To perform this gigantic task, the administration of these countries, besides creating certain new administrative structures, modified some of the existing ones to suit their democratic purpose. Most of the newly structures were, however, borrowed from the Western countries rather than being indigenous. Thus all the administrative structures of these newly emerged countries were rooted in the Western culture because they were either the legacy of the past or imitation of the West. Incepted in the Western culture and transplanted (with modifications) in an entirely

---

1. Bhattacharya, Mohit, *Public Administration: Structure, Process and Behaviour*, Calcutta: The World Press, 1987, p. 274.

different environment, the administrative organisations developed certain peculiar features. These characteristics of the developing countries may be better explained and understood by dividing them into structural and functional categories. Those characteristics which emerge from the "patterned behaviour" of an administrative system that has become "standardized" are classed as structural features whereas functional features are the "outcome of the interaction of two or more structures" of an administrative system.

STRUCTURAL FEATURES

Following are the chief structural features of the developing countries:

1. Complicated Organizational Structures

Most of the developing countries of today are the product of colonial rule and came into being after the end of colonialism. In other words, they were colonies of one or the other imperial mights (now christened as developed countries) during the hey-day of imperialism. This signifies the fact that the administration in these countries acquired shape and meaning under the impact of the colonial system. This means that the European systems have essentially affected and shaped the structure and the system of administration in these countries. Simultaneously, however, their administrative systems are influenced by the problems of development these countries have been facing after gaining independence. Owing to the diversity in the nature and content of their socio-cultural, economic and political fabric, the problems faced by their administrative systems become unique to each one of them and shape and influence their respective administrative structures. Consequently, the structures of the administrative organizations become highly complex and complicated.

2. Transitionality

Complex administrative structures give rise to another organizational feature of the developing countries viz. the 'transitionality' of their administrative structures. This means that the administrative structures are going through a process of transition. Two reasons may be cited for the transitional nature of their administrative structures. Firstly, since these countries are going through a process of social transformation and reconstruction, the administration, being a part of the overall system, cannot remain in isolation and thus unaffected by these changes. Therefore, their administrative structures are shaped and reshaped in tune with the needs of changing times. Simultaneously the functions performed by them also undergo dramatic changes.

Secondly, due to the rigid attitude of the bureaucracy, the administration fails to realize the desired objectives. Consequently, the administration, to attain the desired objectives, brings relevant changes in the structures of their organizations time and again. This keeps their administrative structures in the stage of constant transition.

For instance, in India the administration has been constantly making relevant changes in its structures in tune with the ongoing process of globalization and privatization. However, the steps taken by the Indian administration have failed to give desirable results owing to the rigid attitude of the bureaucracy.

3. Powerful Bureaucracy

Those developing countries that underwent the imperial experience received the problem of powerful bureaucracy in legacy. Because of being the seat of their native political power being situated far away from where the guidelines, directives and orders were to be implemented and poor communication facilities in those days, the imperial governments were not in a position to control these countries politically. The imperial powers were thus compelled to give the bureaucracy considerable free hand. In this regard Ferrel Heady is correct in saying that "the colonial administrative heritage includes one incidental feature that has lasting effects. The colonial version of British, French, or any other system of administration was suited to the requirements of colonial government rather than government at home".[2] He further argued that the colonial bureaucracy was "...more elitist, more authoritarian, more aloof, more paternalistic. Remnants of these bureaucratic traits have inevitably carried over to the successor bureaucracies in the new states"[3].

After independence, in most of the developing countries, administration was assigned the task of carrying out socio-economic development. This concentrated lots of powers in the hands of the bureaucracy. On the other hand, however, the political leadership in these countries were inexperienced and immature and, therefore, weak. Further, these countries are characterized by political instability thereby making political intriguing a common practice. Thus political leadership has little time to concentrate on their official obligations, thereby giving the bureaucracy almost a freehand even in those matters in which it has merely advisory role. Consequently, in almost all the matters, the bureaucracy is heavily relied upon. All this made the bureaucracy very powerful.

4. Lack of Trained Manpower

Skilled, trained and specialized manpower is a prerequisite for the development of a country. The developed countries of today are developed because they possess skilled manpower – indigenous as well as acquired through influx into these countries on account of brain drain from the developing ones. In so far as the developing countries are concerned, most of them have massive unemployment yet they are deficient in skilled manpower. These countries are typically characterized by lack of trained manpower with managerial skills, developmental orientation, farsighted vision and futuristic perspective.

Besides being not able to create the sufficient skilled manpower, these countries have also to face the problem of exodus of whatever skilled manpower they create. These countries are not able to pay adequately to the skilled manpower. Moreover, in most of these countries, the generalists have far greater say in policy formulation, due to which the technocracy feels neglected.

Ferrel Heady is correct in saying that these countries are "deficient in skilled manpower" which is inevitable for carrying out developmental programmes. He further argued that the problem is not that of "... a general shortage of employable manpower; actually, the typical developing country has an abundance of labour ...

---

2 Heady, Ferrel, *Public Administration: A Comparative Perspective*, New York: Marcel Dekker, 1991, p. 298.
3 *Ibid*

the shortage is in trained administrators with management capacity, developmental skills, and technical competence."[4] He further blamed the existing education system in these countries. He opined that a number of countries for example India and Egypt, "... have sizeable pockets of seemingly highly educated unemployed, who either have been educated in the wrong subjects or are the products of marginal institutions"[5].

5. *Lack of Advanced Technology*

In most of the developing countries, the generalists have far greater say in policy formulation, due to which the technocracy feels neglected. Consequently, there is either lopsided technocracy or there is the problem of brain drain. Resultantly, in these countries, indigenous technological advancement becomes difficult and hence they have to rely heavily on borrowed technology. But in modern times, technology has a very short life span and thus, unless otherwise backed by constant research and development, becomes outdated very rapidly. However, due to the lack of research and development facilities in these countries (which in itself is due to the lack of technocracy) today's latest technology (borrowed) becomes outdated tomorrow. Thus these countries are caught in the 'vicious circle of technological backwardness'

6. *Centralized Administrative Mechanism*

Another characteristic of the organization in the developing countries is that they are highly centralized administrative systems, which mean concentration of formal authority at the top echelons of administrative hierarchy. It is the systematic and consistent reservation of authority at central points within an organization[6]. It is the opposite of dispersal and delegation of authority. This means the centre of authority remains to be one and most of the authority is exercised by that centre. Other levels remain away from the authority and thereby away from the actual exercising of power.

The basic reason behind excessive centralization in these countries seems to be a legacy of the past. As noted earlier, most of the developing countries of today tasted colonialism and one of the important principles of imperialism had been centralization i.e., the colonial administration always emphasized on concentrating most of the authority at the apex. Even after several decades of their independence, these countries have not been able to correct the ills of imperial legacies. Excessive centralization is not an exception and continues to plague their administrative systems even today.

7. *Lack of Popular Participation*

The developing countries are also characterized by the dearth of popular participation, which means direct involvement of the people in the process of administrative decision-making, policy formulation and implementation. According to the Team for the Study of Community Projects and National Extension Service "...it is their full realization that all aspects of community are their concern and the government's participation is only to assist them where such assistance is necessary"[7]. Community participation is

---

4   *Ibid*
5   *Ibid*
6   Allen, Louis A., *Management and Organization*, New York: McGraw Hill, 1958, pp. 157-58.
7   Report of the Team for the Study of Community Projects and National Extension Service, Vol. 1, New Delhi: Committee on Plan Projects, 1957, p. 3.

the pre-requisite for the success of any development plan or programme. As a matter of fact, what to speak of the developmental functions, even the routine administrative obligations cannot be effectively performed in the absence of active involvement of the people. In the words of V. Subramanian, "The success of programme of action depends on response to it of the citizen and particularly the class of people whom the programme is intended to benefit"[8].

Moreover, popular participation is significant from another dimension as well; it is essential to check bureaucratic malfeasances and excesses, which are quite frequent in developing countries. In this regard, what Mishra and Sharma have said is worth citing. To them, "With a view to forestalling the dangers of bureaucratic elitism and totalitarianism, people's participation becomes inevitable"[9]. In fact, people's participation becomes all the more important in a country like India to bridge the gap between the people and the administration and to develop mutual faith among the two.

8. Inadequate Information Machinery

Along with the lack of a suitable pool of skilled manpower, a machinery to gather the information and facts is missing in the administrative systems of these countries. This kind of information machinery is required to gather the information and necessary data for the plan and project formulation. Lack of this kind of machinery adversely affects the process of plan formulation because the system of planning is a very scientific mechanism. Its basis is correct information and facts. Such a machinery is very fundamental for the plan's development. In the want of accurate information at the plan formulation stage, the whole plan will go out of gears when it comes at the stage of implementation.

Besides, goal setting, particularly, the determination of priorities, is a serious problem in these countries because of the lack of accurate information about the available resources. This is the reason that it becomes difficult to make a proper assessment of the overall situation in the economy. Even to determine the aims and objectives of planning becomes a great difficulty and the system of planning with vagueness in goals takes the whole process of development away from the real track.

Lack of advanced information machinery also adversely affects the processes of plan implementation, evaluation as well as feedback. All this puts the entire system of planning out of gears.

FUNCTIONAL FEATURES

Following are the important functional features of the developing countries:

1. Formalism

One of the significant functional features of the developing countries is 'formalism' which means the discrepancy between the theory and the practice. Riggs defined formalism as "...the extent to which a discrepancy exists between the prescriptive

---

8 Subramanian, V., "The Citizen and Planning" in *The Indian Journal of Public Administration*, Vol. XXI, No.3, 1975, p. 357.
9 Mishra, S.N. and Sharma, Kushal, "Ensuring People's Participation in Rural Development Programmes" in *Kurukshetra*, Vol. XXXIII, No.4, 1985, p. 6.

and the descriptive, between formal and effective power, between the impression given by constitution, laws and regulations, organisations charts and statistics, and actual practices and facts of government and society"[10]. It is interesting to note that in the case of developing countries, there is found to be a wide gap between what they formally state and what they actually practise. To Riggs, "The greater the discrepancy between the formal and effective, the more formalistic is a system"[11]. Like heterogeneity, formalism pervades all walks of life including administration.

Describing administrative formalism, Arora has said that "actual official behaviour" in developing countries "...does not correspond to legal statutes, even though the public official may insist on following some of the laws literally. Often they insist on meticulously following some technical provisions of laws and rules, while at the same time overlooking other – usually those that relate to general terms and objectives"[12].

2. Administrative Corruption

Corruption is a deviation from established norms or from what is prescribed. It has been defined as "deliberate and intentional exploitation of one's position, status, or resources directly or indirectly for personal aggrandizement whether it to be in terms of material gains or enhancement of power, prestige or influence beyond what is legitimate or sanctioned by commonly accepted norms..."[13]. It includes material as well as non-material gains. Corruption is a common phenomenon widely prevailing in almost all the developing countries. It is stated to be gravely plaguing their administrative systems to the detriment of the public at large. It is one of the main hindrances in the path of development of these countries. Even the political leadership sometimes feels helpless to contain the problem of administrative corruption.

The basic source of administrative corruption in these countries is the conflict inherent in their administrative culture. Ferrel Heady also identified corruption as one of the peculiar features of the administrative systems in these countries. In his words, "Corruption, on a scale ranging from payments to petty officials for facilitating a minor transaction to bribes of impressive dimensions for equally impressive services, is a phenomenon so prevalent as to be expected almost as a matter of course."[14]

3. Redtapism

Another important functional feature of the developing countries is red tapism. The dictionary meaning of red tapism is 'excessive formalities in official transactions'. It is an outcome of the complicated administrative procedures. Complication of administrative procedures emerged as a result of overlapping i.e., because of the coexistence of the old and the new official procedures. Such procedures involve much paper work moving through many levels of organizational hierarchy thereby causing

---

10 *Ibid*, pp. 91-92.
11 *Ibid*, p. 92.
12 Arora, R.K., *Comparative Public Administration: An Ecological Perspective*, New Delhi: Associated Publishing House, 1996, p. 111.
13 Avasthi, A. and Maheshwari, S.R., *Public Administration*, Agra: Lakshmi Publications, 1971, p. 342.
14 Heady, Ferrel, *op. cit.*, 1991, p. 300.

inordinate delay and frustration. This problem is the product of excessive adherence of the administrative officials who develop the habit of giving more importance to rules and regulations than mankind or human beings.

This functional feature may also be attributed to the bureaucratic model of development adopted in developing countries. While highlighting the features of his bureaucratic model, Max Weber pointed out that "the administrative acts, decisions and rules are formulated and recorded in writing even in cases where oral discussion is the rule or is even mandatory"[15]. However, this feature of the Weberian model gives rise to much paper work and therefore, is time consuming. Even the petty directives moving downward or the trivial reports moving upward have all to be recorded and thus cause unnecessary delay and therefore red tapism.

4. Nepotism

Nepotism means showing special favours or loyalty on the basis of family, kinship relations, caste, creed etc. Thus the officials while discharging their administrative obligations, extend as much help to their kin as possible. Though such behaviour is theoretically proscribed and even condemned, yet it is effectively practised in administrative working. Nepotism is an important characteristic of the administrative systems of the developing countries. It, like red-tapism, adversely affects the efficiency of the administrative systems and hinders the process of development of the society. In fact, it is a societal characteristic, which hangs over to the administrative systems of these countries. The kinship bonds are so strong in such societies that the administrative officials, even though strongly feel against, cannot come out of the clutches of these ties. Merit is often sacrificed at the altar of nepotism and consequently even inefficient persons enter the administration, thereby destroying the efficiency of the administration.

B. DEVELOPED COUNTRIES

After the Second World War, the administrative systems in the developed countries have witnessed some basic changes. These changes can be seen from the point of view of the organization and the scope of their administrative systems. In developed countries, the structure, nature as well as methods of their administrative organizations have undergone changes in accordance with the changing needs of the society. While looking at the scope of the administrative activities, the nature of issues and problems are not only different but also higher in comparison to those of the developing countries. For instance, one of the important problems faced by the administration in the developed countries is regarding the protection of the environment and animal life while these problem are nowhere in the list of priorities of the administration in the developing countries. Further, the problem of urbanization in these countries can be related to the problem of providing better housing facilities, civic amenities and improved services to the citizenry while the administration in the developing countries are still engaged in resolving the basic problems pertaining to the necessities of life like food and shelter.

---

15 Max Weber as quoted in Ravindra Prasad, D., Prasad, V.S. and Satyanarayana, P. (eds.) *op. cit.*, 1991, p. 83.

From the point of view of value pattern and the attitude of the bureaucracy, it is generally observed that the administrative functionaries in these countries are more receptive and responsive. They have a problem solving as well as a people friendly approach. The administration in these countries concentrates more on human beings rather than the rules and regulations.

In view of these two dimensions, the characteristics of the administration in the developed countries can be categorized as those pertaining to their structures and the functions performed by these structures.

STRUCTURAL FEATURES

Following are the structural features of the administration in the developed countries:

1. Stress on Efficiency and Management

Efficiency refers to the ratio of input and output. In administrative terminology, organizational efficiency can be regarded as maximum goal realization with minimum input costs. In sharp contrast to the administrative systems of developing countries, enhancement of administrative efficiency is the most important objective in developed countries. Efficiency can be promoted both structurally and functionally. Structurally, it can be build up by adoption of latest technology, simplification of procedures, administrative reforms, modified hierarchy, decentralization, while functionally it can be developed through orientation courses and the training programmes. The administration of these countries adopts all these measures to promote efficiency.

Direct fallout of the stress on organizational efficiency is that the administration in these countries is becoming more akin to the concept of management. The two terms management and administration are differentiated on the ground of their orientation; thus administration is service oriented while management is efficiency oriented. The administration of these countries tries to bring coherence between these two i.e., it talks of efficient service-orientation of the administration and therefore, the word 'management' is often used in place of 'administration'. This replacement is an outcome of the improvement in the technical aspect of the organization of their administrative systems, which in itself is the result of adoption of new methods and procedures thereby improving administrative efficiency.

2. Impact of Technology

The administration in developed countries is backed by the facility of continuous research and development regarding techniques, methods and procedures adopted by the administration. Besides, their administration also heavily relies on the innovations and advancements in the field of science and technology and is always eager as well as receptive to adopt these changes in its functioning. Impact of technology on the administration in these countries can be seen in two ways. One, it has enhanced their administrative efficiency which is much higher than that in the developing countries. Secondly, it has helped in developing new methods of management and organization.

Now, since the administration in the developed countries utilizes advanced and sophisticated technology even in its routine functioning, therefore, the technocrats have a greater say in their administration. In other words, the influence of technocrats in the administration is enormous.

3. Rational Bureaucracy

Based upon a long experience of the development of the administration, the bureaucracy in the developed countries succeeded in evolving the norms and methods, which can be described as rational. Since the procedures in administration, the style of operation of the bureaucracy and the attitude of the administrative functionaries evolved over a period of long time, that's why it became norm bound. In other words, there are some well-established rules and norms that have become part of their administrative culture. That's why their compliance ensures the rational character of bureaucracy. Ferrel Heady has highlighted the rational character of the bureaucracy in the developed countries as "the public services of a modernized political system will be large scale, complex, and instrumental in the sense that its mission is understood to be that of carrying out the policies of the political decision-makers"[16]. In other words, it will tend to have the Weberian attributes as specified by him for his "ideal type" bureaucracy.

4. Responsible Administration

Due to political stability, mature political leadership, strong mass awareness and mass opinion, vigilant mass media, effective popular participation, pressure groups, political parties organized on democratic lines, the administrative acts in the developed countries always remain under constant scrutiny. Therefore, the feeling of a responsible administration is emerging strongly in the developed countries. This tendency is an outcome, on the one hand, of the re-oriented attitudes and values of the administrative functionaries. On the other hand, people have become more and more demanding.

5. Tendency towards more Democratization

The administrative systems of the developed countries are showing a greater tendency towards democratization and decentralization. The administrative authority instead of being concentrated at the top is largely dispersed over a number of hierarchical levels. Thus the middle and lower ranks of their administration also enjoy the decision making powers over matters of considerable importance and thus have not to look towards the higher politico-administrative echelons even for petty affairs. Consequently, the decision-making and plan formulation activity, instead of being concentrated at the top, is widely dispersed over the entire politico-administrative hierarchy. In this way it ensures involvement of the common people at various levels of administrative decision-making process thereby making the administrative system more and more democratic.

6. Growing Specialization

Another important characteristic of administration in developed countries is growing specialization, which means each structure performing or carrying out a specific function. In other words, specialization in administration refers to more and more

---

16 Heady, Ferrel, *Public Administration: A Comparative Perspective*, New York: Marcel Dekker, 1991, pp. 189-90.

differentiation among its structures and functions. Specialization is the result of growing use of modern technology in administration. Specialization brings role-clarity in organizational functioning thereby reducing the possibility of conflict of legitimacies. It also helps in fixing responsibility of the administrative functionaries. In this regard what Sharkansky said is worth citing: "The organization of government is patterned after the organization of the private sector, in the sense that there is a high degree of task-specialization and that roles are assigned according to the personal achievements of individuals, rather than according to family status or social class"[17].

7. Growing Popular Participation

The level of awareness about the administrative rules and procedures of the people in developed countries is higher in comparison to that of their counterparts in developing countries. Consequently, they largely involve themselves in the decision-making process of administration. This provides a democratic character to the administrative decisions. Along with the higher level of the consciousness of the common people, the administrative functionaries, to a large extent, also adopt encouraging attitude in this direction.

FUNCTIONAL FEATURES

The main functional characteristics of the administration in the developed countries are as under

1. Fair and Impartial Administration

The administrative system in these countries is highly impartial in its working and does not discriminate between any two individuals on the basis of caste, creed, religion, region, colour or for that matter on any other ground. As against the wide spread practice of "nepotism" prevailing in the developing countries, all the people are treated at par by the administration in these countries. While delivering the benefits and services, fair practices are used and no partiality on any ground is exercised. Administrative functionaries do not show nor extend any special favour.

2. Responsive Administration

According to Sahni and Vayunandan, 'administrative responsiveness' means "responding to, reflecting and giving expression to the will of the people"[18]. Responsiveness of administration is measured in terms of how rapidly, promptly and effectively do the administrative functionaries respond to the public calls while discharging their official obligations. The faster the administration responds, the more responsive it is regarded to be. Taken in this sense, the administration in the developed countries is highly responsive. As against this, the administrative functionaries in the developing countries are far less responsive. The administrative functionaries in developed countries do not have the habit of living glorified life, living in fortresses that are difficult for the common people to overcome. They also

---

17 Sharkansky, Ira, *Public Administration: Policy Making in Government Agencies*, Chicago: Rand McNally College Publishing Company, 1975, p. 30.
18 Sahni, Pardeep and Vayunandan, E., *Administrative Responsiveness in India: Perceptions, Analysis and Model Building*, New Delhi: Manohar Publishers and Distributors, 1992, p. 3.

do not meet out masterly treatment to the people nor is their behaviour officious. They act like the friend and guide of the people.

3. Administrative Realism

Administrative systems of the developed countries are further characterized by high degree of realism i.e., there is no or minimum gap between their theory and practice. Unlike the administrative systems of the developing countries, there is no gap between what do they theoretically prescribe and actually practise. In other words, what the administration of these countries formally state in the form of rules and regulations also try to effectively adopt in its actual behaviour.

4. Procedural Simplicity

Procedural complexities give rise to corruption as well as red tapism and thus mar the efficiency of an administrative system. Resultantly, the procedures should be so simple that even common citizens can easily comprehend and follow them. Thus simplicity of administrative procedures has a direct bearing on the efficiency of the administration. Unlike the administration in developing countries, the administrative systems of the developed countries have emphasized on procedural simplicity. Thus the administration of these countries tries to remove every sort of complicacies in administrative procedures.

5
MAIN CONTRIBUTORS TO COMPARATIVE PUBLIC ADMINISTRATION

Several scholars have contributed to the field of comparative public administration. An effort has been made in this chapter to highlight the contribution of two of the more prominent among them viz., Fred W. Riggs and Ferrel Heady.

FRED W. RIGGS

Theories and models of public administration, which mainly developed in the pre-2nd world war phase, were found unsuitable in the developing countries of Asia, Africa and Latin America, which came in to existence in the post war period. Developed in the western world, the theories and models were culture specific and thus were not useful and valid for all administrative systems. These models and theories could not prove helpful in understanding the administrative systems in developing countries because the environment, nature of issues and the problems thereat have been entirely different from those of the western countries.[1] There arose the need, therefore, for developing a set of models and approaches that could be universal or at least be helpful in comprehension of the administrative systems of the newly emerged countries. This prompted the emergence of comparative public administration, during later half of the 1950s and 1960s, which stressed cross-cultural, cross-temporal and cross-national administrative studies. During this period, F.W. Riggs, a prominent and innovative scholar, contributed significantly to the field and developed several analytical models and approaches to the study of public administration in a comparative perspective.

He strongly believed in empirical analysis and interdisciplinary approach and, therefore, relied on, and even borrowed concepts from, various disciplines including Sociology, Psychology, Physics, Biology and Economics and used them in developing his various models. He also borrowed and used several new words from other subjects and even coined a few to convey/ express his ideas. It is rightly observed that the terms used by Riggs to explain his models are peculiarly Riggsian[2]

LIFE-SKETCH

Born at Kuling in China in 1917, Riggs did his BA from the University of Illinois and MA from the Fletcher School of Law and Diplomacy. He completed his doctoral

---

1   Heady, Ferrel, *Public Administration: A Comparative Perspective*, (2nd ed.) New York: Marcel Dekker, 1979, p. 13.
2   Prasad, Ravinder, Parsad, V. S., Satynarayana, P., *Administrative –Thinkers*, New Delhi: Sterling Publishers Pvt. Limited, 1991, p. 235.

research in political science from Columbia University in 1948³. During 1947-48, he joined as lecturer in the City University of New York and held various positions at different places. From 1948-51, he worked with the Foreign Policy Association as a research associate. In 1951, he joined as the assistant to the director of the Public Administration Clearing House in New York where he worked till 1955. He worked as Distinguished Arthur F. Bentley Professor of Government at Indiana University during 1956-67. Besides, he also worked as a visiting professor at several places including at Yale University during 1955-56, at the National Officials Training Institute in Korea in 1956, at the University of the Philippines in 1958-66. During 1957-58, he got a fellowship from the Committee on Comparative Politics of the Social Science Research Council for research in Thailand. During 1962-63, he worked as a senior specialist at the East-West Center, University of Hawaii. In 1963, when the CAG came into existence as a Committee of The American Society of Public Administration (ASPA), he became its chairman and held this position till 1970. From 1966-67, he worked as a fellow of the Center for Advanced Study in Behavioral Sciences, Stanford.[4] After serving in Indiana University till 1967, he joined the Political Science faculty in the University of Hawaii in 1967 and worked there till his retirement in 1987. Even after his retirement, he continued to engage in research and writing. He passed away at the age of 90 on February 9, 2008[5].

F. W. Riggs secured worldwide recognition for his creative and scholarly contribution in the field of comparative public administration, especially in Asian countries like Indonesia, Korea, Philippines, Taiwan, and Thailand where he contributed to the development of public administration. He was awarded the Order of the White Elephant by the King of Thailand in 1983. Besides, he was honoured with the Dwight Waldo Award for his life time achievements in the field of public administration. "He was in Who's Who in the World and in America. His writings were translated into several languages, including Italian, French, Korean, Portuguese, Russian, and Spanish. He lectured on every continent, including in Egypt, Saudi Arabia, Ethiopia, Sudan, and Tanzania"[6].

F.W. Riggs has been a prolific writer. In the field of comparative public administrative and development administration, he wrote numerous articles and published several books. His major publications include *Frontiers of Development Administrative* (ed); *Administration in Developing Countries: The theory of Prismatic Society*; *Prismatic Society Revisited*; *Ecology of Public Administration*; *Applied Prismatic* etc. In the opinion of Ferrel Heady, Riggs's *Administration in Developing Countries: The Theory of Prismatic Society* continues to be probably the most notable single contribution to comparative administration[7]. He has further observed that mere acquaintance with his writings in comparative theory is in itself not an insignificant accomplishment[8].

---

3   http://www.isanet.org-Obituary: Prof.F.W.Riggs-ISA Blog.
4   Prasad, Ravinder, Parsad, V. S., Satynarayana, P., *op cit.*, p. 235.
5   http://www.isanet.org-Obituary: Prof.F.W.Riggs-ISA Blog.
6   *Ibid*
7   Prasad, Ravinder, Parsad, V. S., Satynarayana, P., *op cit.*, p. 235.
8   Ferrel Heady, *Comparative Public Administration: Concerns and Priorities*, in Ferrel Heady and Sybil L. Stokes (eds), *Papers on Comparative Public Administration*, Ann Arbor: Institute of Public Administration, The University of Michigan,1962, p. 4.

MAIN CONTRIBUTIONS

Riggs' main contribution in the field of comparative public administration can be discussed by analyzing his important analytical tools which he utilized to explain his administrative theories. He used structural-functional and ecological approaches in his analysis. The two approaches have been discussed in Chapter-2 of this text.

In order to analyse the administrative systems of developing countries, Riggs developed and utilized some ideal models, which proved helpful in promoting the growth of this discipline from normative to empirical. In his agraria-industria typology, which was propounded in 1957, Riggs classified the societies into two broad categories viz. Agrarian/ agriculture and Industrial societies. The polar types were abstracted from observed realities, with imperial China and contemporary America providing the bases for conceptualizing the agrarian and the industrial, respectively[9]. Riggs was of the opinion that at a given point, all societies transform into industrial from agrarian. The following main structural features have been identified of the two societies.[10]

Sr. No.	Agraria	Industria
1	Dominance of ascriptive values (Recognition of status and customs)	Dominance of achievement norms
2	Particularistic and functionally diffused	Universalistic & functionally specific
3	Stable local groups and limited spatial mobility	High degree of social & spatial mobility
4	Relatively simple and stable "occupational" differentiation	Mature & well developed occupational system
5	Existence of a differential stratification system of diffuse impact	Existence of egalitarian class system based on generalised patterns of occupational achievement

This typology was criticized for being uni-directional from agrarian to industrial societies and for the neglect of transitional societies, which are falling in the stage of in-between the two and possessing the characteristics of both polar societies.

Later on, Riggs developed another typology named 'Fused-Prismatic-Diffracted' to replace the earlier agrarian-industria typology. He classified all societies into three categories – fused, prismatic and diffracted. "Fused" and "differentiated" societies are models constructed deductively from contrasting assumptions about the relationship between structures and the number of functions they perform. A structure is "functionally diffuse" when it performs a large number of functions, and "functionally specific" when it performs a limited number of functions.[11] This categorization is purely ideal and based on his hypothetical assumption to analyze the undeveloped, developing and developed societies. The fused – Prismatic-diffracted

---

9   Arora, R. K., *Comparative Public Administration*, New Delhi: Associated Publishing House, 1996, p. 108
10 *Ibid*
11 Ferrel Heady, *op. cit.*, 4th edition, 1991, p. 91.

models are "ideal type not to be found in any actual society, but perhaps approximated in some, and useful for heuristic purposes and as an aid in the organization of data[12].

To explain the process of transformation of a society, Riggs symbolically used the diffraction of a ray of light through a prism. When a ray of light entered into a prism, it deviates/diffracts from its actual path and when it comes out, it provides a broad spectrum of light. The ray of light before entering into prism represents 'fused' stage, inside the prism 'prismatic' stage, and outside of the prism 'diffracted' stage. The terminology is drawn by analogy from optics – the prism causes the diffraction of undifferentiated fused ray of light into a rainbow spectrum of distinct colours popularly known as VIBGYOR. On the same analogy, Riggs highlighted that diffracted societies at their early stages of development would be fused, in the transitional stage prismatic and finally, in the last stage they would be in a diffracted stage. By utilizing structural-functional approach, Riggs termed the functionally diffuse societies as 'fused' the functionally specific as 'diffracted' and the intermediate societies lying between the two polar types, as 'prismatic'.[13]

Riggs has aptly remarked, "It would be a mistake to think of the fused and refracted models as a dichotomy, like two boxes, into which we could sort every concrete society. Rather, we should think of them as polar types on a scale, with an indefinitely large number of intermediate types between. To make it simple, however, let us imagine a midpoint between these extremes and let us call it the "Prismatic model" because of the Prism which refracts fused light."[14] However, Riggs emphasized that no society can be exclusively called either fused or diffracted; whereas all societies are lying in between the two polar types and thus essentially Prismatic in nature. Riggs explain it by using a scale given in the following figure[15]

X S	T X P	A X
Fused	Prismatic	Refracted

In the above figure X has been placed on three points of the scale to represent the ideal positions of the fused – prismatic – diffracted typology. According to Riggs, "If we could average the characteristics of real societies, we might be able to place them on the same scale, and I would suggest that traditional Siam might be put where I have placed the letter S, modern Thailand near T, P would represent Philippines and A, America. Of course, these are speculative guesses and not the result of any exact measurement…"[16] Logically speaking, it would seem quite clear that no actual society would be either completely fused and completely diffracted; all would be to some degree prismatic in the sense of being intermediate between the two polar types.[17]

---

12 Riggs, "Models in the Comparative Study of Public Administration" (Comparative Administration Group, American Society of Public Administration, 1959), p. 22.
13 Riggs, F.W., *Administration in Developing Countries: The Theory of Prismatic Society*, (Boston: Houghton Mifflin Co. 1964, p. 24.
14 Riggs, F.W., *The Ecology of Public Administration*, New Delhi: Asia Publishing House, 1961 p. 94.
15 *Ibid*, p. 95.
16 *Ibid*
17 Heady Ferrel, *op. cit.*, 1991, p. 91.

Riggs utilized parsonian pattern variables and hypothised that "a diffracted system would rank high in terms of universalism and achievement orientation, a fused model high in particularism and ascription, with the prismatic model inter-mediate in these scales"[18]. Riggs has also developed intermediate categories of pattern variables. Thus, a prismatic society is characterised as an intermediate category between these two by "Selectivism" (position between Universalism and Particularism), "attainment" (stage between achievement and ascription) and poly-functionalism (falling between functionally specific and diffused). Riggs has further observed that the correlation among these variable would be assumed one and need not to define.[19]

The prismatic model, as originally presented by Riggs, is of the same ideal type as that of fused and diffracted models. It represents an intermediate stage between the two extremes of a continuum with a mixture of traits of both. It highlights a society that is semi differentiated standing midway between an undifferentiated (fused) society and a highly differentiated (diffracted) society. It can be represented with the help of following figure:

Functionally diffused	Semi differentiated	Highly differentiated
Fused →	Prismatic →	Diffracted
Differentiation increasing		Differentiation increasing

In *Prismatic Society Revisited*, Riggs further complicated the matter by pointing out a new dimension with regard to his Fused-Prismatic-Differentiated typology. He realised his mistaken view of one-dimensional approach and gave a two dimensional approach in connection with this typology. The earlier dimension was categorizing societies on the bases of degree of differentiation i.e. undifferentiated; semi differentiated and highly differentiated representing fused, prismatic and diffracted societies, respectively. The above figure shows the continuously increasing differentiation from fused to diffracted.

The second dimension later introduced by Riggs has to do with the degree of integration among structures of a society. Besides being differentiated or functionally specific, the diffracted societies also need to be integrated. Thus only differentiation is not the sole criterion for a diffracted society, rather both the dimensions viz. differentiation and integration are inevitable. The second dimension is insignificant in the fused society as it is undifferentiated but integrated. If a society is highly diffracted but poorly integrated, it would qualify to be called a prismatic society rather than a diffracted society. This two-dimensional approach can be effectively presented in the following figure:

Differentiation Scale

Poor differentiation	Semi differentiation	High differentiation
Fused →	Prismatic →	Diffracted
High integration	Poor integration	High integration

Integration scale

---

18 Riggs, *Administration in Developing Countries : The Theory of Prismatic Society, op. cit.,* p. 31
19 Arora, R.K., *Comparative Public Administration, op. cit.,* p. 240.

From the above figure, it is obvious that a fused society is poorly differentiated and highly integrated. Now in a movement from fused to prismatic, one dimension that is differentiation is increasing but integration is decreasing because with the start of the process of differentiation, the bonds of fused society break down and thus increase the possibility of mal-integration or poor co-ordination among fused structures. This process results into the creation of a prismatic society, which is semi-differentiated and poorly integrated. Then in a movement from a prismatic to a diffracted society, both the dimensions are showing an increasing trend because now the process of integration results in establishing new bonds among the structures. Resultantly the diffracted society is highly differentiated as well as highly integrated.

Riggs redefined the prismatic model by expanding it to include any society that is differentiated but mal-integrated. This corresponding reinterpretation of the diffracted model makes it refer to any society that is differentiated and integrated. Hence prismatic and diffracted are no longer models next to one another on a one dimensional scale based on degree of differentiation.[20]

PRISMATIC MODEL

Since prismatic societies share the value patterns of both the polar societies i.e. fused and diffracted, Riggs explained the characteristics of prismatic societies in greater detail. He highlighted following characteristics of the prismatic model:

Formalism

Prismatic societies are characterized by a high level of formalism. It refers to the gap between the 'theoretically prescribed' and 'effectively practiced' norms and values. According to Riggs, formalism refers to "the extent to which a discrepancy exists between the prescriptive and descriptive and between formal and effective power …"[21] In other words, it means the extent to which congruence or incongruence exists between the theoretically stated objectives and their actual performance. The level of congruence between formal theory and its practices represents degree of "realism"; conversely, the incongruence between the two represents formalism. The fused and the diffracted societies have relatively high degree of realism and less formalism but it is contrary in prismatic societies.

On the pattern of diffracted societies, there are well-developed laws, rules and regulations that are supposed to be followed by the administrative functionaries. But in actual practice the behavior of the administrative functionaries is not rational, sometimes they stick to these rules but many times they violate them. Formalistic behavior is caused by "the lack of pressure towards program objectives, the weakness of social power as a guide to bureaucratic performance and a great permissiveness for arbitrary administration."[22] This formalistic behavior of government functionaries promotes their inclination towards corrupt practices. Thus formalism, generally, joins with the process of official corruption.[23]

---

20 Ferrel Heady, *Comparative Public Administration, op. cit.,* p. 92.
21 Riggs, *The Ecology of Public Administration, op. cit.,* pp. 91-92.
22 Riggs, "The 'Sala' Model: An Ecological Approach to the study of Comparative Public Administration", *Philippine Journal of Public Administration,* Vol. VI, 1962, p. 5.
23 Arora, R.K., *op. cit.,* p. 111.

Even though several laws and policies are in place in these countries, these are seldom followed. For instance, in India, smoking in public places is an offence and is prohibited, but it is usually violated. In fact, this is a common phenomenon occurring every now and then.

Heterogeneity

Heterogeneity is yet another aspect of prismatic society. In all walks of life a high degree of heterogeneity prevails. Heterogeneity means, "the simultaneous presence, side by side, of quite different kinds of systems, practices and viewpoints."[24] Heterogeneity is an outcome of the fact that even though the values and practices of the diffracted society are being acquired while those of the fused society are not given up. This is because of the fact that values cannot get replaced abruptly; they represent a mindset which takes time, sometimes even generations/ages to get replaced.

Riggs has highlighted that "the fused and refracted models are relatively homogeneous, but the prismatic model is marked by great heterogeneity."[25] On the one hand there are prismatic cities having air conditioned office building, "sophisticated" intellectual class, well developed communication system and role specificity, but at the same time there is poorly developed village life or tribal life, having traditional view points and outlook and role vagueness and a complete lack of modern facilities of living. The village elders combine various political, administrative, social, economic and religious roles.[26] Riggs has observed, "the mountain tribe and the city office building are extreme types, and in between there are many villages, towns, government offices and back street "hang outs" having distinctive characteristics quite different from both the extremes."[27]

Numerous examples of heterogeneity can be cited in Indian context. For instance, traditional education centres - *gurukuls, madarsas* etc. - simultaneously exist with convent schools patterned on western education system. Further, despite the land records having been computerized in several states, land records are continued to be maintained on traditional patterns as well. Even though there are directives promoting paper-less work and to entertain communications through electronic means, administrative functionaries usually dissuade this practice and emphasize on written communications alongside electronic communications. This is true for both in-house communications as also for communications from the people outside of their departments.

Other aspects of heterogeneity inclue poly-communalism and existence of *clects*, heterogeneity in economics "Poly-normativism" and lack of consensus and power distribution etc.

Poly-Communalism and Existence of 'Clects'

Poly communalism means, "the simultaneous existence in a society of various ethnic, religious and racial groups which live in a relatively hostile interaction with each

---

24 Riggs, *The Ecology of Public Administration, op. cit.,* p. 9.
25 *Ibid,* p. 119.
26 *Ibid*
27 Arora, R. K., *op. cit.,* p. 111.

other"[28] Thus in a poly communal society, caste, class, community and religion play an important role and resultantly a number of "interest groups" would come out. The groups represent the people of a particular community or group and serve their interests. Riggs utilized a "purely artificial word" *clects* for them. The word *clect* combines the traits of 'sects' and 'club' of the fused and diffracted societies respectively. According to Riggs, *clect* "refers to any group which makes use of modern, associational methods of organization, but retains diffuse and particularistic goals of a traditional type."[29] Riggs was of the view that it is impossible "to form a single national association for all those with a specific kind of functional interest in a prismatic society. Instead such a group might form in each community."[30] Such a group is not a clan, but neither is it an "association" in the strict sense of the word since, although it uses associational techniques of organization, its purpose is highly particularistic.[31]

Heterogeneity in Economics: Bazar Canteen Model

Riggs also highlighted existence of heterogeneity in prismatic economy and he termed this prismatic economic structure, "the bazar canteen model"[32] In a fused society 'arena' factors i.e. familial and social considerations, dominate in the economic system whereas in a diffracted society, it is the market factors (factors of supply and demand) that dominate the economy. In a prismatic economy, both of these "arena" as well as "market" factors coexist simultaneously and result in generating "price-indeterminacy". In such societies, it is difficult to have a fixed price for a commodity or service due to the simultaneous interaction and impact of both economic and non-economic factors. Here, prices of commodities or services are affected by the social, cultural and political relationships of buyers and sellers.

The price-indeterminacy promotes a bazar like atmosphere in a prismatic society. In a bazar, there are no fixed prices and bargaining is involved in each transaction. The bargaining is regulated only by personal relationships and not by the market factors of supply and demand. For instance, a good friend or a relative may be able to buy some commodity more reasonably than a stranger. Thus, the economic organizations in a prismatic society generally act like "subsidized" canteens– which provide goods and services at a price lower than the average to the members of a privileged group and the persons who are "politically influential". Moreover these economic structures, many times, also operate like "tributary canteens" – in which the under privileged or the members of outside group are forced to pay higher prices.[33] The concept of price indeterminacy can be extended to include not only goods and services, but all factors of production such as labour, capital, land, time, money[34] etc.

---

28 *Ibid*, p. 113.
29 Riggs, *The Ecology of Public Administration, op. cit.*, p. 126.
30 *Ibid*
31 *Ibid*, p. 127.
32 Riggs, "The Bazar Canteen Model" in *Philippine Sociological Review*, July- October,1958 Nos3&4, pp. 6-59
33 Arora, R. K., *op. cit.*, p. 114.
34 Riggs, The Bazar Canteen Model, *op. cit.*, pp. 13-19.

Poly-Normativism and Lack of Consensus

Yet another dimension of heterogeneity in a prismatic society is the displacement of traditional values by new ones, which Riggs called "poly-normativism". Poly-normativism is an outcome of the simultaneous existence of traditional norms of the fused society and the "new" sets of norms from the diffracted society. "If a society is poly normative and normlessness is wide spread, a substantial divorce appears between the formal and the effective, between theory and practice, between the law and its implementation, and between authority and control."[35]

In such a situation, there is a lack of consensus on the effective norms of behavior in a prismatic society. The poly normative character of the prismatic society results into dissensus (lack of consensus) on the fundamental goals of the state. But in fused and diffracted societies, there exists a high degree of consensus on the fundamental goals.

In this way, prismatic heterogeneity embraces the geographic urban-rural range, growing class and communal differentiation, the rise of counter elites and revolutionary movements, subsidized and tributary canteens and price-indeterminacy in economy, poly normativism and selectivism in administration and the existence of *clects*.[36]

Overlapping

Another important characteristic of prismatic model is overlapping. It refers to "the extent to which formally differentiated structures of a diffracted society coexist with undifferentiated structures of a fused type."[37] In a fused society, multiple number of functions are performed by some traditional structure while in a diffracted society one structure performs one prominent function. Thus in both cases there is no problem of overlapping because in these societies whatever is available is also effective. But in prismatic societies, new structures are created on the pattern of the diffracted model but the traditional structures also remained in practice. Arora has observed, "In a prismatic society, new or "modern" social structures are created, in essence the older or undifferentiated structures continue to dominate the social system."[38] In India, higher and technical education are a peculiar example where several institutions/ agencies in the course of time have been created and there is considerable confusion about the role and jurisdiction of most of them.

SALA MODEL

The word *sala* is a Spanish word borrowed by Riggs, which represents government office in Latin-American countries. Its general meaning is simply "room." "In normal usage *sala* applies to personal rooms in a home, to religious and public halls, but also and particularly, to government offices."[39] The Prismatic bureaucrats are designated as *sala* officials or *sala* men by Riggs. The counterpart of *sala* in diffracted societies

---

35 Riggs, *Administration in Developing Countries: Theory of Prismatic Society*, op. cit., p. 183.
36 Riggs, *The Ecology of Public Administration*, op. cit., pp. 127-128.
37 Riggs, *The 'Sala' Model: An Ecological Approach to the Study of Comparative Public Administration*, op. cit., p. 5.
38 Arora, R. K., op. cit., p. 112.
39 Riggs, F. W., *Administration in Developing Countries: The Theory of Prismatic Society*, op. cit., p. 268.

is termed as "bureau" whereas in fused societies it is termed as "chamber". Riggs spelled out some features of the *sala* model 'the typical bureau by reviewing the salient characteristics of the prismatic model, linking them to the logical behaviour of the "*sala* official" and relating them in each case to the criterion of administrative efficiency.[40]

Bureaucratic Recruitment/Nepotism

In the prismatic model, selection of the administrative functionaries is based formalistically on examinations, but in actual practices, non- administrative criterion like family loyalty and kinship relations are given due weight in matters of appointment. It results into the problem of nepotism. According to Riggs, there is "contrast between official duties, in which appointments on merit basis are prescribed and family loyalties which prescribe aid to relatives in finding positions, produces the familiar phenomenon of nepotism."[41] He further remarked that "Nepotism is a prismatic mode of recruitment in which familistic considerations dominate appointments, although the formal rules prescribe non-ascriptive tests."[42] Thus selectivistic recruitment is one of the important features of *sala* model, which highlights the importance of non-administrative criteria.

The examinations remain formalistic to the extent that they measure indeterminate qualities. "The bureau of civil services is unsuccessful in its efforts to administer examinations and civil service recruitment to the extent that the legislators intervene successfully."[43] The appointments and promotions of *sala* officials are made with a view to strengthening empires rather than to select a best qualified person for a given post.[44] Frequent adoption of non-merit considerations in the prismatic *sala* model ultimately affects the administrative efficiency. Excessive "bureaucratisation" in the prismatic model itself, not only provides incentives for officials to bypass the formal rules of a "merit system", but also allows them to fringe these rules with impunity.[45] Thus selectivistic recruitment and allocation of benefits, responding to pressure from *clects*, is a fundamental feature of *sala* model and reveals the importance of non-administrative criteria.[46]

Institutionalized Corruption

Contrary to price determinacy in the market model, the implications of price indeterminacy for administrative efficiency in prismatic model are more serious. It results into administrative corruption, low official salaries and diminished productivity. Low economic level in the prismatic model results into low salaries of the *sala* officials, which ultimately promotes their inclination towards other corrupt practices. Thus corruption becomes instutionalized in the *sala*. These corrupt practices

---

40 Ibid, p. 269.
41 Ibid, p. 137.
42 Ibid, p. 273.
43 Riggs, *Ecology of public administration, op. cit.*, p. 107.
44 Ibid, p. 108.
45 Riggs, F. W., *Administration in Developing Countries: The Theory of Prismatic Society; op. cit.*, p. 273.
46 Riggs, *The Ecology of Public Administration, op.cit.*, p. 138.

lead to exploitation and social injustice in these societies. According to Riggs, "some officials enjoy positions which enable them to extort bribes and other favour from interest groups. Part of this extra intake must be passed on to superiors or influential members of the prismatic bureaucracy who furnish protection... those subordinates who pay the most tribute to their superiors expect to be promoted most rapidly, in grateful recognition. Thus *sala* sanctions reward inefficiency, for what could be more efficient as a means of rule application than the practice of accepting money to suspend the application of a rule?"[47] In this way institutionalized corruption is an important feature of the *sala* model.

Influence of Clects

The existence of *clects* in a poly-communal prismatic society, influences the character of *sala* officials. Various non-administrative criteria such as the strong family ties and kinship relationship and loyalty towards the members of ones community deviates the *sala* officials from administrative rationality. Along with this the 'place of birth' and "old school ties" also act as powerful loyalties which also influence *sala* official to compromise administrative duty. The *clects* keep interests of their members above the national interests. The *sala* officials also show their allegiance to the *clects* belonging to their own community. This leads to promote non-rational considerations in the administrative working. The *sala* or its agencies develop close relations with particular *clects*, or starts functioning like a *clect* itself. In such circumstances, the *sala* functions primarily in the interest of some particular groups but it continues to pay lip service to achievement and universalistic norms.[48] Thus responding to the pressure from *clects* is a fundamental feature of the prismatic *sala*.

Normlessness or Dissensus in Sala

Poly-normativism, which is an important characteristic of the prismatic model, further, affects the prismatic sala officials. Due to the simultaneous existence of 'new'set of norms of diffracted bureau with the older traditional norms, it results in 'dissensus' or 'normlessness' situation. This "normlessness" situation in a prismatic society affects the prismatic-sala model because in such a system, officials publicly claim to follow objective, universalistic and achievement oriented norms but in actual practice they follow more subjective, ascription oriented, and particularistic modes of conduct.[49] Thus in these administrative systems, officials theoretically pretend to adopt western rationalistic norms (universalistic) in their working, but in practice they stick to the traditional norms and realities (ascriptive values). "Even the citizen, in his relationship with the sala, is poly-normative – ready to disregard official rules for his own benefits, and yet stressing the idea that government conduct should be of a strict legal rational character.[50]

Riggs pointed out that "the *sala* official while formally adhering to one set of specific norms, may secretly reject them as meaningless or not binding... officials can adhere publicly to the norms of objective, achievement oriented standard ..., but privately subscribe to more subjective, ascriptive-oriented standards ... He can

---
47 Ibid, p. 270.
48 Arora, R.K., *op. cit.*, p. 113.
49 Arora, R.K., *op. cit.*, p. 115.
50 Ibid

publicly castigate bribery and corruption, but secretly encourage them. He can insist, one moment, on a strict and literal enforcement of regulations but the next movement wink at their open violation"[51]

Disengagement of Authority and Control

The prismatic *sala* model is further characterized by disengagement of authority and control. The authority structure is generally highly 'centralized' but the control mechanism is found disengaged from the authority structure, which is very much rooted in the heterogeneous character of the social system. Due to the poly communal and poly-normative character of the prismatic society and the existence of *clects* in it, the behaviour of the *sala* officials is controlled more from the side of the society than the apex authority structure. In other words, the control system in prismatic societies is localised and dispersed. The degree of disengagement of power- the separation of authority and control is greater in the *sala* than in either chamber or office. [52] This lack of integrity between authority and control results in to administrative inefficiency.

Bureaucratic Domination over Political Leadership

Another characteristic of the prismatic *sala* model is pertaining to the domination of bureaucracy over political leadership. It is mainly because the bureaucracy in these societies is assigned the cumbersome task of social transformation and socio-economic progress, which ultimately results into enhancing the powers of the bureaucracy. But the polity in these societies, apart from being illiterate, ignorant and weak, is not in a position to bridle the bureaucracy particularly in the wake of their enhanced powers. This situation in the prismatic societies is characterized by Riggs as 'unbalanced polity'.

APPRAISAL

Riggs has an important place in the field of comparative public administration. The ecological approach developed by him touches wider horizons in the discipline of public administration and thus studies the mutual interactions between the administration and the environment in which it is embedded. Along with this, the nature of his ideal models is also deductive. Both, the approaches and his ideal models proved helpful in understanding the problems of developing countries. It needs to be mentioned that his models are ideal but they served the heuristic purpose and thus proved helpful in promoting the interest of the scholars and practitioners in understanding the ground realities. The *sala* model of Riggs is really of much significance particularly in understanding the administrative systems in the developing countries. Though the contribution of Riggs is significant yet he is not free from criticisms.

To explain his concepts Riggs utilized new terminology, which is peculiarly called 'Riggsian'. Apart from assigning different meanings to the words already in vogue, he also coined a number of his own words. Coining of new words is not bad, if the existing vocabulary fails to clarify the words/concepts. But assigning different meaning to the words, which are already in vogue, may create confusion in instead

---

51 Riggs, *Administration in developing countries: Theory of prismatic society; op. cit.*, p. 277.
52 *Ibid*, p. 281

of clarifying them.[53] Along with this, in the lust for providing a scientific character to his models, Riggs borrowed a number of words liberally from the physical sciences. However it seems doubtful that the borrowed terminology could prove helpful in providing them a scientific character.[54]

Riggs is also criticized on the ground of lack of change orientation in his models. In this connection, Hahn-Been Lee criticized the Riggsian models as equilibrium models, as they can prove helpful in preserving a system rather than carrying any change in it. Thus Lee highlighted that the Riggsian models are hardly helpful in administering changes in a system.[55]

Riggsian categorization of societies into fused, prismatic and diffracted societies, in the want of quantitative indicators, is somewhat imaginary and based on some assumptions. Some critics argued that Riggs failed in developing a measuring rod as a result of which, the identification of prismatic or diffracted societies becomes very difficult. The reader, following Riggsian analysis, may tend to associate prismatic conditions with every situation he knows. Hence in the want of empirical evidence, the validity of such imaginations or assumptions is questionable.

FERREL HEADY

LIFE SKETCH

Born on February 14, 1916, Ferrel Heady received his degree of A.B. & A.M. from Washington University, St. Louis, Missouri in 1937. Later on, he completed his doctoral research from the same university in 1940. He started his academic career in teaching and joined the University of Michigan in 1946, where he worked for 20 years. During this period apart from teaching, he worked at other administrative positions like the Director of the Institute of Public Administration of this University. He also worked as the Director and Chief Adviser of the Institute of Public Administration at the University of Philippines during 1953-54 and had administrative experience in both the American state and national governments. In 1965, he became a Senior Specialist at the University of Hawaii's East- West Centre[56].

In 1968, he became the President of the University of New Mexico and worked there till 1975. After this, Ferrel Heady returned to teaching and research in the areas of political science & public administration at the University of New Mexico. He retired from this University in 1981, after getting the status of Professor Emeritus. In 1992, he completed a Fulbright Senior Lectureship in Comparative Public Administration in Columbia. In addition to serving as ASPA President, Heady was one of the founders of ASPA's Section on International and Comparative Administration.

Even after his retirement, he continued to travel frequently on assignments to Latin American Countries. He also continued to teach public administration courses

---

53 R. K. Arora, *Comparative Public Administration*, op. cit., p. 129.
54 Kishankhana, "Contemporary models of positive public administration: An assessment of their utility and exposition of inherent fallacies": *Philippines Journals of public administration* Vol. xviii, No.2, April 1974, p. 103.
55 Hahn Been Lee, "From ecology of Times," *International Review of administrative Sciences*, Vol. Xxxiii No.2, 1967, p. 1-13.
56 http://64.91.142.87-ASPA's Presidential Biographies

& presented papers at national and international conferences. In 1994, he received the Prestigious Dwight Waldo Award for career contributions to the literature and leadership of public administration. He passed away on August 17, 2006, at the age of 90.[57]

Ferrel Heady was a prolific writer. *Public Administration: A Comparative Perspective* and *Papers on Comparative Public Administration* (books) and *Comparative public Administration: Concerns and priorities* (article) are some of his most cited works.

MAIN CONTRIBUTIONS

The contribution of Ferrel Heady in the field of comparative public administration is significant. While working with CAG scholars in South Asian countries, he conducted lot of research with regard to the administrative systems of both developed and developing countries and thus tried to promote the comparative aspect in the study of public administration, which ultimately resulted into widening its horizons. His contribution in both developing and developed countries has been given below:-"

I. Administration in Less Developed Countries:

The Contribution of Ferrel Heady with regard to the administrative systems in less developed countries is as under:

Political Regime Variations:-

Ferrel Heady has discussed the aspect of political regime variations in a comprehensive way. He made an attempt to classify the political regimes prevailing in the less developed countries on the basis of some resemblance and affinities. However, Ferrel Heady has accepted that in this classification, it is not possible to give place to every country. In the mid-1960s, he classified the political regimes in these countries into six categories. Later on, he revised the classification and divided the regimes into two broad sets – Bureaucracy Prominent Political Regimes and Party Prominent Political Regimes. Each of the two categories has a further four-fold classification.[58] Examples in each category are cited from various developing countries by Ferrel Heady. A brief description of these two sets is as under:

Bureaucracy-Prominent Political Regimes

As the name applies, in such types of regimes bureaucracy occupies the central position in the power game. Most of the powers are concentrated into its hands and all the decisions at the political level are taken by it. It may have various forms which are again divided by Ferrel Heady into following four categories:

Traditional Elite Systems

The dominant political elites in these countries are the ancestors of the earlier ruling families and owe their power to the traditionally established social system. Such a system may either be based on inherited monarchy or draw legitimacy from the religion. These are the countries, which have not yet passed through the stage of drastic societal transformation. In this category Ferrel Heady has incorporated some countries like Jordan, Morocco, Iran etc. and he further pointed out that the number of

---

57 http:///elibrary.unm.ed-Ferrel Heady.
58 Ferrel Heady, *op. cit.*, p. 298.

countries is diminishing. Currently such systems have been replaced in Afghanistan, Ethiopia, Kampuchea, Libya and Laos. While differentiating among the traditional elite system, Ferrel Heady pointed out two orientations – ortho-traditional regimes and neo-traditional regimes. Saudi Arabia exhibits the earlier regime whereas Iran exhibits the latter. In the first category of regimes, the political elite owe their power to their ruling monarchical families. In such systems, political activities are almost banned and competitive politics is not allowed. Political parties and pressure groups are either weak or non-existent.

Besides, there exists no mass-mobilization. In such regimes, the army and civil bureaucracy are heavily relied upon to carry out desirable change and to resist unwarranted/unwanted changes. Further in the second category of regimes, the political elite owe their power to traditional legitimizing source i.e. religion. In such a system though religious leaders dominate yet they have to rely on trustworthy laymen to handle the business of political offices and for staffing the military and civil bureaucracies. Like the ortho traditional regimes, these political regimes have to depend on the competence and effectiveness of their bureaucratic officials for their survival.[59] Thus in these traditional elite systems the ruling elite has to rely on army and civil bureaucracy as they help in safeguarding and promoting their interests. The administration in these regimes is the main apparatus for action but its traditional character resists its efficiency.

Personalist Bureaucratic Elite Systems

In the personalist bureaucratic political regimes, power is concentrated in one person and they are called caudillo or strongman regimes. 'Caudillo' is a Spanish word that means leader or chief. He generally belongs to a military background and rarely a civilian. In essence it is a one-man show but for regime stability, he further depends on bureaucracy. According to Ferrel Heady, such regimes were most common in Latin American countries during the 19th and 20th centuries and in modern times these systems are available in the countries of sub- Saharan Africa viz., Algeria, Burundi, Central African Republic, Equatorial Guinea, Liberia, Nigeria, Sudan, Congo, Uganda and Zaire.

In such regimes, decision-making power is centred on the personalist leader and thus he takes majority of the administrative decisions. He is the hub of all political power. All the high-ranking officials are appointed by him, not on the basis of merit rather than on the basis of self- defined criteria. The fundamental criterion of their appointment is their personal loyalty and commitment to the regime ideology. He keeps a direct and constant vigil on the high-ranking officials He rewards those officials with increased pay and other incentives like promotion who are loyal and dedicated to him whereas those who are not supportive of him are punished in the form of demotion or dismissals. Ferrel Heady is of the opinion that the life span of such regimes is highly unpredictable.[60]

Collegial Bureaucratic Elite System

In such a regime, the political power is concentrated in a collegial body consisting of the professional bureaucrats who usually have military backgrounds. The members

---
59 Ibid, p. 314-15.
60 Ibid, p. 322.

of such collegial military regimes come from almost the same military ranks. The leader of such a military coup enjoys a special position in the group. Sometimes the persons from civilian backgrounds are also incorporated but there remains the pre-dominance of military officials. Nicaragua is the example of this kind of mixed political leadership. As per Ferrel Heady, the current and most notable examples of collegial military regimes are Argentina, Chile, Indonesia and South Korea.

The leaders of such regimes though try to overhaul civil bureaucracy, launch programmes to affect changes in the bureaucratic apparatus and administrative reform but at the same time they understand their limitation of dependence on non-military administrative system. In such systems the people's participation in the political activities is the least. There remains a complete lack of an opposition party.

Pendulum System

The political regimes falling in this category are distinct from others. It is because they oscillate like a pendulum back and forth between the two categories of regimes. In this category Ferrel Heady has incorporated the political regimes of those developing nations whose political systems are swinging periodically back and forth between the categories of bureaucratic elite and polyarchal competitive regimes. According to him, Argentina, Brazil, Peru, Nigeria and Turkey, are the prominent countries belonging to the pendulum category.

If this kind of oscillation happens many times within a short span, it may affect both categories of regimes. One aspect of such political situation is that the bureaucracy especially when it is military type, is continually in a position to reassert dominance if it is currently subordinated to party control. Moreover with the change in the shift, there is change in orientation. In this regard Ferrel Heady has observed that stress on the maintenance of political stability and the law and order situation or its restoration if disorder has become widespread, is the most common orientation.[61]

Party Prominent Political Regimes

Party prominent regimes are those in which political party or parties with differing ideology, membership, structural base etc. enjoy the central position in the operation of political regimes. Ferrel Heady has divided such political regimes in the developing countries into four categories viz.-polyarchal competitive systems, dominant party semi competitive systems, dominant party mobilization systems, and communist totalitarian systems. In this categorization, the role of bureaucracy seems to be different in all these political systems. A brief view of all these party prominent political regimes is as under:

Polyarchal Competitive Systems

The political systems of these countries are akin to the parliamentary and presidential models of the Western Europe and the United States. In these countries, well-organized political groups remain in competition to capture political power. But unlike the other regimes types, there is lack of well-defined and cohesive political elites. Political power tends to be more dispersed. There exists social mobility and dynamism that

---

61 *Ibid*, p. 297.

promotes competition. The people to some extent participate in the election process. The political leaders make direct appeal to the public and make commitment and promises to gain political support. The politicians receive pressure from particular interest groups for special consideration. The governmental programs emphasize on short- range objectives in various fields viz. education, welfare, and health. The formulation of long term programmes with the objective to promote major social and economic reform are rare and less effective. In such polyarchal competitive systems, the government does not have enough power to levy and collect taxes and implement laws and regulations. Public administration must be carried on without consistent political support. The bureaucracy itself may become one of the focuses for competition among contending political groups in such political regimes.[62]

The number of countries in this category reduced extensively during the 1960s and 1970s, but sufficiently increased further in the 1980s and early 1990s. According to Ferrel Heady, the important examples in this regard are Argentina, Brazil, Chile, Greece, Pakistan, Philippines, Turkey and Uruguay etc.

Dominant Party Semi-Competitive Systems

In such types of political regimes, the actual powers are monopolized by a single dominant party up to a sufficiently large period. It does not mean that there is no existence of other parties. Other parties do exist and are also legal in character. But the dominant party stands victorious by sweeping all other parties generally in all elections, though this dominant party is non-dictatorial and can be given sufficient challenge by a rival political party at the polls. According to Ferrel Heady Mexico's Partido Revolucionario Institucional (PRI), the National Front party of Malaysia and to some extent the Congress Party in India, has been the vital examples of such a dominant party in the recent past.

Dominant Party Mobilisation Systems

Such kind of political regimes are available in Algeria, Bolivia, Ghana, Guinea, Mali, Mauritania and some other Western African States. In the politics of such nations, permissiveness is less but coercion is high. The dominant party is generally the sole party that is legally recognized. Other parties are either non-existent or they have to take permission. While providing permission, a number of restrictions are imposed on them in order to keep them weak. In such regimes ideology is more doctrinaire and more and more emphasis is laid on it. Here more emphasis is given on demonstrating great loyalty towards the regime by the masses. The political future of such regimes is shaky and unstable, thus in such regimes, emphasis is laid on developing a strong mass base by deeply penetrating its roots in the society so that the faith of the society's key groups can be won. Such a party has to depend on the commitment and support of the bureaucracy not only for better performance but also for mass mobilization.[63]

---

62 Chaturvedi T.N., *Comparative Public Administration*, New Delhi: Research Publication, 1999, p. 36.
63 *Ibid*, p. 37.

Communist Totalitarian Systems

Except for the Soviet Union, rest of the communist countries are included under this categorization. It is still a matter of debate whether these countries can be called developing or not. The communist regimes of East Europe have undergone drastic political changes that resulted in the alteration of their single party system and their totalitarian characteristics. Up to early 1990s, the communist system was replaced by a democratic government system in a number of communist countries viz. Romania, Poland, Czechoslovakia, Hungary and Bulgaria etc.

In comparison to their non-communist counterparts, other Afro- Asian and Latin American countries with communist regimes viz., North Korea, North Vietnam, Cuba, Kampuchea (Cambodia), Laos etc. have experienced minor modifications in their earlier set-up and thus retained their commitment to Marxist –Leninist ideology and a totalitarian political system. In these communist countries, the political power is concentrated in a single party. The party ideology is the centre of all activities. No importance to the legitimacy of open opposition is given in these systems.

Ferrel Heady has pointed out that in the communist regimes, the administrative apparatus is highly complex and kept under direct supervision of the party at various levels. It is responsive to the small circle of elitist leadership at apex level. In such regimes, the state bureaucracy and the party bureaucracy are not only parallel but also interlocked. While recruiting the administrators, more emphasis is laid on political loyalty in comparison to expert knowledge. Like the other societies, the scarcity of resources for the rapid industrialization and economic development also plague the administrative machinery in these countries. The matter is further complicated by emphasizing more on the responsiveness of the administrative officials to the party apparatus. It leads to the problem of continuous conflict between party units and the administrative officials held responsible for implementing particular programmes. This situation results in loss of organizational efficiency. Such situation further curtails the initiative taking power of the administrative officials and their willingness to conduct experiments.[64]

Common-Administrative Patterns

Ferrel Heady's role is quite significant in identifying some prominent features designated as "typical" of administrative systems in the developing countries. Ferrel Heady has observed that the importance of the administration has been recognized in the context of development in these countries. But the existing administrative machinery in these countries is not appropriate for managing development programme because of its deficiencies. Most of the striking features highlighted by Ferrel Heady are indicative of the grave administrative deficiencies of these countries. Ferrel Heady has pointed out following five[65] main features of administration currently found in these countries:

Imitative Rather than Indigenous Administrative Patterns

Ferrel Heady has observed that the basic pattern of administration in most of these countries is imitative rather than indigenous. It is mainly because in the post–

64 Ferrel Heady, *op cit.*, p. 404.
65 *Ibid*, p. 299-302.

independence era, almost all these countries have imitated their earlier colonial administrative system with a few incidental features borrowed from some other systems. Most of them have adopted the modern style of western bureaucratic administration. All of them failed in developing their own indigenous administrative institutions and structures. These imitated bureaucratic pattern of administration without giving due considerations to the necessary adaptations in the entirely changed atmosphere proved unsuitable in combating the challenging tasks of development in the post-independence phase in comparison to that, if it were fully home grown/ indigenous. It is because the colonial administration had a definite motto of exploitation and not to carry out development. In this way, one of the most typical features of the administrative systems in most of these developing countries is that their administrative patterns are not indigenous or homely grown rather they are imitated on the pattern of their earlier colonial administrative pattern. Thus the administrative systems of these countries are not appropriate to carry out development.

Bureaucracy with Unskilled Manpower

Another important aspect relating to the administrative systems of these countries highlighted by Ferrel Heady is that the bureaucracy that is essential for developmental programmes in these countries, lack technically qualified manpower. In these countries, the size of employable manpower is very high but there is an acute shortage of expertise and skilled manpower needed to carry out the challenging tasks of development administration. The public services in almost all of these countries are found over staffed particularly at the lower rungs of administration. But at the higher level there is scarcity of trained administrators with high degrees of managerial capabilities.

For this deficiency of trained manpower in most of these countries, Ferrel Heady has blamed their education system. In his words "A number of countries, for example India and Egypt, have sizeable pockets of seemingly highly educated unemployed, who either have been educated in the wrong subjects or are the products of marginal institutions."[66] Moreover the problem is further aggravated due to the policy of reservation in civil services for certain minority group as in India. It has ultimately restricted the entry of otherwise qualified candidates. He further remarked that it is difficult to fill the gap between supply and demand of trained manpower at the top administrative positions in these nations. He indicated that strenuous training efforts could be the alternative in this regard.

Non-Achievement Orientation of Bureaucracy

Another important characteristic feature of these administrative systems divulged by Ferrel Heady is the non-achievement orientation of bureaucracy in these countries. According to him bureaucracy in these nations lacks a production-oriented attitude. It is mainly because the bureaucratic behaviour in these transitional societies is very much influenced from the ascriptive values of their traditional past. These values are yet to be abandoned though the social structures have experienced a drastic change. Thus their more attachment with ascriptive values rather than achievement norms explains much of their behavioural aspect.

---

66 *Ibid*, p. 300.

These considerations directly affect the personnel processes viz., recruitment promotions, disciplinary action, dismissals etc. in these countries. Though they adopt merit system in personnel matters but the non-merit considerations (like familial or kinship) are openly practiced. Ferrel heady further highlighted that corruption is still another aspect related with the non-achievement orientation of bureaucracy of all of these countries. While commenting on another socially significant practice of these countries, he pointed out that in these countries public services are utilized as the alternative to overcome employment or to provide social security to the personnel.[67]

Widespread Discrepancy between Form and Reality

Still another characteristic pointed out by Ferrel Heady regarding the administrative systems of these countries is the widespread discrepancy between form and reality. It is called 'formalism' by Riggs. In other words, formalism characterizes the administrative systems of these emerging nations. As a result there exists a high degree of incongruence between what they formally prescribe and actually practice. He further pointed out that these gaps are tried to be bridged by framing laws but they are rarely implemented in these nations. Besides, there are rules for personnel regulation but are generally bypassed and attempts of power delegation are made with control remaining at the apex.

Operational Autonomy of Bureaucracy

Another important feature of these administrative systems highlighted by Ferrel Heady is pertaining to the operational autonomy of bureaucracy. On the analogy of colonialism, bureaucracy in these newly liberated nations also enjoys extra-ordinary powers near to monopoly without having any effective check on it. However in the entirely new set up its masters have undergone a complete change. In this context Ferrel Heady has observed that, "colonialism was essentially rule by bureaucracy with policy guidance from remote sources and this pattern persists even after the bureaucracy has a new master in the nation."[68] The post-colonial era witnessed the enormous increase in bureaucratic powers in these countries mainly because of assigning the task of development to it. But at the same time, the political leadership in these nations was immature, shortsighted and narrow in outlook and thus not in a position to exercise an effective check on the bureaucracy. This increase in bureaucratic powers, results in providing it almost a free hand in carrying out its obligations because political leadership in these nations is too weak to bridle it. [69]

II. Administration in More Developed Nations

Besides commenting on the administrative systems in the developing nations, Ferrel Heady has also discussed the administration of the developed nations. He not only pointed out the general characteristic of their polity and administration but also traced out some variations in their administrative systems. A brief description of these aspects is as under:

---

67 Bhale Rao, C.N. *op cit.,* p. 76.
68 Ferrel Heady, *op. cit.,* p. 302.
69 Bhale Rao, C.N. *op cit.,* p. 76-77.

Shared Political and Administrative Characteristics

Ferrel Heady has highlighted the following characteristics[70] that are shared by the modernized polities of Western Europe and elsewhere:
1. Patronizing of governmental organizations, after the private ones in order to promote task-specialization and assignment of political roles in strict accordance with achievement rather than ascriptive norms.
2. Standardization of Political decisions which are mainly based on rational and secular character.
3. Wide expansion of political and administrative activity in all major spheres.
4. High degree of involvement of common masses in political and administrative affairs.
5. Direct correlation of political power to legitimacy.

Some of these characteristics[71] have counterparts in the nature of public bureaucracies of developed nations, despite having some variations in the patterns of bureaucracy:
1. Complex and large bureaucracy, having distinct sub-units and is oriented towards implementing the policies of the top decision-makers effectively.
2. Specialized bureaucracy attracting highly specialized manpower which reflects both task-specialization and wide range of governmental activities.
3. Highly professionalized bureaucracy, both because of its own members and by other participants in the policy process.
4. The bureaucracy of these modern polities tends to effectively receive policy directions that come from other functionally specific political institutions.
5. Fully developed bureaucracy having role specificity due to the maturity and stability of their political systems.

Variation in the Administrative Systems of Developed Nations

In comparison to the total percentage, variations among the developed nations are very less. Ferrel Heady has tried to trace out some significant variations among these nations. He classified these nations into following four categories:
  i) 'Classic' Administrative Systems;
  ii) Administration in 'the Civic Culture';
  iii) Adaptive Modernizing Administration;
  iv) Administration under Communism.

In the first category Ferrel Heady has basically discussed France and Germany. In addition to this, he selected five other administrative systems and made them a focus of his attention. He selected Great Britain and United States and Japan and considered these countries as examples of "first tier" on the development continuum. He also selected the Russian Federation in the Commonwealth of Independent States and the People's Republic of China as examples of "second tier" on that

---

70 Ferrel Heady, *op.cit.*, p. 190.
71 *Ibid*, p. 190-91

continuum.⁷² He divided all these five countries in to the last three categories of the above classification, a brief description of which is as under:

(i) 'Classic' Administrative Systems

In this category, Ferrel Heady incorporated basically the administrative systems of France and Germany and several other countries of Western and Southern Europe viz. Italy, Spain, Austria, Switzerland, Belgium, Netherlands and Ireland, as their administration also share many of the attributes found in France and Germany. He called their administrative systems as "classic".

In this category Ferrel Heady focused his attention on the administrative systems of France and Germany. He pointed out that the political culture of both these countries are alike mainly in two respects - firstly, both remained victims of long political instability (about more than two centuries) that resulted into abrupt, drastic and frequent political changes due to the different political orientations of successive political regimes. For instance, since 1789, France has remained three times a constitutional monarchy, an empire twice, once a semi dictatorship, and five times a republic and most of the transformations were an outcome of violence.

At the same time Germany also experienced even more disruptive changes like the establishment of a unified reich under Bismarck in 1871, the German Empire in 1918, the Weimer Republic after World War I, Nazi dictatorship during the 2ⁿᵈ World War, division between West and East Germany after the 2ⁿᵈ World War, and reunification again in 1990. Thus like France, the German political heritage is one of disunity, frustration and lack of stability.⁷³ Secondly, in sharp contrast to this political instability, there remained administrative and bureaucratic continuity during all the political regimes in both the nations.

In these countries, the bureaucrats enjoy a respectable place in society. A bureaucrat is viewed as government official rather than a public servant. The civil services in both these nations are career services, generally chosen in an early part of their life and continue till they retire. The civil servants in both the nations enjoy security of tenure until or unless some disciplinary action is taken against them. It can be taken strictly in accordance with the detailed procedures of disciplinary action by the higher authorities in case of default on the part of the administrative officials. The civil servants draw handsome salaries that are intended to maintain their status. Other fringe benefits like promotions, family allowances, various social security arrangements, gratuity and retirement benefits in the form of pension are lucrative. The civil servants in both the nations play a significant role in active politics.⁷⁴

But in comparison to the civil servants of Germany, their counterparts in France enjoy more freedom in political matters. They are comparatively free to join political parties and to take active part in the promotion of their activities.

(ii) Administration in 'the Civic Culture'

In the second category, Ferrel Heady has incorporated the administrative systems of Great Britain and United States of America. Basically it was Almond and Verba who utilized the term "the civic culture" for the administrative systems of USA, Great

---

72 Ibid, p. 221.
73 Ibid, p. 193.
74 Chaturvedi, T.N., op. cit., p. 34.

Britain and some other countries that were earlier British colonies. These countries of Great Britain and the USA share not only a common political heritage but also have a lot of likeness in their administrative systems. In these countries, political culture and political structures are congruent, thus the political system is highly stable and its legitimacy is well established.[75]

Ferrel Heady has opined that unlike Germany and France, the historical past of their political development is relatively that of stability. Over the years in their past, these countries have utilized the incremental approach in the growth and development of their political institutions. Resultantly, the polity of these nations did not experience any violent discontinuity and abrupt changes. Thus, in these nations political changes were almost continuous and stable. This incremental and gradualist pattern of political development in these countries ultimately has its serious impact on their administrative systems. The adjustment between the two remained good. As an outcome of the political stability in these nations, the administration does not have to carry out the whole burden of the government alone. However, the top-ranking bureaucracy in both these countries play influential roles in the decision making process of the government.[76]

In the political cultures of both the nations, common people take effective part in the activities of administration. The administration in these countries effectively responds to the needs of the common masses and is subjected to strong political control. Public accountability in both these countries is exerted through a number of channels; hence the bureaucracy in these countries is characterized by a high degree of responsibility. The social forces have a substantial influence on the bureaucracies in both these countries. Moreover the citizenry is vigilant and contribute effectively in the working of administration.

(iii) Adaptive Modernizing Administration

Ferrel Heady has incorporated the administrative system of Japan in third category. He pointed out that whatever may be the measuring scale of development, "Japan is the most outstanding and possibly the only non-western nation which clearly has achieved recognition as highly developed..."[77] The defeat and surrender of Japan at the end of the 2nd World War, resulted in the emergence of new patterns in its politics and administration which were given shape in the newly drafted constitution in 1946, which become effective in 1947. Prior to this the services of civil bureaucracy were limited to few hands. They were the servants of the emperor. Article 15 of this constitution declares: "All public officials are servants of the whole community and not of any group thereof." Moreover in 1947, a new civil services law was also enacted which not only described the detailed reform provisions but also caused the establishment of National Personnel Authority with a guaranteed semi-autonomous status. These constitutional provisions tried to democratize the post war Japanese civil services. The Japanese civil services increased in number remarkably (about eightfold) from 1940s to mid-1970s but the administrative reforms of 1980s in Japan

---

75 Ferrel Heady, *op. cit.*, p. 221-22.
76 Chaturvedi, T.N., *op cit.*, p. 34
77 Ferrel Heady, *op. cit.*, p. 221.

in the light of privatization and liberalization resulted in de-emphasizing the role of government. It had an adverse effect on the strength of the civil services[78].

The higher civil service in Japan constitutes a small group. The civil service in Japan is a career service that attracts the talented and brightest youth. The higher civil servants not only effectively contribute in the decision making process of the government but also play an active role in political life. Thus it is characterized by multi-functionalism in its operations. It is politically very active and persistently remains the prime mover of policy initiatives particularly for the better health of the society. The post war civil service in Japan is also characterized by continuity and stability despite the tremendous administrative changes and reforms during occupation and later.[79] After retirement the civil servants in Japan, enjoy better opportunities for their placement[80].

(iv) Administration under Communism

In this categorization Ferrel Heady has incorporated erstwhile USSR and the People's Republic of China. Ferrel Heady pointed out that the erstwhile USSR had two important characteristics since the Bolshevik Revolution till 1985. First was the concentration of political power in the Communist party and "the other was that this reality of one-party rule was disguised behind an elaborate facade which borrowed the phraseology of liberal democracy and pretended to be a constitutional federal system—with elections, legislative and executive organs, and agencies of state administration."[81] USSR ushered in a new political era in 1985, when Mikhail Gorbachev was selected as the general secretary of the Communist party. During his regime, drastic measures viz. Glasnost (openness) and Perestroika (restructuring) has gained momentum as key indicators of his reforms. This resulted in the substantial alteration in the Russian politics and administration. The hold of communist party over administration was drastically changed. As an outcome of these reforms, USSR had disintegrated in 1991, Gorbachev resigned and ultimately this county went out of the world map[82]. It is the most important incident of the 20th century.

The Russian Federation inherited the USSR's role in international affairs and Boris Yeltsin became its president. "The Russian Federation was by far the largest of the Soviet Union republics, consisting of almost three-quarters of its landmass, having over half of its total population, and possessing a high proportion of its raw materials, energy resources, heavy industry, and scientific/engineering personnel."[83] To strengthen his institutional base, Yeltsin launched a three point strategy – "first, he initiated a referendum to create an elected Russian Federation Presidency... His second move was to convert the chief administrative positions in the major cities of Moscow and Leningrad into elective offices as well. Thirdly, he fulfilled a campaign promise to eliminate the Communist party apparatus paralleling official state agencies..."[84] Thus during this phase, were efforts made to de-emphasize the

---

78 Ibid, p. 239-41.
79 Ibid, p. 243.
80 Chaturvedi, T. N., *op cit.*, p. 34.
81 Ibid, p. 249.
82 Chaturvedi T. N., *op. cit.*, p. 35.
83 Ferrel Heady, *op cit.*, p. 249.
84 Ibid, p. 253.

centralized state planning, to revamp the state bureaucracy, to replace the control of the Communist party, greater exposure of the economy to market forces but the results are not very encouraging.

Further, on the basis of the combinations of current measures of achievements and future probabilities, Ferrel Heady incorporated the People's Republic of China in the '2nd tier' of developed countries. The People's Republic of China was established in 1949. Ferrel Heady has highlighted that since its beginning, there persisted two consistent themes – "one is a determination to politicize the bureaucracy and make it responsive to party direction, using various devices. Most fundamental is the practice of putting party members in most of the important governmental positions... the second theme is decentralization by the transfer of administrative powers to the lowest feasible level. This diffusion strategy is designed to prevent the buildup of a non-productive administrative superstructure and at the same time strengthen local initiative and responsibility."

Thus the bureaucracy in the Chinese Communist regime is not heavily relied on and there remains the tendency to curb bureaucratic powers. While making the bureaucratic appointments, more stress is given on political loyalty. Thus party control on bureaucracy is very heavy in china. But the post-Maoist leaders, especially Deng Xiaoping has viewed some reforms in this direction that were further continued by the post –Deng leaders. They were interested in creating the modern civil service system but without removing the control the Chinese Communist Party (CCP). In this context Ferrel Heady has remarked that they have "… called for the adoption of Western principles of personnel management, such as recruitment by examination, position classification, and performance evaluation. At the same time, the concept of political neutrality is rejected and loyalty to the CCP is stressed as a basic requirement." It is obvious that the overriding considerations of the regime still prevails in China, thus the position of bureaucracy could not improve to a sufficient extent. The party still exercises its tight control over the working of administration.

EVALUATION

The contribution of Ferrel Heady in the discipline of comparative public administration is very significant. He responded to the needs felt by many students, teachers and researchers who had chosen to explore the fascinating problems of comparison among different nations, both developing and developed. He succeeded in guiding and directing the budding scholars in the discipline of public administration. He conducted a lot of research and his research efforts are more specifically focused on the administrative systems of developing countries. Besides highlighting the common administrative patterns and political regime variations in these countries, Ferrel Heady pointed out that development has been recognised as a fundamental goal in these countries. He also discussed the ideology of development adopted in most of these countries having twin goals of nation building and socio-economic progress. He also discussed the basic features of the politics of development in these countries. At the same time he also traced the salient features of administration and polity in the developed countries and discussed the regime variations in these countries. In addition to this, he also studied the closely related fields of comparative public administration such as development administration and comparative public policy. His recent contribution to the literature on societal change has been taken into account in the discussion of concepts of system transformation. His basic approach for the study continues, "to bring within the range of consideration administrative systems that have wide variations among them, and to make the task manageable by focusing on public bureaucracies as common governmental institution and by placing special emphasis on relationship between bureaucracies and political regime types."[85]

---

[85] Heady, Ferrel, *op. cit.*, 2001, p. vi.

6
ADMINISTRATIVE SYSTEM IN UNITED KINGDOM

The United Kingdom incorporates Great Britain and Northern Ireland and Great Britain includes England, Scotland and Wales. It has a long historical past as it has evolved over a number of years. Its constitution is unwritten and flexible. The law of the land is based on statutes, common law and traditional rights. Over the years, the UK has adopted the incremental approach as far as the growth and development of its political and administrative organizations is concerned. It was mainly because unlike France, the UK did not experience any sort of violent discontinuity and abrupt changes. The changes that took place both in the administration and polity were almost continuous and stable. Resultantly, most of the institutions in the UK are an outcome of the revolutionary process.

The British system is characterized by supremacy of Parliament. Being unitary in character, all the powers of the government are concentrated in the hands of the Centre. There exists the parliamentary form of government where the executive powers theoretically rest with the monarch and practically exercised by the cabinet headed by the Prime Minister. It is also known as a constitutional monarchy. The Parliament is bi-cameral in nature and consists of two houses –House of Commons and House of Lords. The members of the former have an added advantage over the members of the latter specifically in terms of financial matters. Thus, the legislative powers in the UK are prominently enjoyed by the members of House of Commons. However, the House of Lords being a permanent chamber enjoys more time to debate public issues in comparison to the House of Commons. The administration operates directly under the executive. The bureaucracy of the UK is modelled on the pattern of Weberian model. The system of rank classification has been adopted in Britain. The civil servants in the UK enjoy a lot of respect in society. They are career civil servants and enter into service early on and work till their retirement. The political rights of civil servants at the higher level are more restricted in comparison the lower level functionaries. Civil servants in the UK are not specifically denied the right to strike under law but strike by civil servants is a disciplinary offence. The retirement age for civil servants in the UK is 62 to 65 years.

The doctrine of 'Rule of Law' constitutes the fundamental characteristic of the British constitution. It refers to the fact that the law is supreme and hence the government must operate in consonance with the law. For the redressal of the grievances of the common citizens, there exists the mechanism of parliamentary commissioners. Being unitary in nature, the units of local government derive their authority from the central government and they can be created and abolished for administrative convenience.

In the present chapter an endeavour has been made to discuss *the salient features of the administration, political executive, local government, and control machinery of the UK* in detail.

(A) ADMINISTRATIVE FEATURES

The British administration is a result of a long drawn process as Britain has come out of a monarchical form of government to a democratic set up through a process of evolution. The incremental and gradualist approach of political development in the U.K. has its serious impact on its administrative system. Thus most of the features of the British administration are of evolutionary in nature. Following are the prominent features of the British administration:

1. Evolutionary Character: One of the important features of the British administrative system is its evolutionary character. It has grown like an organism over a period of time. Most of the administrative structures, procedures and institutions are not the product of one day, rather an out come of a series of traditional developments. In the want of some political upheavals, its basic framework has experienced no fundamental revolutionary change. Thus, unlike France and Germany, the British administration is an outcome of slow and gradual change. The greatest consequence of gradualism was that "… the administrative system also was able to take shape feature by feature in a way that reflected the political changes and was consonant with them. Political and administrative adaptations were concurrent and fairly well balanced, but the political theme was dominant."[1] Thus the evolutionary character of the British administration has contributed to what one observer called its 'labyrinthine complexity.'[2] Hence the British administrative machinery has evolved strictly in accordance with the changing circumstances and the present structure bears its testimony. Consequently the British administrative system is popularly known as a 'Living organization'. While discussing this aspect Prof. Steel has observed, "The character of contemporary public administration in Britain has been strongly influenced by the fact that the system of government has developed gradually with only a few sharp breaks in its evolution. Many of the important institutions and processes have their origins in the nineteenth century and earlier."[3]

2. Rule of Law: Another important feature of British administrative system is 'Rule of law'. It means that essentially no one is above the law and that no one can be punished or otherwise be made to suffer except as provided by the law[4]. It implied the supremacy of law in England. It is defined by an English jurist, as "the supremacy or dominance of law, as distinguished from mere arbitrariness, or from some alternative mode, which is not law, of determining or disposing of the rights

---

1 Heady, Ferrel, *Public Administration: A Comparative perspective (6th ed)*, New York: Marcel Decker, New York, 2001, p. 222.
2 Steel, D.R., "Britain" in Ridley, F.F. (ed.), *Government and Administration in Western Europe*, Oxford: Martin Co. Ltd, 1979, p. 21.
3 *Ibid*, p. 18.
4 Neumann, Robert G., *European Government (4h ed)*, MC. Graw Hill Book Company, New York: 1968, p. 25.

of individuals."⁵ Resultantly no one is above the law and all are treated equally by law. Partial treatment is found deficient in the administrative working and all the services are delivered to the common citizens without any discrimination. The administrative officials discharge their obligations strictly in accordance with the law of the nation and the arbitrary use of powers is found lacking. Thus, the main emphasis of this principle is freedom from arbitrariness⁶ as the rights of the people of Britain are secured by the administration through the rule of law. The citizens, the courts, the administrative officials and private individuals are all subject to it. The monarch who 'can do no wrong' is the sole exception.

3. **Responsible Administration:** the administration in Britain is highly responsible to the public. The British administration effectively responds to the needs of the common people and is subjected to strong political control. Public accountability is exerted through a number of channels. The most significant among these is the individual and collective ministerial accountability. Ministers, being the spokesmen of their respective departments, are held accountable in the Parliament for their departmental affairs. It is mainly because all actions of the department are taken in the name of the minister and the civil servants remain anonymous, so the former has to own the entire responsibility of the department. Within the department, attention is paid to ensure that the minister is not exposed to parliamentary criticism and this possibility has a major impact upon the way in which decisions are taken.⁷ Any Member of Parliament can ask questions to any minister and then the minister concerned is supposed to provide a satisfactory answer failing which he has no option but to resign. The minister, in turn, can take disciplinary action against the guilty officials for their acts of omission and commission. In this way there is a convention that ministers are responsible to the Parliament for all the actions of their departments, a doctrine that is of crucial importance in determining the relationship of the executive to the legislature and that between ministers and their civil servants⁸. They can, therefore, be called to explain and justify what has been done in their name and they are liable to be held responsible, and ultimately may be censured by the Parliament.⁹ If a minister is held accountable because of a personal mistake, the responsibility will, as a rule, be confined to him and the stability of the rest of the cabinet may not be affected. For instance, "when Chancellor of the Exchequer High Dalton imprudently revealed to a favoured journalist certain facts about the forthcoming budget message - a gross breach of custom and possibility of law - he resigned in the ensuring storm without shaking in any way the solid foundation of the Attlee government."¹⁰

Moreover, the cabinet is also collectively responsible to the Parliament. In the words of Lord Salisbury, it means, that "each member [of the cabinet] who does not resign is absolutely and irretrievably responsible, and has no right afterwards to say

---

5   Lord Hewart as quoted in Bhagwan, Vishnu and Vidya Bhushan, *World Constitution*, New Delhi, Sterling Publishers Pvt. Ltd., 1991, p. 24.
6   Neumann, Robert G., *op. cit.*, p. 25.
7   Steel, D.R, *Britain* in F.F. Ridley (ed.), *op. cit.*, p. 24.
8   *Ibid*, p. 18.
9   *Ibid*, p. 55
10 Neuman, Robert G., *op. cit.*, p. 81.

that he agreed in one case to a compromise, while in another he was persuaded by his colleagues."[11] Collective responsibility is feasible only if there is a high degree of cabinet solidarity. It is because all the cabinet members sail in the same boat and they sink and swim together. The principle of collective responsibility thus limits the power of individual members of the cabinet as a whole. It helps to channel the ambitions of politicians and make them less disruptive of the group co-operation that is essential to effective and responsible government[12]. Thus, cabinet ministers both share in a collective responsibility for the general policies and record of the government and bear an individual responsibility for the actions and record of that portion of the administrative-machine placed directly in their charge.[13]

Besides, the media also plays an important role in exercising a check over the malfunctioning of administration. Further, the administration operates under the constant vigil of other social forces like political parties and pressure groups. Moreover, the citizenry is vigilant and contribute effectively in the decision making process of administration. Hence the bureaucracy in these countries is characterized by a high sense of responsibility.

4. **Geographical Decentralization**: Geographical decentralisation is another important characteristic of British administration. The unitary character of the British government highlights a general view of its being highly centralized. In one way this view holds true as there exists supremacy of Parliament and all public bodies are subordinate to it. However, it is not true that the United Kingdom is governed from London. It is mainly because, in case of the central government, a vast majority of the civil servants work outside Greater London and most of the important services are provided by the local authorities to the common citizens. Most of the central departments and other national organizations operate through a well-developed network system of regional and local offices. Though formal authority of decision making in such offices rests with the minister, yet in actual practice such decisions are taken by officials who operate within the framework of centrally drawn up rules and procedures but who enjoy extensive discretion.[14]

Unlike USA and India, which are federal in character, Britain, like France is unitary in character. Therefore, it is characterized by 'lack of elected regional tier of governments.' Consequently, local authorities are the 'principal operating agencies of the government' in Britain. However, even though these local bodies draw their powers directly from the Parliament (and hence are dependent on it) and the central government constantly supervises their working, yet 'these bodies retain a very high degree of autonomy both in setting priorities and in settling how services should be rendered, which is reflected in wide variations in standards and practices in different parts of the country.'[15]

Moreover, in Britain, the government has taken a serious view of the peculiarities of the various geographically separated units i.e. Scotland, Wales and Northern

---

11 Harold Laski as quoted in Neumann, Robert G., *op. cit.*, p. 82.
12 Moodie, Grame C, *The government of Great Britain (3rded)*, London, Methuen and Co. Ltd., 1971, p. 102.
13 *Ibid*
14 Steel, D.R., *Britain* in F.F. Ridley (ed.), *op. cit.*, p. 33.
15 *Ibid*, p. 34.

Ireland. The administration of these separated units faces regional peculiarities in comparison to the British system. The affairs of Scotland and Wales have historically been managed by the Secretary of State for Scottish Affairs and the Secretary of State for Welsh Affairs respectively (Ministers in the British Cabinet). However, recently (in late 1997), the British Government introduced legislations to establish a Scottish Parliament and a Welsh Assembly. On 6th May, 1999, the first election for these bodies was held. The Welsh Assembly opened on 26th May, 1999 and the Scottish Parliament opened on 1st July, 1999. Today most of the functions discharged by the devolved legislatures were previously performed by the Scottish and Welsh offices.[16]

On the other hand, the history of Northern Ireland has remained chequered in the sense that sometimes it has been amalgamated with the British system by providing for a separate Secretary of State in the British Cabinet while at others it had its own legislature and executive to administer its affairs. Thus, it had its own Parliament and prime minister from 1921 to 1973. But in 1973, to control the disturbing situation, the British Government imposed direct rule and its affairs were handed over to a Secretary of State for Northern Ireland. By mid-1990s, efforts were made by the successive British governments and U.S. to restore peace in Northern Ireland. Ultimately, on 10th April, 1998, 'Good Friday Agreement' was made with the intervention of U.S. Senator George Mitchell. Resultantly, in December, 1999 a devolved government was restored in Northern Ireland. The agreement provides for a 108 member elected Assembly. But, in October, 2002, Northern Ireland's devolved Institutions were again suspended and the powers were reverted to the Northern Ireland office. Again elections to the Northern Ireland Assembly were held on 7th May, 2007 and full powers were restored to the devolved institutions on 8th May, 2007. However, powers relating to policing and justice were transferred to the Assembly in April, 2010.[17]

5. **Important Role of Select Committees:** The role of select committees of the British Parliament is significant in the administrative working of Britain. Though these committees are prevailing in most of the democratic countries of the world yet they are relatively more active and keep greater vigil over the administration in Britain. A select committee usually consists of "about fifteen or twenty MPs chosen to reflect the party balance in the House of Commons that is appointed to investigate and report to the House of Commons on particular issues."[18] Public Accounts Committee and the Expenditure Committee are two important committees of Parliament that deal with expenditure. The former was established in 1861 and investigates the cases of alleged mal-administration and thus is the traditional watchdog of government expenditure. Likewise, the latter, which was established in 1971, plays a crucial role in controlling public expenditure. Other such committees are select committee on Nationalized Industries, select committee on Statutory Instruments, select committee on Overseas Development, select committee on Sciences and Technology etc. Along with this, there exists a number of cabinet committees, departmental committees and the committees of local government. Besides co-ordinating the administrative working of various departments, they also keep a constant vigil

---

16 www.state.gov/r/pa/ei/bgn/3846.htm.
17 http://en. Wikipedia.org-Northern Ireland Assembly.
18 Steel, D.R., "Britain" in F.F. Ridley (ed.), *op. cit.*, p. 57.

on their working. Further, there exists inter departmental committees which play a prominent role in the smooth working of administration. These committees operate within limits, which are laid down by the government.[19] In 2001, the quorum of each committee was standardized to three Members or a quarter of the membership, whichever is the larger[20]

These committees conduct detailed enquiries into the administrative working and scrutinize the issues under consideration. In the process, they reveal several weaknesses, inadequacies and malfunctioning of the administration. The reports of these committees are discussed and debated in the British Parliament. Since the criticism by these committees is taken very seriously by the British Government, they (the committees) become an important instrument of control over administration. Thus, the very fear of being censured by the committees keeps the British administration on its toes.

6. **Honest and Transparent Administration:** the British Government has taken due care of making the administrative procedures and functions more and more transparent. To this end, the procedures are simplified and excessive formalities are avoided. Existing laws are frequently reviewed and are also amended accordingly to provide for greater transparency and popular participation. While framing rules and regulations, adequate attention is given to make the system as transparent as possible. The developments taking place in Britain during about the last two decades stand witnessed to this fact. Thus, for instance, Margaret Thatcher took a number of initiatives during her regime to promote efficiency and to ensure administrative accountability. She introduced the concept of "Financial Management Initiative" in the eighties. On this edifice, her successor, John Major, introduced the concept of the Citizen's Charter in June, 1991. He introduced a White Paper in Parliament that "encompassed the principles guiding the Charter, viz., openness, standards, information, choice, non-discrimination and accessibility, to which were later added courtesy and helpfulness, putting things right, value for money and consultation with citizens." The Citizen's Charter aims at "...demanding from the government and service organizations the fundamentals of accountability, transparency, quality and choice of services by them to the people." This Charter is more or less a voluntary commitment on the part of government and service organizations towards the citizens. In the U.K. there exists about 42 national charters and about 10,000 charters of local government services at various stages of enforcement. In Britain, citizen's charters are written and available in all languages i.e. in English, Gurmukhi, Punjabi, Gujarati, Bengali, Hindi, Chinese, and Vietnamese etc. so that even the minorities living in England can be provided with the information of their rights in the languages they better understand. The most important point that needs to be mentioned here is that after the formulation of the Citizen's Charter, the Prime Minister submits a report to the Parliament every year about the progress of the charters prepared by respective ministries in a comparative perspective.[21] The introduction of 'Charter Mark Scheme' (1992) constituted another milestone as it "introduced assessment of service standard

---

19 *Ibid*, p. 60.
20 siteresources.worldbank.org/...Holding the Execu The Accountability Function of the UK Parliament.pdf
21 Steel, D.R., *Britain* in F.F. Ridley (ed.), *op. cit.*, p. 60.

based on ten criteria which included, besides the earlier mentioned principles, fair treatment, effective use of resources, innovation and accessible complaint and redress system."[22] These Charter Marks are awarded to those personnel belonging to different organizations who discharge their services efficiently and satisfactorily to the citizens, and as a result, their nominations are sent by those citizens who avail of the services.[23] If the standards are not maintained or if the delivery of service is delayed, "the concerned department has to pay compensation ranging from Pounds 5 to 75 for not honouring the commitment."[24] The charter was again rechristened in 1998 by the Tony Blair government and it launched the 'Service First Programme' with a view to transform and modernize public services as part of the wider dispensation of better government.[25] In 2006, the Charter Mark Scheme was taken up for a comprehensive review by constituting the Bernard Herdan Committee. Pursuant to the recommendations of its report, not only this scheme was modified but a new scheme Known as 'Customer Service Excellence' was launched in 2008. Like the Charter Mark Scheme, under the new scheme also, public service organizations are encouraged to seek Customer Service Excellence through a formal independent process based on following five criteria: costumer insight, culture of organization, information and access, delivery and timeliness & quality of service.[26]

7. **Efficient Civil Services:** The British civil service is an example of efficiency and neutrality. Many of its principal features were developed in the 19th century when the scale of government was small and its functions were of regulatory nature. But with the passage of time, the nature of the State in Britain, as in most of the other countries, underwent a drastic change. Consequently, there has been a qualitative as well as quantitative change in the functions of administration. However, despite this increase in their activities, the efficiency and neutrality of civil servants in Britain has remained unaltered and they still enjoy a high degree of respect. Concerted efforts are made to ensure their efficiency and neutrality. They are highly paid career civil servants and are recruited on the basis of an open competitive examination which is the responsibility of an independent civil service commission. Since 1968, the Commission has been a part of the Civil Service Department that is headed by the Prime Minister but enjoys complete independence in selection matters.[27] In addition to this, considerable emphasis has been laid on their training. Of late, therefore, the informal training (by means of practical experience of working under the supervision and guidance of senior staff) is being supplemented by formal training since 1945. Through formal training, an effort is made to equip them with latest technological advancements with an aim of developing their efficiency and through informal training, *inter alia* moral values are being inculcated. They are also assured of several more or less automatic promotions and on the basis of the recommendations of the Fulton Committee Report (1968) greater flexibility in promotion has been introduced but seniority remains important.[28]

22 Srivastava, I. C, *op. cit.*, pp. 31-32.
23 Roy, C.N., *op. cit.*, p. 803.
24 *Ibid*
25 Srivastava, I. C, *op. cit.*, p. 32.
26 http://www.arc.gov.in/12_Report.pdf
27 Steel, D.R., *Britain* in F.F. Ridley (ed.), *op. cit.*, p. 40.
28 *Ibid*, pp. 43-45.

As a result of these concerted efforts, the members of civil services discharge their duties with commitment, devotion and efficiency. They are serious and sincere towards the administrative obligations assigned to them. They are committed to the national cause. The degree of goal realization is sufficiently high in Britain.

8. Effective Co-ordination: The British administration is further characterized by existence of effective co-ordination. The geographical decentralization of the British administrative system enhanced the importance of co-ordination particularly in setting priorities and careful planning of public spending and with regard to settling disputes between various branches of government and the smooth running of the administrative machinery.[29] In Britain, the cabinet is the chief co-ordinating agency and there exists the cabinet secretariat for its assistance. Traditionally, the cabinet secretariat has been extending all possible services to cabinet and its committees. Of late (since 1960s), however, it has become more instrumental and has started providing the base for a number of senior government advisers and special units for important areas of decision making. Most important, however, has been the creation of the Central Policy Review Staff (CPRS) in 1971, which physically and constitutionally is a part of the cabinet office and is mainly concerned with offering advice to ministers which will help them to relate their policies and decisions with the government's strategy as a whole.[30]

In case of financial matters, the Treasury plays a prominent role in co-ordinating the entire administrative-working by exercising tight control over public expenditure. Since mid-19th century, it has developed an elaborate system for controlling departmental spending that is linked closely to the requirements of annual parliamentary appropriation procedures. In 1961, a new system of public expenditure planning, known as the 'Public Expenditure Survey System' has been introduced, which worked as a planning device till 1974. But since 1974, it has been modified so that it also has a role to play in controlling spendings.[31]

9. Growing Tendency towards Administrative Reforms: In the last two decades, there seems to be a tendency of comprehensive administrative reforms in Britain in consonance with the 'New Public Management'. The reforms in the public sector have been designed for the qualitative improvement of management. The introduction of the citizen's charter in the U.K. is primarily based on the rising concern of administration regarding client-orientation and treating citizens as customers rather than as beneficiaries. Conservative governments under Margaret Thatcher and John Major and the Labour government of Tony Blaire have showed a serious concern for widespread restructuring of the public sector under the strategy of 'privatisation'. Efforts have been made to create new hybrid forms of myriad organisations based on public-private partnership. Such efforts led to the publication of a White Paper on 'Modernising Government' in March, 1999. The White Paper set out a programme of reform that was to be the future agenda not only for the government but also for the series of new measures that were to be implemented in years to come.[32] Besides, there has been a significant

---

29 *Ibid*, p. 36.
30 *Ibid*
31 *Ibid*, p. 57.
32 Dixit, Manoj, Jaya Chaturevedi and I.H. Syed, *Public Administration*, Lucknow: New Royal Book Co., 2003, pp. 232-237.

development in the field of Information and Technology (I.T.). The I.T. based e-governance in England contributed significantly in promoting direct interface between citizens and government. Moreover, the efforts of the government in the direction of framing the Freedom of Information Act reflect the seriousness of the government towards administrative modernization and reformation[33].

In addition to this, the introduction of Performance and Innovative Unit (PIU) as a part of the UK's drive for 'better and more joined up government' is an endeavour to promote better linkages between policy formulation and implementation. "The PIU aims to improve the capacity of the government to address strategic cross- cutting issues and promote innovation in the development of policy and in the delivery of government's objectives."[34]

10. Bureaucratic Administration: Another characteristic of the British administrative system is its bureaucratic character. In England bureaucracy is not only mature but also highly experienced. It may be noticed that due to the long administrative experience, bureaucracy in England succeeded in evolving rational norms and methods. This has been rendered possible largely because of the relative political stability in England for, due to political stability the political masters have been able to concentrate on governance aspect. Consequently, the administrative structures, procedures, the style of working and the attitude of bureaucracy have evolved and taken shape gradually over a long period of time. Thus, since the bureaucracy in England is highly norm bound, it is relied upon by the political leaders heavily. It plays a significant role in policy making as well as in its implementation. The British system operates under a convention that imposes upon the official and the minister clearly understood mutual obligations based on the principle of impartiality and anonymity.[35] They serve their political masters i.e. the ministers of different governments with equal devotion and skill.

11. Generalist-Specialist Controversy: Like in India and unlike in France, the generalists-specialists controversy is still in vogue in Britain. Traditionally, specialists and professionals have worked outside the realm of policy making. They have been employed in separate hierarchies outside the line of management in the department.[36] It is mainly because of two reasons. Firstly, in Britain it is widely considered that specialists are not suitable to discharge the duties which an administrative functionary at the top echelons is expected to. Administration is seen as a process of arbitrating between special interests of various pressure groups and the experts within departments. The successful administrator, therefore, needs to be detached from any particular field and through his training and experience he needs to be

---

33 The Labour Party in its election manifesto for the 2001 election made a commitment regarding the introduction of a Freedom of Information Act. "The key proposals involve creation of a general statutory right of access to official information and records and a corresponding duty placed on the government to publish more information at no charge as a matter of course." *Ibid*, p. 236.
34 *Ibid*, p. 235.
35 Heady, Ferrel, *Public Administration: A Comparative Perspective (4 ed)*, New York: Marcel Decker, New York, 1991, p. 227.
36 Steel, D.R., *Britain* in F.F. Ridley (ed.), *op. cit*, p. 47.

able to find a balance between different interests. Secondly, since the ministers are most of the times amateurs, it is argued that they need the advice and assistance of such officials who are able to translate the ideas of experts into simplified terms that the amateur minister can understand easily. Such officials should also be apt in operating the government machinery and in implementing ministerial wishes.[37]

However, with the increasing *technologisation,* in the last two decades a fundamental change in the attitude towards the specialists and professionals is being perceived the world over and Britain is not an exception to this. Thus, of late, in Britain also, the role of specialists in administration is increasing. The specialists having technical knowledge are gaining almost equal respect as that of generalists.

12. Effective Local Administration: In British, there emerged a complex network of independent units of urban and local governments towards the end of the 19th century. For instance, the old London city had a metropolitan local government system since 1888. The local government has a well-defined structure and it has a multi-functional character. In Britain the whole of the country is divided into different types of local government units, the range and activities of which are sufficiently large.[38] The central departments do not themselves provide many public services; rather the local government units are the principal operating agencies. Most of the essential services such as education, welfare, housing, police and fire services etc., are discharged by the local authorities[39]. Their powers are laid down by the parliamentary acts and decisions and they are controlled and regulated directly by the central government. Certain decisions of the local bodies require ministerial approval and the independence of local bodies is limited to that extent. In addition to this, the central government provides for over 50 percent of their current expenditure. Though, in the recent past, the government has made a number of attempts to increase central control over issues that were previously left to local discretion, even then these bodies enjoy a sufficient degree of autonomy.[40] Thus, local government authorities are very closely linked to the central administration in their operations, but organizationally they have retained their independence.[41] The British system guarantees them a degree of autonomy within the legal framework.

(B) BRITISH EXECUTIVE

Britain is a constitutional monarchy where the monarch is the titular head and the cabinet headed by the prime minister is the real head. The monarchy is hereditary in character. The British administration is run in the name of the Monarch yet his position is merely that of honour. In actual practice, it is the British Prime Minister and his cabinet that governs the nation and is thus the real executive. In fact, the British executive comprises of the monarch, the cabinet and the prime minister. The three are discussed below in succession.

---

37 *Ibid,* p. 48-49.
38 Smith, Brian C. and Jeffrey Stanger, *Administering Britain,* Glasgow: William Collins Sons and Co. Ltd., 1976, p. 35-36.
39 Steel, D.R., *Britain* in F.F. Ridley (ed.), *op. cit.,* p. 23.
40 *Ibid,* p. 34.
41 Moodie, Graeme C., *op.cit.,* p. 177.

I. THE MONARCH

Great Britain is a constitutional monarchy i.e., constitutionally, the monarch is the head of the State of the United Kingdom. The British monarch is quite an old institution. It is an institution which is more widely known than understood. It is undoubtedly the most unique of all the political institutions of Great Britain. The British monarch/king[42] or more correctly, the Crown, is the counterpart of the Indian president. Though, whereas the former is hereditary and the latter is elected, the two play almost an identical role in their respective spheres. Though the terms 'king' and the 'Crown' are often used interchangeably, but the two are different in the sense that the king is a person whereas the Crown is an institution[43]. As against the king, the term crown "represents the sum total of the governmental powers and is synonymous with the executive"[44]. The British Government is run under the command of the Queen (the present monarch) and is called 'Her Majesty's Government'. Even a political party sitting on the opposition benches in British Parliament is designated as 'Her Majesty's Most Loyal Opposition'[45]. Further, instead of being called the citizens of Great Britain, the Britishers are called the subjects of the king.

Though monarchy in Great Britain is hereditary – the Crown is inherited by the heirs of the House of Hanover – yet succession to the throne can be altered by the Parliament and it has actually been done a number of times. The law relating to the monarch has been developed by both convention and statute. Rules regarding the succession to the throne are laid down in the Act of Settlement (1701) and were subsequently reaffirmed in the subsequent Succession to the Crown Acts and in the Acts of Union with Scotland and Ireland. Though males are preferred over females but the later are not excluded from the succession and the present holder of this office, Queen Elizabeth II, is the seventh queen of England. The king must belong to the Church of England and Roman Catholics and those who marry Roman Catholics are disqualified. If the sovereign is minor (under 18 years of age), the royal functions are to be discharged by a Regent, the next person over 21 years in the line of succession. "In the event of illness (not amounting to total incapacity

---

42 The term 'king' is here used as a term common to either sex. But the head of the State is now a queen.

43 This distinction is reflected in the announcement at the time of death of a king when it is said, "The king is dead, long live the king!" This announcement implies that the king is dead but the king who has died is a person. The latter part of the announcement implies 'long live the institution or the office which one monarch has passed on to the other'. The Crown is an artificial or juristic person that knows neither birth nor death; it cannot be dethroned nor can it abdicate, as it is an institution. What dies is the person (king or monarch) and the office that this person represented (Crown) continues and continues uninterrupted even at the time of the death of a king. This distinction is also reflected in Blackstone's statement: "Henry, Edward or George may die, but the king survives them all". What he meant was that the king as a person was like other mortals, subject to death but that kingship as an institution did not cease to exist even for a minute.

44 Wade and Phillips as quoted in K.R. Bombwall (1971), *Major Contemporaries Constitutional Systems*, Ambala: Modern Publications, p. 39.

45 Maheshwari, S.R., *The Civil Service in Great Britain*, New Delhi: Concept Publishing House, 1976, p. 1.

or absence from the United Kingdom), the Sovereign may appoint Counsellors of State to exercise such of the royal functions as may be conferred on them by letters patent"[46].

In ancient times, all the powers were enjoyed by the king absolutely, who exercised them unquestionably. This signified the concept of absolute monarchy. So, the king reigned as well as ruled. But the Glorious Revolution of 1688, was a landmark and acted as a dividing line in the British Constitutional history. Thereafter, the British monarchy confronted far-reaching changes, which resulted in transferring of most of the powers of the king to the Parliament and to a large extent to the cabinet. Consequently, now, the monarch has been left with "...the smallest amount of residuary powers and in British politics, counts for practically very little. The transfer of sovereignty from the king to the Parliament has been almost complete. The major break-through was made at the time of the Glorious Revolution but it has been continuing since then"[47].

These transferred powers are now exercised by a composite body called the Crown, which incorporates the king, the cabinet and the Parliament and all three combined make an abstract concept of supreme authority[48]. Hence, the personal powers of the king have diminished and those of the Crown have increased. In other words, the powers of the king have been institutionalized. The king has merely to give his or her formal assent to the decisions taken by the cabinet and the Parliament. It resulted into reducing the king to a nominal head. Due to this change in position the king still reigns, but he has gradually ceased to rule. Now, the king personally has nothing to do with any affair of the government and hence the popular saying, "The king can do no wrong". The king must abide by the advice of his prime minister even in matters affecting his private life and "some admirers of Parliamentary Sovereignty have maintained that even if the Parliament were to send to the king his death warrant, he would have no alternative but to sign it"[49].

The position of a reigning queen is exactly the same as that of a king, but while a king's spouse is called queen, the husband of a reigning queen is never called king. Queen Victoria's husband Prince Albert received the title *Prince Consort* in the later years of his life. But this title has not been received by the husband of Queen Elizabeth-II and is not likely to, because to history – conscious Englishmen, this designation is forever tied to the memories of Victoria and Albert[50].

POWERS

The monarch is the chief executive in Great Britain. In abstract theory the powers of the monarch are very extensive and formidable. Her formal powers include "... most activities of government, as laws are passed in her name, taxes are collected by Her Majesty's Inspectors, convicted criminals are sent to Her Majesty's prisons,

---

46 Harvey, J. and L. Bather, *The British Constitution and Politics* (5th ed.), London: Macmillan Education Ltd., 1984, pp. 199-200.
47 Goyal, O.P., *Comparative Governments*, New Delhi: Macmillan India Ltd., 1985, p. 102.
48 Kapur, Anup Chand, *Select Constitutions*, Chandigarh, 1970, p. 41.
49 Goyal. O.P., *op. cit.*, p. 103.
50 Neumann, Robert G. (1968), *op. cit.*, p. 70.

and she appoints ministers and judges, and confers honours"[51]. Bagehot also wrote in 1872, that the queen "could disband the army, she could dismiss all the officers from the General Commanding-in-Chief downward; ... she could sell off all our ships of war and our naval stores; she could make peace by sacrifice of Cornwall, and begin a war for the conquest of Brittany ..."[52]. The extent of her formal authority may be classified as under:

1. Executive Powers

The monarch is the supreme executive of the State and in this capacity has to ensure the execution of all laws enacted by the Parliament. The monarch also directs and supervises the work of the administration. All the higher executive and administrative officers such as the prime ministers, members of the cabinet and other ministers as well as other higher officers of the government including judges and ambassadors are appointed by the monarch. The judicial officials as well as the officers of the army, navy and the air force are appointed by the monarch. The monarch holds the supreme command of the armed officials. The monarch also enjoys unlimited powers to remove officers (except judges) and discharge employees. The monarch conducts the country's foreign relations, can declare war, conclude peace and make treaties with foreign powers and performs the diplomatic functions and receives ambassadors and ministers from foreign countries. "Practically everything else, significant or insignificant, is asserted to have been done by him"[53].

2. Legislative Powers

The king is also an integral part of the Parliament and all law-making powers are vested in the "King-in-Parliament". It is the king who bestows peerages and thus largely determines the composition and character of the House of Lords. The orders-in-council are still issued in the name of the Crown. "The statues are enacted by the king's most excellent Majesty, by and with the advice and consent of the lords Spiritual and Temporal and Commoners, in this present Parliament assembled and by the authority of the same. The Crown summons, prorogues and dissolves the Parliament."[54] The session of every new Parliament starts with a speech from the throne. All the bills passed by the Parliament are laid before the king for his assent and they become Acts only when such assent has been declared and notified. The crown, through his officers, called ministers, guides and controls the Parliament in preparing the king's speech and it also decides what bills shall be introduced in the Parliament. The Parliament conducts business during the pleasure of the crown. After dissolving the Parliament, it is the king who orders fresh elections.

3. Judicial Powers

The Crown also acts as the 'foundation of justice'. The king can appoint the judges to the regular courts. All arrests are made and all criminal prosecutions are launched in the name of the Crown. The king also enjoys the prerogative to grant pardon and

---

51 Sallis, Edward, *The Machinery of Government: An Introduction to Public Administration*, London: Holt, Rinehart and Winston Ltd., 1982, p. 85.
52 Quoted in Neumann, Robert G., *op. cit.*, pp. 70-71.
53 Goyal. O.P., *op. cit.*, p. 101.
54 *Ibid*

reprieve. However, the powers of the Crown in this field are very limited. This is perhaps because the Court of Star Chamber "...set up by Henry VII, the Court of High Commission of Elizabeth I and the Bloody Assize of James II left so much of bad odour in the mouth of Englishmen that they sought to control the powers of the Crown in this field more ardently than in other fields"[55]. Thus, though he can appoint the judges but is deprived of any power to remove them except, of course, on the request of both Houses of Parliament. The king also cannot create new courts nor can he alter the organization and procedure of any court. Further, the king is also deprived of the power to change the number, tenure or pay of judges.

4. Powers of the Crown as Fountain of Honour

The Crown is stated to be the fountain of honour. It bestows titles, honours, distinctions and decorations on those who have rendered meritorious service to the State or have distinguished themselves in the fields of science, arts or letters. Certain honours such as the Order of the Garter, the Order of Merit and the Royal Victorian Order are reserved for being conferred by the Sovereign. In consultation with the prime minister, he creates hereditary and life peers to: a) honour persons for public service; (b) provide more representation to a particular party in the Upper House; (c) allow persons having specific qualification to take part in the deliberations of the Chamber; (d) find a place in Parliament for a person whom the prime minister wishes to include in his cabinet; (e) resolve a deadlock between the House of Commons and House of Lords[56].

5. Ecclesiastical Powers

The monarch is the head of the Church of England and in this capacity appoints archbishops, bishops, and deans, cannon and other ecclesiastical dignitaries. It summons the conventions of Canterbury and York and as the head of the Anglican Church, gives assent to the bills passed by them as is the case with the Acts of Parliament. The Crown is also the head of the Church of Scotland. The Crown also hears appeals from all ecclesiastical courts. Generally, he issues the *conge d'elire* -- the writ of election for deans and cannons. The *conge d'elire* is the letter missive designating the persons to be elected as deans and cannons leaving no discretion to the electors[57].

POSITION

Theoretically, the monarch being the Head of the State of United Kingdom possesses vast powers. However, the actual powers of the monarch are extremely limited. The monarch is merely a symbol of the government and State with a ceremonial or ambassadorial role to play. The king has to act merely as a constitutional head. "In theory, he still has a wide range of powers and prerogatives, which have never been formally abolished. However, all these powers and prerogatives have either fallen into disuse or they have to be exercised in accordance with established political

---

55 Gupta, B.B., *Comparative Study of Six Living Constitutions*, New Delhi: Sterling Publishers Pvt. Ltd., 1974, pp. 143-44.
56 Harvey, J. and L. Bather, *op. cit.*, p. 209.
57 Gupta, B.B., *op. cit.*, p. 144.

conventions"[58]. In fact, the powers constitutionally conferred upon the king are actually exercised by the cabinet/prime minister and the former has to abide by the advice rendered by the cabinet/prime minister. Much water has flown down the Thames since the days of royal absolutism when the ministers advised and the king decided and wielded considerable authority. Presently, the situation is altogether different. With "… the rise of liberal and, later, democratic ideas, the increased power of the Parliament, and the accompanying need to devise peaceful constitutional means of changing government policy and personnel made it possible to preserve the monarchy only by steadily restricting its actual powers to govern."[59] It has been realized, in effect, by extending the doctrine of ministerial responsibility to mean that, in most of the areas of government, "…the monarch should exercise his or her powers only upon the advice of ministers supported by the House of Commons… the power to govern rests squarely with ministers, whose advice the monarch must normally accept, and who derive their authority to govern from elections and not hereditary right"[60]. In Britain, the rule of responsible government prevails and it demands that the executive should be responsible to the people through the Parliament. It was, therefore, considered desirable to get all the acts got countersigned by a popular minister – who shall be responsible to the Parliament – of the Crown and hence the doctrine of ministerial responsibility was made applicable.

Whether it is the selection of the prime minister or the appointment of the ministers or the dissolution of the Parliament, there is virtually very little room left for the discretion of the monarch. The two party system has left no choice for the monarch to exercise any discretion in regard to the selection of prime minister. The monarch is obliged to call the leader of the majority party in the House of Commons to form the government and later to endorse the list of ministers prepared by the prime minister. During the last whole century, perhaps there were only three such instances when there arose a need for the monarch to make real choice regarding the selection of prime minister[61]. And even in these circumstances, the monarch's choice 'in effect lay only between two men', and it appears "… that the monarch in fact did no more than ratify the decisions or preferences of the various party leaders concerned. Should similar situations arise in the future, moreover, there is ground for arguing that the monarch would more clearly leave the decision to the parties themselves"[62].

Constitutionally, dismissal of the ministers is regarded as the prerogatives of the king. But, given the two party system, this prerogative can hardly be used by the king in real practice. This power was, in effect, last exercised by the king in 1783 – when George III dismissed the government of Fox. Since then no other king has ever repeated this act and "… if it is ever to be attempted by the king today, it would

---

58 Goyal, O.P., *op. cit.*, p. 103.
59 Moodie, Graeme C., *op. cit.*, 1971, p. 91.
60 Ibid
61 These included: in 1923 and 1957, when a Conservative party government had to obtain a new prime minister before its own choice of successor had been made and in 1931, when the National Government was formed under MacDonald. For details please refer Harvey, J. and L. Bather, *op. cit.*, pp. 205-06.
62 Moodie, Graeme C., *op. cit.*, p. 92.

create a revolutionary crisis"[63]. The idea of providing the power to actually dismissing the prime minister could not find favour in a democratic country mainly because of two reasons-firstly, the sovereign can't be better qualified to judge a situation than the prime minister, who is supposed to run the government. Secondly, it is necessary to take a long view. "A Government is selected for five years and some time during that period it may have to take unpopular measures; but it can always hope for a return to favour before it has to seek re-election"[64]. Further, there are several agencies to judge the acts of the prime minister in case some unconstitutional is being done by him. Among others, these include the internal dynamics of his party, the opposition, the media, the people, the judiciary and the like. All these exert considerable pressure upon him and let him not act in an arbitrary manner.

Dissolution of the Parliament is another field in which the king is asserted to have discretionary powers. Sometimes it is argued that the monarch possesses the constitutional right to refuse to dissolve the Parliament. However, it is the prime minister and not the king who is responsible to and the leader of the House of Commons and by dint of this is the best judge as to when should be the House dissolved. Therefore, any amount of royal discretion in the question of dissolution of the House seems needless. Historically also, during the century approximately, this power has not been actually exercised by any of the monarchs. It is true that all enactments of the Parliament require royal assent for becoming law. It is, however, equally true that the king has not withheld his assent to any bill passed by the Parliament for the last about two centuries and "... it is difficult to believe that it would ever be done now. If it does happen, it is clear that there could a revolutionary crisis"[65].

Thus, the real position of the monarch is that of a titular head wherein he does not exercise any power except or without the advice of the minister concerned. In other words, the British Monarch has no 'power'. He has been reduced to a 'nominal head' like the Indian President. It also means that he has no political responsibility. As he always acts on the advice of his ministers, so for every public act done in his name, the responsibility goes to the minister concerned or to the whole cabinet.

INFLUENCE

From the above, it should not be misconstrued that the king has been devoid of all powers. Undoubtedly, in certain matters he does act exactly as an automation would act, yet in many others he is certainly more than an automaton. He definitely possesses very few powers yet he wields considerable influence and it is difficult to swallow the comments of Sir Sidney Low that the Crown in British politics is a *convenient working hypothesis*. Obviously, he is much more than that.

Walter Bagehot remarked in his famous treatise *The English Constitution* that the king possesses three rights viz. the right to be consulted, the right to encourage, and the right to warn, to which he added, "And a king of great sense and sagacity would want no others"[66]. The monarch is informed about all the problems facing the nation

---

63 Goyal, O.P., *op. cit.*, p. 104.
64 Harvey, J. and L. Bather, *op. cit.*, p. 207.
65 Goyal, O.P., *op. cit.*, p. 103.
66 Quoted in Neumann, Robert G., *op. cit.*, p. 73.

and the decisions taken by the cabinet. The monarch can also tender advice to the government on any problem facing the country, which, given the respect the king in Great Britain commands coupled with the quantum of experience that he would accumulate through the years of his reign, will carry considerable weight and no government would be able to ignore that easily. Further, the king can encourage the prime minister if he is doing something commendable. In a country like the United Kingdom, where the press is free and the people are enlightened, any favourable comments from the Buckingham Palace about the acts of the government would considerably boost the morale of the government in addition to making the public opinion in favour of the government. Such an act of the monarch can be particularly helpful for the prime minister and his government when he is taking a good step and the opposition is not letting the government to take that step. Conversely, if the prime minister is taking some such step – particularly taking in case when his party commands a large majority support in the House of Commons – that may prove harmful to the interests of the country, the monarch can warn the prime minister. Such a warning will have an adverse effect on the popularity of the government.

Thus, it may be concluded that the king in Britain is a constitutional head and in that capacity, has to abide by the advice rendered by the prime minister and therefore, actually possesses very few powers. However, there are no two opinions about the fact that the king commands a great respect and honour and therefore, wields considerable influence in the British polity as well as society. The monarch deliberately takes a non-party political stance, and this has helped it both to survive as an institution and to become a national symbol.

II. PRIME MINISTER

The United Kingdom has a parliamentary form of government and one of the key features of this form of government is the existence of two sets of executive viz. nominal and real. In the United Kingdom, the monarch is the symbolic or constitutional head whereas the real head of the government is the prime minister. He is the leader of the majority party in the House of Commons. His party has entered the electoral fight under his leadership, and the people who voted for it have thereby unmistakably voted for his premiership[67]. He holds one of the most powerful political offices in the world. If any single person today occupies a position of supreme governing power in Great Britain, it is the prime minister. He is the principal adviser to the Crown and thus also the principal inheritor of its powers[68]. Hence the prime minister holds a position of unmistakable supremacy. However, despite this there has been a difference between the influences exerted by different prime ministers in the history of the United Kingdom. In this connection, it need not be forgotten that the quantum of influence which the British prime minister, and for that matter any other executive, wields depends, at least to some extent, on the personality of the person holding this position. "If he is a strong like Sir Winston Churchill, Harold Macmillan or Harold Wilson, he will imprint his stamp on the cabinet. If he is endowed with fewer leadership capacities, like Lord Rosebery or Lord Salisbury, the entire course of his cabinet will be lacking indecisiveness"[69].

---

67 Neumann, Robert G., *op. cit.*, p. 78.
68 Moodie, Graeme C., p. 96.
69 Neumann, Robert G., *op. cit.*, p. 74.

EVOLUTION

Like most of the other institutions of Britain, the office of prime minister is an outcome of a mere accident. It came into existence during the Hanoverian period. Walpole was the first British prime minister who was asked by George I to preside over cabinet meetings since the king lacked knowledge of English and was least interested in English affairs. Till the beginning of the last century, this office remained unknown to law[70]. The law of the country did not know the prime minister as such until 1905. It was by an Act in 1906, which provided a definite and exalted rank to the prime minister by fixing the order of precedence in state ceremonials. Later, a number of other constitutional changes took place and a number of statutes passed like the Chequers Estate Act, 1917, the Ministers of the Crown Act, 1937 etc. which ultimately enhanced the powers of this office[71]. These Acts, though, have recognized the constitutional position of the prime minister, yet they failed in conferring any legal power as such. Whatever powers the prime minister exercises are derived from constitutional conventions. Therefore, the power and authority of the prime minister rest upon extra legal basis.

APPOINTMENT

The appointment of the prime minister is the most important function of the monarch. After every election, the monarch appoints one person from amongst those who have been elected to the House of Commons – earlier the prime minister could be appointed from amongst the Lords also, as we will see later – as prime minister of the country. From this it seems that the monarch has a real prerogative to appoint anyone from amongst the Members of the Commons as prime minister. But the real situation is entirely different. The monarch is bound by convention and has to appoint the leader of the majority party in the House of Commons as prime minister. The monarch cannot use any discretion in this matter and will not be able to do that so long as the two party system prevails in Britain. Should the prevalent two party system collapses in Great Britain, the monarch may have to make a personal choice in appointment of the prime minister. Thus, for instance, the monarch may be obliged to use her discretion if a general election results in a hung Parliament – a situation wherein no political party can claim majority support in the House of Commons. The monarch will make her own choice in that situation as has been done by the Indian president a number of times during the last decade of the previous century. However, under the normal circumstances the choice of the prime minister is made by the electorate. Both the major parties declare their leaders far in advance of the elections and people are fully aware who will be their prime minister if they vote for a particular party. Thus, so long as the two party system prevails, "it may be stated that the people of Britain elect their Prime Minister no less than the American people elect their presidents"[72].

In any case, it is imperative that while making a choice for the prime minister, the monarch should keep herself away from party politics. The monarch should

---

70 Bhagwan, Vishnu and Vidya Bhushan, *World Constitutions*, New Delhi: Sterling Publishers Pvt. Ltd., 1991, p. 65.
71 *Ibid.*
72 Neumann, Robert G., *op. cit.*, p. 75.

take all possible precautions to keep herself away from the party politics and to be non-partisan. Jennings has aptly summarized the role of the monarch at the time of selection of a prime minister. To him, the task of the monarch is only "...to secure a Government, not to try to form a Government. To do so would be to engage in party politics. It is, moreover, essential to the belief in the monarch's impartiality, not only that she should in fact act impartially, but that she should appear to act impartially"[73].

As stated above, one of the essential qualifications for being appointed as prime minister of Britain is that the person should be a member of the Parliament. Thus all prime ministers from Robert Walpole till the present incumbent have been members of either of the two houses of Parliament. This has been rendered essential by the doctrine of ministerial responsibility. If the prime minister is not a member of the Parliament, he/she would not be able to attend the sessions of the Parliament and thus also would not be able to respond to the queries of the members. Resultantly the principle of ministerial responsibility would be diluted. Thus, by convention, the king had to choose prime minister from amongst the members of either of the two houses.

Gradually, however, it also came to be realized that the prime minister should belong to the House of Commons and not to the House of Lords[74]. This was because it was apprehended that the House of Lords has least parity with the House of Commons. Thus the word Parliament had come to be identified more and more "... with the House of Commons. It was in the House of Commons that the representatives of the people sat and the House of Lords was neither representative nor responsible ... ministerial responsibility to Parliament could be made real and effective not in the Lords but in the Commons"[75]. This realization brought a major shift in the existing policy regarding the selection of prime ministers. As a consequence of it, in 1923, Mr. Baldwin (who hailed from the House of Commons) was preferred to Lord Curzon (who was in the House of Lords at that time), despite the later being the most eminent Conservative leader at that time. Thenceforth, it has become a convention to appoint a prime minister from the House of Commons only[76].

FUNCTIONS

The Parliamentary enactments in Great Britain do make mention of the prime minister but do not specify his functions. He derives all authority only from conventions. In this context, Jennings says that, it is a singular constitutional law, " ... which knows of the Prime Minister because he is three times mentioned in statutes [the Chequers Estate Act, 1917; the Ministers of the Crown Act, 1937; and the Physical Training and Recreation Act, 1937], but can say of him only that he has no powers

---

73 Quoted in Goyal, O.P., *op. cit.*, p. 93.
74 Earlier the prime minister could be appointed from either of the two houses. Thus, during the period 1837 to 1902, six of the prime ministers chosen were from the House of Lords. But, several problems were encountered in the conduct of legislative business during the tenure of these six prime ministers. Thus, after the resignation of Lord Salisbury in 1902, nobody hailing from the House of Lords has been appointed prime minister of Britain.
75 Goyal, O.P., *op. cit.*, p. 93.
76 Jaya Plan, N., *Modern Governments*, New Delhi: Atlantic Publishers & Distributors, p. 44.

whatever..."[77]. Even the Ministers of Crown Act, 1937 though granted him a salary and a pension on retirement but remained silent in regard to "... who shall be Prime Minister or what he shall do"[78]. Despite that, however, the prime minister in Britain is by far the most powerful person and wields great authority. The extent of the powers possessed by him can be seen from the following description of his functions:

1. Appointment/Selection of Ministers or Formation of Council of Ministers

One of the most important functions to be performed by the prime minister right after being appointed so is the formation of the council of ministers. There are about a hundred ministerial ranks to be filled from amongst his party men in both Houses of Parliament. This process also includes the formation of cabinet "... the inner group of some twenty people meeting regularly under the chairmanship of the prime minister and sharing constitutional responsibility for all conduct of government"[79]. Those appointed must be or become (either by winning a by-election or being made a peer) members of either House. Constitutionally, appointment of ministers is one of the important powers of the prime minister and he is stated to have freedom in this matter, "no prime minister, however, can be as free politically as he is constitutionally"[80]. Though the prime minister enjoys comparatively a free hand yet the formation of council of ministers is not an easy job. He has to give due consideration to the claims and views of the leading members of his party. Occasionally, the prime minister has to weigh the views of the king in cabinet formation. Sometimes, he deletes a name or adds a name to suit the king's wishes.

Besides these difficulties, there are certain constitutional and conventional limitations within the ambit of which the prime minister has to work while formulating the ministry. These have been well summed up by Harvey and Bather[81] and are listed below:

1. While no statute requires that a minister should be an MP or a peer, there is a well-established convention to that effect.
2. The Ministers of Crown Act, 1964 limits the maximum number of ministers and Parliamentary Secretaries who can sit in the House of Commons to 91, thereby ensuring indirectly that there is a nucleus of ministers in the Lords.
3. Where the head of a department is in the House of Lords, his immediate deputy must be in the Commons, although the converse does not always follow.
4. Certain offices are invariably filled by members of the House of Commons, either because they have considerable political significance or because most of the discussion of their work is carried on there. Such posts include those of Chancellor of the Exchequer, Home Secretary and the Secretaries of State for Social Services, Education, and Science, Trade, the Environment, and Employment.
5. The Lord Chancellor, the Attorney-General and the Solicitor-General must be lawyers.

---

77 Jennings, Sir Ivor, *The Law and the Constitution*, London: The English Language Book Society and University of London Press Ltd., 1973, p. 70.
78 Harvey, J. and L. Bather, *op. cit.*, p. 221.
79 Moodie, Graeme C., *op. cit.*, p. 89.
80 *Ibid*, p. 97.
81 Harvey, J. and L. Bather, *op. cit.*, pp. 222-23.

6. Unless there is a coalition government, the principle of political homogeneity has to be followed.
7. Ministers must have the essential personal qualities of competence and honesty. An incompetent minister soon becomes an embarrassment to the prime minister. The Parliament, particularly the House of Commons, which was once called "the world's most exclusive club" often put the ministers in very precarious situations of which only ministers with great sagacity can steer clear. Thus, the ministers must be capable of persuading the Parliament to endorse their actions.

Hence, while forming his council of ministers the prime minister has to work under several constraints and compulsions, yet it is also true that despite these limitations, he enjoys considerable freedom and, except in a few cases, it is his will that ultimately prevails. Thus, it may be said that the prime minister "... is free to build as he wishes so long as the administration as a whole is reasonably representative of the principal political forces within the party and so long as he does not leave any sizable body of influential people outside the administration in a position to make trouble."[82]

2. Allocation of Portfolio

Having formed the council of ministers, the next important task of the prime minister is to allocate portfolios among his team-members. This is the prime minister's prerogative and makes him immensely powerful vis-à-vis his ministerial colleagues. However, this power is also by no means unrestricted. He has to give weight to the wishes of the prominent and senior party leaders who have preference for some specific departments and at times are relentless. For instance, Henderson was not ready to take anything except the Foreign Office in the MacDonald ministry whereas the later was not ready to put the former in charge of this ministry. However, the premier had to yield as the exclusion of Henderson from the ministry was out of question[83].

Sometimes, the prime minister has to confer ministerial berths even on his opponents within the party. In this regard, Attlee's gesture of placing Aneurin Bevan in charge of health portfolio may be cited as an example. In the similar way, "Harold Wilson muted the opposition of Frank Cousins (who had favoured unilateral disarmament) and of R.H.S. Crossman, an often oppositional left-wing intellectual, by taking them into his first government"[84]. Sometimes, there are also recommendations from the crown that he is usually obliged to honour. At some occasions, he is compelled to compromise the administrative acumen and talent to pacify the claims of some prominent party leaders. "It may be possible to pass over one or even two prominent party leaders, and it may be essential to ignore some of the claims of those who expect office, but the prime minister cannot, politically, ignore all of them even if he should wish to"[85].

In this way, it becomes obvious that though allocation of portfolios is the exclusive privilege of the prime minister but he has to work under certain constraints and sometimes even to include such faces in his ministry whom he does not like very

---

82 Moodie, Graeme C., *op. cit.*, p. 97.
83 Neumann, Robert G., *op. cit.*, p. 76.
84 *Ibid*, pp. 76-77.
85 Moodie, Graeme C., *op. cit.*, p. 97.

much. However, if he disregards the wishes of prominent party leaders, he should be prepared for problems in future. In this connection, it is noteworthy that the said constraints are more at work in the case of allocating portfolios among his senior colleagues and the prime minister is relatively freer in the case of allocation of less important posts of the ministry.

3. Shuffling of Portfolios and Dismissal of Ministers

Now-a-days elections in Britain are not fights between the two parties but between their prime ministerial candidates. Thus, if the government fails, it is regarded to be the failure of the prime minister more than the party in power. From this, it directly stems that the prime minister should possess the authority to analyze and evaluate the performance of his ministerial colleagues and, if upon such analysis and evaluation, finds some minister inconvenient or less capable of conducting the affairs of one department, to transfer him to some other. In other words, the prime minister reserves the right to shuffle and reshuffle the portfolios among the different ministers. The prime minister has also been authorized to drop someone from the ministry, if the latter is incapable to discharge his responsibilities or if some of his action brought embarrassment to the government or if there is some fundamental disagreement on some policy matter. However, in such a situation it has been more usual to demand the resignation from the minister concerned instead of resorting to dismissal. In any case, such decisions are unpleasant and the prime ministers generally "... like their Cabinet to appear united and usually try to avoid too many dismissals or transfers. Prime Ministers do use this power selectively to show their authority and to bring particular party factions into line"[86] and a few instances of dismissals do exist. In the recent political history of Britain, the action of Mr. Macmillan in 1962 in which he made 24 governmental changes overnight including the removal of 7 ministers may be cited as an example. This is, however, a rare incident and such ruthless dismissals ought to be avoided. Margaret Thatcher also exercised this power in 1981 and "... removed from her Cabinet one leading 'wet', the Chancellor of the Duchy of Lancaster, Norman St John Stevas, who was known to be opposed to the Prime Minister's hard-line monetarist economic policy"[87].

4. Chairman of the Council of Ministers

The position of prime minister in cabinet is quite often equated with that of the chairman of board of directors. But there is one significant difference between the positions of the two. Whereas the latter is elected by the board of directors, the former is not elected by the cabinet, rather it is the prime minister who chooses his team (cabinet). This makes the *primus inter pares* a real boss of the cabinet. In fact, the conglomerate impact of the powers of prime minister to select the ministers (after his appointment as prime minister), to allocate portfolios to them and the power of dismissal of ministers is that he is rendered far superior to his ministerial colleagues. He convenes and presides over the meetings of the cabinet. It is he who decides, not only when the cabinet shall meet but also what it shall discuss. His role is crucial in setting the agenda of the cabinet meetings and he can accept or reject the proposal

---

86 Sallis, Edward, *op. cit.*, p. 88.
87 Ibid

made by its members for discussion. Although the views of the all members count, yet the prime minister's decision is the final word. The prime minister also acts as the guide of the cabinet and is responsible for establishing effective co-ordination among the policies of different ministers. Therefore, it becomes clear that the prime minister is the undisputed leader or chairman of the cabinet. Highlighting the position of the prime minister in relation to the cabinet, Lord Morrison has observed that though all the cabinet members stand on the same footing, "... speak with equal voice, and on rare occasions when a division is taken, are counted on the fraternal principle of one vote, yet the head of the Cabinet is Prime inter pares, and occupies a position which so long as it lasts, is one of exceptional and peculiar authority"[88].

Conventionally, the prime minister has got some overriding powers over his cabinet colleagues. Thus, he enjoys the right to communicate directly with his Cabinet colleagues and their subordinates. He also has "...the authority to take decisions in matters falling within the jurisdiction of his Cabinet colleagues and sometimes he does that even without consulting his Cabinet colleagues and they are left with the difficult choice of either accepting the policy announced by him or to lose their valuable leader"[89]. The dominant role of the prime minister in policy formulation has also been highlighted by Moodie. To him, "subject to cabinet ratification, he may make important decisions on his own and, by announcing them publicly in his capacity as chief spokesman for the government, make the ratification more likely"[90]. It is by virtue of the exercise of these powers that some scholars prefer to call the British political system the "prime-ministerial form of government" rather than the "cabinet form of government".

5. Determination of the Structure of Cabinet Committees

In the capacity of the chairman of the council of ministers, the prime minister not only determines the size of the cabinet but also the structure and size of the its (cabinet) committees. He presides over several of these committees while the rest are presided over by the cabinet ministers of his liking. The members of these committees are also selected by him. Though the cabinet committees seldom come in to the limelight, "... they are the places where most Cabinet business is transacted. Their composition is therefore crucial to the outcome of decisions"[91]. Thus, by selecting the chairman and the members of the cabinet committees, he can favour his own views where there are policy differences in the cabinet. All this further consolidates his position vis-à-vis the cabinet, particularly its recalcitrant members.

6. Leader of the House of Commons

Provided he did not belong to the House of Lords, the prime minister used to be the official Leader of the House of Commons. In that capacity, he made decisions regarding the general business of the House during the sessions. However, with the successive and gradual increase in his functions, it was deemed desirable to relieve him of this function. Consequently, he is no longer the official Leader of the House

---

88 Ibid, p. 97.
89 Goyal, O.P., *op. cit.*, p. 99.
90 Moodie, Graeme C., *op. cit.*, pp. 97-98.
91 Sallis, Edward, *op. cit.*, p. 88.

and this duty is now assigned to some other minister. Yet he is still the leader of his parliamentary party and controls the business of the House through the party whips. Further, if the House wishes to express its views "...on those national issues which over-ride party divisions e.g., events concerning the Royal Family or the death of a distinguished statesman, the Prime Minister acts as its spokesman. On such occasions, the Leader of Opposition usually underlines the unity of the House by adding his own observations"[92].

7. Channel of Communication

The prime minister is the principal, and sometimes the only medium of communication between the cabinet and the sovereign as well as between the Parliament and the sovereign. As discussed earlier, the queen possesses a constitutional right to be informed about and consulted on all major policy matters be they internal or foreign affecting the British interests. The queen must also be apprised of the international events and the stance taken by the British government on those happenings. All this is, however, conveyed to the queen by the prime minister. Though there is no bar on the ministers to talk to the sovereign but it is not expected of them to discuss public affairs with the latter behind the back of other ministers. Further, all the messages of the cabinet are conveyed by the prime minister to the monarch. Conversely, it is the prime minister who presents the views of the queen, if any, on some policy matter before the cabinet. Though such views are not binding on it, the latter (cabinet) is obliged to consider those views before taking any decision on that policy. Sometimes, the queen also sends messages to the Parliament. These messages are also routed through the prime minister. In this way, he acts as direct channel of communication between the cabinet and the monarch.

8. Chief Adviser to the King

Constitutionally, all the functions in Great Britain are discharged by the monarch and nothing can be done without the ratification of the monarch. However, ratification by the monarch is merely a formality. The monarch is only the nominal head and has to exercise all the constitutionally conferred powers in consultation with the prime minister. In normal circumstances, the monarch cannot do anything what has not been advised by his prime minister and cannot deny what he has been advised to do by the prime minister. Resultantly, an intimate relationship develops between the monarch and the prime minister and usually most prime ministers have a regular weekly audience with the former. What is important is that he can render advice to the king even without any sort of consultation and discussion with the cabinet.

9. Power of Dissolution

The prime minister enjoys the power to dissolve the House of Commons and by this power, he regulates the business of the House. Unlike many other political systems, there has no fixed date for general elections in British system providing they are held "...within the five-year term. The decision 'to go to the country' rests with the Prime minister. It is an important power, as it allows the Prime Minister to consult

---

92 Harvey J. and L. Bather, *op. cit.,* p. 227.

public opinion polls and to choose the best time for his or her party to be returned to office"[93]. This power of dissolution in the hands of the prime minister also puts the members of the House, his party colleagues and even his cabinet colleagues on his mercy as dissolution means new elections without the certainty of returning to the House, or the Government or the Cabinet as the case may be.

10. Representative of the Nation

The prime minister also acts as the representative of the nation. He represents his nation at the national and international levels. Occasionally, he attends and participates in international conferences and meetings where he presents his views as the leader of the nation. His views, presented at such conferences or at any other platform are regarded to be the views of the nation. He also remains in direct contact with the prime ministers of commonwealth countries, though the utility of such contacts and communications has been on the decline[94].

POSITION

The position of the British prime minister is a formidable one which is clearly reflected from the functions and powers discusses above. He is the centre of the government and the rest of the governmental machinery revolves around him. He manages the sovereign, the cabinet and the House of Commons. He maintains party solidarity and thus keeps the party united. He also manages the electorate by keeping the atmosphere of success all round[95]. Thus, the British prime minister holds a position of unmistakable supremacy and he is the pivot of the British administration.

Indeed, the primacy of the prime minister is the fundamental principal of the British cabinet system. Various scholars have given different (miek,¡) to explain the position of the British prime minister. He has been rightly described as the "keystone of the Cabinet arch". Prof. Munro described him, "the captain of the ship of the state" whereas Prof. Laski called him "the pivot around which the entire government machinery revolves". While describing his position in the cabinet, Lord Morley has written, "although in the cabinet all its members stand on equal footing ... yet the head of the Cabinet (the prime minister) is *primus inter pares* and occupies a position, which, so long as it lasts, is one of exceptional and peculiar authority"[96]. But Prof. Carter is of the view that prime minister is much more than *primus inter pares*. To him, elevation from the position of a cabinet minister to that of prime minister is not "merely a change of place but a change of dimension"[97]. Similarly, Jennings holds that "he is not merely *primus inter pares*. He is also not even *inter stellas lunaninores* [as Harcourt has held]. He is rather a sun around which planets revolve"[98].

The position of the prime minister in the administration of the United Kingdom becomes clear from the above statements of the eminent scholars. The importance of

---

93 Sallis, Edward, *op. cit.*, p. 88.
94 Goyal, O.P., *op. cit.*, p. 96.
95 *Ibid*
96 Quoted in Jennings, S.I., *Some Characteristics of the Indian Constitution*, Madras: O.V.P., 1953, p. 126.
97 Carter, B.E., *The Office of the Prime Minister*, London, 1956, p. 343.
98 Jennings, S.I., *op. cit.*, 1953, p. 200.

the prime minister has further increased in view of the recent developments in the field of science and technology and the recent changes in the international order. "Radio and television bring him more frequently than any other politician into the homes of the people, who therefore, see in his personality the embodiment of the party and, in times of emergency, the trustee of the national cause"[99]. Besides, the acts of insurgency and threats thereof by certain militant outfits like the *Al-Qaida* etc. and the wars against the so-called militant states of Afghanistan and Iraq have heightened both the threats as well as position of the British prime minister along with the American president. It is, therefore, obvious that the prime minister occupies the key position in the British constitution; and almost all recent developments have tended to increase his authority. However, the extent of his powers depends upon the capacity, capability and the personality of the prime minister. History stands witness to the fact that as prime ministers, persons with dominating personalities enjoyed more powers and wielded greater influence in the British administration. Thus, the power enjoyed and exercised by various prime ministers has remained relative. Dynamic and dominating personalities like Pitts, Peel, Disraeli, Gladstone, Lloyd George, Harold Macmillan, Harold Wilson and Churchill have exercised more powers in comparison to the weaklings like North, New Castle, Liverpool, Campbell Banherman, Lord Resebery or Lord Salisbury.

In nutshell it may be stated that the British prime minister enjoys a special position in Britain. Further it depends upon the personality and character of the person holding this office, which determines how he carried out the challenging tasks of this office.

Deputy Prime Minister

The post of deputy prime minister need not necessarily exists in Britain. Its existence depends on the preferences of the prime minister and his or her party regarding the form/kind of organization they want. The Blair Government has created a separate department known as the office of the deputy prime minister in 2002. In case of a sudden vacancy in premiership, there is no automatic sucesssion from the post of deputy prime minister in Britain. Moreover when the prime minister is outside the nation, the deputy prime minister does not enjoy any additional powers. The position has often been used as an honorific.[100]

Departments of the United Kingdom Government

The departments are the main agencies to implement the governmental policies that are duly authorized by the British Parliament. A department generally operates under the headship of a minister. The permanent officials, even, head some departments particularly those where the questions of policy normally do not arise. They carried out their functions with the assistance of various local authorities, statutory boards, and a number of government sponsored organizations. The change in the government, may caused to affect some radical changes in the policy of the government. But the number of departments and their corresponding functions may or may not undergo any change. However the constantly increasing scope of activities of the government

---

99 Harvey, J. and L. Bather, *op. cit.*, 1984, p. 229.
100 *Ibid*

in various fields in the last few decades has resulted in the creation of a number of new departments. These departments of the United Kingdom government can broadly be divided into two categories: ministerial departments and non-ministerial departments. The holders of the ministerial department offices may be known as 'Secretary of State' or ' Ministers' who are in complete charge of a government department. The non-ministerial departments are usually headed by senior civil servants. They also include the holders of traditional offices like Lord President of the Council, Lord Privy Seal, the Paymaster General and the ministers without portfolio[101].The holders of the non-ministerial departments either have no or limited departmental duties. Generally they are supposed to discharge special duties that are assigned to them by the prime minister from time to time.

III. COUNCIL OF MINISTERS

Britain is a classical example of the parliamentary form of government in which the cabinet headed by the prime minister acts as the real executive whereas the monarch operates as the nominal head though all the powers are exercised in his name. Thus the core of the British constitutional machinery is the cabinet. Being the real executive, it operates like the pivot of the whole political machinery. It acts as the supreme directing authority of the government and provides unity in the British system. In the British government it is the cabinet that performs the executive function of policy-making and co-ordination. Several scholars have used colourful phrases to describe the pivotal position which the cabinet in Britain possesses. Thus, Ramsay Muir calls it "the steering wheel of the ship of state" and Lowell describes it as the "keystone of the political arch". Sir John Marriott feels that cabinet is the "pivot round which the whole political machinery revolves". According to Bagehot cabinet is a "hyphen that joins the buckle that binds the executive and the legislative departments together". L.S. Amery highlighted that the cabinet is "the central directing instrument of government".

From the above phrases, the position of the cabinet in the British administration can be easily visualized. The cabinet is a linking instrument between the legislature and the executive wing of the government and is considered the nerve centre of the government and administration in Britain.

EVOLUTION

The British cabinet is a product of a series of long historical developments in Britain. It is an offshoot of the Privy Council, the origin of which itself was embedded in the Curia Regis of Norman Period. The Privy Council was meant to render advice to the king on various administrative matters. Its members were selected at the discretion of the king. Over the years its size expanded and it became difficult for the king to take the opinion of all its members, so he started taking opinion of only his close and confident members of the Privy Council. For instance, Charles-II (1660-1685), selected 5 members who were his close associates for rendering advice, which, was popularly called 'CABAL' after the first letter of their names. Thus, the

---

[101] Research Board (ed.) "How Britain is governed," *Research Publication in Social Science*, Delhi, 1979, p. 38-9.

British cabinet was a vague institution and could not acquire an appropriate shape till the Glorious Revolution of 1688[102].

The actual beginning of cabinet system can be traced to the cabinet of 1697, which was popularly known as 'Sunderland's Junta'. Further, the passage of the Act of Settlement in 1701 resulted into the establishment of parliamentary supremacy[103]. Up to mid-18th century no scholar, except Bagehot, made a mention of it. It was Bagehot who made a reference to the cabinet system in his book for the first time in 1867. With the passage of time, the cabinet system gained popularity and currency. But it was only in 20th century that the cabinet became the pivot of British politico-administrative system by gaining more powers and acquiring appropriate shape[104].

ORGANISATION OF THE CABINET

The process of cabinet formation in Britain starts with the formal selection of the prime minister by the monarch. The monarch generally calls the leader of the majority party in Parliament to form the government and designates him as the prime minister. Now, the prime minister prepares a list of persons to be designated as 'ministers' and the body comprising of all these ministers is called 'ministry'. There are about a hundred ministerial positions[105] which every prime minister fills from amongst his party men in the two houses of Parliament, though usually a lion's share is grabbed by the members of the Commons. All those appointed as ministers must be or become the members of either of the two houses of Parliament.

The ministry consists of four different categories of ministers viz. the cabinet ministers, ministers having independent charge of specific administrative departments, ministers of state and parliamentary secretaries. While the ministers of the first two categories are appointed by the monarch, those belonging to the latter two categories are appointed by the prime minister. However, it is only the first category of ministers viz. cabinet ministers who are included in the cabinet – the inner group of some twenty ministers holding important portfolios, who regularly meet under the chairmanship of the prime minister and share constitutional responsibility for all acts of omission and commission of the government. Though the composition of the cabinet is decided by the prime minister, yet some of the ministers holding "… important portfolios like the Chancellor of Exchequer, the Secretaries of State of Home, Foreign Affairs, and the Commonwealth are invariably its members"[106].

---

102 Bhagwan, Vishnoo and Vidya Bhushan, *op. cit.*, 1991, p. 49.

103 *Ibid*, p. 50.

104 *Ibid*

105 Moodie gives the breakup of these ministerial positions as under: "Up to fifty of them will be ministers. Thirty will be heads of the various administrative departments and offices. The rest will be either non-departmental ministers, such as the Lord Privy Seal, or Ministers of State. Neither of these are in charge of departments, but the latter are attached to large and important ones and are usually given some special responsibility; one of the Ministers of State in the Foreign Office is specially concerned with the work of the United Nations. In addition, all the main departments will have one or more parliamentary secretaries or undersecretaries to assist the ministers in, particularly, the parliamentary aspects of their duties. The most important members of the administration, however, are those senior ministers who are included in the cabinet…" Moodie, Graeme C., *op. cit.*, p. 89.

106 Maheshwari, S.R., *op. cit.*, p. 3.

PRINCIPLES OR SALIENT FEATURES OF THE BRITISH CABINET

As has been seen, the cabinet in Great Britain has been in existence since long. Over the years, there has also been a tremendous change in its functions and role. From merely an advisory body, the cabinet in Great Britain has become the real executive. During the long time span of its existence, the cabinet has developed certain principles or salient features for its effective and smooth working. Some of the most important of these are listed below:

1. The Monarch is Not Part of the Cabinet

As has been seen historically, the cabinet was created to assist the monarch and was, in real sense of the term, subordinate to the latter. It only performed the advisory role and it was not obligatory for the monarch to accept the advice rendered by the cabinet. Further, initially, the monarch also used to preside over the meetings of the cabinet. Gradually, however, the monarchs started avoiding the cabinet meetings. King George I in particular ceased to attend its meetings. During his reign, the cabinet meetings were presided over by one of the cabinet members – precursor of the modern prime minister – and the cabinet decisions were conveyed to the monarch after the conclusion of the meeting. This practice continued during the reigns of George II and George III. By that time, it became a convention of keeping the monarch out of the cabinet meetings and to convey and get the decisions of the cabinet ratified by monarch. This function was performed by the prime minister. Hence, conventionally, the monarch is no longer part of the cabinet nor does he attend the meetings thereof.

2. Close Affinity with the Parliament

Great Britain is one of the ideal examples of two-party system; one party – enjoying majority support in the House of Commons – rules while the other performs the role of opposition. After elections, the chosen leader of the majority party – whom the monarch appoints prime minister – receives a formal invitation from the Buckingham Palace to form the government. The prime minister than prepares a list of persons from amongst his party men, whom the monarch appoints as ministers. The only qualification for getting appointed as minister is that the person should be a member of either the House of Commons or the House of Lords. However, sometimes even those who are not members of either of the two Houses are appointed ministers, but in that case the person appointed as minister will have to become member of any of the two Houses within a period of six months. In any case, for becoming minister it is essential to be a Member of Parliament. Further, the ministers are required to be present in the Parliament during when it is in session and to answer the questions raised by the members of the Parliament. In other words, the ministers are responsible for all acts of the government towards the Parliament. Again, the cabinet survives only till it enjoys majority support in the House of Commons and in the event of losing majority support, the government will have to resign. What can be directly inferred or deduced from the above is that unlike in the United States, there is a close relationship between the cabinet and the Parliament.

3. Ministerial Responsibility

The ministers are directly responsible to the Parliament for all acts of omissions and commissions of theirs as well as the officials subordinate to them. The ministerial responsibility is two-fold – individual and collective. Individual responsibility is one where the ministers are responsible to the Parliament for the works of their department where as collective responsibility is that where ministers collectively share and own the policy and actions of the government. In Britain, every minister is bound by "cabinet's individual responsibility". He is required to consult the cabinet before taking any decision because his erring/wrong decisions can bring trouble to the whole cabinet. If he failed in doing so, he will be held accountable for his personal mistake or worse. As a rule the, responsibility will be confined to him only and the stability of the rest of the cabinet may not be affected. For instance, "when Chancellor of the Exchequer High Dalton imprudently revealed to a favoured journalist certain facts about the forth coming budget message – a gross breach of custom and possibility of law-he resigned in the ensuring storm without shaking in any way the solid foundation of the Attlee government"[107]. Moreover, since the cabinet operates like a well-knit unit, so it is also essential for the cabinet ministers that they must agree or support the cabinet decisions. In case of disagreement with the cabinet decision, the minister concerned has no option but to resign. "Lord Morley and Burns resigned in 1914, as they could not approve the decision to war. In 1938, Anthony Eden resigned because he did not agree with the foreign policy of Chamberlain".[108] Besides, the ministers are responsible for their own personal conduct and also the running of their department. So if a minister's reputation is destroyed by a scandal (for example when it was revealed David Mellor had an extra-marital affair), they usually resign. If their department is involved in a scandal or revealed to be extremely incompetent, (for example the A-level marking scandal of 2002 when Estelle Morris was the minister involved), they resign.

As far as collective responsibility is concerned, it is the Sine qua non of the cabinet system. Here the cabinet is responsible to the House of Commons for its deeds collectively. It is supposed to win the confidence of the House of Commons as it remains in office as long as it enjoys its confidence. In case of loss of this confidence, the cabinet as a whole has to resign. Thus the cabinet operates like a well-knit unit and stand and fall. In other words, "what collective responsibility means is that when, after a full discussion, a decision is made, it becomes binding upon all members including those who opposed to it in the discussion."[109] If a decision is taken by some minister with prior consultation of the cabinet, then the whole cabinet and not the minister concerned would be responsible for its consequences. The Cabinet meets on a regular basis, usually weekly on a Thursday morning, notionally to discuss the most important issues of government policy, and to make decisions which they are bound to by "cabinet collective responsibility". This is a convention that ministers must support the decisions made by the government. If a minister cannot support government policy in public, they must resign.

---

107 Neuman, Robert, G., *op. cit.,* p. 81.
108 Bhagwan, Vishnoo and Vidya Bhushan, *op. cit.,* 1991, p. 54.
109 Bombwall, K.R., Major Contemporary Constitutional Systems, Ambala Cantt., Modern Publications, 1971, p. 58.

Collective responsibility is feasible only if there is a high degree of cabinet solidarity. It is because all the cabinet members are sailors of the same boat and they sink and swim together. The principle of collective responsibility thus limits the power of individual members of the cabinet as a whole. It helps to channel the ambitions of politicians and make them less disruptive of the group co-operation that is essential to effective and responsible government.[110] Thus the cabinet ministers bear both kinds of responsibility to the House of Commons.

4. Leadership of the Prime Minister:

Further, the cabinet operates under the leadership of the prime minister. He is recognized as the keystone of the cabinet arch. Though all the ministers enjoy equal status and stand on almost equal footing, yet the decision of the prime minister is final. He resolves all sort of conflict at the level of cabinet. The whole cabinet operates under his general direction and kind supervision. He is responsible for maintaining harmony and co-ordination among the cabinet ministers. He gives sufficient weight to the views and opinions of the ministers but in case of difference of opinion the decision of the prime minister prevails. Thus he operates like an umpire of the cabinet.

5. Secrecy:

The cabinet operates on the doctrine of secrecy. Generally the meetings of the cabinet are held "in camera" and what transpires in these meetings is not open to the press. Utter secrecy is maintained regarding its proceedings and they are not made open to the public. So all the ministers are supposed to maintain the confidentiality of the internal business of the cabinet. It is either the prime minister or some authorized spokesman of the party only who can reveal some information or give some hints about what happened inside it. The upholding of secrecy by the cabinet ministers could assist in maintaining party solidarity. It is evident that the non- observance of secrecy and party solidarity by the cabinet ministers can invite risk to them. Resultantly, all support and co-operate each other. Moreover, they speak in one tune and work in unison.

6. Political homogeneity:

Political homogeneity is still another characteristic of the British cabinet. The prime minister generally selects all the cabinet ministers from his own political party. This leads to provide a homogeneous character to the British cabinet. Resultantly all the ministers hold almost similar views and the difference of opinion rarely arise among them. The formation of cabinet on party line helps the ministers to work like a team and thus ensures the unity of purpose. The political homogeneity of the British cabinet helps in getting majority support on almost all policy issues raised by the cabinet in the House of Commons. It is because of this fact; the coalitional government does not find favour in Britain. Moreover, the party based character of the British cabinet is also quite helpful in maintaining secrecy of its proceedings and the collective responsibility of its ministers.

Functions of the Cabinet: The British government is generally described as the cabinet form of government. It is because the cabinet in Britain constitutes the core

---

110 Moodie, Grame,C., *op. cit.,* p. 102

of the entire governmental machinery. Thus it has to discharge a multiple number of functions. The cabinet ministers perform multifarious activities both in individual as well as collective capacity. In fact the British cabinet is the real authority that exercises all those powers which are vested in the Crown. The important functions of the British cabinet can be discussed under following heads:

1. *Determination of policies and the fulfillment of details:* The cabinet being a deliberative organ plays a significant role in determining the major policies of the government both at home and abroad. At the time of general election, both parties present the broad issues that need policy before the electorates in the form of political manifestos. After coming to power, these issues or problems prevailing at national and international level are translated into policies after long and thoughtful considerations. "All governments are concerned with protecting vital national interests, maintaining the peace and at the same time the challenge of the inevitable changes and events which occur in the world scene."[111] Thus the cabinet frames different policies pertaining to national and international affairs after having a lot of deliberation on such issues. Once the cabinet takes such decisions, they become binding on all the ministers irrespective of their personal likes or dislikes. Moreover, the cabinet not only determines these policies rather it is also responsible for the fulfillment of their minute details. It is mainly because the cabinet is considered as the real policy making organ of the British government.

2. *Chief co-ordinator of policies of different departments:* The British cabinet plays a significant role in co-ordinating the policies of different government departments. For the effective implementation of the governmental policy it is inevitable to have co-ordination between/ among the affected departments. It is because the government operates like a well co-ordinated unit. Moreover, the government works through a number of departments and their operations affect each other. They can't be separated into water-tight compartments. For instance a proposal to raise the school-leaving certificate age (related to the Department of Education), would also affect the Departments of Employment, Defense, Health and Social Security, Home Affairs etc.[112] Thus the cabinet tries to bind various government departments through the policy string. It decides broad issues that affect different departments at the level of policy. It ensures that the work of different departments does not overlap and they do not adopt contradictory policies. Thus it tries to iron out all the differences among them. However, the problem of co-ordination has become serious in recent times particularly due to consistently increasing complexities in the governmental working. Besides, the number of governmental departments has also increased substantially. Thus, the task of co-ordination becomes more and more challenging in recent times.

3. *Legislative Functions:* The cabinet also plays a significant role in guiding, managing and controlling the legislative business of the Parliament. It initiates most of the legislative bills and fulfills their details. "Most of the bills which are initiated, steered, explained, defended and ultimately passed in the Parliament

---

111 Padfield, Colin F., *British Constitution*, London, W. A. Allen & Co. Ltd., 1972, p. 115.
112 Harvey, J. and L. Bather, *op. cit.*, 1984, p. 243.

are government bills, prepared by the cabinet."[113] Even the speech of the British Monarch that spells out the major policies of the government, at the beginning of every parliamentary session, is prepared by the cabinet. The cabinet is further responsible for drafting all the ordinances (order-in- council) proclaimed by the Monarch, when the Parliament is not in session. It also regulates the business of the House of Commons. "When will the Commons meet and what matters it shall discuss and how much time will be given to different matters-all these are decided by the cabinet"[114] The prestige and authority of the British cabinet has further enhanced with regard to legislative affairs due to the prevalent practice of delegated legislation particularly in recent times. In present days, due to the increasing burden of legislation on the Parliament, most of the legislations are passed by it in 'skeleton forum', the details of which are later on filled by the cabinet. Thus the British cabinet enjoys enormous powers as far as the legislative business of the nation is concerned.

4. *Exercise effective control and supervision over governmental working:* Legally the authority of the Crown is vested in the British Monarch, but in actual practice he cannot exercise this authority without the consent of the cabinet. In real sense, it is the cabinet that is the actual user of the King' authority. Being the chief user of these powers, it is responsible for the smooth governance of the nation. Thus, it maintains an effective supervision and control over the entire governmental machinery. The cabinet ministers are in charge of the respective departments of the government and are responsible for managing their affairs. Being the political head of their department/ministry, they exercise a tight control and supervision over their business. They are supposed to implement the respective policies of the government in letter and spirit framed by the cabinet. Any deviation from it may cause their removal. Thus the whole administrative machinery operates under the direction and supervision of the cabinet.

5. *Chief Controller of the Finance.* Further, the cabinet exercises a strict control over the purse string of the nation. The Chancellor of the Exchequer, a prominent cabinet minister is in charge of budget preparation. He chalks out the outlines of the budget on the basis of the preliminary estimates presented by the respective departments. The cabinet ultimately finalizes the outline of the budget prepared in association of the other departments. The cabinet also takes decisions regarding the imposition of taxes and their collectior.. It is the cabinet that decides the tax structure of the government. In other words, it is the cabinet that decides which fresh charges (taxes) are to be imposed, which are to be abolished, which are to be increased and which are to be reduced. The cabinet plays a significant role in the passage of the budget and the execution of the budget. It conducts both pre and post budget scrutiny and try to remove every possibility of misappropriation.

6. *Take decisions on major unforeseen situations:* Along with its routine working, the cabinet has to take a number of decisions regarding unforeseen problems and situations. Such problems may arise both at home and abroad. The cabinet is

---

[113] Hari Hara Das, *Comparative Government and Politics*, Himalaya Publishing House, Delhi: 1994, p. 253.
[114] Bhagwan, Vishnoo and Vidya Bhushan (1991), *op. cit.*, p. 59.

required to take frequent decisions to bring changes in the national economy in consonance with the global changes. Various problems concerning environment protection also need urgent cabinet decisions. The situations created due to the natural calamities may even require such cabinet decisions. Besides, the British cabinet has to take a number of frequent decisions with regards to foreign affairs.

THE CABINET OFFICE

In Britain, the cabinet office, popularly known as the secretariat, came in to existence in 1916, to handle the business of British cabinet. It includes basically the permanent officials and mainly acts as a recording and informing centre. It directly works under the control and supervision of the prime minister. It acts as the chief co-ordinator of policies of different departments. Traditionally the cabinet secretariat extends all possible services to the cabinet and its committees, taking minutes and recording decisions that are transmitted as impulses for action throughout Whitehall. It has started to play a more positive role since the 1960s. Today, its prominent functions incorporates circulation of the memoranda, and other documents required for cabinet or its committees business, preparing agenda for the cabinet meetings, recording of discussions and circulating the minutes, keeping in touch with the progress of action on decisions and safeguarding the security of documents etc[115].

Along with this, Central Statistical Office (CSO) that is an integral part of the British cabinet is also attached to it. It is "... charged with the collection from departments of statistics relating to the national economy, their analysis and their preparation as an agreed body of statistics to assist the government in formulating its economic and financial body."[116] Moreover, in 1971, a Central Policy Review Staff (CPRS) has been created as a physical and constitutional part of the cabinet secretariat and is mainly concerned with offering advice to ministers that will help to relate their policies and decisions with the governmental strategy as a whole.[117] It also operates under the direction and supervision of the British prime minister. Besides, in Britain the opposition party also is headed by a similar group that is popularly known as the Shadow Cabinet.

(C) LOCAL GOVERNMENT*

Like its constitutional history, the local government in Britain has also been evolutionary in character. Though it has been in existence since long, yet its present institutions started acquiring shape during the Industrial Revolution Era. The British local government is adapting itself according to the changing circumstances.[118] This is substantiated from the fact that the process of reorganizing the local government

---

115 Research Board (ed.) How Britain is governed, *op. cit.*, p. 35-6.
116 *Ibid*, p. 36.
117 F.F. Ridley, *Government and Administration in Western Europe* (ed.), Oxford: Martin Co. Ltd., 1979, p. 36.
118 Barthwal C. P., *Understanding Local Self-Government*, Lucknow: Bharat Book Center, 1997, pp. 11-12.

* Local Government in the United Kingdom has already been published in the Journal of Constitutional and Parliamentary Studies (ICPS), New Delhi, Vol 39, No. 1-4, 2005, pp 115-134.

structure is still going on. Since Britain has a unitary system of government, the local government operates under the direct control of the central government. However, it enjoys considerable operational autonomy. Further, the local government in Britain is multi-functional in nature. The local government institutions discharge a wide variety of services. "They not only perform usual functions of a local body, such as drainage, refuse collection and disposal, education, street-lightening, assisting in disability and welfare and providing leisure services but are also responsible for providing transport, undertaking strategic planning, police function, fire services and construction and maintenance of highways."[119] Because of this fact these bodies are "...often described as 'omnibus' rather than 'ad hoc'."[120]

Evolution

The institution of local government in Great Britain has a long elongated history. It was even in existence when the central government was non-existent. Its rudiments are deeply rooted into the British history. During Anglo-Saxon times, shires, hundreds of townships and boroughs, having their specific local authority, were parts of the local government. In the Norman period, the shires became counties, hundreds disappeared, and feudal lords occupied townships.[121] "The borough descended from those towns of the Middle Ages which acquired special powers and privileges either because these were commercially prosperous or otherwise important."[122] With the passage of time old townships emerged as the parish. Thus, at the close of Middle Ages, county, borough and the parish were the three main units of British local government. The justices of peace, who were appointed by the Crown, ran the administrative business of these counties. These institutions of local government continued in existence during the period of Tudors, Stuarts and Hanoverians and survived until the beginning of the industrial revolution in the early part of the 19th century.

As an outcome of the Industrial Revolution, thickly populated industrial areas came into existence in England, which demanded better civic amenities. Consequently a number of special districts, boards, commissions etc. were set up to meet out the specific requirements of these areas. But the mushroom growth of different kinds of local units ultimately resulted in chaos with regard to their jurisdiction and authority conflicts in the later part of the century.[123] This situation was described as, "chaos of areas, a chaos of franchises, a chaos of authorities, and chaos of rates."[124] To remedy the situation of chaos in the working of local government units, some radical action on the part of the British government became inevitable. Resultantly, the Parliament passed the Local Government Act, 1888, which tried to provide a new perspective to the county government and led to the creation of historic counties

---

119 *Ibid*, p. 12.
120 Smith C. Brain and Jeffrey Stanyer, *op. cit.*, p. 113.
121 Nigam, S. R., *Local Government*, New Delhi: Kitab Mahal Private Ltd., 1968, p. 10.
122 Barthwal, C. P., *op. cit.*, p. 14.
123 Nigam, S. R., *op. cit.*, p. 10-11.
124 Rathbone and Pell as quoted in Barthwal, C.P., *op. cit.*, p. 15.

and administrative counties though the earlier was not a part of local government. Further, this Act made the provision of elected county councils (for administrative counties) and also transferred the powers of the justices of peace to these county councils.[125] The Act of 1888, also exempted the most populous boroughs from the jurisdiction of the counties in which these were located and designated them as county boroughs. The powers of both (administrative county as well as borough) were conferred upon them.[126]

In this series of efforts, the British Parliament also passed the District and Parish Council Act, 1894, by which it abolished most of the special districts. This Act replaced these special districts with the urban and rural districts of the county and assigned them such functions as were earlier performed by the special districts or other local government units.[127] The Act made the provision of a duly elected (by the ratepayers) council for each district. This Act also rejuvenated the rural districts by making provision of parish councils (having population less than 200). The rural parishes having less population were without councils and they were to hold parish meetings.[128] To further rationalize the British local government system, the Parliament passed the Local Government Act, 1933. This Act made an effort to eradicate all sorts of anomalies in the field of local government. Being a comprehensive Act, it tried to rationalize the structure, powers and functions of various local government units.[129] However, the old structure established at the end of the 19th century continued in existence and basically remained same until a complete overhauling of it took place in April, 1974. Though in-between, a number of Commissions - Local Government Boundary Commission 1945, Local Government Act, 1958, Royal Commission 1969 etc. were constituted but their recommendations could not be effectively taken into consideration either on one pretext or the other.

In the post-Second World War phase, the local government in Britain underwent at least three major reorganizations. The successive reorganizations were efforts in the direction of promoting more rationalization. The three reorganizations - the reorganization of 1970s, the reorganization of mid-1980s and the reorganization of 1990s - are briefly discussed below.

Reorganization of 1970s

The new Conservative government of Sir Edward Heath argued for a two-tier structure for metropolitan areas as well as the rest of England. In this regard, Local Government Act, 1972, which became effective on 1st April, 1974, was passed. The re-organization of local government in England was followed by Wales in the same year. Scotland had the same structure introduced in 1975, except that the upper tier units were known as regions. But the case of Northern Ireland was different as it already had a two-tier local government system. The British Parliament, in sharp

---

125 Nigam, S. R., *op. cit.*, p. 11.
126 Barthwal, C. P., *op cit.*, p. 16.
127 Nigam, S. R., *op. cit*, p. 11.
128 Barthwal, C. P., *op. cit*, p. 16.
129 Nigam S.R., *op. cit.*, p. 11-12.

contrast to the three constituents of Great Britain, replaced the two-tier system of Northern Ireland by a single-tier district council system in 1973. Thus, the early 1970s is considered as the phase of re-organization in the history of the British local government.[130] The re-organized structure of local government in England was an improvement over the earlier in following respects:

1. The re-organization rationalized and streamlined the whole structure of the British local government and made it comparatively simplified by curtailing the number of local authorities that resulted into expansion in the size of the new units.
2. It eliminated the town-county dichotomy by abolishing the rural district. However, districts still remained there but they were either purely urban or purely rural.
3. The re-organization rationalized the size (in terms of population) of local government units. The metropolitan counties were to be established in the areas having population exceeding 10 lakhs; a non-metropolitan county in areas having population of more than five lakhs, a metropolitan district in areas having population near about two lakhs fifty thousand and a non-metropolitan county district in areas having population around one-lakh.
4. The re-organization further streamlined the system of election to the local bodies. It provided that except in the case of the metropolitan districts (where 1/3 of councillors would be elected after every year), elections of all local bodies would be held on the first Thursday in May (unless the Home Secretary fixed another date) after completing a fixed tenure of four years.
5. The re-organization also promoted the democratic element of the British local government. Except in London, the office of aldermen, who were earlier elected indirectly by the councillors, was abolished.[131]

Reorganization of Mid-1980s

The re-organization which provided for six metropolitan counties for the local government of England were later on abolished by the Margaret Thatcher's Conservative government in 1983. The local government of London, which is almost different from the rest of the country, contained Greater London Authority having London borough and the City of London as its parts during the re-organization in 1974. But the Thatcher government also abolished the Greater London Council.[132] In 1986, the Greater London Council and the six metropolitan counties were abolished leaving the boroughs and districts to operate as single-tier units. The structure of local government in Britain in the aftermath of the reorganization efforts of mid-1980s is depicted in Figure-1.[133]

---

130 Barthwal, C.P., *op. cit.*, p. 19.
131 *Ibid*, p. 20.
132 *Ibid*, p. 20 & 23.
133 Barthwal, C.P., *op. cit.*, p. 24.

Local Government Structure[134]

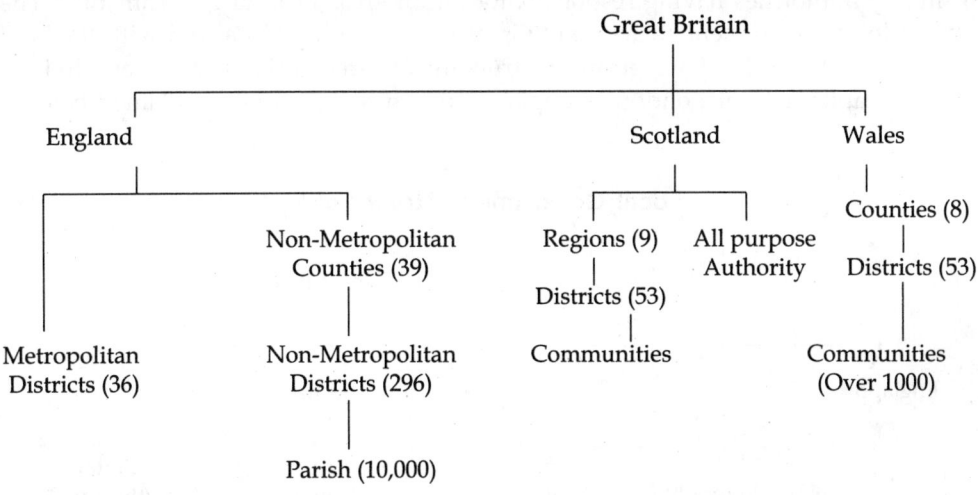

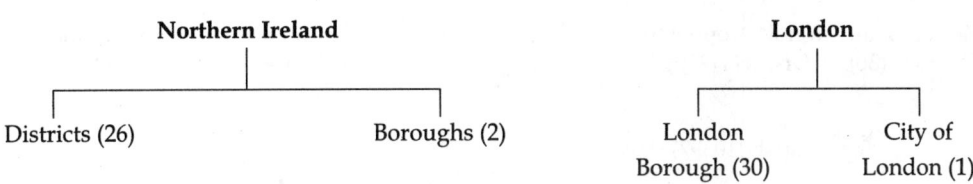

Figure-1

Reorganization of Mid-1990s

By the mid-1990s, it was realized that the two-tier system of local government was also not much efficient either. Thus, in 1996, the two-tier system was changed in Scotland and Wales. In Scotland, it was replaced by a single-tier system of council areas whereas in Wales by a system of unitary authorities. Northern Ireland already had a single-tier structure. However, the situation in England remained rather more complex as in some parts there existed two-tier system whereas in others there existed single-tier structure of local government. Local Government Commission in England (LGCE) in the 1990s reviewed the administrative structure of non-metropolitan areas and recommended that some areas retain the existing two-tier structure and others be set up as single-tier Unitary Authorities (UAs). Metropolitan districts were not included in the Local Government Re-organization (LGR) and have retained their post-1986 status. But in 2000, the London Boroughs were brought under the control of the Greater London Authority. Following the LGR in the 1990s, major changes came

---

134 Present local government structure includes Isles of Scilly.

into existence to make administrative adjustments according to the needs of the areas concerned. The salient feature of this re-organization was regarding the introduction of unitary authorities having responsibility for all areas of local government.[135] The present local government structure of Great Britain can be visualized with the help of Figure-2.[136] The local government structure of Great Britain, Northern Ireland and the Capital city of London as depicted in Figure-2 is briefly explained below:

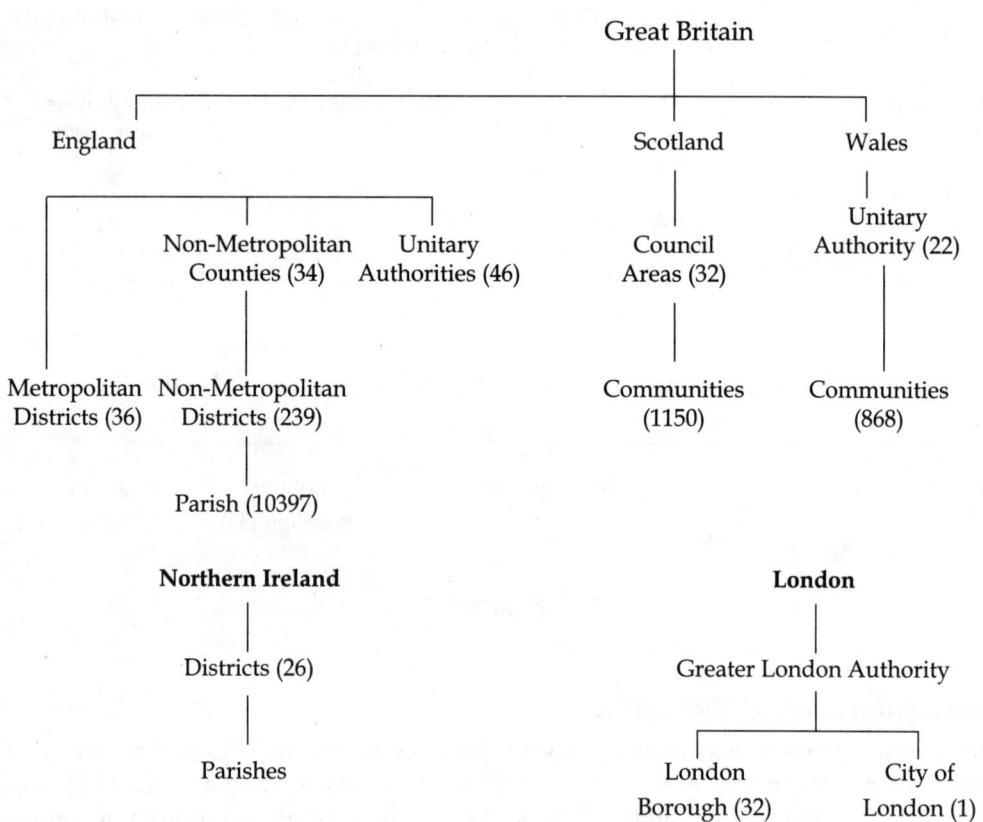

Figure-2

(I) Great Britain

The local government structure of the three constituent parts of Great Britain viz. England, Scotland and Wales, is explained in this section.

---

135 See website *www.Statistics.gov.uk/geography/parishes.asp*
136 The graphical presentation of the British local government is based on its description given in website http://en. Wikipeadia. org/ wiki /Local_ government_ in_ England.
137 Present local government structure includes Isles of Scilly.

England

England has no separate governing body for the whole of it other than that of the Government of United Kingdom. It is subdivided into 9 regions. One of these regions is Greater London. It has an elected Assembly and a Mayor. The Greater London is a very active region. In sharp contrast to this, the remaining 8 regions of England have unelected Regional Assemblies and Regional Development Agencies, which play a very minor role. However, all these 9 regions have their own system of local government, which can be broadly divided into two parts viz. the local government structure in Greater London and the local government structure in the remaining 8 regions.[138]

Excluding Greater London, three different types of local government units are in vogue in England viz. *the non-metropolitan counties* (which are also sometimes referred to as shire counties or merely counties), *the metropolitan districts*, and *the unitary authorities*. The first type has a two-tier structure (and is divisible into non-metropolitan districts) while the second and the third have a single-tier structure. At present, in England, there are 34 non-metropolitan counties, 36 metropolitan districts and 46 unitary authorities. The 34 non-metropolitan counties are divided into 239 non-metropolitan districts. The non-metropolitan districts have been further divided into more than 10,000 parishes. The three types of local government units are explained below.

Non-Metropolitan County

England has metropolitan (usually urban) areas and non-metropolitan (usually rural) areas. The non-metropolitan areas have at their apex non-metropolitan counties and these are usually created in an area having a population of more than five lakhs. Before the reorganization of the mid-1990s, there were 39 non- metropolitan counties. However, due to the creation of an additional unit of local government viz. unitary authorities (by this reorganization), their number has been reduced to 34. Every non-metropolitan county has a council that is elected directly by the residents of the respective non-metropolitan county for a period of four years. The non-metropolitan county councils are divided into electoral divisions, each of which is represented by a county councillor. However, the Local Government Act, 2000, allows these councils to have multi-member county divisions. Any candidate, who has attained 21 years of age and is a British citizen, is eligible for election. There exists a functional classification between non-metropolitan counties and non-metropolitan districts. The non-metropolitan counties are responsible for more strategic services such as education, libraries, main roads, social services, trading standards and transport etc.[139]

Earlier, the councils had no split between executive and legislative functions; all the functions were vested in the county councils and were exercised usually through their committees/sub committees. In 2000, the Parliament passed the Local Government Act to force councils to move to an executive based system "... either with the council leader and a cabinet acting as an executive authority, or with a directly-elected mayor, either with a mayor and cabinet drawn from the councillors; or a mayor and council manager. There is a small exception to this whereby smaller

---

138 http://en.wikipedia.org./wiki/locaLgovernment_in_the UnitedKingdom.
139 See website www.just do something, net/xsc. asp? Uri=/home/ hsw /local gov / structure.

district councils (population of less than 80,000) can adopt a modified committee system."[140]

Non-Metropolitan Districts

As discussed above, non-metropolitan counties are a two-tier system and are divided into non-metropolitan districts. At present there are 239 non-metropolitan districts whereas their number before the reorganization of the mid-1990s was 296. The non-metropolitan districts are usually created around a population of about one lakh. The people living in a non-metropolitan district elect their representatives and constitute a non-metropolitan district council. The non-metropolitan district councils are divided into wards for election purposes. Generally, they have a four-year term. But they even have a choice either to have whole council elections or one-third of their Councillors elected each year in non-county election year. The members of non-metropolitan district council (that have selected for whole council election) are elected directly by the voters for a period of 4 years and their election is based on relative majority system.[141]

The councillors devote most of their time to the service of local authorities. The councillors' duties include direction and control of council affairs, making important decisions, monitoring timely progress of authority's activities etc. The councillors do not discharge the work of the council themselves and so are responsible mainly for appointment and oversight of officers, who are delegated to perform most tasks. Local authorities now a-days have to appoint a 'CEO' with overall responsibility for council employees and who operate in conjunction with department heads.[142] Besides, the general powers with regard to the promotion of economic, social, and environmental well being of their area, the district councils are responsible for leisure, environmental health, housing, garbage collection, local roads etc.

Parish

In England a parish or a community (also called 'civil parish') is the lowest unit of local government. However, they are not counted towards the tier-system of the local government units in the United Kingdom.[143] They are the counterparts of the village panchayats in India. Parishes do not cover the whole of England and mostly exist in rural and small urban areas. Parishes vary greatly in size.[144] Though usually parishes do not exist in large urban areas, however, exceptions do exist.[145] Presently, there are more than 10,000 parishes in England, and 1150 and 868 communities in

---

140 http://en.wikipedia.org/wiki/Local_Government in_UnitedKingdom
141 *Ibid*
142 See website www.just do something, net/xsc. asp? Uri=/home/ hsw /local gov / structure.
143 The absence or presence of local councils does not count towards whether a district is unitary or not. Councils such as districts, counties and unitaries are known as principal local authorities in order to differentiate them in their legal status from parish and town councils, which are not uniform in their existence.

See the website http://en.wikipedia.org/wiki/Local_government_in_the_United_Kingdom
144 Thus, some of them cover tiny hamlets with populations of less than 100 while some are very big such as Hereford and covers towns with populations of tens of thousands. http://en.wikipedia.org/wiki/Civil_parish_(England)
145 For instance, in Birmingham there exist a parish 'New Frankley'. *Ibid*.

Scotland and Wales, respectively. In Greater London, however, the local government legislation specifically prohibits the establishment of parishes.[146]

Parishes are usually administered by parish councils[147] called a town council or a city council. Parish councils are run by volunteer councillors who are elected for a period of four years. Any person who is 18 years of age can cast his vote and any British citizen who has attained 21 years of age can contest the election. The number of councillors differs from parish to parish. Some parishes are deemed too small to have a parish council and instead have a parish meeting. In such cases, usually, however, a few parishes are grouped together and share a common parish council[148].

Usually, the parish councils play only a minor role; however, some large parish councils have a role similar to that of a small district council. They have to perform certain local functions prominent among them being the provision and upkeep of certain local facilities such as allotments, parks, playgrounds, footpaths, village halls, public clocks and for litter collection. Recently, parish councils have been given new powers to provide traffic calming, community transport, and crime prevention measures.[149] They also have a consultative role in planning.[150]

Metropolitan Districts

Before 1986, there existed a two-tier structure of local government in metropolitan areas in England. It had 6 metropolitan counties and these were divided into 36 metropolitan districts. However, with the abolition of metropolitan counties in 1986, there remained only a single-tier local government structure in metropolitan areas in England thereby leaving 36 metropolitan districts. A metropolitan district is created in an urban area having a population of about 2-4 lakhs. Each metropolitan district has a metropolitan district council elected by the residents of the respective metropolitan district.[151] The members of the metropolitan district council are elected for a period of four years. The separation of executive-legislative functions is also applicable in the case of metropolitan districts.

The metropolitan district councils are responsible for education, environmental health, emergency planning, housing, garbage collection, construction and maintenance of roads in metropolitan areas etc. They also enjoy general powers particularly with regard to the promotion of economic, social, and environmental well-being of the metropolitan area.

Unitary Authorities

The Local Government Reorganization in the 1990s led to some major changes in the local government system of England. For instance, in some areas, it introduced

---

146 *Ibid*
147 In England they are known as 'parish councils'. In Wales the equivalent body to a parish council is termed a community council. In Scotland the administrative counties were sub-divided into parishes, but these lacked their own councils. Now, Scotland also has bodies called community councils, but these are not equivalent to and have fewer powers than the English parishes and the Welsh communities. Ireland also has civil parishes and these are divided into town lands. *Ibid*.
148 *Ibid*
149 *Ibid*
150 http://en.wikipedia.org/wiki/Local_government_in_the_United_Kingdom
151 http://en.wikipedia.org/wiki/Districts_of_England

a single-tier system of unitary authorities having almost all responsibilities for local areas. This is opposed to a two-tier system where local government functions are divided between different authorities. Between 1995 and 1998, these were established across the country in different areas particularly in medium-sized urban areas and currently, there are 46 unitary authorities in England. Usually, the unitary authorities have an elected council. Their members are elected for a period of 4 years. Any person who is 18 years of age can cast his vote. Anyone, who has attained 21 years of age and is a British citizen, is eligible for contesting election.[152] In England, many cities and large towns are now administered by unitary authorities, with the local council responsible for running all local services, combining both county and district functions.[153]

Scotland

The earlier two-tier structure of local government in Scotland was largely replaced with a unitary system by the Local Government (Scotland) Act, 1994. This Act led to the abolition of the existing structure of 9 regions and 53 districts and replaced them with a structure of 29 single-tier unitary authorities. However, the three single tier Islands Area Councils (Orkney, Shetland and Western Isles) remained unchanged. These changes came into existence in 1996. Since April 1996, therefore, Scotland has been divided into 32 units known as council areas, whose councils are single-tier structures. The power vested in these authorities is administered by elected councillors. The councillors are elected for a period of 4 years. For election purposes the council areas consists of electoral wards. At present there are about 1,200 elected councillors of all the authorities. Each authority elects a Provost to chair meetings of the authority council and acts as a figurehead for the area. The office of the Provost is roughly equivalent to that of the English Mayor. The four prominent cities of Scotland viz., Glasgow, Edinburgh, Aberdeen and Dundee have a Lord Provost rather than a Provost, although they discharge essentially the same services. In Scotland, Glasgow is the largest unitary authority with more than 60,000 inhabitants whereas Orkney is the smallest one, with less than 20,000 people living there. The unitary authorities in Scotland carry out basically all-municipal services.[154]

Each council area in Scotland is divided into communities. Earlier, in Scotland the administrative counties were sub-divided into parishes, but these lacked their own councils. Now, Scotland also has bodies called community councils, but these are not equivalent to and have fewer powers than the English parishes.[155] A majority of communities have their community councils that are elected directly by the voters. However, these communities are not considered as a tier of Scottish local government.[156] At present, there exists approximately 1150 such councils. They discharge a number of activities basically related to local infrastructure and community events e.g. playgrounds, bus shelters, village halls, footpaths, flower beds, Christmas celebrations.[157]

152 See website www. just do something, net/xsc. asp? Uri=/home/ hsw /local gov / structure
153 http://en.wikipedia.org/wiki/ unitaryauthority
154 www.do something, net/xsc. asp? Uri=/home/ hsw /local gov / structure
155 http://en.wikipedia.org/wiki/Civil_parish_(England)
156 *Ibid*
157 *Ibid*

Wales

Another integral part of Great Britain is known as Wales. Since April 1974, Wales had a two-tier system of 8 counties and 37 districts. But in April 1996, these were replaced by a unitary system comprising of 22 unitary authorities. Out of these, 8 unitary authorities have county borough status (reflecting their existence as large population centres) whereas the rest 14 have a county status (reflecting at least some aspect of rurality). Each authority has a council. The councillors are elected for a period of four years. For election purposes, the Welsh unitary authorities consist of electoral divisions. The unitary authorities are responsible for all local authority functions[158].

The Welsh unitary authorities are divisible into communities. Like parishes of England, the communities in Wales are lowest unit of local government and the two are almost equivalent bodies. At present there are 868 communities in Wales and cover the whole of Wales.[159] Most of the communities of Wales have a directly elected council to manage their affairs. The community councillors are elected for a period of 4 years like parish councillors and they usually select one person from amongst themselves as chairman. The local community councils in Wales discharge some basic services like litter bins, maintenance of parks and graveyards etc.[160]

(II). Northern Ireland

After the reorganization of October 1973, the two-tier local government structure of Northern Ireland was replaced by single-tier structure consisting of 26 districts known as 'district council areas'. This system remained unaffected by the later local government reorganizations in the UK. At present, there exist 26 districts in Northern Ireland.[161] The districts in Northern Ireland are mainly based in a main town and generally incorporate urban and rural areas surrounding that town. Each district of Northern Ireland has a council that is directly elected by the voters. The tenure of the members of district councils is 4 years. The district councils are unitary administrations and are responsible for all areas of local government. Like England, Ireland also has civil parishes and these are further divided into town lands.[162]

(III) Government of London

Local government of a nation's capital is generally different from the other cities. For instance, the local system of New Delhi is not akin to that of the other three metropolitan cities of India viz. Mumbai or Kolkata or Chennai. On the same analogy, the local government of London always remained different from the other cities of the United Kingdom. Before the reorganization of the mid-1980s, the local government of London consisted of Greater London (covering an area of about 1580 sq. kms. in and around London), which is one of the nine regions of England. Greater London comprised of London boroughs and the City of London. But the Margaret Thatcher government in 1983 abolished the Greater London council (GLC)

---

158 www.Statistics.gov.uk/geography/parishes.asp
159 http://en.wikipedia.org/wiki/Civil_parish_(England)
160 *Ibid*
161 http://en.wikipedia.org/wiki/Local_Government_jn_ United_Kingdom
162 http://en.wikipedia.org/wiki/Civil_parish_(England)

on grounds of alleged inefficiency and it ceased to exist on 1st April, 1986. Its functions were transferred to the borough councils and the corporation of the City of London. Thus, after the abolition of Greater London council, a single-tier structure of local government was created in London. But in 2000, the necessity of a two-tier structure was again realized. Thus, the elected component for Greater London was revived in the form of Greater London Authority (GLA) in 2000[163]. The present structure of the government of London is as under:

Greater London Authority (GLA)

The GLA came into existence by the Local Government Act, 2000 and started its working from 3rd July, 2000. Today it administers an area of about 1580 sq. kms of Greater London. All the London boroughs and the City of London are now brought under its control. The basic purpose behind its creation is to improve the level of co-ordination among various London boroughs. Though the newly created GLA is comparatively weaker than the GLC, yet currently it enjoys some powers that were never enjoyed by the later. Today it has the right to appoint members of the Police Authority for the Metropolitan Police Services. GLA consists of an elected Mayor and 25 members Assembly.[164] The headquarters of the GLA is at City Hall in Southwark.

The Greater London Authority is different from the corporation of London in the respect that the earlier controls the whole area of London whereas the later controls only one square mile of the city. The Mayor of London is separate from that of the Lord mayor of London. The former acts as the actual head of the whole region of London whereas the later acts only as a ceremonial head of the city of London.[165] The two constituents of GLA (the Mayor of London and the London Assembly) are briefly discussed below.

Mayor of London

Mayor of London acts as the head of the Greater London Authority. He is the only directly elected Mayor in England. He enjoys a fixed tenure of four years. It was only in May, 2000, that for the first time elections were conducted for this post in England. Ken Livingstone (the former leader of GLC from 1981-86) was the first elected Mayor of London. He was re-elected to this post in the elections held in 2004. The Mayor of London is supposed to discharge a wide variety of functions. He is mainly responsible for providing transport facilities, police and fire-fighting services, strategic planning and economic development of the whole region of London. The Mayor is further responsible for proposing the policy and the authority's budget and making appointments to the capital's strategic transport and development bodies.[166]

London Assembly

The London Assembly is an elected body and consists of 25 members. "Its 14 members are directly elected from the 14 constituencies, each with one member, and the rest 11 are elected from party lists to make the total members from each party proportional

---

163 http://en.wikipedia.org/wiki/Greater_London_Authority
164 *Ibid*
165 www.Statistics.gov.uk/geography/parishes.asp
166 http://en.wikipedia.org/wiki/Greater_London_Authority

to the votes cast for that party across the whole of London. But the 'AM' (Additional Member) title is attached after the names of those members of the Assembly who are elected from party lists."[167] The London Assembly exercises supervision and control over the Mayor of London. It enjoys the power to scrutinize the mayor. Its basic purpose is to hold the Mayor of London accountable. It scrutinizes the actions and decisions taken by the Mayor of London. It can conduct any sort of investigation and enquiry. It also enjoys the power to amend the budget of the Authority and to initiate new proposals.[168]

City of London

It covers an area of about one sq. miles and is situated in the heart of the British capital. It is primarily a business and financial center. "It is the ancient core of the modern leviathan. It is the historic entity... it has remained to this day with its ancient boundaries virtually intact and its old form of municipal government practically unchanged for several centuries."[169]

The city corporation is the local authority of the city of London and for a long time it remained least affected from the reforms made by the successive governments. It is mainly because "...the city of London has very influential and wealthy people. They have vested interests which are strong enough to resist reforms"[170]. The structure, functions and the powers of the city corporation are laid down by the Local Government Act, 1889. The corporation governs the city of London through a Lord Mayor and three separate bodies viz., the court of common council, the court of aldermen and the court of common hall. Lord Mayor acts as the chairman of all these bodies. A brief view of which is as under:

The Court of Common Council

It is the real governing body of the city. It is in-charge of all the administrative and executive powers of the city. It consists of 132 common councillors, 24 aldermen and one Lord Mayor.[171] The councillors are elected directly by the city electors annually. The aldermen are elected for life directly and are irremovable. For election purpose, the city is divided into 25 wards, each having one alderman, and varying number of common councillors. The court of aldermen selects the Lord Mayor of London out of the two aldermen nominated by the Court of Common Hall annually. Being the first citizen of the city, he performs a number of ceremonial functions. The meetings of common council are held fortnightly. But much of its work is discharged through various committees."[172]

The Court of Aldermen

It is considered as the second chamber of the city corporation. It consists of the Lord Mayor and the 24 aldermen. The important function of this court is to select one person as Lord Mayor annually out of those two aldermen who were nominated

---

167 www.Statistics.gov.uk/geography/parishes.asp
168 Ibid
169 Nigam S. R., *op. cit.*, p. 47.
170 Ibid, p. 48
171 Barthwal C. P., *op. cit.*, p. 26
172 Nigam S. R., *op. cit.*, p. 48-49.

by the Court of Common Hall.

The Court of Common Hall

It is primarily an assembly of Lord Mayor, 24 aldermen, and liverymen. "Liverymen are persons who are members of associations of craftsmen, such as of goldsmiths and fishmongers." [173] In fact, it is a town meeting of all the important persons of the city. The prominent function of this Court is to nominate two aldermen annually, out of which the Court of Aldermen can select one as the Lord Mayor of London. It also selects some important officials like Sheriffs and Chamberlain.[174]

The city corporation is responsible for performing multifold nature of functions viz., regulation and control, environmental, transport, education etc. It provides a number of civic amenities like sanitation, street lighting, maintenance of roads and streets, maintenance of parks, drainage, health services etc. to the city dwellers. "It is the sole sanitary authority for the port of London, its duty being to inspect the passengers and crews of all vessels putting in at the Port of London. It is responsible for maintaining the four cross-river bridges on the Thames. It has certain duties under the Shop's Act and, the Weight and Measures Act... it maintains its highly efficient police force. It is only the city of London, in Greater London, which is not policed by Scotland Yard. It maintains the famous Guildhall School of Music."[175]

London Borough

Another part of the local government of London consists of 32 actual boroughs. Each London borough has an elected council. For election purposes each borough is divided into borough wards. The elected members of the council elects one of its members as head who presides over the council and is known as Mayor. London Borough councils performs many functions of local nature such as maintenance of schools, maintenance of roads, births, deaths and marriage registrations, inspection of weights and measures, and a host of social welfare functions. The protection of environment is also an important function of the London Borough councils.

(D) CONTROL OVER ADMINISTRATION

Like India, Britain is a democratic state where the holders of public offices are accountable to the people for the authority exercised by them. To check the misuse of power, abuse of public authority and to safeguard the public interest, various forms of accountability have been devised by the British administration. In the words of L.D. White, public accountability is the "sum total of the constitutional, statutory, administrative and judicial rules and precedents and the established practices by means of which public officials may be held accountable for their official actions."[176] The machinery for controlling the administration in Britain is very much complex and moreover, it is quite advanced in comparison to other countries. Due to the existence of such an effective control mechanism, the public officials in Britain work with a very high degree of public responsibility. The administration in Britain is controlled internally as well as externally. Internal control is one that is

---
173 *Ibid*, p. 48.
174 *Ibid*
175 *Ibid*, p. 48.
176 White, L.D., *Introduction to the Study of Public Administration*, p. 495.

fitted within the administrative machinery and work automatically as the machine operates, whereas the external control upon the administration is from the outside. In Britain, the executive exercises its control internally whereas the Parliament and the judiciary exercise the external control. A brief picture of the control mechanism in Britain is as under:

I. Legislative Control: The British Parliament constitutes the most important mechanism or instrument to control the administration effectively. It is not only confined to the preparation of laws but also interferes in the operational working of administration. It is the Parliament in England that approves all the administrative policies. In Britain, there is no law, which it cannot make or unmake. So far as the legality of these laws is concerned, it is supreme and sovereign. No court can question the legality of its Acts. It is because there exists the 'doctrine of sovereignty of Parliament'. The significance of parliamentary control over administration has been aptly summarized by Steel in the following words:

At the heart of the system is Parliament. It is the forum in which the representatives of the electorate attempt to influence the activities of the executive and in which they can raise their constituents' grievances. Its ability to do these things stems from the fact that it lays down the functioning of all public bodies and provides them with the means of carrying them out. Parliament is not only important in itself; it also influences all the other institutions and procedures of redress. Thus the courts exists not to challenge Parliament but to enforce its will similarly although there are now other important channels, such as ombudsmen and administrative-tribunals, they have all been fitted with what is still essentially a parliamentary system[177]. The British Parliament exercises control over the administration in the following manner

1. **Determination of Policies and Laws:** Laws and the policies framed by the Parliament are an effective means of exercising control over the administration as the laws determine the administrative structures and procedures. Even in times of subordinate legislation, which Lord Hevert described as *New Despotism*, legislation, as a means of controlling administration, has not lost its significance altogether. This is because the broad guidelines are still provided by the legislature and the executive merely fills in the details.

    Further, laws and policies before being passed in the House, undergo a lot of debates and discussion. Besides criticizing the underlying policy of the bill/policy proposal, the Members of Parliament during the course of such debate and discussion may also indicate the failures of the government in general.

2. **Parliamentary Questions:** In a parliamentary system, parliamentary questions are an important tool to exercise surveillance over the administration. In a democratic country like England, the role of Parliamentary questions is significant in making the government accountable directly to the Parliament and through the Parliament to the people. Any member of Parliament can ask questions or seek information from the ministers on matters of public interest. If the Member of Parliament just wants to obtain information he may seek a written reply that is printed in the official record of proceedings. But if he wants to raise an issue publicly and to be able to ask a supplementary

---

177 Steel, D.R., "Britain" in F.F. Ridley (ed.), *op. cit.*, p. 54.

question to the minister's reply, the question is tabled for oral answer.[178] The questions may either be concerned with limited interests or may involve issues of national importance. The minister concerned collects the material for answering these questions with the help of the officials and secretaries of his department. Thus, the underlying purpose behind asking questions is to seek information and elicit facts on public issues.

Generally, the question time in the House of Commons starts at 2.35 p.m. and continue till 3.30 p.m. on the first four days of the week. To prepare the answer to a question two days' notice must be given. The questions may even be sent by post. But generally they are submitted at the Table Office in writing.[179] If an oral question is desired, "…the question must be marked with an asterisk; questions without asterisks are treated as requiring a written answer. Any member may ask up to two oral questions and any number of written questions a day. About 24,000 questions, written or oral, are answered in each session."[180]

'Question-time' is largely a development of the twentieth century in Britain. It is significant in putting the government on track and keeping the administration on its toes. It is essential in making the administration alert towards its acts of omission and commission. The former Prime Minister Earl Attlee has observed, "... I always consider that question time in the House is one of the finest examples of real democracy... The effect of questions to the minister and still more questions asked publicly in the House is to keep the whole of civil service on their toes."[181] Hence, the parliamentary questions asked during the question time keep the British administration under a constant vigil and thus serve the purpose of asserting the supremacy of the Parliament.

3. **Adjournment Motion:** It is an important device of exercising day-to-day control over the administration. The underlying purpose behind this motion is to attract the attention of the House of Commons towards a matter of urgent nature and of public importance. But introduction of this motion in the House requires the prior permission of the Speaker. If admitted, the ordinary business of the House is suspended and an immediate debate takes place on the matter for which this motion is moved. Thus, it is an extraordinary device that disturbs the normal business of the House for discussing such matters. "An adjournment motion is generally taken as a question of confidence in the government and is, therefore, taken up seriously. A vote at the end of debate may amount to censuring of the government and government may be asked to resign."[182]

4. **No-Confidence Motion:** No-confidence motion is another important weapon in the hands of the opposition to exercise an effective control over the working of government. The council of minister will remain in power as long as it enjoys the confidence of the House of Commons. If the House expresses a lack of confidence

---

178 *Ibid*, p. 56.
179 Research Board (ed.), *op. cit.*, p. 85.
180 *Ibjd*, p. 85.
181 Robson, W.A. (ed.), *The Civil Service in Britain and France,* London: the Hogarth Press, 1956, p. 20.
182 Narang, A.S., *Comparative Government and Politics,* New Delhi: Gitanjali Publishing House, 1999, p. 87

in the council of ministers, the government has no option but to resign. This motion can be brought in the House either due to the general poor performance of the government or its failure on some particular front (specifically when the whole policy of the government or a part of it, comes under fire). Even "An individual Minister can be attacked for deficiencies in his Department and the severity of disapproval may force his resignation."[183]

5. **Budgetary Control:** In a parliamentary system, the executive is required to take prior sanctions of the Parliament before appropriating public money. In fact, the executive cannot spend even a single penny without its prior approval. When the budget is presented before the Parliament, the Members of Parliament get an opportunity to review the administrative working by criticizing the policies and misdeeds of the government. In Britain also, the Parliament enjoys the opportunity to criticize the working of each department in great detail during the passage of budget particularly when the demands for grant are put to vote. "Motions of amendment or rejection of the budget may be taken as lack of confidence against the government requiring it to resign."[184] Hence the debate on annual budget is an important instrument in the hands of Parliament as it provides an opportunity to the opposition to reveal deficiencies in the overall working of the government.

6. **Select Committees:** In Britain, the select committees are considered as the most effective means of 'controlling' the administration.[185] A select committee consists of about "fifteen or twenty MPs chosen to reflect the party balance in the House of Commons, that is appointed to investigate and report to the House of Commons on particular issues...the present system of committees was established in 1971, following an experiment into the desirability of extending this kind of review."[186] A select committee is required to examine a subject that the House assigned to it. After conducting a detailed scrutiny, the committee presents its report to the House. However, its recommendations may or may not be accepted by the later. Some committees like Public Accounts Committee (PAC) and the Expenditure Committee (EC) are set up under the standing orders of the House. The work of PAC is more precisely related to the routine administration in comparison to the other committees. This committee acts as a traditional watchdog over the governmental expenditure. This committee considers and examines the report of the Comptroller and Auditor General. The EC is supposed to suggest economy in the governmental expenditure. For the specialized work there are occasions to create special committees. A few committees viz. Committee on Nationalized Industry and Committee on Science and Technology etc. are appointed in each session.[187] These committees make investigations about the administrative issues and prepare their reports that are submitted to the Parliament.

---

183 Curtis, M.R., *Central Government: An Introduction to the British System,* London: Pitman House, 1970, p. 44.
184 Narang, A.S., *op. cit.,* p. 87.
185 Smith Brian C. and Jeffrey Stanyer, *op. cit.,* p. 218.
186 Steel, D.R., "Britain" in F.F. Ridley (ed.), *op. cit.,* p. 57
187 Smith Brain C. and Jeffrey Stanyer, *op. cit.,* p. 219.

7. **Audit:** The British Parliament also exercises its control over public expenditure through the instrument of audit. Britain was the first country to have public accounts audited in order to find out if Parliament's sanctions were honestly and faithfully adhered to. The Comptroller and Auditor General of England audits all government accounts and ensures that money spent by the executive confirms/matches with the money granted by the Parliament. Thus, he cheeks all sorts of irregularities and misappropriations made by the executive. He presents a report to the Parliament in this regard. With the widening of the scope of the activities of the Comptroller and Auditor General through the National Audit Act of 1983,[188] the role of audit in Britain has further increased in tightening the bridle of the executive.

II. Executive Control: Being the real executive in Britain, the cabinet headed by the prime minister plays a crucial role in streamlining and exercising control over the administrative machinery. Though all the acts of the government are performed in the name of the Monarch, but factually, it is the cabinet which makes all the decisions. The control exercised by the executive over the administration acquires a number of forms. First, it decides all the policies, rules, regulations and procedures with regard to the working of the administration. Thus, the cabinet plays an instrumental role in determining the operational working of the government. Secondly, the cabinet exercises its control over the administration through its power of appointment and removal of key administrative functionaries at the top rungs of the administration. Thirdly, the entire administration of Britain is divided into a number of departments and each of these is politically headed by a minister called Secretary. Through the hierarchical channels, the ministerial authority wades through the entire department. All the administrative officials are thus guided and directed by the in-build control mechanism fitted within the administrative hierarchy. Fourthly, the executive exercises its control through the practice of 'delegated legislation'. Due to the paucity of time with the legislature, it passes an Act in a skeleton form and the executive is required to make the detailed provisions of the Act in consonance with the spirit of the Act. Through this authority to legislate, the executive regulates the behaviour of the administrative functionaries. Fifthly, the control of Treasury over the administration is very strict in England. It is because; in England public funds are kept in the Exchequer Account at the Bank of England. On the request of the Treasury, the Bank transfers sums from the Exchequer to the supply account of the Paymaster General, indicating the services in respect of which the issues are to be made. The heads of the various departments get funds to meet their bills by issuing 'payable orders' on the Paymaster General. By maintaining suitable registers, the heads see that 'payable orders' do not exceed the budgetary grant. In this way, the administrative activities are determined and regulated by the Treasury.

Besides, the 'Tribunal of Enquiries Act' 1921, also authorizes the British executive to conduct enquiries regarding those administrative functionaries involved in mal-administration. In case their fault is proved, it can take suitable actions against them. Moreover, the launching of the Citizens Charter system by John Major, the former prime minister and the later developments like IT revolutions in this field by his

---

188 Rowat, Donald C. (ed.), *Public Administration in Developed Democracies: A Comparative Study*, New York: Marcel Dekker. Inc. 1988, p. 81.

successor Tony Blair have proved significant in maintaining transparency (and thus controlling the administration) particularly in the implementation and evaluation of administrative programmes. It is helpful in establishing a direct control of the prime minister over the administration.

III. Judicial Control: Although the judiciary in England enjoys no power to question the validity of statutory laws, yet it enjoys the power to review executive actions[189] due to the prevailing doctrine of the sovereignty of Parliament and can intervene into the administrative lapses. The courts do have the power to declare the administrative actions *ultra vires* if they are not in consonance with law. Thus the judiciary in the United Kingdom has to ensure that the executive respects the will of the Parliament. The fundamental principle of judicial review in Britain is *ultra vires* and the courts enjoy the power to prevent the executive from "…exceeding its powers or from failing to exercise its powers in accordance with any procedures or conditions that may be laid down by statute. Not only can they restrain the executive on these grounds, they can also require it to undertake duties that have been prescribed by Parliament."[190] Thus, the judiciary in Britain restricts the scope of maladministration to a great extent and imposes several restrictions on the administration to follow the parliamentary laws. The courts in Britain intervene in administrative matters on the following main grounds.

1. Every official is required to operate within the specified geographical limits and the authority entrusted to him. If he exceeds his administrative power either beyond that specified geographical area or beyond the authority entrusted to him, his deeds will be declared *ultra vires* and hence null and void. Thus *lack of jurisdiction* is a prominent ground of judicial intervention in the administrative matters.

2. In Britain all powers are derived from law. Statutory laws prescribe the extent and limits of powers of different public functionaries. But there may be a possibility of misinterpretation or faulty interpretation of a law. A public servant may misconstrue the law. He may impose some conditions/obligations on the citizens that are not required by law. If a law is misconstrued or wrongly interpreted by a public servant and some obligations are imposed on some citizens then his deeds are challengeable in any court of law. In technical terms, it is called *misfeasance*. The court intervenes into the matter not only to provide a correct explanation of law but also to declare the actions of the administrative official *ultra vires*.

3. While analyzing a situation, there may be the chances that the administrative officials may cause some *error in fact-finding*. He may either ignore the actual facts or knowingly avoid them. This may affect the interests of a citizen adversely. In such cases, the courts intervene in the administrative matters and try to rectify the error in discovering the actual facts.

4. There may also arise the possibility of *malfeasance* on the part of some government official. Malfeasance means that an administrative official may utilize his authority either vindictively to harm some another or to attain some personal end. In

---

189 Rowat Donald C. (ed), *op. cit.*, p. 80.
190 Steel, D.R., "Britain" in F.F. Ridley (ed.), *op. cit.*, p. 62.

that case the courts can intervene and punish the official if he is found guilty of abusing his authority.
5. The law lay down some procedures which the officials have to follow while discharging their administrative obligations. But there may be some occasions when the public officials may violate the prescribed procedures thereby causing *error of procedure.* In such cases the courts get an opportunity to intervene into administrative matters to question the legality of actions of such officials.

Forms of Judicial Control or Remedies

Thus, the courts can intervene in the administrative functioning on any of the above-mentioned five grounds. In the event of intervention, the courts take resort to any of the following courses of action:

1. *Judicial Review of Administrative Acts and Decisions:* In England, the acts and decisions of the administrative officials can be challenged in a court of law on the grounds of usurping jurisdiction beyond ones limit, vindictive use of authority or misuse of power. However, unlike U.S.A., the scope of judicial review in England is limited as is not extendable to all the administrative actions. In Britain, it is limited in three ways: "firstly, many classes of administrative acts and decisions are excluded by statutes of Parliament from the scrutiny of the courts; secondly, many others are excluded by rules evolved by the courts themselves, i.e. by judicial self-limitations; and thirdly, certain other matters are excluded procedural difficulties."[191] Hence the judiciary in England enjoys the power of review of administrative actions but to a limited extent.

2. *Statutory Appeal against Administrative Acts and Decisions to the Courts:* The aggrieved citizens in England enjoy the right to appeal to the courts or to a higher administrative-tribunal against the illegal acts and decisions of the administrative officials. However, it is noteworthy that the courts in England are expensive and their procedure, apart from lengthy, is dilatory also. In this regard Robson has observed that in Britain though the aggrieved citizen, "...has, recourse to the courts but this is expensive, lengthy and generally intimidating and the courts have traditionally been reluctant to intervene in many areas of decision making."[192] So most of the appeals against the illegal administrative actions are made in the administrative tribunals. But if the aggrieved party is not satisfied with the decision of a tribunal, it can file statutory appeal to the courts of law.

3. *Suits against the Crown:* The Crown in England enjoyed immunity from any legal action up to 1947. Thus, it could not be sued except through the procedure of petition of right i.e. by its own permission. The aggrieved party could file suits for damages only against the administrative officials i.e., the suits were liable against them personally. But if an official (particularly working at lower rungs of administration) was not in a position to bear the burden awarded by the court to the aggrieved party, the court had no option but to send him in jail for debt.

---

191 Robson as quoted in Sharma, M.P. and B.L. Sadana, *Public administration in Theory and Practice,* Allahabad: Kitab Mehal, 1996, p. 687.
192 Steel, D.R., "Britain" in F.F. Ridley (ed.), *op. cit.,* p. 63.

But it was not an effective relief to the aggrieved party. Obviously, this suited neither the officials nor the public and the State came under lot of fire.

Consequently, as an outcome of the long agitation, the Crowns Proceedings Act was passed in 1947, which permits the citizens to sue the Crown. Thus, now the British Crown is liable for the misdeeds of its officials.[193] However, despite the passage of this Act, the Crown is still not fully liable to the courts for the wrongful acts of its officials.

4. *Suits against Public Officials:* In Britain, the formal head of the state i.e. the Monarch enjoys legal immunity and is not liable in any court of law. He is completely immune from all sorts of legal liabilities in respect of his/her acts either done in personal or public capacity. Along with this, the judicial officers, in their judicial capacity are also immune from legal proceedings with regard to their acts of commissions as guides of courts.[194] "Even if their action be erroneous, malicious, or not in the honest exercise of their office, they are immune from liability. In case of judges of the superior courts, even if the judge exceeds his jurisdiction, he incurs no personal liability"[195]

As far as non-judicial officials are concerned, in matters of torts, they (all servants of the Crown and public officials) can be held personally liable for their wrongful deeds. However, in matters of contracts, they cannot be personally sued if they made contracts in their official capacity. In such cases the remedy for the aggrieved party is to sue the crown through the procedure of petition of right.[196] "The Public Authorities Protection Act, 1893, however protects acts of public officials done in pursuance of an act of Parliament from challenge in a civil proceeding after a short period of limitation. Finally, as regards the criminal liability of the officials, it is the same as of private individuals."[197]

5. *Extraordinary Remedies:* Originally, the extraordinary writs were granted by the Sovereign on the ground of inadequacy of ordinary legal remedies. However, "In course of time these writs came to be issued by the High Court of Justice as the agency through which the Sovereign exercise his judicial power and these prerogative writs were issued as extraordinary remedies in cases where there was either no remedy available under the ordinary law or the remedy available was inadequate."[198] Presently, these remedies are issued by the courts of competent jurisdiction and are available to the citizen in extra ordinary circumstances. The extraordinary remedies are designed to ensure that public functionaries do not misuse their authority, make errors of law or refuse to exercise their powers. These extraordinary remedies include *Habeas corpus, Mandamus, Certiorari, Prohibition* and *Quo-waranto* and are explained below.

   a. *Habeas Corpus:* It literally means 'to produce the body of. It is always issued in the form of an order of a court. This writ is an important safeguard of

---

193 Sharma, M.P and B.L.Sharma, *op. cit.*, p. 690.
194 *Ibid*, pp. 692-3
195 *Ibid*, p. 693.
196 *Ibid*
197 *Ibid*
198 Basu, Durga Das, *Introduction to the Constitution of India* (13lh ed.), Prentice Hall of India, New York: Englewood Cliffs, 1990, p. 123.

individual liberty and proved helpful in justifying the cause of detention of a person if he is illegally detained by another. In Britain, there are various writs that go by this name, but in historical and political terms, the most important among them is the habeas corpus and *subjiendum recipienbum*.[199] The writ of habeas corpus is issued against a person who has detained another, requiring him to produce the latter before it in order to know the cause of his detention and to set him free if the claim of his detention is found forfeited.[200]

b. *Mandamus:* Literally Mandamus means a command or mandate. This writ is issued at the discretion of the court and not as a matter of right. It is issued in the form of a command by a court to a public official or any inferior court or any authority to do something that he has failed to do yet. Through this writ the court can compel the public functionaries to discharge their legal duties, which they are knowingly avoiding. Thus, the writ of mandamus commands a public official to do that, which was a part of his duty, but he still failed to do it.[201]

c. *Prohibition:* Literally prohibition means 'to prevent from doing something.' It is a judicial writ as a court of sufficient jurisdiction issues this writ only to a judicial or quasi-judicial body. Through this writ the higher court prohibits the lower courts/tribunals from doing something. This writ imposes restrictions on the operational working of the lower courts/tribunals. It prevents them from usurping jurisdiction with which they are not vested. This writ commands them not to do anything beyond their jurisdiction or with which they are not vested.[202] Prohibition is different from mandamus in that while the former can be claimed as a matter of right whereas the later can't be and that while mandamus is positive in nature (as it is a directive to do something that is part of the duty of an official) whereas prohibition is negative in nature (as it prohibits from doing something illegal).

d. *Certiorari:* Literally it means 'to be certified' or 'to be made certain'. It is a writ issued by a superior court to an inferior court to transfer the proceedings of a case pending with it in order to give a more effective judgment. This writ is issued against the judicial acts only. Hence, through this writ the higher court ensures the certification and return of some proceedings pending with a lower court, to determine their legality and to quash them if it failed to follow the doctrine of natural justice. In other words, the writ of certiorari means "…the direction of a superior court to an inferior court for transferring the records of proceedings of a case pending with it for the purpose of determining the legality of proceedings and for giving more satisfactory effect to them than could be done in the inferior court concerned."[203] Thus, the writ of certiorari is something more than the writ of prohibition in the sense that the later is preventive in nature only whereas the former is both preventive and curative.

---

199 Sharma, M.P and B.L. Sharma, *op. cit.*, p. 695.
200 Awasthi, A., *op. cit.*, p. 31.
201 *Ibid*
202 Bhagwan, Vishnoo and Vidya Bhushan, *op. cit.*, p. 690.
203 *Ibid*, pp. 690-91.

e. *Quo-warranto:* It literally means 'by what warrant or authority'. The court, by using this writ enquires into the legality of claim of any person to a public office. This writ is thus meant to try and examine one's claim to an office. Here the burden of proof to prove his claim remains on the claimant. If his claim asserted to an office or franchise is found forfeited, then the court ousts him from its enjoyment. In other sense, this writ is issued by the court "... to enquire into the legality of the claim which a party asserts to an office or franchise and to oust him from its enjoyment, if the claim be not well founded or to have the same declared forfeited."[204]

IV. Tribunals and Enquiries: The increase in governmental activities resulted into the creation of administrative tribunals under some special provisions to adjudicate the disputes between the administration and the citizens. These are created with an objective to secure an impartial, and fair judgment in cases of appeal against discretionary decisions of public authorities. Today, there are more than 2000 tribunals in Britain, prominent among them include: Agricultural Land Tribunals, Rent Tribunals, National Insurance Local Tribunals, Transport Tribunals, National Health Service Tribunals, Industrial Tribunals, Medical Appeal Tribunals and Supplementary Benefits Appeal Tribunals.[205] These tribunals operate in an informal way that is desirable for handling various complaints of the citizens. "The distinctive feature of tribunals and enquiries is that they are less formal and cheaper than the courts and are able to reach decisions more quickly. They also permit a higher degree of specialization than is possible within the present judicial system."[206] The decisions of the tribunals are binding particularly in matters of social security and taxation. In most of the tribunals, decisions are taken by a panel consisting of a chairman, who is legally qualified but who may do this work in a part-time capacity.[207]

In England, the administrative tribunals are mainly of two types. The first type of tribunals "... carry out an impartial review of a case and make a decision that is legally binding upon both parties: these are most common in fields such as social security and taxation." The second type of tribunals operate "... in a number of areas, notably planning, there is a provision for the holding of a public inquiry before a final decision is taken. They are held by a representative of the minister who follows a quasi-judicial procedure before making his recommendation to the minister, but the latter is then free to accept or reject it."[208] Such enquiries are not much costly but their reports are not binding.

Tribunals are purely neither administrative nor judicial in nature. They adopt a simplistic procedure in sharp contrast to the complicated one as followed by the ordinary courts and try to test the issues before them by weighing the relative merits of both parties. Thus, since they adopt informal and simplistic procedure, they are less costly and consume far less time than the ordinary courts of law. In the recent years, the importance of such tribunals has significantly increased and now generally they are regarded as informal courts of law.

---

204 *Ibid*, p. 691.
205 Smith, Brian C. and Jeffrey Stanyer, *op. cit.*, p. 230.
206 Steel, D.R., "Britain" in F.F. Ridley (ed.), *op. cit.*, p. 64.
207 Sallis, Edward, *op. cit.*, p. 242.
208 Steel, D.R., "Britain" in F.F. Ridley (ed.), *op. cit.*, p. 64.

7
ADMINISTRATIVE SYSTEM IN THE UNITED STATES

The United States of America came into existence as a breakage of Britain's 13 American colonies from the United Kingdom in 1776. These states combined themselves together as a federal country known as the United States of America. During the 19th and 20th centuries, 37 new states were added to this federation making the total number of states in the US fifty. In American history, the Civil War (1861-65) and the Great Depression of the 1930s are the two most traumatic experiences. Encouraged by victories in World Wars I and II and the end of the Cold War in 1991, the US has succeeded in establishing its hegemony throughout the world. Its economy is marked by steady growth and low rates of unemployment and inflation. It has registered rapid advancement in the field of technology.[1] The US philosophy of Liberal Economy is getting wide recognition even in the communist countries. Several countries, including India, Russia, and China are engaged in carrying drastic transformations in their economies in consonance with its popular philosophy of liberalization, privatization and globalization. Today, the US is a federation of 50 States. It has a written constitution and the powers are clearly divided between the Centre and the federating units. In political terms, the US is a democratic republic where the head of the government is elected. There exists presidential form of government in which all the executive powers are vested in the executive. Its legislature, popularly called Congress, is bicameral and consists of the House of Representative (the lower house) and the Senate (the upper house). As against the other parliamentary democracies of the world, in America the Senate (the upper house) is considered as more powerful chamber than the House of Representatives (the lower house). Its strength is constant (100) and every federating unit, irrespective of its size, sends two members to it. Apart from this, there exists an independent judiciary, which enjoys sufficient power of judicial review. It is a custodian of the fundamental rights of the citizens and the US Constitution. All the three organs of the government in America are closely interwoven with each other through the doctrines of Separation of Power and Checks and Balances.

In the present chapter an endeavour is made to highlight a detailed view of salient features, chief executive, local government, control machinery of the US administrative system.

---

1   http://www.nationmaster.com/Country/US/background.

(A) ADMINISTRATIVE FEATURES

The US system is a continuously "... changing organism which has been matured by the unending process of trial, error and corrections."[2] This has been rendered possible due to the political stability in that country, which has not undergone any violent and abrupt changes during the past over two centuries. Consequently, the political institutions have evolved over a period of time through the process of gradualism and incrementalism. This incremental and gradual pattern of political development in the US has a positive impact on its administrative system. In this regard Ferrel Heady has observed, "The greatest consequence of gradualism on public administration was that the administrative system also was able to take shape feature by feature in a way that reflected in the political changes and was consonant with them. Political and administrative adaptations were concurrent and fairly well balanced..."[3] In this background, the salient characteristics of the US administration are as under:

1. The Impact of European Settlements

Before the arrival of the Europeans, the US was originally inhabited by the Native Indians. During the 16th and 17th centuries, the Spanish, the Dutch and the English settled in different parts of what is today known as the US. They settled in various prominent cities of the present day America, prominent among them being Jamestown, New Amsterdam, New York city etc. This was followed by extensive British settlement during the late 17th and 18th centuries.[4] The European settlers changed the life-pattern and ideas of the original inhabitants of the country a great deal and imbibed in them the spirit of liberty and rights. These settlers brought with them new values, new hopes, new expectations and new ambitions, which resulted in shaping a new form of social and administrative organization. "The early settlers of America had brought with them certain institutions of their motherland. They worked these institutions in their homes. One of these institutions was the English Common Law, which embodied those fundamental rights of the individual, which even the King must respect."[5] The notion of 'no taxation without representation' was also one of the key ingredients of the views and ideas which these settlers brought with them. In the economic field, they brought the ideas of entrepreneurship and spendthrift, which proved significant in flourishing trade and business in the US. The imprints of the ideas can be viewed on the US politico-administrative as well as social life.

2. The British Impact

During the 17th and 18th centuries, a large number of Europeans migrated to America and settled there. Among these settlers, majority of the immigrants were from the British Isles "...who regarded themselves as transplanted Englishmen. They were inheritors of the English historical experience... During the century and a half of the colonial period, these Englishmen in the New World gradually formed their own views as to their rights vis-a-vis to the British Crown and the government in

---

2   Bhagwan, Vishnoo and Vidya Bhushan, *World Constitutions*, New Delhi: Sterling Publishers Pvt. Ltd., 1991, p. 3.
3   *Ibid*, p. 222.
4   http://en.wikipedia.org/wiki/United_States
5   Bhagwan, Vishnoo and Vidya Bhushan, *op. cit.*, p. 5.

the homeland."⁶ Therefore, the British ideas got more currency in America during its formative years. Their impact is visible on the socio-political life of the people in America. While writing the US Constitution, the American founding fathers "... brought to their task a comprehensive knowledge of and attraction to a variety of historical political experiments and statements of political philosophy which guided them in devising the innovative features which produced an obviously American political edifice on the British foundation."⁷ For instance, the US local administration and government, in its structural and functional terms, is considerably influenced by the British administrative system. These local public corporations fully reflect the impact of Anglo-Saxon jurisprudence. The idea of having a constitution was also derived from the British, though it is a separate matter that whereas Britain has an unwritten constitution, the U.S has a written one. The notion behind it was that the government and administration could be a very advance, if the system is based on some constitutional principles. Moreover, 'rule of law', which has remained a central aspect of British political philosophy, was adopted as a prominent political value in the US and became a salient feature of the US administration.

The American government and administration continued to bear the British imprint at least till the nineteenth century. However, towards the close of the nineteenth century and then in the early twentieth century, an effort was undertaken to purge the US administration and to remove the 'irrelevant elements' of this impact. This effort was undertaken in the background of the widely raised slogan 'Reverse English.'

3. Impact of the Ideas of Hamilton, Jefferson and Madison

Though the thirteen American colonies declared themselves independent States in July 1776, they finally got independence in 1783, when the British recognized their independence by the treaty of Versailles. However, the US Constitution could not be enacted and adopted before 1787. During this period, a long debate continued on the form and content of the administrative system. There were many tall and important personalities who contributed significantly in this debate and amongst these, Alexander Hamilton. Thomas Jefferson and James Madison are considered to be prominent.

Hamilton was a conservative, who emphasized on commercialism as the base of a strong nation. He advocated a centralized system, where powers should be used for the protection of national business. On the other hand, the administrative philosophy of Hamilton accepted the importance of the middle class (workers class). Hamilton was also of the view that the US must be a federal country where the federated units should be given wide powers. However, Hamilton was also not in favour of making the Federal government dependent on the states. Thus, during the presidency of George Washington, at the urge of Alexander Hamilton, the then Secretary of Treasury and a staunch supporter of a strong national government, "...a far-reaching commitment was made and carried out that the government at the center would create and maintain its own administrative agencies for the execution of national policy, and would not rely on state agencies as instrumentalities for day-

---

6 *Ibid*, p. 395.
7 *Ibid*, pp. 395-96.

by-day operations."⁸ He also advocated that there should be a strong chief executive. According to him, "a feeble executive (by contrast) implies a feeble execution of government. A feeble execution is but another phrase for a bad execution; and a government ill- executed... must be, in practice, a bad government."⁹ Hamilton also held the view that the bureaucracy should be exceptionally well-paid "... since the assistance provided by the bureaucracy to the chief executive is of paramount importance..."¹⁰

The philosophy of Thomas Jefferson, who has been regarded as the founder of the public administration in America, was based on rationality, individualism and liberty. He advocated the idea of limited government and decentralized administration. This idea was expressed in Thomas Jeffersonian saying, 'Good government is that which governs the least'. Another dimension of this idea is that the governments should not interfere in the social life and economic transactions. In terms of economic organization he proposed agrarian democracy, striving for a peaceful family life with independent peasants' proprietorship. His ideas led to the creation of national government in America with checks and balances and division of powers.¹¹

James Madison, who was the major author of American Constitution, said that "I am not a friend to a very energetic government. It is always oppressive. It places the government more at their ease at the expenses of the people."¹² Thus, he was not in favour of a strong government and was an advocate of liberty. To him, "... instability, injustice and confusion introduced into the public councils, have, in truth, been the mortal diseases under which popular governments have everywhere perished; and these continue to be the favourite and fruitful topics from which the adversaries to liberty derive their most specious declamations."¹³

From the above discourse, it is obvious that though there were some obvious contradictions in the ideas of these founding fathers yet these (their ideas) deeply influenced the US administration.

4. Separation of Powers

The doctrine of separation of powers implies that the powers of a sovereign government should be split between two or more strongly independent entities, preventing any one person or group from gaining too much power. Though there is no direct reference to this doctrine in the Constitution yet it is one of the cardinal principles of US administration. This doctrine was propounded by a French philosopher Montesquieu in 18th century. He was not in favour of concentration of legislative, executive and judicial powers in one hand as he had been a witness to its negative consequences. He believed that because all these powers were concentrated in the hands of the French Monarchs they behaved in a despotic manner. Similarly, the US founding fathers were fearful that the concentration of legislative, executive and judicial powers in

---

8 *Ibid*, p. 396.
9 Sahni, Pardeep, "Understanding Administrative Theory: A Perspective" in Dhameja, Alka (ed.), *Contemporary Debates in Public Administration*, New Delhi: Prentice-Hall of India Pvt. Ltd., 2003, p. 25.
10 *Ibid*
11 *Ibid*
12 Drinker, Catherine as quoted in *Ibid*, p. 26.
13 *Ibid*

one hand or office might lead to tyranny. Therefore, they adopted this doctrine and vested the three powers in the Congress, the President and the Courts respectively. Thus, unlike the parliamentary form of government, where there is an overlapping and close relationship between the legislature and the executive (as the latter is part of the former), in the US there is no direct relationship between the executive and legislature (because the former is not part of the latter). The President has almost no direct control over the business of Congress nor responsible to it. Constitutionally, the Congress is the real legislative organ and it can even legislate against the wishes of the President. He can only persuade and request the Congress for enacting or not enacting a particular law. The judiciary is also independent of both the Congress and the President as once appointed, the judges are almost irremovable. In sum, the freedom of the Congress and the president is partly maintained by the fact that "… they are separately elected, and are held directly accountable to the public. There are also judicial prohibitions against certain types of interference in each others' affairs. Judicial independence is maintained by life appointments, with voluntary retirement, and a high threshold for removal by the legislature."[14]

In the US, besides at the Federal level, the doctrine of separation of powers is also applied at the state and local levels and also governs the mutual relations of the various levels of governance The American states also mirror the executive/legislative/judicial separation of the federal government. Major cities even tend to adopt the same practice. But in general, the arrangements at the local and regional level vary far widely. In many American states and local governments, executive authority and law enforcement authority are separated where citizens are allowed "…to directly elect public prosecutors (district attorneys and state attorneys-general). In some states, judges are also directly elected. Many localities also separate special powers from their executive and legislative branches, through the direct election of police chiefs, school boards, transit agency boards, park commissioners, insurance commissioners, and the like."[15]

5. Checks and Balances

However, since government is an organic whole, so a complete separation of the three organs of the government into watertight compartments would be neither feasible nor advisable nor workable. It is mainly because an absolute separation of the three wings of the government would mean that the three wings would frame their respective citadels and may pull the government in divergent directions thereby defeating the very purpose of 'government.' Keeping this in view, the US founding fathers adopted another doctrine of 'checks and balances. This phrase "checks and balances" was also coined by the same French Philosopher, Montesquieu. In a system of government with multiple branches having separation of powers, "…"checks" refers to the ability, right, and responsibility of each power to monitor the activities of the other(s); "balances" refers to the ability of each entity to use its authority to limit the powers of the others, whether in general scope or in particular cases."[16]

In the US administration, the powers of one organ are so devised as to exercise a check upon the powers of others. In other words, the doctrine of separation

14 http://en.wikipedia.org/wiki/Separation of powers
15 Ibid
16 Ibid

of powers is implemented through the doctrine of checks and balances. The US founding fathers established a well balanced system among all the three organs of the government at the federal as well as state levels. For instance, "...laws can be passed only by the legislatures, but the executive can usually veto them; executive appointments require 'legislative confirmation; treaties negotiated by the President must be approved by the Senate; and the courts are checked, for example, by possible impeachments of judges and denial of funds."[17]

6. Strong Executive

The US Constitution provides for a presidential form of government where the President enjoys substantial powers. Today, the US President enjoys a strong position, and the powers and importance of this office have greatly increased in comparison to earlier periods. Today, the US President is "... one of the most influential chief executives of any contemporary nation, partly because he leads one of the world's super powers, and partly because of the constitutional scope of the office."[18] With the rise of the US as a superpower in the previous century, the US President became one of the most powerful persons of the world. During the Cold War period, he was sometimes designated as "the leader of the free world" and had a parallel in the Secretary-General of the Soviet Union. However, with the disintegration of the erstwhile Soviet Union, the world became uni-polar with the US as the sole superpower and the US President has become "the most powerful person on Earth."

It is noteworthy that the US founding fathers were not in favour of such a strong president and, therefore, made the provision of an indirectly elected president. However, later on due to the emergence of strong political parties - Republican and Democrat - the presidential election has now become almost direct. Resultantly, the US presidency is a very powerful position. Along with this, a number of other developments/factors that took place over the years further contributed in the enhancement of his powers. Thus, the Supreme Court has sufficiently enhanced his powers particularly in all those matters where the constitution was silent and has vested all the implied powers in the executive. The statutes of Congress further made an addition to his powers. Moreover, the conventions and usages also proved significant in enhancing the powers of his office.[19] His popularity emanates from the enormous powers, he enjoys. He presides over the "... executive branch of the federal government - a vast organization numbering about 4 million people, including 1 million active-duty military personnel."[20] The US President is the chief executive officer of the country. He is both the head of the state and the head of the government. Unlike the parliamentary democracies, he is neither a part of the US Congress nor responsible to it. He is directly responsible to the people who elect him. Besides, he enjoys security of tenure and can't be removed from his office except through the process of impeachment (in the Congress), which is a very rigorous process.

---

17 Ferguson, John H. and Dean E. McHenry, *The American Federal Government* (8th ed.), New York: McGraw Hill Inc., p. 32.
18 Heady, Ferrel, *The United States* in Rowat, Donald C. (ed.), Public Administration in Developed Democracies: A Comparative Study, New York: Marcel Dekker, Inc., 1988, p. 397.
19 http://en_wikipedia. Org./wiki/president_of_the_United_States
20 *Ibid*

The process of impeachment can only be initiated if charges of serious nature are levelled against him.

7. Federal Structure

A 'federal country' is defined as a State having constitutionally provided two levels of government: the central or federal level and the state level. The two levels of government derive their powers directly from the constitution and none has any authority to intervene into the jurisdiction of the other in normal circumstances. Presently, the US is a federal country of 'self-governing regions' (termed as 'states'). Taken in the sense of multi-layer governance, federalism has a long history in the US. Thus, even before independence there "... were local, colonial and British central [governments]. Ever since, the layers have been local, state and national."[21] In 1776, the 13 colonies declared their independence from Great Britain and constituted a league of friendship, which also continued till the end of the War of Independence (1783). "The original political structure was a confederation in 1777, ratified in 1781 as the Articles of Confederation. After a long debate, this was supplanted by the Constitution in 1789, forming a more centralized federal government."[22] The US Constitution adopted federalism as an administrative device to suit the geographical, economic, social, cultural, ethnic, and other regional diversities. In addition to the original 13 states, during the 19th century many new states entered into the confederation taking the total number of the federating units to 50[23].

Under the Indian Constitution the centre-state relations are governed by three lists (the Federal List, the State List and the Concurrent List) and the residuary powers rest with the Federal government. In sharp contrast to this, the US Constitution provides for only one list which mentions the powers of the Federal government; all the powers not mentioned in this list rest with the states. The US Constitution imposes restrictions on the powers of the federal government and limits them to certain areas like defense, foreign affairs, the issuing and management of currency, the management of trade and relations between the states etc. "In addition to these explicitly, stated powers, the federal government — with the assistance of the Supreme Court — has gradually extended these powers into such areas as welfare and education, on the basis of the "necessary and proper clause" of the Constitution."[24] Thus, as against the Indian federation in which the Federal government has overriding powers, the position of states is more powerful in comparison to the Federal government in its US counterpart. In case of any conflict between the two levels of governance, the US Constitution has provided for an independent judiciary.

8. Impact of Liberalism

Americans were deeply influenced by the liberal philosophy of John Locke, the famous British liberalist. It was the liberal ideas of John Locke which motivated and guided them in throwing off the yoke of British rule. In fact, John Locke propounded the liberal philosophy to stabilize the Glorious Revolution in Britain but they were adopted

---

21 Ferguson, John H. and Dean E. McHenry, *op. cit.*, p. 33.
22 http://en.wikipedia.org/wiki/United_States
23 *Ibid*
24 *Ibid*

and used by the Americans against themselves (the British). During the enactment of the US Constitution, the liberal philosophy guided the founding fathers such as Wilson, Andrew Jackson & Jefferson along with the stalwart of American leadership, George Washington, a great deal. Resultantly, the US emerged as a liberal democracy where the ability of elected representatives to exercise decision making power "... is subject to the rule of law and moderated by a constitution which emphasizes the protection of the rights and freedoms of individuals and minorities and which places constraints on the extent to which the will of the majority can be exercised."[25]

Impact of liberal philosophy on the US administration can be witnessed from the fact that the US Constitution provides freedom of speech and expression, freedom of Press, right to private property and privacy, equality before law, grants universal suffrage, limits the authority of the government and protects rights of the citizens and restricts the State intervention into individual affairs.

9. Independent State Administration

America, being a federal country, has constitutionally created two levels of governance viz. the federal government and the state governments. Both the levels of governments enjoy constitutionally bestowed distinct jurisdictions and operate in their respective spheres of activity. However, in sharp contrast to India, in America, the federated units have their own respective constitutions and possess relatively more autonomy. Consequently, in the US, the state governments have the greatest influence over people's daily lives. "Each state has its own written constitution and has different laws. There are sometimes great differences in law and procedure between the different states, concerning issues such as property, crime, health, and education."[26]

According to the US Constitution, certain aspects relating to sovereign interests have been transferred by each state to the federal government while retaining the remainder for itself. The other tasks like "... education, health, transportation, and other infrastructure are generally the responsibility of the states. Over time, the Constitution has been amended, and the interpretation and application of its provisions have changed. The general tendency has been toward centralization, with the federal government playing a much larger role than it once did."[27]

10. Changing Profile of Civil Services?

In contrast to the French and British civil service, the US civil service has been characterized by the absence of "career". Historically, in the US "... the orientation has been towards shorter-term or "program" staffing."[28] Thus, they have been selected for specific programmes. However, during the past some time, there has been limited experimentation "...with "career" rather than "program" selection and advancement devices"[29] and creation of Senior Executive Service (SES) in 1978, may be cited an example in this regard. But after two decades of experience, the SES has received mixed evaluations, and there is considerable doubt that it is producing a service-

---

25 http://en.wikipedia.org/wiki/Liberal_democracy
26 http://en.wikipedia.org/wiki/United_States
27 http://en.wikipedia.org.wiki/States_of_the_United_States
28 Rowat, Donald C, *op. cit.*, p. 405.
29 *Ibid*

wide category of administrative generalists with more clear-cut lines for promotion to positions of high level administrative responsibility."[30]

Unlike in India and France, the civil servants in the US enjoy relatively low social prestige and status and the reasons for this have been more than one. Under the impact of liberalism, historically, the Americans have attached more value to individual liberty. Thus, the activities undertaken by the administration have been regarded to be encroachments on individual liberty. Therefore, the "American citizens tend to look upon the public bureaucracy with suspicion and distrust, so that they are more intent on trying to make the civil service responsive and subservient than in building up bureaucratic self-esteem."[31] Secondly, in the US more value has been attached to private entrepreneurship than governmental activity and hence the managers of the former acquired prominence in comparison to the latter. The absence of career system in civil services has been another contributory factor for low social prestige of the civil servants in the US.[32] However, with the creation of SES, there seems to be some perceptible change in the positive direction in the popular perception towards the civil servants.

About the civil servants, the Americans have dichotomous views. Their personal views about the civil servants mismatch with the general popular perception. Thus, for instance, "they tend to disapprove of government sponsored welfare programs in general, but to approve of specific programs such as food stamps, aid to dependent children, or health care for the poor."[33] In other words, though the personal encounters of the citizens with the civil servants have been satisfactory, yet the people are not ready to change their mindset of a popular negative perception about them. In this regard, what Heady has observed about the civil servants in the US seems to be true. According to him: "the civil service has gradually become more competent in its composition and more professional in its outlook, in response to the demands placed upon the government for performance..."[34]

11. Impact of Pressure Group

Pressure groups are the bodies of persons who share some common purpose and try to influence public policy. They are found almost in every nation and exert a significant influence over the administrative working and the US is no exception to it. In fact, in the US, the pressure groups[35] are more dominant and their numerical strength is also greater in comparison to most of the other countries. Their number

---

30 Heady, Ferrel, *Public Administration: A Comparative Perspective* (6th ed.), New York: Marcel Dekker, Inc., 2001, p. 234.
31 Heady, Ferrel, *The United States* in Rowat, Donald C, *op. cit.*, p. 408.
32 *Ibid*
33 *Ibid*, p. 415.
34 *Ibid*, p. 416.
35 "In America, the title "pressure group" has all-but been replaced with the title "interest group"... The word "interest" is seen as being less forceful than the word "pressure" which could hint at vaguely undemocratic tendencies and processes as a pressure group. Pressure groups should not be seen as rivals to *political parties* in America but the two groups do complement one another."[35] http://www.historylearning site.co.uk/pressure groups_in_ america. htm.dated, Ocotber 18, 2005.

has significantly increased during the second half of the previous century, particularly since the end of the Second World War. This has been mainly because of the widening scope of government activity over the years and its penetration into the every aspect of society. Further, due to the increase in complexities of life, individual's power to influence the governmental outcome, along with his power to secure his objective privately, has diminished.[36]

The pressure groups have both positive and negative impact on the administration. They control the administration and do not let it become oppressive and autocratic. They keep vigil on the administration and act as a watchdog of the interests of their respective social groups. Secondly, they provide crucial information to the administration which the administration, sometimes, do not possess. They procure this information due to their informal character. This helps the administration in making better policy decisions. However, these groups also exert pressure upon the administration for getting their interests incorporated into policy decisions. Since there are several such groups simultaneously exerting pressure upon the administration and thus pulling it in different directions, it, quite often, becomes difficult for the administration to maintain a balance among these groups. Another negative aspect associated with the pressure groups is that those groups which fail to get their demands incorporated in the policy decisions become hostile and create problems for the administration.

Whenever the administration attempt to regulate some social, political, or economic activity, those affected, lobby the administration not to take actions that would adversely affect them. For instance, "... when President Reagan announced his re-armament programme and the construction of the neutron bomb, the Nuclear Freeze Groups began a series of protests attracting significant public support." [37] Likewise, President Clinton was pressurized by both logging groups and environmentalists "...when the loggers wanted parts of Washington State opened to them whereas the environment groups protested that rare species found there were likely to become even rarer. A compromise that satisfied both groups was arrived at: some logging, but stronger protection for those areas not opened to logging."[38] It is also believed that 'George W Bush's current hard-line against Iraq in August 2002, was 'influenced by pressure groups representing the military.' "A report by the World Policy Institute based in New York, states that the President's policy may have been influenced by some of his advisors who have close ties to the "military-industrial complex."[39]

12. Diverse but Well-Developed Local Government

In the US, local government is a state subject.[40] Thus, the provision of local government is separately made by the constitution of all the states. Obviously, therefore, there

---

36 *Ibid*
37 *Ibid*
38 *Ibid*
39 *Ibid*
40 Since the passage of the tenth amendment of the US Constitution, local government ceased to be a federal subject and as such belongs to the states. Hence the state legislature enjoys power of establishing local government units and determines their structure, powers and functions.

exist variations in the system of local government prevailing in different states and the local government units along with their powers and functions in different states bear hardly any uniformity. Thus, "local units, such as counties, townships, municipalities, and special districts are organized in 50 different ways, because laws providing for their establishment and working derive primarily from the 50 state constitutions."[41]

However, it needs to be mentioned here that despite the inherent diversities in the local government units in different states, they exhibit some basic similarities. Broadly, there exist the general-purpose and the special-purpose local government system in the US. The earlier category of local government units performs some common nature functions while the latter category local government units are created to perform some specific function. Among the first category of local government units are included the counties, the cities, towns, townships etc. The second categorization incorporates those local government units which are specifically established to discharge some specific function usually known as special districts. These districts are usually named after the function they discharge such as school districts, natural resources districts; fire protection districts; urban water supply districts; housing and community districts; sewerage districts; park and recreation districts, hospital districts, libraries districts; health districts and airport districts etc. They are found almost in all the US states with few exceptions.

(B) Political Executive

In the US, the executive comprises of the President, the Vice-President and the President's Cabinet. In the present section, these three functionaries along with the administrative departments of the Federal government are discussed in detail.

PRESIDENT

As contrary to the then existing system of parliamentary government, the United State of America after gaining independence, adopted the presidential system of government. Unlike the parliamentary form of government, the presidential form of government does not differentiate between the nominal and real executives; rather it is characterized by a single executive viz. the President who is both the head of the nation as well as the head of the state and all the executive powers are vested in him. US was the first country that adopted the presidential system of government. Thus, it is regarded as the precursor or forerunner in creating the office of the President. The President in USA is a democratically elected official and the most powerful personality of the United States. He enjoys the status of chief legislator, chief executive of federal government and commander-in-chief of the armed forces. With the rise of US as superpower in the previous century, the American President became one of the most powerful persons of the world. In the post-Second War bipolar world phase, which was also designated as cold war period, he was sometimes designated as "the leader of the free world," a phrase that is still invoked today. With the disintegration of the erstwhile Soviet Union, the world became uni-polar with the US as the sole super-power, the US President has become "the most powerful person on Earth" and is recognized as the most renowned figure of the world.

---

41 Barthwal, C. P., *Understanding Local Self-Government,* Lucknow: Bharat Book Center, 1997, p. 65.

Initially, the U.S. constitutional fathers were not in favour of such a strong president. Therefore, though the US Constitution vested substantial powers on the President, but the position of the President was kept weak by providing for his indirect election; initially, the President was to be elected indirectly by an electoral college. However, later on due to the emergence of strong political parties- Republican and Democrat - the presidential election has now become almost direct. Thus, today he enjoys a great measure of popular support. Along with this, a number of other developments/factors that took place over the years further contributed in the enhancement of his powers. "Among these factors are the rise of political parties, Supreme Court Decisions, and Congressional actions granting new authority to the president."[42] The Supreme Court has sufficiently enhanced his powers particularly in all those matters where the constitution was silent. Thus, the Supreme Court vested all the implied powers in the executive. The statutes of the Congress further made an addition to his powers. Moreover, the conventions and usages also proved significant in enhancing the powers of his office. As a consequence, today the U.S. President enjoys a strong position and the powers and importance of this office greatly increased in comparison to earlier period. Barrack H. Obama currently holds the office of the President of the US. [43]

Qualifications

The US Constitution clearly prescribes the requirements to hold the office of the president. Constitutionally, three qualifications have been laid down for a person to be eligible for being elected as President. Thus, he must be:

(i) natural-born citizen of the United States,
(ii) at least 35 years of age, and
(iii) a resident of the United States for a period of 14 years.

There has been no dispute regarding these qualifications for this office for quite a long time. But in the recent years a controversy has emerged regarding the requirement of native born citizenship. "Some commentators argue that the clause should be repealed because it excludes qualified people based on technicalities, and fails to appreciate the contributions made by immigrants to American society... Occasionally, constitutional amendments are proposed to remove or amend this requirement, but have not been successful."[44] Consequently, the above three qualifications are valid till date.

Salary and Perks

The U.S. Congress determines the salary and other emoluments of the President by its statutes. Once decided by the Congress, they cannot be increased or diminished during the term of the President. Originally his salary was fixed $ 25,000 per year in September, 1789. But due to its constant revision from time to time, it varied accordingly. In March, 1873, it was doubled in comparison to the previous one. In March, 1909, it was raised to $ 75,000 per year. In January, 1949, it was further

---

42 White, Robert, *American Government: Democracy at work* (2nd edition), New York: D.Van Nostrand Company, Inc., 1963, p. 185.
43 http://en_ wikipedia. Org./wiki/president_of_the_ United_ States
44 *Ibid*

enhanced to $ 1,00,000 per year. Again in January, 1969, became double the previous one and made $ 2,00,000 per year. Recently, in the year 2001, it was again revised. Now, since its revision from January, 2001, the U.S. President has been getting a salary of $ 4,00,000 per year.[45]

Along with this, currently the President also enjoys many non-salary perks like the White House as a place for living and working. His personal offices are housed in it. He uses several specially built Boeing 747s while travelling abroad. They are comfortable enough and enable him to discharge all his office work even on board. He makes use of an armoured Cadillac limousine that is well equipped with bullet-proof windows and tires while travelling around Washington. Besides, there exists the presidential helicopter for making somewhat longer trips around the Washington area.

In addition to this, there are certain other benefits which the President continues to enjoy even after leaving the office. Thus, fringe benefits like free mailing privileges, free office space, the right to hold a diplomatic passport and budget for office help and staff assistance, are continuously enjoyed by the President even after leaving his office.[46] Till recently, the President of US and his family were provided security cover by the State. However, the life-term and all time protection by the Secret Service extended to the presidents and their families after leaving office has been withdrawn recently. Up to 1997, all former Presidents and their families "...were protected by the Secret Service until the President's death. The last President to have lifetime Secret Service protection is Bill Clinton; George W. Bush and all subsequent presidents will be protected by the Secret Service for a maximum of 10 years after leaving office."[47]

Immunities

The U.S. President enjoys complete immunity from any court procedure. He cannot be arrested for any sort of offence. No court of law can issue orders against him to perform any act. He can be removed only by impeachment. After his removal from the post, he is liable to a treatment equal to that of an ordinary citizen of the United States.

Tenure and Re-eligibility

The U.S. Constitution provides for a fixed tenure of four years and the re-eligibility of the President for second term. George Washington, the first U.S. President, was re-elected for the second term but he firmly rejected the possibility to contest election for third term. Since then a tradition of "no third term" was emerged in America. But this tradition was violated during the Second World War. At this time, President Roosevelt was re-elected for the third and fourth consecutive terms in 1940 and 1944. In this connection, the Twenty-Second (Constitution) Amendment came into effect in 1951 and the provisions of this Amendment were first applied to Dwight D. Eisenhower. Through this, Amendment the total term of a President was limited to a maximum period of ten years. Thus, it restricted the re-eligibility of the incumbent

---

45 *Ibid*
46 *Ibid*
47 *Ibid*

to this office for the third term. In case a permanent vacancy is created to this office either after two years or more than two years, the Vice-President who succeeded to this office will have two more chances to contest election but if it is created before the completion of two years, in that case the successor to this office will have only one chance to contest election for this post. Since the passage of this Amendment, four President viz., Dwight D. Eisenhower, Ronald Reagan, Bill Clinton and George W. Bush have served for two full terms. The only President who served more than eight years was Lyndon Johnson.[48]

Impeachment Process

The U.S. President is elected for a period of four years and enjoys security of tenure. This is because he cannot be removed from office except through the process of impeachment (in the Congress), which is a very rigorous process. The process of impeachment can be initiated if charges of serious nature are leveled against him. A proposal to this effect is brought in the House of Representatives. If this House passes the proposal with a special majority, then it is sent to the second chamber viz. the Senate. During the impeachment process, the Senate acts as a judicial tribunal and it is presided over by the Chief Justice of Supreme Court. After consideration of the proposal, if the Senate also convicts the President by 2/3 majority of its members present and voting, the president has no option but to resign. However, as is obvious, this method of impeachment is very cumbersome and, therefore, once elected, the US President is almost irremovable. The fact that till date not even a single president has not been removed by this method in America stands witness to this fact.

For the first, time impeachment were brought against President Andrew Johnson but it fell by one vote in the Senate. Second time, it was brought against President Richard Nixon in 1974 in the Watergate scandal case. But before the completion of the impeachment process, President Nixon resigned. Third time it was brought in case of President Bill Clinton in the Monica-Levinsky sex scandal case. The Congress conducted enquiries with the help of an independent advocate Kenneth Star. However, the facts of this case were found true. But most of the U.S. people did not feel it as a big enough excuse to merit impeachment. Moreover, President Clinton apologised publicly to his family and the nation for this act. Resultantly the resolution could not be passed in the Senate.

Succession

Constitutionally, the Vice-President succeeds to the office of President if a vacancy is created either due to his death, resignation or removal from office (by impeachment or conviction). In fact, the line of succession to this office consists of 17 government officials. It begins with the Vice-President and ends with the Secretary of Veteran Affairs.[49] In so far as the vacancy to this office due to the President's disability was concerned, originally, the Constitution was silent. This void was filled by the passage of twenty-fifth (Constitution) Amendment by the Congress. Section 3 of this Amendment provides that in case of President's disability, the Vice-President will

---

48 *Ibid*
49 http://en_ wikipedia. Org./wiki/Piesident_of_the_ United_ states # Sucession

act as the 'Acting President'. Besides, Section 2 of this Amendment provides that if the office of Vice-President falls vacant, the post is filled by the President's nominee subject to the approval of the Congress. In 1973, due to the resignation of the then Vice-President Spiro Agnew, Gerald R. Ford was selected as the first Vice-President by this Method.[50] Moreover, in the next year he succeeded to the post of President because of the resignation of President Nixon (due to his involvement in Watergate scandal). It was a classic example in the U.S. history where a person rose to this office without contesting election.

Oath

According to Article II (Section 1, Paragraph 8) of the US Constitution, the new incumbent, before entering into President's office must take the following oath: "I do solemnly swear that I will faithfully execute the Office of President of the United States, and will to the best of my ability, preserve, protect, and defend the Constitution of the United States." Since 1937 (after the ratification of Twentieth (Constitution) Amendment), the oath of office is sworn in to the new incumbent by the Chief Justice of United States on 20th January. This day is popularly known as the inauguration day. Prior to the ratification of this Amendment, the new incumbent used to take oath on 4th March of the year following the presidential election. After taking oath, the President delivers an inaugural address. In his address he sets out the tone for the administration.[51]

Presidential Powers

The US President is the chief executive officer of the country. He is both the head of the state and the head of the government. Constitutionally, all the executive powers are vested in him. In addition to this, vast plethora of powers has been vested in him through the various Supreme Court decisions (which has vested all the implied powers in him), the statutes of Congress, and the conventions and usages. His popularity emanates from the enormous powers, he enjoys. He presides over the "... executive branch of the federal government – a vast organization numbering about 4 million people, including 1 million active-duty military personnel."[52] In addition to his executive powers, he also enjoys a lot of legislative and judicial powers. A brief view of his powers is as under:

Legislative Powers

The doctrine of separation of powers, which was adopted by the founding fathers in the US, postulates separation of legislative, executive and judicial powers. In the US the three powers are vested in the Congress, the President and the Courts respectively. Thus, unlike the parliamentary form of government, where there is an overlapping and close relationship between the legislature and the executive (as the latter is part of the former), in the US there is no direct relationship between the executive and legislature (because the former is not part of the latter). The President has almost no direct control over the business of Congress nor responsible to it. Constitutionally, the Congress is the real legislative organ and it can even legislate

---

50 http://en. Wikipedia. Org/wiki/Vice_President_of_the_United_States_of_America
51 http://en wikipedia. Org./wiki/president_of_the_ United_ states
52 *Ibid*

against the wishes of the President. He can only persuade and request the Congress for enacting or not enacting a particular law.

However, the actual practice is different and the President enjoys and exercises several legislative powers. In fact, it has been rightly said, "despite the constitutional provision that 'all legislative powers' granted to the federal government are vested in the US Congress, the president, as the chief formulator of public policy, has a major legislative role."[53] Hence in modern times, he operates as a 'Chief Legislator'. His legislative powers are discussed below:

1. Veto Power:

Under certain circumstances, the US President has been constitutionally empowered to veto the bills passed by the Congress. Under these circumstances, the veto power of the US President becomes real and substantial. The US President may exercise the veto power in the following chief manners.

(i) *Pocket veto:* When a bill is submitted to the President, he may opt neither to sign it nor to return it- within 10 days - for reconsideration of the Congress (excluding Sundays and holidays). He may simply let the bill lie on his table till the expiry of ten days. During this period, if the Congress is adjourned, the bill fails to become a law. This method is known as the *'pocket veto'* of the US President. This veto is an effective tool in the hands of the US President to grab legislative powers. It is because this veto power of the President is converted into *'absolute veto'* during the last ten days of the session of the Congress. It is a customary that, the Congress passed numerous bills and resolutions towards the end of the session to clear up its arrears where the President enjoys the opportunity to exercise his absolute veto power. A considerable number of "… last minute bills can thus be killed by the President if he is against them and the fact is that this power has been frequently used by the various Presidents."[54]

(ii) *Qualified Veto:* When a bill is presented to the President, in place of giving assent to it, he may return the bill to the House of Congress in which it was originated with or without his objections. Both the Houses of Congress are required to reconsider this bill. However, if each House passes it by two-thirds majority again, then it becomes a law without the signatures of the President. Thus, the two-thirds majority of each House of Congress only overrides the qualified veto. But if it fails to obtain the two-thirds majority, the proposed legislation dies. In general, it is very much difficult in America to take two- thirds majority again on a bill rejected by the President. So the fate of most of such bills is nothing but death. Between 1789 and 1925 "… the Presidents used their direct veto at least 6,000 times, out of which only 36 bills rejected by the President were re-passed by two- thirds majority of the Congress."[55]

Thus the veto power is a significant legislative power of the U.S. President and is an important weapon to influence Congressional actions. The early Presidents

---

53 *Ibid*
54 Vishnoo Bhagwan and Vidhya Bhusan, *op. cit.,* p. 43.
55 *Ibid*

used it very sparingly. But the later ones, important among whom being Cleveland, Franklin Roosevelt, Truman and Eisenhower, made frequent use of this power. In fact, two Presidents - Cleveland and Franklin Roosevelt - have used two-thirds of all veto powers since Washington. On the other hand, eight presidents did not use the veto power at all during their terms of office.[56]

2. Presidential Message:

In the parliamentary form of government, the executive is part of the legislature. The prime minister and the ministers sit in the Parliament and take part in the legislative processes. The fact remains that most of legislations are initiated by the executive. It is because the executive is in better knowledge as to what legislations are required. However, such an inter-linkage is absent in a presidential system like that of the US and, consequently, the U.S. President is empowered to recommend legislations to the Congress. The U.S. President may send messages to the Congress proposing some legislative measures. This message basically incorporates the major legislative or policy recommendations of the President for enacting laws on the issues of immense importance. The President may also personally appear before the Congress to deliver the message. Initially, this practice was seldom followed, but the recent presidents, particularly since Wilson, have increased the practice of appearing in person to give messages. The personal appearance of a president invites the attention of the Congress as well as the public.[57] Thus, the presidential messages are a potent source for originating a number of Congressional laws. "Much of the legislation dealt with by the Congress is drafted at the initiative of the executive branch. In annual and special messages to the Congress, the president may propose a legislation he believes is necessary. The most important of these is the annual State of the Union Address traditionally given in January."[58]

Constitutionally it is not binding on the Congress to enact laws on all the massages sent by the President; however, the Congress usually accepts the legislative recommendations of the President. Thus, the Presidential messages strengthen his hands as a legislative leader. In case the Congress does not accept his messages, the President has another option available to him in the form of making an appeal to the electorate. He can make a direct appeal to the nation to win popular support for his legislative proposals. If the legislative proposal is in the favour of the nation, public opinion is formed in favour of the President, which in a developed country like the US, even the Congress can't dare to ignore. In this way, the President can compel the Congress to enact the requisite legislation.[59]

3. Special Sessions:

The U.S. President also enjoys the power to call a special session of the Congress. Earlier, this practice of calling special Congress sessions was very common. In 1913, the Congress passed most of the important laws in the special sessions called by President Wilson. President Roosevelt convened a special session in 1933, popularly

---

56 Goyal O.P., *Comparative Governments: UK, USA, USSR, Japan, China, Switzerland*, New Delhi: Macmillan India Limited, 1985, p. 222-23.
57 White, Robert, *op. cit.*, p. 205.
58 http://en wikipedia. Org./wiki/president_of_the_ United_ states #Legislative_powers
59 *Ibid*

known as the 'Hundred Day Session'. But after the ratification of the twentieth (Constitution) Amendment, the need of such a session has been significantly reduced.[60] Due to the insertion of a new calendar under this Amendment the interval between regular sessions has been narrowed. In such sessions, the Congressmen are also deprived of their usual allowances including the T.A. and D.A. It has a deterring effect on Congressmen. Resultantly, they discourage the President not to use this power frequently to discomfort them.[61] After the ratification of this Amendment, special sessions of the Congress have been rarely convened. Of course, some special sessions of the Congress like the one convened at the outbreak of War in 1939 are exceptions.[62]

4. Delegated Legislation:

Delegated legislation, which Lord Hevert designated *New Despotism*, is a common phenomenon in modern democracies and the US is no exception to it. Thus, like the other executives of the world, it has also enhanced the legislative powers of the US President. The Congress often delegates powers to the President under this practice to frame rules and regulations (within the ambit of the limitations mentioned therein) that have the effect of law. Due to the time constraints, the U.S. Congress generally passes a law highlighting its broad outlines and the President is authorized to provide for its detailed provisions. The practice of delegated legislation has enormously enhanced the legislative powers of the U.S. President. The rules and regulations framed by the President under this practice called 'executive orders' have the equal force of law as those framed by Congress. "President Roosevelt is supposed to have exercised this power extensively. He is said to have issued 3,703 executive orders during his presidential career prior to 1944. During the same period the Congress passed only 4,553 laws".[63]

In addition to this, the recent Presidents have established a Constitutional Liaison Officer to improve the working relationship and to avert conflicts between the President and the Congress. Moreover, his aides play a crucial role in taking a serious note of all the legislative activities going on in the Congress and inform the President from time to time. They also try to persuade the Representatives of both parties and the Senators to support administrative policies.[64]

5. Patronage:

In addition to the above-listed formal methods, the President also exercises his influence over legislation through informal or indirect means. Thus, for instance, he enjoys the power to appoint a large number of persons in the Federal services. In 2003, more than 3000 executive agency positions were subject to presidential appointment.[65] The presidential 'patronage' is nothing but the practice of seeking jobs for political supporters. His power to appoint persons to political positions is an

---

60 Goyal O.P., *op. cit.*, p. 222.
61 Bhagwan Vishnoo & Vidya Bhusan, *op.cit.*, p. 44.
62 Kapur, Anup Chand, *Select Constitutions* (7th ed.l), Chandigarh, 1970, p. 329.
63 Vishnoo Bhagwan & Vidya Bhusan, *op.cit.*, p. 45.
64 http://en *wikipedia. Org./wiki/president_of_the_* United_ states #Executive_powers
65 http://en_ wikipedia. Org./wiki/ president_of_the_ United_ states #Legislative_powers

important weapon in the hands of the President to bargain with the Congressmen.⁶⁶ Through this power the U.S. President tries to oblige the Representatives and the Senators of the Congress by extending favour (of political appointments) to their near and dear ones. In lieu of extending special favour, he maintains his hegemony in the Congress and gets his legislative proposals passed in it. In case he finds that the Congressmen are refusing to support his proposals, he can threaten them to withdraw the patronage extended to their supporters.

Executive Powers

The U.S. President is the chief executive officer of the country. Unlike the President of India or the Crown in Britain, he is the real executive i.e., rather than the executive powers being exercised in his name by some other agency, he himself exercise these powers. He is both the head of the state as well as the head of the nation. Thus, his powers are very extensive and are conferred upon him by the Constitution as well as by the Supreme Court directives and the Congressional legislative enactments. Being the chief executive of the federal government, he is concerned with the management of national affairs. His executive powers are discussed below.

1. Chief Administrator

Being the head of the government and the State, the U.S. President is the custodian of the constitution and enforces all the laws enshrined in it. As chief administrator, he guides, directs and controls the activities of the apex administrative officials directly operating under him. He is also responsible to ensure the execution of all the laws passed by the Congress and all the decisions taken by the federal courts. Maintenance of law and order in the country constitute another important responsibility of the President. Thus he safeguards the rights and property of the American citizens.⁶⁷

He is also liable for the smooth management of national affairs. Thus, he has to ensure democratic and republic government to the federal government as well as to the government of every US state. He even safeguards the interests of the respective state governments. If he perceives any threat to the democratic and republic governance in any US state he is empowered to initiate action on his own. However, in the event of domestic violence in a state he can't initiate any action on his own. For taking action in such a situation, a request either from the state legislature or from the Governor (if the legislature is not in session) of that state is a pre-requisite.⁶⁸

2. Commander in Chief

Unlike the President of India who is the nominal Supreme Commander of the Indian armed forces, the US President is the Supreme Commander of the US armed forces in reality. Constitutionally he shares "... power over the military establishment with Congress, which may make rules, appropriate money, and declare war."⁶⁹ He appoints the top military officials, which are, however, subject to the ratification by

---

66 White, Robert, *op. cit.*, p. 205-06.
67 Bhagwan, Vishnoo & Vidya Bhusan, *op. cit.*, p. 38.
68 *Ibid*
69 Ferguson, John H. and Dean E. McHenry, *op. cit.*, p. 320.

the Senate.[70] But the President can remove them at his will. Though the President alone cannot declare war but, being the Supreme Commander of armed forces, he can surely create a situation in which the Congress is left with no other option to approve war. This is evident by what Ferguson and McHenry have observed: "a President, by belligerent use of the Armed Forces, may involve the country in a state of war, leaving Congress no option but to declare war."[71] For instance, in 1941 Congress had to declare war against Germany. The reason behind it was that long before this declaration of war, U.S. Navy started firing on submarines threatening conveys to Britain.[72]

In the event of declaration of war, the military powers of the President are substantially increased. He becomes the ultimate authority to manage and direct war operations. It is he who decides how the military will move and how many troops will be deployed at which place. The U. S. Congress may grant even broader powers in connection with the safety and security of the nation. For instance, Congress delegated unfettered powers to President Roosevelt during World War II. Likewise, substantial powers have been conferred upon President George Bush to fight against Osama-bin Laden after the terrorist attack on Pentagon and World Trade Center on 11 September 2001 and more currently in 2003, Congress extended enormous powers to the President in the war operations against Saddam Hussein in Iraq.

3. Foreign Relations

US President has a vital role to play in matters of relations with foreign countries. It is the constitutional responsibility of the President to establish and maintain relations of the United States with foreign nations. "The Constitution gives him authority to make treaties (with the consent of two-thirds of the Senate), to appoint diplomats and consuls (subject to ratification by a Senate majority), and to receive foreign diplomatic and consular representatives."[73] Therefore, he is the central figure who represents America at the international level and also shapes its foreign policy.

In this capacity the President appoints ambassadors and other diplomatic officials but also receives foreign ambassadors and other public officials. He also makes treaties with foreign nationals, which are, however, subject to the confirmation by the Senate. In fact, he is the sole in-charge of negotiating all foreign treatises and agreements but they must need ratification by two-thirds vote of the Congress. Theoretically, this is a significant limitation on the powers of the President because in the event of non-ratification of any treaty entered into with some foreign country by him, his position will really become very awkward. However, in actual practice the possibilities of such an occurrence are very remote. First, because the Senate is also aware of the fact that such a step would not be in the national interest of the country. Secondly, these treaties are placed before the Senate for ratification at such a stage where it becomes difficult for the Senate to reject them.[74] Moreover, President has another weapon whereby he can even by-pass the Senate in case he senses some

---

70 Ibid
71 Ibid
72 Kapur. Anup Chand, *op.cit.*, p. 321.
73 Ferguson, John, H. and McHenry, Dean, E., *op. cit.*, p. 321.
74 Vishnoo Bhagwan & Vidya Bhusan, *op. cit.*, p. 39.

hostility from the side of the Senate. Thus, he can, for instance, enter into 'executive agreements' with foreign countries. "Executive agreements are pledges of certain action by executives of two countries."[75] The US President can enter into agreements with chief executives of the foreign nations without the consent of Senate. For instance, Gentlemen's Agreement between President Theodore Roosevelt and the Emperor of Japan can be cited as an example in this regard.[76]

Besides, the President maintains his official contacts with foreign nations through his Secretary of State. At many occasions, he himself attends the summit conferences where chief of states meet for direct consultation. Thus, President Woodrow Wilson headed the American delegation "...to the Paris Conference at the end of World War I; President Franklin D. Roosevelt met with Allied leaders during World War II; and every president since then has sat down with world leaders to discuss economic and political issues and to reach bilateral and multilateral relations."[77] Along with this, the US President safeguards the interests of foreigners in America and the Americans abroad through his Departments of State and Defense. Thus, the observation of Ferguson and McHenry seems true that like the military affairs the President dominates the field of foreign relations also.[78]

4. Appointments

The US President enjoys the power to appoint several federal officials to key administrative positions. This power of appointment of the President is of paramount significance because "through it the President commands the allegiance of a great number of Federal officers and secures the support of many national legislatures for his programme."[79] These appointments basically fall under two broad categories -appointments that need ratification by the Senate and others which do not. In the earlier category the President appoints the Secretaries of the executive departments, judges of the Supreme Court, military officials, ambassadors and other diplomatic officials, members of various Bureaus, Boards and Commissions and other officers of the United State. These officials are appointed on the patronage basis and factually involve the prominent party leaders and those who helped the President in winning the election. Such appointments are usually made for a period of four years and need to be ratified by the Senate and to that extent the power of appointment of these officials is limited. However, in case, the party to which the President belongs enjoys majority in the Senate, his power of making these appointments becomes almost absolute. In any case, usually, except some controversial cases, the Senate extends its confirmation to the appointments made by the President. "Over the years, the Senators have used their right of approving appointments to produce a co-operative appointment power with the President"[80] In the second category the President appoints civil servants strictly according to the civil service rules and in such appointments the Senate's approval is not required. In this category appointments are based on ability and experience of the candidates. "In 2003, more than 3000 executive agency

---

75 Ferguson, John, H. and McHenry, Dean, E., *op. cit.*, p. 322.
76 Kapur, Anup Chand, *op. cit.*, p. 273.
77 http://en_wikipedia.Org./wiki/president_of_the_United_states #Executive_powers
78 Ferguson & Mc Henry, *op. cit.*, p. 321. 19.
79 *Ibid*, p. 318.
80 White, Robert, *op. cit.*, p. 196.

positions were subject to presidential appointment, with more than 1200 requiring Senate approval."[81]

5. Power of Removal

The US Constitution clearly highlights that the President can appoint Federal officials with the consent of the Senate but as far as their removal is concerned, it is completely silent. Thus, it is not clear whether the President has the power to remove an officer and in case he possesses this power, he can exercise it with or without the consent of the Senate. In this context the critics are of the opinion that if the consent of the Senate is essential while appointing an officer then why it should not be compulsorily at the time of removal. In this regard Congress has made two attempts in 1867 and 1876 to exercise a check over the power of removal of the President.[82] But the Supreme Court made these efforts futile in the *Meyers case* and made it clear that the President can remove the officials without the consent of the Senate.[83] Hence the *Meyers* verdict made the power of the removal of Federal officials of the President unqualified. Consequently, today, the President enjoys unlimited removal powers except with regard to (i) judges of the Federal courts (who can only be removed through impeachment), (ii) members of the various Boards and Commissions and (iii) the employees/officials appointed under Civil Service Rules.[84]

6. Management of Financial Affairs

In the US, theoretically, the Congress controls the finances of the nation but in actual practice it is the President who enjoys significant powers regarding the management of financial powers. Through the budget, the President ultimately regulates the entire machinery of administration and thus ensures his supervision and control over administration. He maintains his direct control and supervision over the financial matters through his staff agency viz., the Office of Management and Budget (OMB). The OMB is responsible for managing the financial affairs of the nation under the direction and control of the President. As an expert agency, it prepares the budget, which is presented before the Congress for being approved. The Congress enjoys the power to amend it. In fact, the Congress enjoys greater powers in comparison to the Parliaments of India and Britain as later can only reduce the budget proposals placed before them to be approved whereas the former can both increase and decrease the budgetary proposals placed before it for being approved. However, usually, the budget presented before the Congress is approved as such. This is because the budget is prepared by a specialized agency and technical in nature, so most the Congressmen, who are laymen in financial matters, are not able to understand its intricacies and technicalities.[85] Moreover, in the event of the party to which the President belongs, is enjoying majority in the Congress, the budget proposals are ratified by the Congress without any problem.

---

81 http://en *wikipedia. Org./wiki/president_of_the_* United_ states # Executive_powers
82 Vishnoo Bhagwan & Vidya Bhusan, *op. cit.,* p. 41.
83 Goyal O.P., *op cit.,* p. 218.
84 Kapur, Anup Chand, *op. cit.,* p. 320.
85 Vishnoo Bhagwan & Vidya Bhusan, *op. cit.,* p. 46.

Judicial Powers

Like the Indian President, the US President also enjoys certain judiciary powers. Thus, for instance, like the Indian President who appoints the judges of the Supreme Court and High Courts, the US President appoints the judges of the Federal courts. However, unlike the Indian President who makes these appointments on the recommendations of the Council of Ministers, the power of appointing judges of the Federal courts of the US President are real. Again like the Indian President, the President is also constitutionally empowered to grant pardon and reprieves to those convicted by the Federal courts. Thus through these powers he can affect the decisions of the Federal Courts. A Pardon generally provides immunity to the convict from all charges leveled against him against the breach of federal laws. "A pardon declares that the person pardoned is innocent of the crime, and it generally restores all rights which are lost to convicts."[86] The scope of his pardoning power is quite extensive as he can pardon any convict except one convicted by impeachment. A reprieve simply means the suspension or postponement of penalties awarded to a person. The President grants it usually on humanitarian grounds. The President even enjoys the power to grant amnesty. An amnesty is granted to a group of offenders. For instance, Jefferson provided amnesty to all those who were convicted under the Alien and Sedition Acts of 1789.[87] However, whereas the Indian President, being the constitutional head, possesses these powers only theoretically, the US President exercises these powers in reality.

Position

From the above, it becomes obvious that the US President enjoys a central place in the American administration. Being the real head of the State and government, he enjoys a great deal of real and effective powers which make his position really very strong. While some of these powers like power of appointment, power to veto Congressional bills, power to negotiate treaties, the right to pardon etc., have been bestowed upon him by the Constitution itself, others have been devolved to him by the Congress and the courts. The devolution of powers by the Congress and the courts have been rendered essential by the circumstances. The Congress made an addition to his powers and contributed significantly in enhancing them through its statutes. The judicial interpretations also contributed in further accumulating his powers by assigning all such powers to the President where the Constitution is silent. Again the emergent situations in American scenario from time to time like Great Economic Depression of 1930s, World War II and the Cold War between the USA and the former Soviet Union for a long period further proved significant in enhancing his powers enormously. The recent changes at the global level viz., the emergence of a uni-polar world due to the collapse of the erstwhile Soviet Union have further made his position stronger at the global level.

Unlike the countries having parliamentary form of government like Britain and India, where there exists a difference between the head of the State and the head of the government, the two positions are clubbed together in the US and there the President is both the head of the State and the head of the government. In the earlier

---

86 White, Robert, *op. cit.*, p. 203.
87 Ferguson & Mc Henry, *op. cit.*, p. 323.

capacity he is a symbol of the State, so his presence is inevitable on a number of ceremonial occasions like receiving and congratulating scientists, inventors and authors, lightening the Christmas tree, commending the Red Cross, endorsing the Boys Scouts, opening of fairs, tunnels, and bridges etc.[88] In this capacity, he also represents the State at national and international levels. As head of the government, he serves in several capacities and thus has to discharge a number of responsibilities. As chief administrator, he maintains his direct control and supervision over the executive departments and other agencies involved in the management of administrative affairs. He is the custodian of the rights and properties of the citizens who look to him for safeguarding their interests. As the chief manager of the national economy, he is solely responsible for the management of economic affairs of the country and safeguard American economic interests at international level. Thus, he mobilizes public opinion, influences economic development and organizes government. In military and foreign affairs, his authority is also quite extensive particularly in the conduct of war and in negotiating treaties with foreign nations. Hence in both the capacities - as head of the State and as head of the government - the President enjoys a significant position.

There is also a significant difference between the Indian and British Prime Ministers and the US President. Thus, whereas the formers are elected from a particular parliamentary constituency and later on, by dint of being chosen the leader of the majority/largest political party in the lower house, are sworn in as prime ministers, the US President is elected not from a particular constituency and in fact, fights the election for the Presidency. His election is almost direct and all the voters caste their votes in the presidential elections in his name. In this way, the position of the US President is relatively stronger in comparison to the Indian and British Prime Ministers. Thus, he is the pivot of the American politics. He is the chief leader of the Party, the position that he gained through election on party lines. Thus, he is actively involved in party politics. He guides and directs the party men in formulating policies and programmes of the party. He is the chief of the party both inside and outside the Congress. Thus, his overall position in the party is very strong and his contacts with the fellow party men in the Congress are very intimate. He enters into a lot of bargaining with them. Resultantly, he maintains his hold in the Congress and in this way influences several legislative proposals. "Under the impact of the rise of the modern welfare state, the Congress is also compelled to delegate to the President the power to legislate and such delegation is very large in times of emergencies."[89] Besides, the US President is the chief spokesman of the nation and the leader of the 'free world.' He leads the nation at national and international levels and thus reveals the "real sentiment and purpose of the country." [90] He speaks on the behalf of his nation so his voice is considered as the voice of the American people. In recent times he has really emerged as the leader of the free world. In fact, in the uni-polar world headed by the US, the position of the US President is so strong that his statements are keenly observed throughout

---

88 Johnson, Claudius et. al., *American National Government*, New York: Thomas Y. Crowell Company, 1964, p. 418.
89 Goyal, O.P., *op. cit.*, p. 223.
90 Johnson, Claudius et. al., *op. cit.*, pp. 420-21.

the world. It is mainly because of the fact that today, "the economic and military power of USA has increased the position of US President in international politics also significantly because he is the chief formulator of US foreign policy, whether one likes or not, has become very important in world affairs today."[91] In modern times, the US President enjoys hegemony not only in America but also on most of the nations of the world. It can be aptly remarked that "... politically the President is certainly the most important power in Washington and, furthermore, is often one of the most famous and influential Americans even outside that city."[92] It is mainly because of his this position that even the election of the US President is very keenly observed not only by the American people but by the whole world.

Recently, the media and press have further played a significant role in raising his influence and position at the national as well as international levels. The speeches delivered by the President at the national and international platforms directly telecast/broadcast and reach the people throughout the world. He can be directly heard on radio and television. It even brought the US Presidents into the homes of not only the millions of Americans but also to the innumerable people across the globe. Hence the media also contributed a lot in making his position more strong and making him a global figure.

However, there are no two opinions that the personal qualities and traits and the circumstances contribute a great deal in making the chief executive of a country relatively strong and weak. Thus, like the British Prime Ministers, there have been several strong and weak Presidents in the US also and this has been attributed to their respective personal qualities and the circumstances under which they worked. The Presidents with dynamic personalities in the US history like Theodore Roosevelt, Woodrow Wilson, Cleveland Jackson, Franklin D. Roosevelt etc. contributed significantly in raising the position and influence of this office, whereas the weak personalities like Hoover, William Taft, Warren Harding, Calvin Coolidge etc. could not establish their effectiveness particularly in party affairs and in the rest of the managements.[93] In nutshell, it may be concluded: "much of the President's authority accrues by virtue of factors beyond the formal powers. Prestige, as chief representative of the American people and as leader of his political party, makes him a strong leader, if he chooses the role and has the personal qualities to fill it."[94]

VICE-PRESIDENT

The US Constitution also makes provision for the office of the Vice-President. The qualifications to hold this office are equivalent to those of the President. He is the first successors in the line of presidential succession. In case of vacancy to the office of the President, the Vice-President holds the office of the President. "Eight Vice-Presidents have assumed the Presidency upon the death of the President, and one upon the President's resignation."[95]

---

91 Narang, A.S., *Comparative Government and Politics*, New Delhi: Gitanjali Publishing House, 1999, p. 139.
92 http://en_wikipedia. Org./wiki/president_of_the_United_states # Constraints_on_Presidential_power.
93 Ferguson & Mc Henry, *op. cit.*, p. 328.
94 Ferguson, John, H. and Mchenry, Dean, E., *The American Federal Government*, (8th edition), New York: McGraw- Hill, Inc. 1965, p. 308.
95 http://en. Wikipedia. Org/wiki/VicePresident_of_the_United_States_of_America.

The mode of election to this office is similar to that of the President. Formally, the vice-presidential candidate is nominated by the party convention. He is elected by the presidential electors. After the ratification of twelfth (Constitution) Amendment, the presidential electors cast two ballots - one for the presidential candidate and another for the vice-presidential candidate. A vice-presidential candidate gaining absolute majority of total votes becomes the Vice-President. If no candidate gains absolute majority, then the senate elects one out of the two candidates (securing highest scores) as Vice President.[96] Unlike the President, the Constitution does not specify an oath of office for the Vice-President. "Since 1974, the official residence of the Vice-President and his family has been Number One Observatory Circle, on the grounds of the United States Naval Observatory in Washington, DC."[97] Prior to the ratification of the twenty-fifth (Constitution) Amendment, there was no provision to fill the vacancy created to the office of Vice-President either due to resignation or death of the existing Vice-President. Resultantly, the office remained vacant till the next presidential elections. However, after the ratification of this Amendment, the Vice-President has to be nominated by the President in such circumstances. Thus, section 2 of the 25th Amendment provides that whenever there is a vacancy in the office of the Vice-President, "...the President shall nominate a Vice-President who shall take office upon confirmation by a majority vote of both Houses of Congress.' Gerald Ford was the first Vice-President selected by this method, after the resignation of Spiro Agnew in 1974; after succeeding to the Presidency, Ford nominated Nelson Rockefeller as Vice-President."[98]

It is customary for the presidential candidate to suggest some names for the vice-presidential candidate by keeping in view the geographic or ideological balance. The Constitution also restricts that both a presidential and vice-presidential candidates should not belong to the same state. "In practice, this requirement is easily circumvented by having the candidate for Vice-President change the state of residency as was done by Dick Cheney who changed his legal residency from Texas to Wyoming in order to run for election as Vice President alongside George W. Bush."[99]

Role of the Vice-President

Constitutionally, the role of the Vice-President in America is not very much significant. He performs only a limited number of functions which are as under-

Firstly, the Vice-President acts as the president of the US Senate. Being its president, he can't influence the working of Senate in the passage of legislations. Constitutionally, he is restricted from voting except in case of ties. Thus, he enjoys only the casting vote in case of deadlock in the Senate. For instance, recently, in 2001, "... as the Senators were divided 50-50 between Republicans and Democrats and thus Dick Cheney's casting vote gave the Republicans the Senate majority."[100] Generally, the Vice-President does not chair the meetings of the Senate and the Senate chooses a president *pro tempore* to work in this capacity in his absence.[101]

96 Vishnoo Bhagwan & Vidya Bhusan, *op. cit.*, p. 56.
97 http://en. Wikipedia. Org/wiki/Vice President_of_the United_States_of_America
98 *Ibid*
99 *Ibid*
100 *Ibid*
101 *Ibid*

Secondly, he succeeds to the office of the President in case of vacancy to this office. The permanent vacancy may be caused due to the death/resignation of the President, or due to his removal through the process of impeachment. The vacancy may be an outcome of his disability due to illness or on some other grounds. In this case the nature of vacancy would be temporary. In USA, two instances can be cited when the vice-president acts as the Acting President till the removal of the presidential disability. First when Ronald Reagon underwent surgery to remove cancerous polyps from his colon in July, 1965 and secondly when George W. Bush underwent a colonoscopy procedure requiring sedation.[102]

Thirdly, he presides over the counting process of the ballots of the electoral college on 6th January of the year following the election year, in the presence of both Houses of Congress and declare the results for the presidential and vice-presidential candidates. "In this capacity, only four Vice-Presidents have been able to announce their own election to the presidency: John Adams, Thomas Jefferson, Martin Van Buren and George H.W. Bush."[103]

From the above it is obvious that the position of the Vice-President in the US is uninfluential. It is because his office has not been assigned any significant role to perform. "John Adams, the first Vice-President, described it as "the most insignificant office that ever the invention of man contrived or his imagination conceived."[104] Some other occupants of this office also have similar kinds of observations with regard to this office. "Roosevelt called it as an office unique in its functions or rather in its "lack of functions".... Wilson described the position of the Vice-President as "one of anomalous insignificance and curious uncertainty." President Roosevelt once opined that he would rather be a professor of History than Vice-President."[105] However, in recent years this office has attracted some attention particularly after the initiative taken by President Roosevelt. "In 1933, President Franklin D. Roosevelt raised the stature of the office by renewing the practice of inviting the Vice-President to cabinet meetings, which has been maintained by every President since."[106] In 1941, he even incorporated Henry Wallace, the then Vice-President in his cabinet. The successive Presidents like Eisenhower also contributed in enhancing the influence of this office. "Once elected, President Eisenhower raised the stature of the vice-presidency further when he ordered Vice-President Nixon to preside at Cabinet meetings in his absence."[107] By keeping in view the necessity of knowledge regarding national security issues, the US Congress made the Vice-President one of four statutory members of the National Security Council in 1949.[108] Since 1949, the Vice-President has been working as a member of the National Security Council. In addition to this, recently the other functions of the holders of this office are "... as a spokesperson for the administration's policy, as an adviser to the President, and as a symbol of American concern or support. Their influence in this role depends almost entirely

---

102 Ibid
103 Ibid
104 Ibid
105 Vishnoo Bhagwan & Vidya Bhusan, *op. cit.*, p. 57.
106 http://en.Wikipedia.Org/wiki/Vice_President_of_the_United_States_of_America.
107 Ibid
108 Ibid

on the characteristics of the particular administration. Cheney, for instance, is widely regarded as one of George W. closest confidantes."[109]

President's Cabinet

The Cabinet constitutes an integral part of the executive branch in the US federal government. It consists of all the heads of federal executive department. Originally, it was found lacking in the Constitution. In the US, it came into existence, with the creation of some departments of the federal government by the US Congress for the management of governmental affairs. Each department was kept under the charge of a Secretary and the Presidents over the years started taking consultations with them. These Secretaries, heads of the respective executive departments, along with the US Vice-President constitute the 'President's Cabinet'. At present there are 15 Secretaries of the various executive departments. The US President is, although, independent in the selection of the heads of the executive departments, yet he has to keep into view a number of considerations like, position and influence of a person in the party, efforts to please some pressure groups and the expertise, competence and administrative abilities of a person etc. at the time of their selection.[110] Usually, the cabinet members are the former or current senators, representatives or the governors of US states or are the prominent members of their political parties. But due to the doctrine of 'separation of power' in USA no cabinet member can simultaneously hold an office in the Congress and Judiciary.[111] However, all these appointments made by the US President need approval of the Senate by a simple majority The cabinet members, being the appointees of the US President, acts as his mere subordinate. They enjoy office till the term of the President. They hold their office during his pleasure as he enjoys the power to remove them. Even the Congress can also remove them through the process of impeachment. But they are accountable only to the US President for their acts of omission and commission and not to the Congress. They attend the cabinet meetings that are usually held (once in a week) and participate in the discourse which is highly informal in nature. They can discuss any matter raised in the meeting but ultimately the will of the President prevails. They can only tender their advice to the President which may or may not be acceptable. However, it needs to be mentioned here that since the beginning of the President Roosevelt's period, the role of the US Cabinet declined substantially particularly in the field of policy making. It is mainly because the Presidents since than started operating through his Executive Office rather than the cabinet. At present, the non-cabinet members like the chief of White House, Director of the Office of the Management and Budget and the National Security Advisor play a dominant role in policy making and thus enjoy power more than some of the cabinet members.[112]

Federal Executive Departments

In the US, the federal executive departments are extended arms of the executive to discharge various line functions of the federal government. These departments generally came into existence by an Act of the Congress. The heads of these

---

109 *Ibid*
110 Goyal, O.P, *op. cit.*, p. 227
111 http://en. Wikipedia.Org/wiki/united_ states_cabinet.
112 *Ibid*

departments are appointed by the President with the consent of the Senate. Each Secretary, being the head of his department is responsible for managing the affairs of his department with the help of permanent staff of his department. "He has important duties in determining departmental policy, appointing and removing officers, and settling disputes and appeals."[113] At present there exists 15 federal executive departments in the US.

Other Executive Office Agencies

The Executive Office of the President consists of the immediate staff of the US President, in addition to the supporting staff (of multiple levels). The Executive Office has been gaining significance since the period of Franklin Roosevelt. Today this Office enjoys more powers in comparison to the President's Cabinet. Within the Executive Office of the President, there exist a number of bodies. A few of them are as under[114]:

- White House Chief of Staff
- White House Press Secretary
- United States Office of Management and Budget
- United States National Security Council
- United States Trade Representative
- Office of National Drug Control Policy
- Council of Economic Advisers
- Council of Environmental Quality
- Domestic Policy Council
- National Economic Council
- Office of Administration
- Office of Faith-Based and Community Initiatives
- Office of National AIDS Policy
- Office of National Drugs Control Policy
- Office of Science and Technology
- President's Critical Infrastructure Protection Board
- USA Freedom Corps
- White House Military Office

(C) LOCAL GOVERNMENT

The US is a federal country and its Constitution demarcates the jurisdiction of the Federal government and the states that are substantially independent from the Federal government in their internal working. Like India, local government in the US also falls within the purview of states and its relationship with the state government is unitary rather than federal. It is quite obvious from the tenth amendment of the US Constitution. Hence the determination of the structure, powers and functions of the local government units rests with the respective states. The legislatures of the states

---

113 Ferguson & Mc Henry, *op. cit.*, p. 317.
114 http://en.Wikipedia.Org/wiki/Executive_Office_of_the_President.

are quite independent in creating, modifying or even abolishing any unit of local government. Consequently, the local government units along with their powers and functions in different states bear hardly any uniformity; rather are characterized by a great deal of diversity. In this regard, Barthwal has rightly observed, "local units, such as counties, townships, municipalities, and special districts are organized in 50 different ways, because laws providing for their establishment and working derive primarily from the 50 state constitutions."[115] However, it needs to be mentioned here that despite the inherent diversities in the local government units in different states, they exhibit some fundamental alikeness.

Broadly, the US local government system can be categorized into two categories: the general-purpose local government system and the special-purpose local government system. In the first category are included those local government units which are established to perform some functions of common nature. Prominent among them are Counties and within them there exists some other such units i.e. Villages, towns, townships and cities, which discharge the assigned functions in their respective local area. According to US Census Bureau, there exist about 36000 general-purpose local government units below the county level.[116] The second categorization incorporates those local government units which are specifically established for a special purpose in a particular area. For instance, school districts, social services districts, transport districts and natural resources districts etc. The two types of local government units are discussed below in detail.

I. GENERAL-PURPOSE LOCAL GOVERNMENT UNITS

As is obvious, this categorization of local government system includes those local government units which are established in the broader interest of the public to discharge some functions that are highly general in nature. Amongst these general-purpose local government units, county is the top most and most prominent. All the states are first divided into counties. In the area of the county there are the cities"... which are important units of local government. Filling out the picture presented by the counties and cities are innumerable minor jurisdictions in which people find government operating so near to them as if were at their doorsteps. These minor units are towns, townships, villages and districts."[117] Each local government unit operating at a particular place is required to carry out some general nature functions. A brief description of the different general-purpose local government units is as under:

A. COUNTY

County is an important unit of US local government and finds its existence in almost all the US states except Connecticut and Rhode Island and in Washington, D.C. County in the US is a British legacy. A US county is a unit of local government which is smaller than a state but generally larger than a city or town. The actual term "county" describes them in 48 of the 50 states; Louisiana uses the term "parish" and Alaska uses the word "borough." Including them, "...there are 3,086 counties

---

115 Barthwal, C. P., *op. cit.*, p. 65.
116 *Ibid*, p. 67.
117 Nigam, S. R., *Local Government* (3rd ed), New Delhi: S. Chand & Company Pvt. Ltd., 1987, p. 148."

in the United States, an average of 62 counties per state. The state with the fewest counties is Delware (three), and the state with the most is Texas (254). In many states, counties are subdivided into townships or towns and may contain other independent, self-governing municipalities."[118] The population size of different counties varies from state to state. Some counties are overpopulated whereas others are scarcely populated. Los Angeles County in California is an example of the earlier category and Loving County in Texas is an example of the latter. Average population size of a county is around 67,000. It is interesting to note that in the US about 89 percent of the total population is served through counties.[119]

A county is governed through a central governing body which is popularly called County Board. The name and the composition of the governing body (County Board) vary from state to state. In some states namely New Jersey, New York, Michigan, Virginia etc., the membership of the board is large (varies between 40-50). It is because in these states, representation is provided to every town or township or a city ward falling within the jurisdiction of the county and one or more representative from each is accommodated. In contrast, the County Board is comparatively smaller in size (usually its membership is three) in those states where its members are directly elected by the voters of the county. Such kinds of boards are found in more than two-thirds of the US counties. However, in either case, the governing body is almost everywhere elective. The tenure of county boards in different states is also variable. In common practice, it varies between 2-4 years.[120] The county boards meet at the court house, headquarter of the respective county government.

The county board is presided over by a chairman or president who is usually elected by its members. However, in some states the county judge (or some other official designated for this purpose) may also act as ex-officio chairman. In either case, the chairman handles the overall business of the board. He not only presides over the board meetings but also enjoys the power to sign all official documents. He enjoys the right to vote on all county matters. Though he holds a prominent position and status in the management and administration of county affairs, his actual powers pertaining to county administration are relatively restricted. It is mainly because most of the county work is discharged through a number of committees that it maintains.

POWERS AND FUNCTIONS OF COUNTY BOARDS

The county boards carry out their administrative obligations in accordance with the constitutions of their respective states and the laws framed by them. The county boards are also governed by the special laws framed by the respective state legislatures with regard to them. Generally, these boards operate in dual capacities—firstly as the executor of state laws (being the agents of the state government) and secondly, promoter of the local nature services (for the general welfare of the county residents). Their powers and functions can broadly be categorized as - administrative, legislative and judicial. A brief description of these functions is as under.

A. Administrative - The county boards are primarily responsible for making appointments and to some extent the removal of the county personnel. Being the

---

118 http://wikipedia.org/wiki/ County_%28 United_States%29,
119 Barthwal, C. P., *op. cit.*, p. 67.
120 Nigam, S. R., *op. cit.*, p. 120.

custodian of the county property, like jails, hospitals, almshouse, court house etc; they also maintain their safety and security. These boards purchase and construct county buildings and lease them out. They make necessary arrangements for the construction and maintenance of highways, roads and bridges. They provide licenses for certain trades and occupations such as liquor selling, operating hotels and inns etc. They supervise and maintain control over the county's poor relief and other charitable works. They make necessary provisions for the fulfillment of the vacancies of the elective office-bearers.[121]

B. Legislative - In terms of legislative functions, the boards enjoy sufficient powers to frame byelaws for regulating the county business. Hence they are legally authorized to frame necessary rules and regulations pertaining to the county affairs. Moreover, since these boards are authorized to adopt budget, they can even levy taxes for all authorized county purposes, make appropriations and incur indebtedness.[122]

C. Judicial - The judicial functions of these county boards have been reduced and are not of much significance. Presently, only a semblance of these functions remains and institution of proceedings through their resolutions against their legislative and administrative actions may be included in this category.[123]

OTHER COUNTY OFFICIALS

In addition to the county boards, the constitutions of different states also provide for a number of elective offices for the management of county affairs. These offices though share responsibility with the county board but operate completely independent of its authority. In no way they are subordinate to the county boards. It is mainly because the holders of these offices in each county are also elected by the county voters. Prominent office bearers of these offices include: sheriff, prosecutor, county clerk, coroner, treasurer, auditor and tax assessor. A brief description of these elective officers is as under:

1. Sheriff - The Sheriff in a county is the insignia of the power of the state. He works as the chief police official and thus holds an important administrative position in the county. He is in charge of maintaining law and order and thus preserving peace in the county. His duties are to apprehend the debt defaulters and to execute the court orders in this regard. His tenure varies from state to state (between 2-4 years). "The sheriff is the custodian of the county jail, he summons witnesses, arrests indicted persons, sells the property of private persons for taxes of debt under judicial order and executes the processes of the courts."[124]

2. Prosecutor- Another important elective official in a county is the prosecutor. In some states he is designated as the county attorney. He is entrusted with the task of instituting and conducting criminal prosecutions. He renders legal advice to the county officials. In matters of civil cases, he represents the county. Thus, he plays a significant role with regards to the judicial processes of the county.

3. County Clerk - County clerk, usually, acts as the secretary to the county board in different states. He is mainly responsible for managing and regulating the affairs of

---
121 Ibid, pp. 120-21.
122 Barthwal, C. P., *op. cit.*, p. 74.
123 Ibid, p. 75.
124 Ibid, pp. 72-73.

the county board meetings. He issues notices for inviting such meetings, notes their minutes and maintains the necessary record of their proceedings. He is the custodian and storehouse of the county records. He acts as a vehicle of communication in two ways - between the county and the state government and between the county board and county residents. He is also charged with the responsibility of conducting free and fair county poll. He is also the superintendent of the courthouse and holds the responsibility of its upkeep.[125]

4. *Coroner* - The coroner is generally charged with the responsibility of up-keeping and maintaining the records of those who had died either due to any sort of violence or under some suspicious circumstances. He may or may not be trained in the science of medicine. It is because it is not an essential qualification for this elective office. There has been a lot of hue and cry to abolish this office in some of the states arguing that the duties of this office should be assigned to an appointed medical examiner.[126]

5. *Treasurer* - The treasurer as its name implies is the custodian of all county funds. He holds the responsibility of collecting the county taxes.

6. *Auditor* - Scrutiny of the county accounts which is an important task is assigned to the auditor. In this connection, he not only holds the responsibility of preparing a periodical statement of finances but also issues warrants on the treasury.[127]

7. *Tax Assessor* - The tax assessor has been assigned the task of enlisting all taxpayers in the county. He is charged with the responsibility of not only assessing the value of property possessed by the county inhabitants but also levying of taxes accordingly.[128]

In addition to these elective offices the county boards also appoint the professional staff on merit considerations, to run the county business smoothly. These professionals include - health directors, inspectors of weight and measures, probation officers, welfare superintendents etc.

B. CITIES

The area of each county is further divisible into a number of cities which constitute another important unit of local government in the US. On an average over 19,000 cities are found in all the US states. Though the cities vary in terms of their population yet the population size in most of them is less than 75,000.[129] In the US, the cities are prominent units of local government because majority of the US population resides in them. For governance purposes, there exist three main plans (types) of city government viz., mayor-council plan, the commission plan and the council-manager plan, in the various US states. These three plans of city governance differ from each other in terms of their relations between executive and legislature. A brief description of these governance plans is as under:

1. MAYOR-COUNCIL PLAN

It is the most popular and the oldest kind of city government and is found in smaller as well as larger US cities. As its name symbolizes, it consists of mainly two

---
125 Nigam, S. R., *op. cit.*, p. 122
126 *Ibid*
127 Barthwal C. P, *op. cit.*, p. 73.
128 *Ibid*, p. 74.
129 *Ibid*, p. 74.

bodies - mayor and the council. These two organs of this plan of city governance are discussed below:

A. Mayor: In this city government plan, the mayor acts as the chief executive. In the US cities mainly two types of system with regard to the mayor are found in existence. In cities operating on the pattern of mayor-council plan, there exists either the weak mayor system or the strong mayor system. A brief of both is as under:

a) *Weak Mayor System* - The city councils in this system enjoy sufficient powers over the mayor, who generally acts as the formal head of the city administration. Being the formal head, he enjoys least powers in terms of his control over the city administration. Resultantly, his role is highly ceremonial in nature. His position is sufficiently weak with regards to the implementation of administrative policies. He enjoys least say in matters of appointments. He appoints the officials subject to the approval of the council. Resultantly, the officials hold their office at the council's pleasure. For administering the affairs of most of the city departments, there exist various boards and commissions, the member of which are either directly elected or elected by the council. The council enjoys the right to issue ordinances to direct the administrative working. The mayor can veto such ordinances. But in case of veto the council can override it by two-thirds majority.[130]

b) *Strong Mayor System* - In sharp contrast to the weak mayor system, there exists a strong mayor system in some US cities. In this system, the mayor operates as the actual head of the city administration with a weak council. He enjoys significant powers with regard to appointment of administrative officials of different departments. In matters of appointments council's ratification is not required. The officials carry out their administrative obligations under his direct supervision. He appoints the officials as per the civil service rules. All the administrative officials hold their office during his pleasure. He holds the responsibility of preparing the city's budget. The legislative business of the council is subject to his veto power that can only be overridden by 3/4 votes of the council.[131]

Tenure - The election of the mayor is direct and thus the city voters elect a person from amongst themselves as mayor. He is eligible for re-election. His tenure is not fixed in all cities and varies between 2 - 4 years in small and large cities respectively. However, he can be removed before the expiry of his tenure. Besides, he may also be legally disqualified by the judiciary. He is even liable to be removed by the State Governor on grounds of misbehaviour, breach of law, adoption of corrupt practices, neglect of duty etc.

Powers and Functions - The city mayor is responsible for carrying out legislative, executive and judicial functions. A brief description of his powers and functions is as under:

1. *Legislative* - The city mayor presides over the council meetings but it is not a common practice. He is empowered to convene special meetings of the city council.

---

130 Nigam, S.R., *op. cit.*, pp. 127-28.
131 *Ibid*, p. 129.

He enjoys the right to send messages to the council. Generally, the council gives due weightage to such messages. For the passage of some ordinances on some particular issues, he can send requisite recommendations to the council. The ordinances passed by the council need ratification by the mayor. He may either give his assent or veto them. He may even send them back to the council for reconsideration. His veto can be overridden if the council re-passes the ordinances by a two-thirds or three-fourths majority (as the case may be).[132]

2. *Executive Powers* - The mayor enjoys the power to appoint and remove certain important city officials. Through this power, he maintains his control over city administration. He can appoint and remove a number of city officials either with or without the consent of the council. He co-ordinates the essential public services in the city. He exercises supervision for the smooth enforcement of state laws and the local ordinances. He is also responsible for the preparation of annual city budget.[133]

3. *Judicial Powers* - In comparison to his earlier powers in the judicial sphere, his recent judicial powers have been largely curtailed due to the development of an independent court system over the years. However, "even now, he is usually a magistrate, and in some cities he exercises minor civil and criminal jurisdiction."[134] He also enjoys some powers of remitting fines and penalties of the defaulters of the city ordinances.

Position - The mayor acts as the figure head of the city. Being the fatherly figure of the city, he discharges a lot of social duties. He presides over various city functions organized locally and thus, represents the city at different occasions. He participates as well as addresses public gatherings of the city residents. He hears public complaints against the city administration and tries to redress them. "He knows very well that he is considered by many as *the father of all his people* who can ease every sorrow and right every wrong. So women come to him for help in solving their domestic problems and reformers come to him with the request to make everybody virtuous."[135] He welcomes the VIPs in the city. In modern times, a tendency is emerging in some of the US cities towards making his position comparatively stronger. In real sense, his position depends upon his personality and his power to take initiative. In addition to this his position is further strengthened depending upon his capability to win the confidence and support of the council.

B. The Council - In the council-mayor plan another important chamber is the council that constitutes its legislative wing. Prior to the 19th century, it enjoyed significant powers in the governance of US cities but during the nineteenth century its powers were significantly curtailed. Some of its powers were withdrawn by the state governments while others were handed over to the mayor and the different commissions and boards. But still this body has a significant place in the governance of the city. Today most of the cities have unicameral city councils.[136]

---

132 Barthwal C. P, *op. cit.*, pp. 85-86
133 Nigam S.R., *op. cit.*, p. 131
134 *Ibid*
135 *Ibid*, p. 132
136 *Ibid*, pp. 133.

Composition - The city councils have great variations in terms of their membership. Usually small councils are given preference in most of the US cities in order to promote prompt decision making. The members of these councils are elected through direct election by the city voters. In most of the US cities, the qualifications for the councillors are well prescribed. The members of different councils are elected for a varied period ranging between one to six years. Most of the cities are divisible into wards (also called districts) for election purposes. However, in some cities elections are held on city-wide basis. As per the charter, the city councils meet once a week usually in the evening to ensure maximum participation. A presiding officer who may either be elected by direct election or indirectly by the councillors chairs the council meetings. In some cities, the mayor serves as the presiding officer, being the ex-officio member of the council. The quorum of council meetings also varies from city to city. The mayor can even call a special session of the council either on his own initiative or on the request of a specific number of members.[137]

Powers - The city council draws its powers from the state laws. It has a direct concern for the effective city governance. It is mainly concerned with the responsibility of maintaining law and order in the city and plays a crucial role in the preservation of peace in the city. In this connection it enjoys the power to pass ordinances in accordance with the state laws. It also owns the responsibility with regards to the promotion of general welfare of the public. In other words, "the council may make, amend or repeal ordinances relating to health, parks, fire protection and buildings... The council may also make ordinances relating to beggars, vagrants, fighting and disorder in the streets, public amusements, intoxication, markets, gambling, bathing places, suppression of immorality, the use of fire-arms and firecrackers in the streets and so forth."[138]

In some cities it enjoys the power to initiate the budget while in others not. Usually the executive is required to seek its approval on budgetary matters. Thus, it exercises its control over the city administration through its power of budget authorization. "It can cut salaries and allowances; and by threatening officers with reductions, councillors can ensure the appointment of their friends and political supporters to posts in the city administration."[139] However, the financial powers of the council are limited to a greater extent. It is mainly because it can't make appropriations, levy taxes, and incur debts at its will. In this regard it has to operate in accordance with the provisions prescribed by the state laws or the charters. "As to taxation, the council may levy only those kinds of taxes which are authorized by the municipal charter. With regards to debts, it may be mentioned that it can incur debts only for specific purposes and up to the amount fixed by state laws."[140]

2. THE COMMISSION PLAN

The commission plan highlights another type of city government system in the US. It first came into existence in 1901. The disaster situation (fierce storm) of the Galveston city in Texas led to the emergence of this form of city government in

---
137 *Ibid*, pp. 133-34.
138 *Ibid*, p. 134.
139 *Ibid*, p. 135.
140 *Ibid*

America. It attained much popularity in the beginning of the 20th century. But later on its popularity declined substantially and now it is found in a few states viz., -Birmingham, Idaho, St. Paul, Kansas, North Dakota and Texas etc.

In this type of city, government powers are vested in a small body called commission. Its membership varies between 3 to 9 in different cities. However, in most of the US cities it consists of five members (also called commissioners). All the commissioners are elected through direct election. The tenure of these commissioners also ranges between 2-6 years. In some cities all the members of these commissions are elected at one time while in others they are elected at different intervals and thus retire accordingly[141]

The commissioners are responsible for the entire city management. They operate in twin capacities i.e. collectively they constitute the legislative wing of the city government while individually they act as heads of the departments of the city administration. In the earlier capacity, they approve ordinances for the better governance of the city whereas in the later capacity they bear the responsibility of managing the affairs of their respective departments. They can even appoint the personnel for various boards and commissions operating under them. They maintain supervision and control over the staff operating under them and issue necessary direction for the effective management of city affairs. In fact, a commissioner enjoys complete powers in connection with the department assigned to him.

The cities operating under this plan usually have five departments viz., public affairs; accounts and finance; public safety; street and public improvement; parks and property,[142] each under the charge of a commissioner. The names of these departments vary from city to city. In addition to this, these departments also differ in their scope/area of operation in different cities. In most of the cities, these departments are assigned to its members by the commission itself keeping in view their interest and ability. However, in some US cities, it is the city voters who elect commissioners for specific departments by a direct election.

Mayor - One of the commissioners is elected as the mayor of the commission. In some cities he is selected amongst the commissioners by themselves while in others the city voters elect him by direct voting. Usually, he is the head of public affairs department. He calls the commission meetings and chairs them. However, he does not enjoy overriding powers over his colleagues. His legislative and executive powers are almost equal to his colleagues. For instance, he can't veto the bills passed by the commission. Moreover, his powers regarding appointment also correspond with those of his colleagues. Thus, his position and status are not better than that of his colleagues. His basic role is to maintain co-ordination in the operational working of his colleagues. However, being the nominal head of the city, he enjoys some influence that differentiates his position from that of his colleagues.[143]

3. THE CITY-MANAGER PLAN

It is the third type of city government found in the US. It is considered as an improvement over the commission plan. In this type of city government there

---

141 *Ibid*, pp. 137-38.
142 Barthwal C. P., *op. cit*, p. 9.
143 Nigam S.R., *op. cit.*, p. 139.

exists a professional officer, called the city manager who is entrusted with the task of effective and smooth city governance. In the first decade of 19th century it was first introduced in a city named Staunton in the state of Virginia. Later on it was adopted by another city named Dayton in Ohio in the year 1914. This plan gained currency over the years and was adopted by a number of other US cities.[144] In fact, this city government consists of following three actors: the council, the mayor and the city manager. A brief discussion of these is as under:

The Council - In the city-manager plan, the council constitutes the legislative wing. Its members are elected directly by the city voters whose number varies between three to five in most of the US cities that have adopted this plan. The term of its members also varies between two to four years. Being the legislative body, it is held responsible for managing the city affairs smoothly. It regulates the operational working of city administration through maintaining its general supervision. It lays down the requisite policies in different spheres, approves ordinances and regulates financial appropriations. "It levies taxes, votes appropriations, authorizes borrowings, grants franchises, creates and abolishes departments and investigates the financial transactions and other official acts of any official or department."[145] For the management of city's affairs it is accountable to the people. The most important function of the council is with regard to the selection of a competent person as the city manager. The council even enjoys the power to remove him.

The Mayor - Like the commission plan, the mayor in this plan is quite weak and acts as a nominal head. In most of the cities, he is elected by the council members from amongst themselves, but in some cites the voters directly elect him. He invites the council meetings and chairs them. He approves the council decisions but has no veto power. Being the formal head, he represents the city at ceremonial occasions. During emergency he may be entrusted with the task of maintaining peace. His remuneration exceeds in comparison to that of the other councillors.[146]

The City Manager - In this plan, the city manager is the most important functionary and occupies a vital position in the city administration. He is selected as the city manager by the members of the council. While selecting him to this post, the council pays a lot of attention towards the ability, training, personality and previous experiences of the person concerned. Usually the council selects such a person to this post who is technically sound particularly in the art of managing city affairs. He is a highly paid functionary in comparison to the other city officials. He is entrusted with the task of smooth and effective implementation of state laws and the ordinances passed by the city council. He is accountable to the council for his acts of omission and commission. The council can oust him from his post. Thus, he holds his office during its pleasure.

In the administrative field, the manager operates as the kingpin of city administration. He holds the power of appointment and removal of the personnel and the heads of various city departments. He is entrusted with the task of good governance of the city's administration. Thus, he maintains effective co-ordination

---

144 *Ibid*, p. 141.
145 *Ibid*, p. 143.
146 *Ibid*

among the different city departments. In fact, the entire city administration operates under his direct supervision and control. He enjoys all powers to direct the various administrative branches and their staff. He is also entrusted with the responsibility of preparing various development plans and the city budget and puts such proposals before the council for its consideration. He enjoys the right to attend the council meetings to explain and defend his proposals.[147]

For the success of this form of government, the city manager is supposed to win the confidence of the council. Its efficiency mainly depends upon the adequate understanding and mutual trust between the two. Both of them should work together in a harmonious and cordial relationship. The manager should keep in view his limitations that he is merely a servant of the council and work during its pleasure, while at the same time the council should avoid unnecessary interference in his operational working. "His problems compound when he finds that a policy action which is good for the city is opposed by members partly on political considerations and partly because being laymen, they can not understand its real importance. The council-manager form does not provide a satisfactory solution to such situation."[148]

C. TOWNS AND TOWNSHIPS

In addition to the cities, there exists a number of town and townships as the units of local government, within counties of different US states. Such local government units operate within a confined area and thus their jurisdiction is comparatively small. Being at the doorstep, these bodies work in close association with the common people. In all, more than sixteen thousand towns and townships are found in all the US counties. In terms of their population size they have great variations. Almost 50 of these towns and township have a population less than 1000 whereas 4 of them have a population of 2, 50,000.[149]

TOWNS - The area of counties in six New England States viz., Maine, Vermont, New Hampshire, Massachusetts, Connecticut and Rhode Island is further divisible into towns. The town government in the US symbolizes direct democracy. It is because towns in the US are governed through open town meetings consisting of all the registered town voters. To a large extent it is unique and indigenous in nature. Unlike cities, towns in the US do not have individual charters. They receive powers under the general grant of legislative powers by the state. They enjoy legal status and thus "... they can sue and be sued, levy taxes, borrow money and pass ordinances for the good government of the locality... They exercise control over police, water supply, roads and bridges, parks and gardens, hospitals, libraries and markets." [150] Like the county government, the government of these towns also operates in dual capacity—firstly, as the agent of the state and central government and in this capacity it is responsible for "... assessing and collecting certain taxes and enforcing health regulations and so forth."[151] Secondly, it is entrusted with the task of managing local affairs.

---

147 *Ibid*, pp. 143-44.
148 Barthwal C. P, *op. cit.*, p. 97.
149 *Ibid*, p. 77.
150 Nigam S.R., *op. cit.*, pp. 148-49
151 *Ibid*, p. 149,

Town Meetings: As is obvious, town government operates through the town meetings, which consists of all the registered voters of the town. Such towns operate on the lines of direct democracy. Generally, a town meeting is held once in a year in the town hall. However, if inevitable, a special town meeting can also be convened. To ensure the wider participation, an agenda (containing all the issues to be discussed in the meeting) is prepared and widely circulated. The town meetings are evidence to considerable discussion on items mentioned in the agenda. It is mainly because all the powers pertaining to the management of town affairs are vested in it. Here every town voter enjoys the opportunity to have a direct voice in all town matters. Such meetings ensure the participation of every citizen in the enactment of byelaws (relating to police, public buildings, water supply, gas, electricity, highways etc.), appraisal of reports of various town offices, levy and collection of taxes, budgetary discussion and electing town officials.[152]

Unlike the smaller towns, the towns having comparatively higher population, operate on the lines of indirect democracy. It is because in these towns it is rather difficult to call town meetings of all voters. Resultantly, in such towns in place of town meetings, meetings of their representatives are convened. Such towns are divided into various divisions/wards for selecting one or more representative.

Executive body: In the town meeting the city voters select a governing body also known as the body of selectmen. It is entrusted with the task of managing the town affairs. It usually consists of three to five members selected for a period ranging between 1-3 years. However, the selectmen enjoy long tenures mainly because they are eligible for re-election. The town voters generally prefer to re-elect the earlier selectmen at the time of election because of their experience. The selectmen are responsible for smooth governance of administrative affairs of the town and discharge several functions. For instance, they maintain supervision and control over the administrative officials, construct and maintain town roads and safeguard the town property. They issue licenses to different authorities and enter into contracts with a number of bodies. They also make necessary arrangements for holding town meetings and conducting elections. To discharge these functions the selectmen meet regularly.[153]

Like the counties, in town also, besides the selectmen, there exists a number of other administrative officials viz., town clerk, treasurer, assessor, road commissioner, members of school board etc. for managing the town affairs. These officials aid and assist the selectmen in carrying out their administrative obligations. These officials are also selected by the town voters in the town meetings. The town clerk is the chief administrator of the town, who is usually elected for two years. Like the selectmen, he also enjoys a long tenure. He is also re-elected by the town voters time and again. He has the responsibility of noting the minutes of the town meetings and maintains the necessary records of their proceedings. Besides, he also discharges the responsibility of the registrar of marriages and deaths. The treasurer holds the responsibility of tax collection. The assessor is entrusted with the task of assessing the value of state and private property for taxation. The road commissioner has to construct and maintain the town roads and highways.[154] Most of the town functionaries, being honorary

---

152 *Ibid*, p. 161.
153 *Ibid*, pp. 161-62.
154 Barthwal, C. P., *op. cit.*, pp. 78-79.

(as most of them work on part time basis), receive some fees in lieu of the work performed by them.

TOWNSHIPS - The idea of townships is basically rooted in the early part of US history and its remnants can be traced in the 17th century. During this period the early American settlers established townships on the analogy of rural England. Today townships are found in about sixteen US states, prominent among which are Illinois, Indiana, Kansas, North Dakota, Minnesota, Michigan, Ohio and Pennsylvania.[155] "Township is an artificial creation. Usually, it has an area of six square miles. It has very little relationship to community life."[156] The township government operates on behalf of the state and thus enjoys such powers that are handed over to it by the state. Thus, it is responsible for the implementation of laws passed by the state. It may asses and collects taxes on behalf of the state. Along with this, it discharges functions of local nature like establishing parks, libraries and maintenance of hospitals, fire fighting, street lighting etc.[157]

Township Meetings: In some states viz., New York, New Jersey, Illinois, Wisconsin, and Michigan etc., the townships operate through township meetings of all voters (somewhat like towns) while in others like Indiana, Iowa and Missouri etc., they are found non-existent. Here it needs to be pointed out that the authority and sanctity of township meetings are less in comparison to their counterparts in towns. It is mainly because these meetings are thinly attended by the township voters.[158] "In many cases the township officers attend the meeting and take decisions in the name of whole body." [159]

Township Boards: To govern the affairs of townships, there exists a township board as provided by the state laws. Its name differs from state to state. Usually, it comprises of three members who are generally elected. The tenures of its members range between 2-4 years in different states. The powers of these boards are assigned to them by their respective states. Resultantly, these boards differ in terms of their powers from state to state. The board, generally, enjoys more powers in those states where the township meetings are found absent. These boards are required to discharge a number of functions in a township. Usually they have been entrusted with the task of laying down policy, enactment of by-laws, election of township officers, authorization of borrowings and levying of taxes.[160]

Like the towns, there exist several elected officers like chief township officer, township clerk, treasurer, and assessor to assist the township boards. The chief township officer is the kingpin of the township administration. He is entrusted with responsibility of managing the entire township affairs. He is branded with different names like supervisor, trustee or town chairman in different states. Township clerk acts in the capacity of secretary to the township meeting and thus owns the responsibility of maintaining the records of their proceedings. In fact, he is the repository of all records and documents of the township. The treasurer is concerned

---

155 *Ibid*, p. 79.
156 Nigam S.R., *op. cit.*, p. 150.
157 *Ibid*, 151.
158 *Ibid*, p. 150.
159 *Ibid*, pp. 150-51.
160 *Ibid*

with the collection of township revenue. The assessor assesses the property of the township for taxation purposes.[161]

D. VILLAGES/BOROUGHS

In some US states there exist villages or boroughs. In the Midwest and Northwest states, they are known as villages whereas in Connecticut, New Jersey, Pennsylvania and other Eastern States they are called boroughs. Unlike the Indian village, the US village or borough can be compared with the town area-committee or notified area committee of the pre-74th (Constitution) Amendment Act era. The number of such local units in the US is more than 10,000.[162] In the US, "when a rural area becomes semi-urbanized due to the establishment of some industry or due to any other cause, it demands that it be organized into a separate local government unit so that it may have new public services, such as fire-protection, streets paving, lighting and water supply."[163] By keeping in view such demands the state legislature may make-necessary provisions in this regard under law. But before taking such move the state legislature requires that "... the question of incorporation be approved by a popular referendum."[164] Generally, the population of these local units is comparatively low.

To govern and manage the affairs of this local government unit, there exists a small governing body, called village board. Its members are directly elected by the village voters and usually their number ranges from five to seven. The term of its members varies between one to two years. It is headed by a chief executive generally called president. In various states the board members are known by different names such as trustees in New York, assessors in Maine, commissioners in New Hampshire, burgesses in Connecticut etc.[165] The village board is entrusted with the responsibility of managing local finances, streets construction, street lighting, maintaining public buildings and maintenance of law and order. To assist the board in discharging its duties, there also exist a number of other officials at the village level. They include a village clerk, a treasurer, assessors, school officers, overseers, a constable and a police magistrate who acts as justice of peace.[166]

II. SPECIAL PURPOSE LOCAL GOVERNMENT UNITS

In order to have a complete view of the US local government system, it is rather essential to mention the special districts (comparatively new comers) in this field and created to discharge some specific functions. The origin of such districts is basically rooted in meeting the specific requirements of a particular area. These districts are usually named after the function they discharge. For instance, there exists a number of such districts popularly known as school districts, fire-fighting districts etc. They are usually found in existence across the country involving rural and urban areas.[167] They can be created on the initiative of people of that area. The procedure is that "...a certain percent of voters should petition the county board for the creation of

---

161 Barthwal. C. P., *op. cit.*, pp. 80-81.
162 *Ibid*, p. 81.
163 Nigam, S.R., *op.cit.*, pp. 151-52.
164 *Ibid*, p. 152.
165 *Ibid*
166 Barthwal.C. P., *op. cit.*, p. 82.
167 Nigam, S.R., *op. cit.*, pp. 151-52.

a special district. The county board itself may decide the petition or may submit it to the direct vote of the people. If the decision is favourable, a special district is established as a quasi-municipal corporation."[168] These special districts in the US vary in terms of their numbers and types.

In comparison to the other districts, the school districts are more important due to the nature of function discharged by them. They are found almost in all the US states with few exceptions. In all, there exists near about 16,000 school districts in the US. In addition to them, there exist about 30000 other special districts for discharging other specific functions. They may be categorized as natural resources districts; fire protection districts; urban water supply districts; housing and community districts; sewerage districts; park and recreation districts, hospital districts, library districts; health districts and airport districts etc.[169]

A small body that consists of directors or commissioners governs these special districts. Generally, the voters of these districts directly elect them but in some cases the state or county authority designates them. These officials generally work in honorary capacity. The district governing body enjoys legal status, thus can hire and fire its personnel. It can sue and be sued. It can also raise money by way of imposing taxes. For realizing its specific goals, it can take such steps that are required by law.[170]

(D) CONTROL OVER ADMINISTRATION

The modern democratic systems have witnessed a phenomenal increase in the scope of functions of the State the world-over. These added responsibilities are generally discharged by the administration. However, since authority and responsibility are commensurate, it has led to the increase in the powers of the administrative functionaries. But it is equally true that power corrupts and when absolute, absolutely. Thus, this increase in powers of the administrative functionaries has increased the possibilities of their misuse thereby highlighting the necessity of devising proper and adequate control mechanism. However, experience in several countries revealed that any single method of controlling the administrative functionaries has proved futile, a number of alternative control mechanisms have been devised in most of the countries and America is no exception to it. In fact, "...in comparison with many other countries, controls over administration in the United States are exerted through an unusually large number of channels...". The various control mechanisms pressed into service to control the US administration include the Congressional control, the Presidential control, the judicial control, control by the Press and Media etc. These control mechanisms are detailed below:

A. Congressional Control: The Parliament in any democratic country, being the representative organization of the people, has got a natural right and moral responsibility to exercise control over the administration. Thus, like all other democratic countries, the Congress in the US also discharges this responsibility. In fact, the US Congress is the "... most potent source of control, because of its constitutional grants

---

168 *Ibid*, p. 153.
169 Barthwal. C. P., *op. cit.*, p. 101.
170 Nigam, S.R., *op. cit.*, pp. 153-54.

of power, which include direct participation in a variety of administrative matters. Congress through legislation must authorize governmental programs, determine the organizational arrangements for implementation, and decide on the amounts and methods for funding. It has wide ranging investigative and audit powers to insure that administrative performance conforms to legislative intent. Congress has the weapon at its disposal to be the ultimate winner in a prolonged conflict with the chief executive as to the conduct of administration." In this way, it is an instrument in exercising effective control over the administration. Generally, it adopts the following measures in this context:

1. *Control through Policy Making and Framing of Rules and Regulations:* The administration of any country has to operate within the precincts laid down by their respective legislatures. The administration in the US is also obliged to operate within the arena defined by the Congress. The US Congress, being the legislative body, makes policy and enacts laws and statues to govern the administrative affairs. These legal instruments are important weapons in the hands of the Congress to control the administration as they limit the boundaries of administrative actions and operations. Besides laying down the parameters within which the administration has to operate, the administrative actions are also subject to Congressional discussion and scrutiny.

2. *Control through Budget:* Budget is an important instrument in the hands of the legislature to exercise control over administration in a democratic country. By enacting the budget, the legislature defines the limits or scope of activities of the administration as finance is the lifeblood of administration. Thus, the Congress in the US, like the Indian and British parliaments holds the key of administrative activities. In this regard, however, it is important to note that the US Congress possesses even greater powers in so far as budget enactment is concerned as it can both increase and decrease the budgetary proposals. Besides this, some additional provisions in any item of expenditure of any department can be suggested by the Congress.[171]

    In USA, the budget is prepared by the Office of Management and Budget (OMB), a staff agency of the US President, but is approved by the Congress. The executive can spend no money without the approval of the Congress. Thus, most of the administrative actions are regulated and controlled by the legislature due its control over purse string of the nation.

3. *Debate over the Message Sent by the President:* In the countries having parliamentary form of government, the executive is part of the legislature and participates in the legislative proceedings. The relationship between the two is so intimate that most of the legislative and policy proposals emanate from the executive. However, in countries having the presidential form of government, due to the doctrine of separation of powers, there is no direct relationship between the executive and the legislature. Thus, in these countries the executive does not get any opportunity to initiate any legislative or policy proposals and these are the sole prerogatives of the legislature. The most the executive can do is to send

---

[171] Chaturvedi, T.N., *Comparative Public Administration*, New Delhi: Research Publications, 1999, p. 169.

messages to the legislature to enact laws on the issues which it deems essential. Consequently, the US President can also send messages to the Congress in case he wishes to get some law of his choice enacted. He can also personally appear in the Congress to present such a message. However, the Congress is free to respond the way it likes to such a message of the President. In other words, the Congress enjoys the power to reject the presidential recommendations. In case the Congress wishes to honour the presidential message, the recommendation is referred to an appropriate committee of the Congress for the purpose of introducing legislation. Such messages are also given wider publicity through newspapers to generate a nationwide debate on the policies of the government. The Congress thoroughly debates and discusses the legislative proposals introduced in the light of such messages before passing them in the form of laws.

4. *Approval of Appointments and Treaties:* The US Constitution empowers the President to make appointments on several key administrative positions. For instance, he appoints the Secretaries of the executive departments, judges of the Supreme Court, military officials, ambassadors and other diplomatic officials, members of various Bureaus, Boards and Commissions and other officers of the United States. However, these appointments are subject to the approval of the Senate. This means the Senate enjoys the right to withhold its approval to these appointments. Similarly, though the President can make treaties and enter into agreements with foreign countries. However, these treaties are also subject to ratification by the Senate. The power of ratification by the Senate is an effective instrument of control over the administration.

5. *Control through Committees:* The US Congress constitutes a number of committees to effectively discharge its functions. There are two types of committees - Standing Committees and Select Committees. The earlier are permanently established Committees, which are set up at the beginning of every Congress whereas the later are temporary committees, established by the House or Senate to study particular problems. These committees are described as the eyes, the ears, the hands, and very often the brain of the House. Most of the congressional work including making scrutiny of administrative actions is carried through these committees. In fact, "administrative oversight is carried out mainly through the mechanism of legislative committees with limited jurisdictions and with members who are likely to be proponents and defenders of the programs under review."[172] These committees infuse the sense of answerability in the administration. These committees in USA are well equipped to consider measures referred to them. In addition to making recommendations on legislation, the Standing Committees scrutinize administration of laws by the executive branch of the government and thus serve as a potent measure of control over administration.

6. *Control through the Process of Impeachment:* Power of impeachment of key administrative functionaries, including the chief executive, is a very effective instrument in the hands of the legislature in a democratic country. Thus, for instance, in India, the Parliament enjoys the power to impeach the President, the judges of the Supreme Court and the High Courts, the Chairman and Members

---

172 Heady, Ferrel, *The United States* in Rowat, Donald C, *op. cit.*, p. 414.

of the Public Service Commissions, the Comptroller and Auditor General of India etc. This power of the legislature keeps the administrative functionaries on their toes. Similarly, the US Constitution has also empowered the Congress to impeach several key administrative functionaries including the President. Through this power, the Congress gets an opportunity to scrutinize the actions and deeds of the erring administrative officials. The power of impeachment of the Congress serves as a source of control over the administration.

7. *Control by Comptroller General:* In USA, there is no system of prior financial approval to proposals. Generally the pre-audit in USA is conducted within the executive branch. The post audit takes place after payments. The basic aim behind post audit is to check the judgment made by the responsible officer. In the US the Comptroller-General is responsible for all sorts of auditing. He is also required to approve the accounting reforms introduced by the Account General.[173]

B. Presidential Control: Whereas the Congress exercises the external control over the administration, the President, being the chief executive, exercises internal control over the administration. The chief measures adopted by the President for exercising control over the administration are the following:

1. *Control through Appointments and Removal:* The US President exercises his control over administration through the power of making appointments. He is constitutionally empowered to appoint several key administrative functionaries with the approval of the Senate and Junior Federal Services in accordance with the civil service rules. "The power of making appointments is the most important and effective power in the hands of the President. It enables the President to command the allegiance of a huge number of federal officers and secure their support for implementation of his policy."[174] Thus, the President exercises a close watch over the federal employees to streamline the administrative functioning. Besides, he also enjoys unlimited removal powers of the administrative functionaries (in case of misbehaviour, misdeeds, bribery or any other corrupt practices on their part) except with regard to judges of the Federal courts (who can only be removed through impeachment), members of the various Boards and Commissions and the employees/officials appointed under Civil Service Rules, cannot be removed by the President.[175] The powers of appointment and removal of the President act as a great deterrent for the administration.

2. *Control through Budget:* Although the control regarding federal finance is vested in the Congress yet in actual practice, it is the US President who directs and controls the finances. He is considered as the financial manager of the government. He exercises this control through the instrument of budget –both before and after its passage. In the US, the budget is prepared by the Office of Management and Budget (OMB) - which is a staff agency of the President and is responsible to him. It acts on the basis of broad guidelines issued by him. The spending departments submit their estimates to OMB, which scrutinizes these proposals and makes the financial sanctions to them in the light of the guidelines issued

---

173 Chaturvedi, T.N., *op. cit.,* pp. 165-66.
174 Bhagwan, Vishnoo and Vidya Bhushan, *op. cit.,* p. 40.
175 Kapur, Anup Chand, *op. cit.,* p. 320.

by the President. In this way, the President exercises an effective pre-budget control over the administration through OMB.

After the passage of the budget by the Congress, the OMB ensures that the work is completed with economy. In this regard it also issues relevant guidelines (for effecting economies) on behalf of the President. In this way, OMB is an important instrument of the US President which not only formulates and presents the budget to the Congress annually but also ensures its smooth execution after being enacted by the Congress. "OMB is thus undoubtedly the most effective tool available to the president for obtaining information about and exercising supervisory controls over administrative agencies, within the discretionary boundaries set jointly by Congress and the President through a legislative process."[176]

3. *Controls through Administrative Enquires and Investigations:* The President and his executive heads of respective departments can exercise their control on the administration through administrative enquiries and investigations against those who misuse their authority, make misappropriations, adopt corrupt practices or have committed serious mistakes in administration. Such administrative enquiries may be conducted by the enquiry committees constituted by the executive heads or the President. If the case warrants so, the matter may also be referred to the specialized federal level agencies like Federal Bureau of Investigation (FBI), Central Intelligence Agency (CIA) etc. These federal agencies after conducting these investigations sent their report to the President to take appropriate action.

4. *Hierarchical Controls:* Another important means of presidential control over administration is the control through administrative hierarchies and the relationships within them. The US President is elected directly by the people and he appoints secretaries as the heads of various departments who operate directly under him. Internally, each department has an undersecretary and several assistant secretaries to assist the executive head of the department. In each department, the assistant secretary is in charge of a division, a section or a bureau (as the case may be) and a number of career civil servant and lower administrative functionaries operate under him. All these functionaries are interlinked in a hierarchy of superior-subordinate relationship. In this administrative hierarchy, each functionary working at the lower echelon is responsible and accountable to his superior and through him to the chief executive. "Accountability through executive hierarchical channels is pervasive and important in the American presidential system..."[177] Highlighting the significance of President's control over administration through hierarchical channels, Simon, Smithburg and Thompson have observed that if the executive at apex level who is a peoples representative "... can hire and fire his first-line lieutenants, if they can hire and fire their immediate subordinates, and so forth, then the values in administrative decisions will come from the people and flow down this line of command, always enforce on those below by threat of the sanction of dismissal." [178] In that case

---

176 Heady, Ferrel, "The United States"' in Rowat, Donald C, *op. cit.,* p. 401
177 Ibid p.414
178 Simon, Herbert, Donald W. Smithburg and Victor A. Thompson, *Public Administration,* New York: Alfred A. Knopf, 1954, p. 532.

the administrative officials working at various levels will be responsible and accountable to each higher hierarchical level in turn and ultimately to the chief executive.

5. *Control through Delegated Legislation:* The US President also exercises his control over administration through the practice of delegated legislation. Due to the paucity of time with the Congress, it passes laws in a skeleton form and authorizes the President to fulfill the details. In other words, the legislative powers are delegated to the President by the Congress, who frames rules and regulations in the form of executive orders. These executive orders have the equal force of law. In this way, the US President enjoys legislative powers and thus governs and directs the behavior of the administrative functionaries.

C. Judicial Control: The US judiciary enjoys sufficient power of judicial review. The Federal judiciary is the chief interpreter of the Constitution. It acts as the custodian of the Constitution and fundamental rights of the US citizens. It is empowered to review any policy or decision of administration if it is not in consonance with the provisions of the Constitution. If some administrative decision is found inconsistent with law or the Constitution then the judiciary can declare it ultra virus. "The judicial role is enhanced by the well established doctrine that courts in the United States have ultimate authority for constitutional interpretation and by a more activist stance in recent decades towards intervention in matters which have been dealt with by administrative action."[179] Unlike the Continental European nations, the administrative courts in America are non-existent. The US Federal judiciary examines the administrative actions on the following grounds:

1. *Official Jurisdiction:* The administrative officials have to carry out their duties within a specified jurisdiction. If they exercise their powers beyond the defined jurisdiction, their acts, actions or decision, can be challenged in the court of law. On examination, if the court found so, it can ask for a review or it can declare those acts or decisions null and void.

2. *Misuse of Authority:* The administrative officials may utilize their authority to take some personal revenge. Such cases are challengeable in the judiciary. The judges try to define in precise terms what legal authority has been allotted to the erring official and take some punitive action against the guilty.

3. *Examination of Facts:* The US judiciary also examines the factual basis of the administrative decisions due to its power of judicial review. If the decisions are found devoid of facts or having factual inadequacies then the judiciary is empowered to ask the administration to either change such decisions or withdraw them.

4. *Procedural Violations:* The judiciary in the US can even scrutinize the procedures followed by the administration in carrying out its numerous tasks. It tries to find out whether the procedure adopted by the administration is appropriate or not. Any kind of procedural violation can create a serious obligation to bring changes in the administrative policies and decisions.

5. *Control over the Arbitrariness of Administration:* The US judiciary also has the power to determine whether a given action or a class of actions is within law

---

179 Heady, Ferrel, *The United States* in Rowat, Donald C, *op. cit.*, p. 414.

or not. Thus, it exercises a check on the arbitrary actions of the administrative functionaries. Such kind of arbitrariness invites punishments from the courts.

In this way in the USA "...judicial activism can put a stop to administrative abuse of discretion, mandate administrative action when it has been illegally avoided, and protect the rights of underprivileged groups without other means of redress."[180] Thus, judicial control is the most rapidly expanding source of external control over the administration in the US.[181]

D. Control by the Electorate: The electorates who are the makers of a democratic form of government play their significant role in exercising control over the administration. Since the US is an advanced system of democracy, so the electorates are more conscious about their rights and the administrative obligations. Moreover, politically the people are mature enough to check the arbitrariness of the administrative functionaries. Resultantly, any violation of procedure, excesses of power, or non-fulfillment of responsibilities become the subject of popular criticism. Further, the people in the US are highly organized in the form of pressure groups, professional organizations, trade unions and exert considerable influence over the administration. They fight for their rights and against the mal-administrative practices. In this way, the people in the US maintain vigilant check over actions of administrative officials and thus serve as an effective instrument of control over administration.

---

180 *Ibid*, p. 414.
181 *Ibid*

8
ADMINISTRATIVE SYSTEM OF FRANCE

France had experienced great political turbulence since the French Revolution. It had adopted three monarchic, two dictatorial, three imperial and four republican constitutions. Ultimately; the constitution of the Fifth Republic was approved by public referendum on September 28, 1958. The Parliament in France is bicameral, with a National Assembly (577 members) and a Senate (321 members). The members of the National Assembly are directly elected to 5-year terms whereas Senators are chosen by an electoral college for a period of 6 years, with one-half of the Senate being renewed after every 3 years. The French constitution provides for Parliament with restricted and limited powers. It can legislate only on those items which are defined in the Constitution. The National Assembly is the principal legislative body. The Senate's legislative powers are limited and the National Assembly has the last word in the event of a disagreement between the two houses. Quasi-Presidential & Quasi Parliamentary form of government has been established which has a strong President as head of State who is directly elected by people for five years. The Prime minister who is the head of the government is an appointee of the President. The council of ministers is nominated by the president on the recommendations of the prime minister. Prime Minister and members of the council of ministers though are not the members of the Parliament but are responsible to it. A distinctive feature of the French judicial system is the existence of the Constitutional Council which examines legislations and decides whether it conforms to the constitution and it also considers legislations before they are promulgated. The Council particularly protects basic rights when they might be potentially violated by new laws. There is a Council of State to protect basic rights against the administrative action of the state. The bureaucracy in France is a classic example of the Webberian model. The higher civil servants are selected through *Ecole National de Administration* (ENA) on the basis of merit. Unlike UK and India, the civil servants of France enjoy a lot of political rights. They are also conferred with the right to strike. Having a unitary system, France has been characterized by highly centralized decision making, with each of France's department headed by a prefect appointed by the central government. In 1982, the national government passed a legislation to decentralize authority by giving a wide range of administrative and fiscal powers to local elected officials. The French local administration consists of territorial institutions freely governed by councils that are directly elected by the people. For governance purpose France is divisible into small, administratively manageable units that extended up to village. The present structure of local government has now three main levels of decentralized institutions.

In the present chapter an endeavour has been made to discuss *the salient features of administration, political executive, local government and control machinery of* France in detail.

(A) ADMINISTRATIVE FEATURES

France has passed through various political upheavals and most of these upheavals have been violent. Thus since the French Revolution of 1789, "... France has been a constitutional monarchy three times, an empire twice, a semi dictatorship once, and a republic five times, with most of the transitions taking place as the result of violence."[1] Obviously, this resulted in discontinuity in polity and at times even political vacuum during the intervening periods. During the periods of instability, political direction was wanting and offered opportunities to the administrative apparatus in France to usurp powers and act arbitrarily. Moreover, even after taking over, the new regimes required some time to establish their control over the politico-administrative system and during this period also the administrative machine was rendered direction-less; in fact, it could have misled the political powers that be, at such times. It is interesting to note, however, that despite all these turmoil, "... the administrative apparatus that had been created to serve the *ancient regime* transferred and maintained its allegiance to the nation, after the brief interruption of the Revolution late in the eighteenth century, whether its government took the form of empire or republic."[2] In the above background, following are the main features of the French administration:

1. Dual Executive: Ordinarily, the executive powers in a democratic country are vested in one institution or office. Thus, in the US all executive powers are constitutionally vested in presidency. Even in countries having parliamentary form of government such as India and Great Britain, though constitutionally there are two executives but the real executive powers are exercised by the prime minister along with the council of ministers and the other - president or the monarch - act as only the constitutional head. The Constitution of the Fifth Republic though provides for parliamentary form of government yet contrary to the widely prevalent practice, confers upon both the President and the Prime Minister wide executive powers. Though the Constitution-formally vests the two functionaries with different powers by stating that the President will be the "supreme arbiter of the state" and the government, which "shall determine and direct the policy of the nation" (Art. 20), the government's operation is directed by the Prime Minister (Art. 21).[3] Thus, constitutionally, the President is regarded as the guardian of the nation and the Prime Minister with his cabinet looks after the governmental working where the President enjoys sufficient powers to intervene. But this division of powers between the two functionaries is plagued by vagueness. Machin has also observed that the French Constitution is silent in deciding who should rule France, the President or the Prime Minister and his cabinet. According to him, "... the Prime Minister is 'in general charge of the work of the government', which 'direct the policy of the nation' and is answerable to Parliament, it is the President - not chosen by Parliament - who appoints the Prime Minister, can dissolve the National Assembly (the lower house) and holds other

---

1 Heady, Ferrel, Public Administration: A Comparative Perspective (6th edition), New York: Marcel Dekker Inc., 2001, p. 193.
2 *Ibid*
3 Neumann, G. Robert, *European Government* (4th ed), New York: MC Graw Book Company, 1968, p. 295.

powers essential to the functioning of the government."[4] The text thus provides for the creation of a dual executive where both the President and the Prime Minister and his government enjoy real powers but the government is still responsible to the Parliament. However, though this unclarity in the relationship between the President and the Prime Minister is likely to generate problems in their working and this is also likely to have negative repercussions on the administration. But interestingly, this dualism in administration has not led to generate any serious conflicts. "Since 1958, there have never been any fundamental clashes between the President of the Republic and his Prime Minister, the representative of the parliamentary majority."[5]

2. Conflict of Legitimacies: In addition to the conflicting position of the President and the Prime Minister, France exhibits several conflicting tendencies at the administrative level. Thus, for instance, in addition to the inter and intra ministerial conflicts, several conflicts exist between the generalists and specialists, between senior and junior civil servants as well as between those posted in the field and at the headquarters. According to Machin, these conflicts are reflected at three levels: conflicts among the ministries, between ministries and the inter-ministerial agencies and the intra-ministerial conflicts. The first type of conflicts are an outcome of the inter-ministerial collaboration required in different policy areas. For instance every year there is a bitter struggle between spending ministries like Education, Health and Agriculture and the Budget Ministry over the issue of their continuously growing demands for more money and the reduction of public expenditure by the latter. Likewise, the Ministry of Interior has frequent conflicts with the Ministry of Justice over the issue of Public Order. The second type of conflict invariably arises between ministries and inter-ministerial agencies. For instance, excessive legalism emphasized by the council of state and the 'book-keeping mentality' of the court of accounts and the financial inspectorate are widely resented. Thirdly, the internal organization of the ministries is another source of disputes. Conflicts inescapably arise between the various divisions of each ministry, between the various corps in which senior administrator are grouped, between 'specialist' and 'generalist corps, between senior and junior civil servants and between those in headquarter and those in the fields.[6] Though most of these conflicts exist in the administration in general and, in fact, the administration of no country is altogether free from them, but in France these are more 'acute and permanent.' Consequently, "the French administration bears more resemblance to a battlefield than to an army and the competing forces constantly seek the support of allies in society or elsewhere within the state."[7] This definitely has a bearing on the French administration.

3. Centralized Administration: Historically, 'centralization was a natural instinct for all kings of France.' In fact, considering the geography of France, it was, to an extent, a political compulsion since France had several diverse provinces thereby giving it a 'fragile national fabric,' which was sought to be compensated by creating

---

4 Machin, Howard, "France" in Ridley, F.F., *Government and Administration in Western Europe (ed.)*, Oxford: Martin Robertson & Co. Ltd., 1979, p. 75.
5 Meny, Yves, "France" in Rowat, Donald C, *Public Administration in Developed Democracies: A Comparative Study (ed)*, New York: Marcel Dekker, Inc., 1988, p. 275.
6 Machin, Howard, "France" in Ridley, F.F., *op. cit.*, p. 74.
7 *Ibid*

a centralized administrative set-up. Accordingly, the powers of the 'feudal nobility and provincial representative assemblies' were considerably curtailed. Besides, the control of all 'local administrative and financial questions' was concentrated in the hands of royal officials (the *Intendants*).[8] The 1789 Revolution brought a hope of reversal of this tendency of centralization but situation hardly underwent any change. Rather the post-Revolution France exhibited a tendency towards more centralization under the Jacobins and later under Napoleon. "Their faith that popular sovereignty was indivisible - that the general will could only be articulated through one central national representative agency - led to a concentration of all political powers in Paris..."[9]

The tendency towards centralization was also an outcome of the recurrent political discontinuities in France. During the preceding two centuries, France has experienced violent political instability with every successive political regime having different political orientations. For an effective control over the country, every successive regime preferred centralization of powers. The insistence on centralization was so strong that even the local self government was replaced by the local administration. "Even minute problem of local government must frequently be decided on a Central level, and the Central government empresses many functions, which in other countries are partly exercised by other levels of government partly left to private agencies."[10]

But during the early 1970s, in France a tendency towards decentralization started emerging. Actually the process of decentralization of the administrative power began in 1968 itself and it gained impetus during the mid-1970s. The Administrative Reforms Committee of the French National Assembly advocated decentralization of powers. Resultantly, some reforms were introduced in March, 1982, in the direction of decentralization. The Law of March, 1982, succeeded in introducing several changes relating to finance. "Any transfer of state competence to a local authority must be accompanied by a transfer of resources (chiefly fiscal). In practice, local taxes have tended to rise. The reform also extended the responsibilities of the communal, departmental and regional accountants, giving them the status of chief accountant directly responsible to the Treasury."[11] Besides, it assigned the responsibility for a posteriori auditing of local authority accounts to a new court called regional audit chamber. However, while commenting on the process of decentralization, Yves Meny has observed, it seems that a "marble cake model" is replacing a "layer cake model." "This means that decision-making process are becoming more complex even more cumbersome, but also more democratic. The reform of the local financial system, however, has been disappointing, and financial transfers from the State cannot be considered as an adequate substitute."[12] In a nutshell, of late, France has demonstrated an urge towards decentralization of powers and some scanty efforts have also been made in this direction but the situation has not altogether be different from the earlier one as most of the politico-administrative decisions are still taken by the government in Paris and the field agencies are required to implement them with little discretion to make amendments in them.

---

8   *Ibid*, p. 71.
9   *Ibid*
10 Robert G. Neumann, *op. cit.*, p. 309.
11 Meny, Yves, "France" in Rowat, Donald C., *op. cit.*, p. 309.
12 http://www.ambafrance-au.org/article.Php3?Id.article=445.

4. Unitary Administration: Like Britain, the administrative system in France is unitary in character as constitutionally all the powers and authority is vested in the Central government. Though France is divided into 26 regions (which may be compared to the Indian or the US states), these are not constitutional entities, rather are created by the Central government for administrative convenience. The regions have been conferred powers not by the Constitution but by the Central government which may withdraw these powers at will; the central authority may even rename them, redraw their boundaries and even abolish any of them at will. Each region has an elected regional council to perform functions of executive nature bestowed by the Central government. These councils are responsible for the management of regional affairs. The members of each regional council elect one person amongst them as its President, who acts as its chief executive and presides over its meetings. The president of the regional council operates in dual capacities - as the head of the regional administration and as the agent of the Central government. "Regions do not have legislative autonomy, nor can they issue regulations. They do levy taxes (or, rather, the national government gives them a portion of the taxes it levies) and have sizeable, though not considerable budgets."[13]

Though the Parliament in France is bicameral and consists of the National Assembly and the Senate but the bicameral character is not symbolic of the federal character of the country. All the laws for the whole of France are enacted by the Parliament and the regional councils possess no legislative authority. The laws enacted by the Parliament are effective in the whole of France.

5. Autonomous Civil Services: Traditionally, the bureaucracy in France enjoyed more powers mainly because France remained a victim of recurring political crisis and instability. This discontinuity in French politics led to the dependence of political executive on bureaucracy. The conflicting tendencies of republicanism and monarchy further contributed to this phenomenon.[14] Resultantly, wide powers came to be vested in the French bureaucracy. In France, the bureaucrats are viewed as public officials rather than as public servants. They enjoy an important position in French administration and society and wield great powers. They play an active and crucial role in public policy making.[15]

French civil service is a career Service, ordinarily chosen early in life and continued to retirement. Thus they enjoy security of tenure on a lifetime basis. In addition the French civil servants also enjoy a high degree of respect and status in the society. They are the highly paid functionaries and enjoy comprehensive fringe benefits including family allowances, various social security programmes, and generous retirement pensions.[16] Moreover, they are protected from lawsuits arising from their official functions, because the government is responsible for their acts, except those committed in a strictly personal capacity.[17] Though the supervision of the civil

---

13 http://en. Wikipedia. Org/wiki/ List_of_Region_of_France.
14 This is because during the last over two centuries (since the French Revolution of 1789) France has oscillated between republicanism and monarchy several times.
15 *Public Administration: A Comparative Perspective (6th ed)*, New York: Marcel Decker, Inc., 2001, p. 204.
16 *Ibid*, p. 197.
17 Neumann G. Robert *op. cit.*, p. 309.

servants is handed over to a Minister or Secretary of State yet the Minister or the French government does not ordinarily interfere with the operations of the service and thus there is little political interference from the top.[18] A salient characteristic of the French civil services is that they are divided into corps, "...which may themselves be divided into ranks *(grades)* (called *classes* in certain corps). Corps are grouped in four categories named A to D, in decreasing order of educational knowledge theoretically required... Each corps has a set of possible job or task descriptions and may have its own particular statutes."[19] The civil servants in France also enjoy the right to organize trade unions, the formal recognition of which was given by the Civil Service Statute of 1946. The relationship between the State and civil servants has been more clearly defined in recent years. The civil service union movement has grown markedly in the post-War period and strikes by civil servants have become commonplace.[20] Besides, the civil servants in France unlike those of India or England also enjoy a lot of political freedom. They are almost free to join political parties and take part freely in party politics. French civil servants may become candidates "...for elective office, and may serve in most local offices without giving up active duty, but if they run and are elected to the national legislature they must go on inactive status during the term of service, with a right to return later."[21]

6. Increased Role of State in Planning: The emergence of the concept of welfare state at the turn of the 19th century had implications for the entire Europe and America. Thus, what was earlier regarded to be a private affair of an individual came to be recognized as the responsibility of the State thereby increasing the scope of activity of government and administration. France also did not remain unaffected by this phenomenon and demonstrated phenomenal increase in State activity. In addition to this, there have been two other reasons which necessitated State intervention and control economic activity in France. These were: the three major wars (1870-71, 1914-18 and 1939-45) and the 'increased demand for full employment, economic growth and welfare service.'[22] Along with this growing State intervention, a desire towards planning was also discernible. Consequently, during the first half of the previous century, there has been significant advancement towards nationalization of several activities including the education banks. "The Provisional Government (1944-1946) nationalized many key sectors of French economy, established national health and social security systems, created structures for medium term economic planning and controlled prices and credit for day-to-day economic management."[23]

Thus, by the time the Fifth Republic was established, the State intervention into the economic activity had gained considerable momentum and it "... inherited not only a huge administrative machine, an enormous public sector and a vast armoury of powers for economic control, but also a tradition that the state should play a positive and all-pervasive role in society."[24] Achievements of the planned economy

---

18 Ibid, p. 309.
19 http://en.wikipedia.org/wiki/French_Civil_Services
20 *Ibid*, p. 197-98
21 Heady, Ferrel, *op. cit.*, p. 198
22 Machin, Howard, "France" in Ridley, F.F., *op. cit.*, p. 70.
23 Ibid
24 Ibid

received kudos not only from the Communists and socialists but also from the Christian Democrats and General De Gaulle himself. The successors of De Gaulle have continued with the planned economic model.

7. Influence of Technology: In French administrative system, the technocrats are influential and they are even conferred some powers in administrative decision-making. In fact, "the French system traditionally gives equal prestige, influence and rewards to both 'technical' and 'administrative' corps. It also posts some senior civil servants into the departments, whilst in some ministries certain posts are reserved for specific corps."[25] However, due to this simultaneous authorization of the bureaucracy and technocracy, the French administration is plagued by conflict between them.[26] However, the importance attached to the technocracy in France has resulted in the 'technologisation of administration.'

8. Increasing Interaction between Administration and Pressure Groups: Like most of the other developed countries, the pressure groups in France have been active and politically important since long. It is mainly because the level of political consciousness of the French people is relatively high. There are the customary professional organizations of farmers, of small and medium sized enterprises, veteran's organizations, labour unions etc.[27] which genuinely influence administrative decision-making process. The pressure groups enjoy a respectable place, both at the political and social level and are even capable of influencing an administrative system which is often labeled as 'authoritarian.'[28] Machin has observed that French administration operates in a symbiotic relationship with the interest groups. Resultantly, every branch of administration operates in close co-operation with its client interest groups. These groups not only pressurize the administration for providing better services to these groups but also befitted the administration through their continuous advice. In turn, the state is dependent on them for their expertise. In practice, representatives of interest group continuously "... advise and watch administrative activities through a vast network of committee and commissions. Over four thousand of these committees are attached to the ministries in Paris, whilst even in a small department the Prefect has to deal with a hundred or more local committees in which interest groups are represented."[29] In rural areas, farmers' associations play an influential role in this regard and often operate in close co-operation with the Prefect and the Ministry of Agriculture services. Thus, the pressure groups in France are very active and operate at both national and local level and the administration seeks to take all interests into account[30] while making decisions.

---

25 *Ibid*, pp. 74-75.
26 *Ibid*, p. 74.
27 Some Prominent interest groups are - National Council of French Employers (Council National du Patonat Francies, CNPF) a special organisation for small and medium business: the CNPME (Conseil National de Petits et Moyens Enterprises) which is important because of the very large number of small and medium sized business in France, National Federation of farm Syndicate (Federation national des Syndicates des Exploitants gricoles) National Teachers Federation (Federation de e'Education Nationale (EEN), uFEF (National Union of French Students - union Nationale ds Etudiants de France) etc. See Neuman G. Robert, *op. cit.*, p. 284-285.
28 Meny, Yves, "France" in Rowat, Donald C, *op. cit.*, p. 276.
29 Machin, Howard, "France" in Riddley F.F. *op.cit.*, p. 101-102
30 Meny, Yves, "France" in Rowat, Donald C, *op. cit.*, p. 276.

(B) POLITICAL EXECUTIVE

The chief executive of France is dual in character. It comprises of the President of the French Republic and the French Prime Minister. Unlike India where the President is titular head and the Prime Minister with the Council of Ministers is the real head, in France both the President and the Prime Minister are real heads and both enjoy actual powers. Besides, there is also provision for the constitution of the Council of Ministers by the President after consultation with the Prime Minister. These three functionaries viz. the President, the Prime Minister and the Council of Ministers are discussed in detail in the present section.

PRESIDENT: The French President is the real and elected head of French State. Officially he is known as the President of the French Republic. Four French Republics out of the five have had presidents as their head of State. Due to this fact the French Presidency is considered as oldest in Europe. However, the powers, functions and duties of this office during various Republics differed vastly. The modern day President enjoys enormous powers.[31]

Tenure: The French President is directly elected by the French people for a term of 5 years. Prior to 2001, it was 7 years. President Chirac was elected for the first time in 1995 for a period of 7 years and second time in 2002 for a period of 5 years. His term thus expired in 2007. The Constitution of Fifth Republic is silent regarding the eligibility of the President for re-election and the time limit for which he can serve.

Qualifications: The Constitution of Fifth Republic does not prescribe any specific qualification relating to age, sex or nationality of the presidential candidate. Any French citizen who has attained 18 years of age can be elected to this office. But in practice it is not so easy. It is because a person having a high level stature and high degree of repute at the national political level can only rise to such occasions.

Succession: In case of vacancy, the President of Senate succeeds to this office and serves as the interim President till the new incumbent holds this office. The vacancy to this office is generally created due to the death, resignation or incapacity of the President. The incapacity of the President needs the certification of the Constitutional Council. The interim President is usually restricted from taking crucial decisions. Alain Poher is the only person who served in this temporary capacity for two times — firstly, after the resignation of de Gaulle in 1969 and secondly, after the death of Pompidou in 1974.[32]

Impeachment: Article 68 of the Constitution of the Fifth Republic imposes a serious limitation on the President by introducing the process of impeachment. The French Parliament can oust him from his office through this process. However, the procedure of impeachment is not a simple one. It requires that, "he must be indicted only by the two houses of Parliament ruling by identical vote in open balloting and by an absolute majority of the members of the said houses."[33]

---

31 http://en. wikipedia. org / wiki / President_ of_ France
32 Ibid
33 Gupta Madan Gopal, *Government of the Fifth Republic of France*, Allahabad: Central Book Depot, 1963, p. 89.

POWERS: Like the US President, the election of the French President is direct. Thus being the representative of the people, he operates in the capacity of a real head. Resultantly, he enjoys enormous executive, legislative, judicial and emergency powers. A brief account of the powers of the French President is as under-

Executive Powers: Being the chief executive of the French State, he enjoys the following executive powers:

1. *Powers regarding Appointment and Removal*: The French President enjoys sufficient powers with regard to appointment and removal of the key administrative functionaries. He appoints the French Prime Minister and on his recommendations, the members of the Council of Ministers in accordance with article 8 of the Constitution of the Fifth Republic. He appoints ambassadors to foreign countries. He appoints the President of the Constitutional Council and also nominates its three members. He also nominates all the nine members of the High Council of the judiciary. Besides, he also appoints a number of other top civil and military officials. The French President further enjoys sufficient removal powers to control and regulate the behaviour of these administrative functionaries. He accepts the resignation of the Prime Minister and removes the members of the Council of Ministers on his recommendations. He can even remove the top administrative officials belonging to civil or military services.

2. *Powers pertaining to Foreign Affairs:* Unlike the presidents in many other European countries, the French President enjoys sufficient powers in the field of foreign policy especially with regards to ratification of international treatises and making the negotiation with foreign nations. All the treaties made by the government with foreign countries on a number of crucial issues need his ratification. He exerts a sizeable influence in these matters, both formally and due to the prevailing constitutional convention. In France, an important constitutional convention is that the President directs foreign policy, though he must work on that matter with the Minister of Foreign Affairs. According to article 52 of the Constitution, he is to be informed of all negotiation that leads to the conclusion of an international agreement not subject to ratification.[34] Besides, article 14 of the Constitution of the Fifth Republic provides that, "the President of the Republic shall accredit ambassadors and envoys extraordinary to foreign powers; foreign ambassadors and envoys extraordinary shall be accredited to him."[35]

3. *Power of Arbitration:* According to article 5 of the Constitution, he shall see that the Constitution is observed. He shall ensure, by his power of arbitration, the smooth functioning of the public authorities and the continuity of the State. He shall be the guarantor of national independence, territorial integrity and observance of national treaties. Thus the French President enjoys sufficient power of arbitration and if any conflict may arise with regard to any governmental affair, the French President is authorized to resolve it through this power. In such matters the decision of the President is final. Hence in French system it is the President who tries to remove all sorts of confusion in the governmental affairs if any.

---

34 Bhagwan, Vishnoo and Bhushan, Vidya, *op. cit.*, p. 20.
35 http://en.wikipedia/.org/wiki/President_of_France.

4. *Chairman of the Council of Ministers:* Unlike India and Britain- in France, the President presides over of the council of ministers. This provision is specifically made under article 9 of the Constitution of the Fifth Republic. He calls for the meetings of the Council of Ministers and conducts their business. He operates as their chairman. It is noteworthy that in these meetings, the Prime Minister sits as a member.

5. *Commander-in-Chief:* In military affairs the French President further enjoys a special position. According to article 15 of the Constitution of the Fifth Republic, he is the commander- in- chief of the armed forces. As such the French President is responsible for the defense of the nation. He appoints a number of military personnel at strategic positions. Being the commander- in- chief, he enjoys the right to preside over the higher level national defense councils and committees.

Legislative Powers: The legislative powers of the French President are sufficiently extensive. A brief description of his legislative powers is as under:

1. *Power to Promulgate Laws:* The French President enjoys the power to promulgate the laws passed by the Parliament. In other words, he is authorized constitutionally to sign all the acts passed by the French Parliament before they are published as officials. Article 10 of the Constitution of the Fifth Republic provides that, the President of the Republic shall "…promulgate Acts of Parliament within fifteen days following the final adoption of an Act and its transmission to the Government. He may, before the expiry of this time limit, ask Parliament to reconsider the Act or sections of the Act. Reconsideration shall not be refused."[36] Thus it is clear that when a bill passed by the Parliament is presented before the President in France, he has two options either to give his assent to the bill within 15 days or send it back to the Parliament for reconsideration. However, after its reconsideration if it is again passed by the Parliament, the French President has no option except to sign it. "The president has a very limited form of suspensive veto: when presented a law, he can request another reading of it by Parliament; but if the law is presented a second time, he has to sign it."[37] Prior to promulgation of a law he may refer it to the Constitutional Council also.

2. *Power to dissolve National Assembly:* Article 12 of the French Constitution of the Fifth Republic provides that, "the President of the Republic may, after consulting the Prime Minister and the Presidents of the assemblies, declare the National Assembly dissolved." Thus constitutionally, the French President is empowered to dissolve the National Assembly i.e. the lower chamber of the Parliament. But this power can only be exercised by him with the prior consultation of the Prime Minister and the presidents of the both the houses of Parliament. In case the National Assembly is dissolved by the President, its election shall take place between 20-40 days. It can not be again dissolved within a year following its election.[38]

---

36   Ibid
37   Ibid
38   Ibid

3. *Refusal to Grant Permission for Referendum:* Referendum is an important means to generate public opinion concerning some issues of serious nature. Philosophically it is derived from the Rousseau ideas of general will. Article 11 of the Constitution of the Fifth Republic provides that the French President may submit laws to the citizens in a referendum. He may allow or refuse to grant permission to these referendums initiated by the government or the two assemblies of Parliament and his decision in this connection is final. During the period of de Gaulle, the referendum of 1962 (about the universal suffrage) and the referendum of 1967 (about the French Pacific Territories) can be cited as its prominent examples in France. It is noteworthy that the power of referendum can be misused, so this weapon needs to be handled carefully.

4. *Message to Parliament:* The French President is further empowered to send a special massage to the Parliament to enact laws on some issues of public importance. This message can be sent to either Houses of the Parliament. It is clearly provided by article 18 of the Constitution of the Fifth Republic that "the President of the Republic shall communicate with the two assemblies of Parliament by means of messages, which he shall cause to be read and which shall not be the occasion for any debate. Outside sessions, Parliament shall be convened especially for this purpose."[39] If the Parliament is not in session, he can even summon an extra-ordinary session of Parliament with regard to it. These sessions of the Parliament open and close by his decree. Earlier he could personally appear in the Houses of Parliament. But since 1875, the President has been prohibited from entering the houses of Parliament[40]

5. *Power to Issue Ordinances and Decrees:* The French President is further empowered to issue ordinances and decrees under article 13 of the Constitution of the Fifth Republic. Before being issued, these ordinances and decrees are duly deliberated upon in the Council of Ministers. These ordinances and decrees have equal force as that of the laws passed by the Parliament.

JUDICIAL POWERS

Like his counterparts in India and the US, the French President also enjoys the power to grant pardon in accordance with the sprit of article 17 of the Constitution of the Fifth Republic. "The president may grant a pardon (but not an amnesty) to convicted criminals; the president can also lessen or suppress criminal sentences. This was of crucial importance when France had the death penalty: criminals sentenced to death would generally request that the president turn their sentence into life imprisonment."[41] In addition to this, he is the guarantor of the independence of French Judiciary and thus ensures safety and security of its judges. He also presides over the High Council of Judiciary and nominates its members.

EMERGENCY POWERS:

The French President enjoys substantial emergency powers. In case of emergency, his constitutional powers are enhanced exorbitantly and thus in such circumstances

---

39 Ibid
40 Ibid
41 Ibid

he operates with uncontrolled powers. Article 16 of the French Constitution of the Fifth Republic clearly explain these powers of the French President. This article "... allowing the president a limited form of rule by decree for a limited period of time in exceptional circumstance, has been used only once in France by Charles de Gaulle during the Algerian War in 1961, from April 23 to September 29".[42] The intervention of France in the Algerian crisis stands witnessed that the French President can act with out check at the time of emergency. It is mainly because General de Gaulle, the then President of France enjoyed uncontrolled powers during this emergency situation.

If the President views that the independence of the nation, the integrity of its territories, the fulfillment of its international commitments are in danger or under a serious threat, or the proper functioning of the constitutional public authorities is obstructed, he is constitutionally authorized to take appropriate measures in such circumstances. His own assessment of the situation is sufficient to declare it an emergent one. The only constitutional obligation on the French President is to take consultations with the Prime Minister, presidents of assemblies and the Constitutional Council. But constitutionally or legally these consultations or the opinions are not binding on him. Thus, he is not only the best judge of an emergent situation but also constitutionally free to adopt any measures to handle it. Generally he informs the citizens about these measures through a message. In nutshell, it is noteworthy that the French President assumes almost sweeping powers during emergency. However it needs to be mentioned that during emergency period the Parliament meets as a matter of right and the National Assembly could not be dissolved but it does not affect his decisions during this period.[43]

Position:

From the above, it is obvious that like the US President, the position of the French President is very strong. He is the real head of the state and thus, enjoys enormous powers. Today he enjoys even more powers and influence in comparison to his counterparts under the Third and Fourth Republics. It is mainly because the referendum of 1962 (by General de Gaulle) contributed significantly in improving his position particularly by making his election direct. Now he is a direct representative of the French citizens and enjoys their confidence. It led to enhancement of his influence in all spheres including foreign affairs.

The President, further, enjoys hegemony in the French dual executive system (which is an admixture of Presidential and Parliamentary form of the government). Constitutionally he is empowered to appoint the Prime Minister and his power in this regard is real. "In appointing the Prime Minister, his power is unlimited and according to the letters of the Constitution, Fifth Republic Governments would be the nominees of the President rather than of Parliament for all reference."[44] The President is also empowered to appoint the Council of Ministers on the recommendations of the Prime Minister. Unlike India or England this Council of Ministers operates under his control and it is he who presides over its meetings where the Prime Minister

---

42 *Ibid*
43 Bhagwan, Vishnoo and Bhushan, Vidya, *op. cit.*, p. 21.
44 Gupta, Madan Gopal, *op. cit.*, p. 89.

sits as a member. In this regard, it has been aptly observed that, "in France, if the Council of Ministers is the steering wheel of the ship of the state, the President is the steersman, for there the President governs, while the Prime Minister carries out his policy and is answerable for it to the Assembly."[45]

Besides, the President also enjoys a very strong position vis-a-vis the French Parliament. Unlike the Indian or US President, the French President enjoys the power to dissolve the National Assembly (lower House of the Parliament). Constitutionally he is empowered to send massages to the Parliament to enact requisite law on matters of special public importance. He can also send the bills passed by the Parliament for reconsideration. He can even refuse to grant permission to the bills initiated by the government or the Parliament for conducting referendums and his decision is final in this context. Accordingly, the President in French politics, not only overshadows and overpowers the Prime Minister, the Council of Ministers but also the Parliament. However, it is noteworthy that in a number of matters he has to consult the Prime Minister and the presidents of both the assemblies of Parliament. But this advice being non-binding in nature can hardly influence his decisions. The only provision that restrict his powers is the process of impeachment given under article 68 of the French Constitution. "It is laid down that the President of the Republic shall not be held accountable for actions performed in the exercise for his office except in the case of high treason."[46] But due to the complicated procedure of impeachment, this weapon is still an impotent one. As a result, till date no French President has been impeached through this process in France.

In addition to this, article 16 of the Constitution further strengthens his position as it equip him with the real and almost sweeping powers to view, judge and handle an emergent situation. He is not only the sole judge to decide whether a situation is emergent or not but also equally free in taking appropriate measure to handle that situation. In theory, this article (dealing with emergency powers of the President) imparts him the 'temporary constitutional dictatorship'. It is because once emergency is declared his powers becomes unlimited and uncontrolled. Here it can be safely observed, "once armed with emergency powers the President can do anything except amend the constitution or dissolve the Assembly".[47] It needs to be pointed out that the constitution does not provide any safeguard if any President wishes to abuse his emergency powers. "The only check on the President will be his own opinions, fear of losing popularity and a distant fear of impeachment."[48]

Above all, the personality, strength and vigour of the holder of this office further contribute in strengthening the position of the French President. A person like General de Gaulle, the first President of the Fifth Republic "...occupied the deriving seat and has intervened in most fields of domestic and foreign policies. He regarded both Government and Parliament as being agents of the President. He actually governed and took direct decisions even without consulting the Prime Minister."[49] He often used to bypass the Prime Minister and the Council of Ministers and thus, tried to

---

45 *Ibid*, p. 88-89.
46 *Ibid*, p. 89.
47 *Ibid*, p. 91.
48 *Ibid*
49 Bhagwan, Vishnoo and Bhushan, Vidya, *op. cit.*, p. 23.

reduce the French dual executive into a single headed one. Accordingly, "Prime Ministers regarded themselves as the personal appointees of the President and at his disposal. Through this, their ministers were effectively hired and fired by de Gaulle."[50] By virtue of his dynamic personality and his style of functioning he tried his level best in raising the stature of this office. In fact, he ruled as well as reigned in actual practice. However his successor to this office viz., George Pompidou, Valery Giscard d'Estaing, M. Francois Mitterrand, J. Chirac, N. Sarkozy and the current President could not prove their might as much as that of General de Gaulle.

PRIME MINISTER: The French Prime Minister is a functional head of the Council of Ministers in France. He holds the responsibility of discharging the routine affairs of the government. He is the chief advisor of the French President and thus assists him in carrying out his constitutional obligations. The President even discharge his important functions like declaration of emergency, dissolution of the National Assembly, appointment of the members of the Council of Ministers and their removal from office etc. only after consultation with the Prime Minister. This official position entitled 'Prime Minister' was however found lacking in France prior to the Constitution of the Fifth Republic. Earlier one of the minister of the government held the semi-official title of President of the Council of Ministers and was unofficially known as the prime minister. "Even this was something of a misnomer, as it was the President of France who actually presided over the Council of Ministers."[51]

Appointment: Article 8 of the Constitution of the Fifth Republic provides that he shall be appointed by the President. Constitutionally and legally there is no binding on the President in this regard. He is almost free in appointing any person to this office. Usually, a person to this office whose name is agreed upon by majority of the members of the National Assembly is appointed by the President. The incumbent to this office may or may not be a member of the Parliament or leader of any party. But if he is a member of the Parliament or leader of any party, he has to resign from his membership after holding the charge of this office.[52]

Removal:

The Prime Minister can be removed from his office in two ways: either his government tenders its resignation to the President or the Parliament passed a censure motion against him. The French President though appoints him but can not remove him until or unless he tendered his resignation. He holds his office during the pleasure of Parliament and thus remains in office till he enjoys the confidence of the Parliament. The Parliament can force him to resign by disapproving his policy or a part of it or through the passage of a no confidence motion against him.

Functions:

The French Prime Minister constitutionally does not enjoy much power as he is required to carry out the routine affairs of the government. In this capacity he discharges following functions-

---

50 *Ibid*, p. 24.
51 http://en.wikipedia.org/wiki/ Prime_ Minister_ of_ France
52 Bhagwan, Vishnoo and Bhushan, Vidya, *op. cit.*, p. 25-26.

1. *Management and Direction of the Governmental Operations:* The French Prime Minister along with the Council of Ministers owns the responsibility for managing and directing the governmental affairs. He is responsible for deciding all sorts of such details at the level of cabinet. In this connection he can issue necessary directions at the ministerial level also. In accordance with the provisions of article 13 of the Constitution, he is empowered to make deliberations on some regulations and recommend the President to appoint some civil and military officials.[53] He may even delegate such powers to his ministers. He is the only authority vested with the power "...to issue primary regulation through decrees *(decrets)*; that is, measures of a general character, either issued in support of statutes, either issued autonomously, depending on the area. Other ministers may only issue secondary regulations in the form of decisions *(arretes)*."[54] The issuing of these decrees or the decisions of the Prime Minister taken in the executive capacity, are subject to the oversight of the administrative court system. Some decrees may only be issue after taking advice from the *Conseil*.[55]

2. *Execution of Parliamentary Laws:* The French Prime Minister is further responsible for the execution of all the laws passed by the French Parliament. In this process he is assisted by the Council of Ministers in adoption of suitable measures. "The acts of the Premier are countersigned when circumstances so require, by the minister responsible for execution."[56] In other words, he ensures the respectful execution of the Parliamentary laws. He is empowered to issue necessary directions in this regard. In case of any administrative failure or lacuna, the Prime Minister and the Council of Ministers can be held accountable to the Parliament.

3. *Co-ordination of Ministerial Work:* The Prime Minister also plays a significant role in establishing a proper linkage among the operational working of different departments. He maintains it by establishing effective co-ordination among all the departments and thus ensures that the whole governmental machinery operates like a machine. As mentioned earlier, the French administration is characterized by the conflict of legitimacies. Resultantly, the inter-ministerial as well as intra-ministerial conflicts are quite frequent and open which aggravates the task of carrying out smooth administration some what more difficult in France. He tries to overcome this problem through maintaining effective co-ordination among them. He ensures that each department operates with out any short of inter or intra conflict or rivalry. In this way, he maintains the efficient and effective working of the government.

4. *Exercise Control and Supervision over Administrative Machinery:* Another important function of the Prime Minister is to exercise and maintain his supervision and control over the administrative machinery. He establishes his control over the administration through his cabinet ministers and thus enjoys power to issue necessary directions in this regard. The ministers alternatively exercise their control over the administrative officials of their respective department through the civil servants. The civil servants are primarily responsible for the execution

---

53 *Ibid*, p. 26.
54 http://en.wikipedia.org/wiki/ Prime_ Minister_ of France
55 *Ibid*
56 Gupta, Madan Gopal, *op. cit.*, p 95.

of various administrative policies and the laws. In this way the Prime Minister tries to rule out the possibility of any sort of administrative irregularity and thus ensures a smooth and efficient administration.

5. *Liaison with the Parliament:* Constitutionally, the French Prime Minister is not a member of the Parliament but he maintains his close relations with it. He enjoys the right to attend its sessions and participate actively in its debates and discussions. He can even express the desire to pass some necessary legislation and thus enjoys the right to initiate legislation as per the administrative requirements. To consider some agenda of urgent importance, he can even request the President for inviting an extra ordinary session of the Parliament. "Under article 29, only the Premier may ask for a new session before the end of the month following the closure decree."[57] Besides, he explains the governmental position on various issues and thus defends the government on the floor of the Parliament. Thus, "the Premier is the chief spokesman of the government before the Parliament and it is he who is enjoined by the Constitution to make general declaration of policy. He can make proposals for the amendment of the Constitution to the President of the Republic."[58]

Position:

After a careful perusal of his functions, it is obvious that the position of the French Prime Minister in France is hardly comparable to those of his counterparts in India and England. In the semi-presidential form of French government, the position of the French Prime Minister is secondary in comparison to the President who operates as the chief political figure. Unlike the President, he is not a representative of the French people. He is merely a political appointee of the French President and he is almost free in appointing any person to this office. Accordingly, he operates as his subordinate and enforces his will. Further his position is not sound in comparison to the French Parliament. He is not a member or leader of any house of Parliament. But constitutionally he enjoys the right to sit in the Parliament and participate in its discussions. He not only explains the position of the government in the Parliament but also accountable to it for the deeds of his government. The Parliament can remove him from office through censure motion. Hence the French Prime Minister is entrapped in a buffer state that lies between the President - who appoints him and the Parliament that can remove him from office. Resultantly, he has to win the confidence of both - the President as well as the Parliament.[59] The basic reason behind this sandwiched position of the French Prime Minister is that he enjoys neither the support of the Constitution nor that of polity to exert his position strongly.

Again, the position of the French Prime Minister is not very good if it is compared with the Council of Ministers. The French Prime Minister has the least control over the members of the Council of Ministers in comparison to his counterparts in India and Britain. It is mainly because unlike India and Britain, he can neither appoint nor remove them. He is only authorized to select them. However, the French President can even refuse any person selected by him.

---

57 Ibid
58 Ibid, p. 96.
59 Gupta, Madan Gopal, *op. cit.*, p. 96.

Likewise, as far as their removal is concerned, he can only render his advice to the President that is not binding on him. Moreover, in France it is not the Prime Minister but the President who chairs the Council of Ministers. He rather sits only as a member in these meetings. Accordingly, the position of the French Prime Minister is hardly somewhat more than that of a *Primus inter pares* among the members of the Council of Ministers.

However, from the above it can't be derived "...that the office of the Prime Minister has become entirely unimportant. Even with the increased powers of the President, the Prime Minister remains a key figure. A determined Prime Minister can always hold his own and need have little to fear from his President."[60] Further, the French Prime Minister enjoyed significant influence in a situation of *cohabitation* (i.e. when the President is of one party while another party controls the National Assembly). It is because the President has little power to be exercised by him alone.[61]

COUNCIL OF MINISTERS

The Constitution of the Fifth Republic also provides that the Prime Minister and the Council of Ministers shall constitute the government. It further provides that the government shall frame the national policies and shall be responsible for them to the Parliament. In France, though the French President is the custodian of the Constitution and the head of the state but the Council of Ministers is responsible for the smooth governance of the nation.

Composition: The French President appoints the Council of Ministers after consultation with the Prime Minister. Ordinarily the advice of the Prime Minister is given due weight in their selection. The members of the Council of Ministers need not be parliamentarians. If they happened to be the members of Parliament, they have to resign from its membership. "Early cabinets were drawn largely from the civil services, but in order to have ministers capable of working effectively with Parliament, the practice grew of naming deputies of former assemblies, and recently nearly all ministers have come from Parliament."[62] Further the Constitution is silent regarding the number of members of the Council of Ministers but usually its size remains small. Generally it varies between 25-40 members.[63] It incorporates ministers of three categories-

i) Cabinet Ministers or Ministers who heads the department
ii) Secretaries of State
iii) Ministers without portfolio.

The Cabinet that constitutes the pivot of the French Council of Ministers is an extra-constitutional body. There is no mention of it in the French Constitution. Its members (Cabinet Ministers) are the heads of the main departments of the State. It generally consists of a dozen or more senior ministers.[64] Its salient characteristic is that it underwent several alterations and modifications so far as its composition

---
60 *Ibid.*, p. 96.
61 http://en.wikipedia.org/wilci/ Prime_ Minister_ of_ France
62 Wesson, G., Robert, *Modern Governments: Three Worlds of Politics*, USA: Prentice Hall, Inc. Englewood Cliffs, 1981, p. 104.
63 Pickles(D.), *op. cit.*, p. 79.
64 Wesson, G., Robert, *op. cit.*, p. 104.

is concerned. Its role in French policy making is not so vital as in case of India or Britain. It is mainly because in France "the Prime Minister is not really the boss of the Cabinet; on the one hand, the President stands over him; on the other, the finance minister can check policy on his own."[65] In addition to this, the Council of Ministers also involves the junior ministers, also known as Secretaries of State and the Ministers without portfolio. The number of such ministers in France finds a great variation.

Like in other countries, the Cabinet Ministers are the heads of their respective departments/ministries which are mostly created on functional basis. The functions of the French Cabinet are technical, administrative and political in nature.[66] The prominent French Cabinet Ministers are- Minister of Foreign Affairs, Minister of Interior, Minister of Defense, Minister of National Education, Minister of Justice etc. In France, all the ministries are nearly organized on a somewhat uniform pattern. Each is further characterized by having a *cabinet* with in it. "It is headed by a chief *(Chief de cabinet)* and is composed of an assistant chief, a secretary, and several attaches"[67] It is an outcome of 'custom rather than statute'. Its role has changed from time to time and may vary from ministry to ministry. But it is generally viewed as an intermediary between the minister and external political figures on the one hand, and the permanent internal administrative apparatus on the other.[68] The cabinet of each ministry helps the concerned minister in discharging the duties of his department and is accountable to him. Its members are the personal appointees of the minister. However they are paid out of the public fund. They enjoyed tenure as long as that of the minister who appoints them. This cabinet assists the minister (through rendering advice) in the fulfillment or carrying out of his departmental obligations. However the minister is not bound to accept its advice.

Removal

The members of the Council of Ministers can be dismissed by the French President if they lose confidence. The French Parliament can even remove them from office through censure motion. Moreover, the National Assembly can force the Council of Ministers to resign if it rejects either any policy of the government or a part of it.

Meetings

Usually, the Council of Ministers meets twice a week and it is chaired by the French President. Its meetings are generally held in the President's House. All the members of the Council of Ministers attend these meetings. Some times (usually in the absence of the President) the Prime Minister chairs the Cabinet meetings; otherwise he sits in these meetings as a member.

Functions

The Council of Ministers in France discharge following functions:
1. *Preparation and Execution of Administrative Policies:* The French Council of Ministers under the chairmanship of the President decides the various policies pertaining

---

65 *Ibid*
66 Pickles(D.), *op. cit.,* p. 79.
67 Neumann, G. Robert, *op. cit.,* p. 304.
68 Heady, Ferrel, *op. cit.,* p. 201.

to different departments. These policies are prepared by the Council of Ministers by keeping in view the demand of the public and the requirements of the changing times. For this purpose a lots of exercise is made at the departmental level. These policies are then presented before the Parliament for their passage. After being passed these policies are executed by the government (Council of Ministers led by the Prime Minister). More specifically, the minister-in charge of the respective departments are responsible for making necessary arrangements in this regard. Each minister is further accountable to the Council of Ministers for the smooth execution the policy belonging to his ministry.

2. *Powers of Appointment:* The Council of Ministers enjoys a lot of power regarding the appointments of a number of functionaries. It appoints a ambassadors and envoys extraordinary, the Councillors of State, Master Councillors of the Audit Office, representatives of the government in the overseas Territories, general officers, directors of central administration etc.[69] Further, "an organic law determines the other posts to be filled in meetings of the Council of Ministers, as well as the conditions under which the powers of the President of the Republic to make appointments of office may be delegated by him to be exercised in his name."[70] In fact, the President makes most of the appointments on the recommendations of the Council of Ministers led by the Prime Minister.

3. *Legislative Functions:* Theoretically, it is the French Parliament which is the repository of legislative authority and thus is empowered to enact and amend legislations. In practice, the French Council of Ministers also plays a significant role in the field of legislation. The members of the Council of Ministers are though not the parliamentarians, yet they are constitutionally authorized to attend the parliamentary sessions. They take active participation in its deliberations. The Prime Minister even enjoys the right to initiate legislations. The Council of Ministers can also issues decrees that have the same force as that of law. These are enacted in its meetings after consultation with the Council of State. "They come into force upon their publication and become null and void if the bill for their ratification is not submitted to Parliament before the date set by the enabling act."[71] It also frames laws under the practice of delegated legislation.

4. *Functions regarding Financial Matters:* The French Council of Ministers also enjoys sufficient financial powers. It is responsible for the preparation of the nation's budget. It determines what taxes are to be imposed and how the public revenue is to be spent. In comparison to the U.K. and India, the French Parliament has considerably little authority in budgetary matters. It cannot reduce revenues or raise expenditures. Both the Houses of Parliament are supposed to consider the budget with in a fixed time period. (Time period of the National Assembly is limited to 40 days whereas that of the Senate is 15 days). The National Assembly can further consider the budget and if there is no consensus and it is not passed by Parliament with in 70 days, the government can enact it by decree.[72] "The government has also the right to ask Parliament for temporary credits that would

---

69 Gupta, Madan Gopal, *op. cit.,* p. 94.
70 Ibid
71 Ibid
72 Wesson, Robert, G., *op. cit.,* p. 104.

be necessary if the annual finance bill did not become law before the beginning of the financial year to which it referred."[73]

5. *As Co-ordinator:* The French Council of Ministers plays a significant role in co-ordinating the working of its ministers. The ministers are the heads of their respective departments, having their own secretariat staff *(cabinet)* in the form of political appointees to assist them in discharging their administrative obligations. The minister concerned is the overall in-charge of his department and is solely responsible to look after the affairs of his department. The ministers of respective ministries take varied decisions in order to streamline their departmental working. They frame their own rules and regulations in the light of the governmental powers delegated to them by the Prime Minister.[74] All these activities carried out by the heads of the respective departments (ministers) are co-ordinated by the French Council of Ministers as a chief co-ordinator.

(C) LOCAL GOVERNMENT*

In the pre-Revolution France, not much attention was paid towards the development of local government systems and the monarch was the centre of all governmental powers. Before the French Revolution, *Intendents* who worked directly under the Monarch ran the administration. The administration was divided into 30 provinces and each was headed by an *Intendent.* [75]Thus, historically, French administration was highly centralized. After 1789, efforts were made to identify the local government units and to devolve powers to them. Therefore, the actual beginning of French local government can be traced to the post-Revolution era when its basic pattern was laid down. After the French Revolution, the historic provinces (pre-revolutionary units of administration) were abolished and replaced by new administrative units under the laws passed by the Constituent Assembly in 1789 and 1790. Parishes of ancient regime were transformed into communes (municipalities) and France was divided into 83 departments. A department was divided into arrondissements, which were divided into cantons, which, in turn, were divided into communes. In 1959, the French government created another administrative unit called 'region' above the department. However, region became a unit of local government in 1982. Presently, there are 26 such regions, in France.[76] Of these five geographical units of French administration (regions, departments, arrondissements, cantons and communes), arrondissements and cantons are not units of local government. Thus, presently there are three main units of local government in France: regions, departments and communes or municipalities.[77]

In the beginning the local units enjoyed considerable autonomy and had elected councils. They were also given powers to govern the local affairs. But their autonomy

---

73 Gupta, Madan Gopal, *op.cit.,* p. 95.
74 Pickles (D), *op. cit.,* p. 83.
75 Chaturvedi, T. N., *op. cit,* p. 182.
76 Bharttwal, C. P., *Understanding Local Government,* Lucknow: Bharat Book Centre, 1997, p. 122.
77 http://www.ambafrance-au.org/article. Php3? Id article=445

* Local Government in France has already been published in M.D. University Research Journal (Arts) vol 6, No 1, 2007, pp. 1-14.

was considerably curtailed by the Jacobins and later by Napoleon who introduced the Prefect system to consolidate centralization. At the local level, the Prefect, an agent of the Central government, was responsible for managing the affairs at the department level. "...the Napoleonic prefectoral system reflected the basic beliefs that all political issues were national and to be decided by the government in Paris and, therefore, that in provincial France there should be no local government but only local administration."[78] During that time, the Mayors at the communal level were also appointed rather than elected.

After Napoleon, the local units regained their powers and an effort was made to revive them. Though the process of devolving powers to the local units started much earlier but it gained momentum only after 1958, under the Fifth Republic. Article 72 of the Constitution of the Fifth Republic proclaims decentralization on the one hand and deconcentration on the other. The first President of the Fifth Republic General de Gaulle emphasized on the aspect of devolution in 1958. In 1960s, a series of reforms were carried out to neutralize the highly centralized structures through decentralization of powers.[79] "In 1963, the French centralism flexed its muscles and showed signs of flexibility with the establishment of Regional Economic Planning Councils (CODER). In 1972 the regional councils were set up. In the seventies a move was made to amalgamate small sized communes (municipalities) and to devolve more power to them."[80]

Later on, 1982 reforms in connection with decentralization by the Mitterrand socialist government provided a fundamental basis in terms of local autonomy. At this time, the dramatic change was the ideological transformation that reflects a clear deviation from the previous model. Such changes proved helpful in generating respect for local diversity rather than unnecessary emphasis on uniformity. These reforms not only brought changes relating to finance but also extended the responsibilities of the communal, departmental and regional accountants, giving them the status of chief accountant directly responsible to the Treasury.[81]

Region, which was created as a unit of local administration by President General deGaulle in 1959, was abolished after he (de Gaulle) lost the referendum in 1969 and had to quit. This unit was revived as a unit of local government by this law in 1982. The succeeding ten-year period (1982-92) "...witnessed consolidation of advances made and their implementation with continued adjustments"[82]. Another most important step in the direction of decentralization was the State Act of 1992. Further by the law of February 4, 1995, "...an effort was made to readjust the distribution of powers to planning and development of territory in such a way that each category of local government disposes of homogenous competence."[83] The above mentioned three units of local government in France viz. region, department and commune or municipality, are discussed below in detail.

---

78 Machin, Howard, "France" in Ridley, F.F., *op. cit.*, p. 72.
79 Bharthwal, C. P., *op. cit.*, p. 122.
80 Maheshwari, S.R., *The Higher Civil Service in France*, New Delhi: Allied Publishers Ltd, 1991, p. 108.
81 http://www.ambafrance-au.org/article. Php3? Id article=445
82 Bharthwal, C. P., *op. cit.*, p. 122.
83 Agarwal, R.C., "Territorial Administration in France" in *Indian Journal of Public Administration*, April-June 1999, Vol. XLV, No. 2, p. 233.

REGION

France is divided into 26 regions, 22 in metropolitan France and four overseas. Though the regions were created in 1959 to provide a framework for regional town and country planning, yet they became units of local government only in 1982.[84] Thus, it is the topmost and youngest unit of local government. Each region has a regional council that is elected by universal suffrage. The members of the council are elected for a term of 6 years. The number of councillors varies from 31 to 209.[85] The regional council is responsible for the management of regional affairs. It is the decision-making organ of the region. The main functions of the regional council are three fold - formulation of economic plan, economic development, and vocational training and education.[86] In March 2004, the French government announced a controversial plan to transfer to the regions some categories of non-teaching school personnel.[87]

The members of each regional council elect one person from amongst themselves as its president, who acts as its chief executive and presides over its meetings. The president of the regional council operates in dual capacities - as the head of the regional administration and as the agent of the central government. In the former capacity, he is responsible for enforcing the decisions taken by the regional council, ensuring public security, morality and hygiene of the region, appointment of permanent staff, preparation of budget and its submission to the council, supervision of the regional administration. In the latter capacity, he ensures execution of central laws and deals with matters related to police and various other national matters viz. public health, compulsory military services in the region.[88] However, regions do not enjoy any legislative autonomy. "Regions do not have legislative autonomy, nor can they issue regulations. They do levy taxes (or, rather, the national government gives them a portion of the taxes it levies) and have sizeable, though not considerable budgets."[89] For the purpose of infra-structure (education, public transportation systems, aid to universities and research, support for entrepreneurs), the regions enjoy discretionary spending.[90]

Of late, a proposal to impart limited legislative autonomy to the regions is widely considered. However, there is no unanimity on this proposal and, therefore, it remains controversial. "There are also proposals to suppress the local governments of the departments and to folding them into the regions, keeping the departments only as administrative subdivisions."[91]

DEPARTMENT

In the structural hierarchy of local government there exists a number of departments within a region. In France, they are the basic territorial and administrative units of governance. They are roughly analogous to the British counties and are now

---

84 http://www.ambafrance-au.org/article. Php3? Id article=445
85 Agarwal, R. C, I.IPA, *op. cit.*, p. 235.
86 Bharthwal C.P., *op. cit.*, p. 126.
87 Ibid
88 Bharthwal, C.P., *op. cit.*, p. 127-128.
89 http://en. Wikipedia. Org/wiki/ List of_Region_ of_ France.
90 Ibid
91 Ibid

grouped into 22 metropolitan and four overseas regions and subdivided into 342 arrondissements.[92] During Napoleon era, France had 91 departments but now their number is 100 of which 96 are in metropolitan France and four are overseas (Martinique, Guadeloupe, Reunion and French Guiana). They have developed from a partially decentralized local authority (in 1789) to one with full powers of its own (since 1982).[93]

Majority of the departments in France are named after some mountains or rivers. The population size of various departments varies between 80,000 to 3 million approximately.[94] Most of the departments have an area of around 4,000-8,000 sq. km. Area wise the largest department in France is Gironde (10,000 sq. km) and the smallest the city of Paris (105 sq. km). In terms of population, Nord is the most populous (2,550,000) and Lozere is the least populous (74,000).[95] The departments in France are categorized into 4 classes on the basis of their importance. These include - Hors class or special class (top most class), First class, Second class and Third class. The important French cities viz. Nice and Lille belong to the Hors class.[96] The departments are also numbered and their two-digit numbers appear in and on car number-plates.[97] Each French department has a President - who acts as its executive head – and a General Council - which constitutes its legislature and a Prefect, who is appointed by the government.

ROLE OF THE PREFECT

The term 'Prefect' is derived from ancient Rome's nomenclature of *Prfectus Urbi*, who used to be a close confidant of the Emperor.[98] The Prefect enjoys a unique place in French system. He acts as a liaison between the central government and the population of the department. He is an appointee of the Central government and, therefore, represents it at the departmental level. He enjoys full control and authority over the departmental administration and also maintains his supervision over the department's local authorities.[99] He is usually a professional civil servant but is not required to meet any special standards of professional competence.[100] Generally, he is the senior-most civil servant in the local administration. He is liable to be transferred from one department to the other. "For almost 200 years (1800 to 1982), the Prefect held the executive power in the department, but the law of March 1982, modified his/her powers."[101] His office is 'apolitical' although he participates in active politics.

The capital city of a department bears the title of prefecture that constitutes the headquarter of the department. "The Departments are divided into one to seven arrondissements. The capital city of an arrondissement is called the *sous-prefecture*.

---

92 http://en. Wikipedia. Org/wiki/ D%E 9 Departments.
93 http://www.ambafrance-au.org/article. Php3? id article=445
94 Maheswari, S. R., *op. cit.*, p. 112.
95 http://en. Wikipedia. Org/wiki/ D%E 9 Departments.
96 Nigam, S. R., Local Government, Delhi: Kitab Mehal, Pvt. Ltd., 1968, p. 92.
97 http:/en. Wikipedia. Org/wiki/ D%E 9 Departments.
98 Nigam, S. R., *op. cit.*, p. 94.
99 http://www.ambafrance-au.org/article. Php3? Id article=445
100 Neumann G. Robert, *op. cit.*, p. 349.
101 http://www.ambafrance-au.org/ai1icle. Php3? Id article=445

The civil servant in charge is the *sous-prefect*."[102] To assist the Prefect in discharging his duties, a number of officials viz. Sub-Prefects, the Secretary-General and the Chief of the Cabinet are appointed by the Central government. All of them are civil servants and graduated from National School of Administration *(Ecole National d' Administration)*. The heads of divisions, clerks and other employees in the prefecture assist these officials. Outside the departmental capital, the Prefect is assisted by one or more *sous-prefects*.[103]

The Prefect occupies a central position in the French administrative system and plays a dominant role in the departmental affairs. His role can be better explained by dividing it in two main parts: as agent of the Central government and as supervisor of the commune government. In the former capacity, he acts as an extended arm of the Central government and thus serves its interests within the department. He is responsible for maintenance of law and order in the department. He is also accountable for the execution of various policies and programmes framed by the executive at the central level and all the laws enacted by the Central legislature. All officials of the Central government in the department are responsible to him and he controls them and supervises their functioning.

He is the chief co-ordinator of the different state controlled services, having their own officials in the department and thus co-ordinates the activities of department with those of the Central government. Thus, he is also empowered to direct the officials in the department to carry out the orders of their respective ministers within the department. He also acts as an effective channel for both collection and transmission of information required by the various ministries at the Central level. He also plays a crucial role in collection of taxes inside the department. He is also in charge of the highways, bridges, jails, hospitals and census operations within his department. He enjoys power of patronage and thus appoints a number of officials according to civil service regulations. His political role is vital, thus helps the party in power in winning election by using his influence.[104]

In the latter capacity, he acts as the watchdog over the working of commune governments. He is a supervisor of the communal administration. He can issue directions to the Mayor of the commune regarding policy matters and even suspend him for grave breach of conduct. He approves the communal budget. He can even annul any decision of the commune council. He also appoints some commune officials. It may be pointed out that while working as a supervisor of communal government; his operations are guided and directed strictly in accordance with the instructions from the Central government.[105]

GENERAL COUNCIL

There is also a general council *(conseil general)* in each department. It is the legislative and decision making organ of the department. It has the general responsibility for smooth governance of the departmental affairs. It takes important decision and provides the framework for action to be taken. "It is made up of general councillors elected for a six-year term in a two-ballot uninominal majority poll. Each department

---

102 http://en. Wikipedia. Org/wiki/ D%E 9 Departments.
103 *Ibid*
104 Bharthwal, C.P, *op. cit.*, p. 131
105 *Ibid*

is divided into cantons (France has 3,500 cantons) which serve as the constituencies for the election."[106] The councillors are elected directly by the people through a secret ballot. The number of councillors in a council varies from department to department. It is because each canton elects one representative in the departmental council and the number of cantons in different departments is variable. Thus, size of general council corresponds with the number of cantons in that department. All citizens living in the department who have attained the age of 23 enjoy the right to vote. But for contesting the election, the age of the candidate must be 25 years. Election is held on a fixed day, usually in October, throughout the country. The same person cannot be a member of the general council of more than one department.

A person from amongst the councillors chairs the general council. The law of 1982 conferred executive authority for the department on the chairman of the general council.[107] Thus, at present, the president of the general council has replaced the Prefect as the chief executive of the department. He now heads the department's administration. He prepares the ground for the council meetings, chairs them and executes the decisions taken by the council. He is incharge of income and expenditure of the department.[108] "Elected by the councillors for a six-year term, the chairman prepares the council's debates and implements its decisions, including on budgetary matters."[109] The general council usually meets twice a year. The first meeting usually takes place in April and lasts for about a fortnight while the second meeting lasting for a month is called in August or October.[110] However, a special session can be convened by the President of the Republic, by the Prefect, at the request of 2/3 members of the council or by the departmental commission (standing committee of the council).[111] The quorum for general council meetings is half of the total number of councillors plus one. The general council mainly performs the following three-fold functions:

1. It conducts a general supervision over the administrative activities undertaken by the Central government in the department. Being a unitary form of government, the Central government enjoys unlimited powers of supervision and control over the territorial administrative units in the country. However, to promote and maintain cordial relations between the Central government and the general council of the department, there is a convention that in departmental affairs, no action is taken without prior consultation of the council.

2. The council also exercises a general supervision over the administrative affairs of the department. It exercises control over various departmental services viz. public works, public health, drainage, sanitation etc. It is responsible for maintenance of roads, public buildings, fixing the maximum rates of certain types of taxes, fixation of electoral boundaries, the classification of roads and the authorization of sites of markets or fair grounds.[112] Thus, the powers of the council are quite extensive in departmental affairs.

---

106 http://www.ambafrance-au.org/article. Php3? Id article=445
107 Ibid
108 Agarwal, R. C, IJPA, *op. cit.*, p. 235.
109 http://www.ambafrance-au.org/article. Php3? Id article=445
110 Bharthwal, C. P, *op. cit.*, p. 135.
111 Bhagwan, Vishnoo and Vidya Bhusan, *op. cit.*, p. 61.
112 *Ibid*, p. 61.

3. The general council also enjoys jurisdiction over administrative affairs and services of the commune. The settlement of disputes between two or more communes is its prime responsibility. In fact, the general council of a department controls all those affairs that affect two or more communes and in all such matters, the decisions of the general council of the concerned department are final.[113]

To exercise an effective supervision over the administrative affairs of the department, the practice of creating departmental commission, which is a standing committee of the departmental general council, was established in 1871. The purpose behind its emergence was short sessions and long intervals between two meetings of the council. The departmental commission is constituted by the general council in its August session for a period of one year and consists of 4-7 members. It remains active particularly when the general council is not in session. It meets at least once in a month and keeps constant vigil over the activities of the Prefect. It examines the accounts prepared by the Prefect each month and regulates his expenditure against the authorizations voted in the departmental budget.[114]

COMMUNE

Commune is the lowest tier and smallest unit of the French local government. It was in existence even in the pre-Revolution era. In France, commune is an area anything from the size of a thinly populated hamlet or village to a borough or a large densely populated town or metropolis.[115] Thus, the term commune includes the local government of a city, town or village. Though the size and population of various communes differs widely yet irrespective of their size, all are governed by the same municipal code.

The whole territory of the French Republic is divided into communes and every piece of land in the French Republic belongs to a commune. In metropolitan France, the average surface area of a commune is 14.88 sq. km. (5.75 sq. miles or 3,676 acres). The median population of metropolitan France's communes was 380 inhabitants. There are about 21,000 communes with less than 500 inhabitants.[116] In general, a commune can be a "...2,000,000 inhabitants city like Paris, a 10,000 inhabitants town, or just a 10 inhabitants village. What the median population tells us is that the vast majority of the French communes only have a couple of hundred inhabitants; but there also exists a small number of communes that are highly populated."[117] Paris is the most populous commune of the French Republic. There are six communes in the French Republic with no inhabitants at all. These six communes are on the battlefield of Verdun: Beaumont-en-Verdunois, Bezonvauz, Haumont-pres-Samogneux, Louvemont-Cote-du-Poivre, Cumieres-li-Mort-Homme and Fleury-devant-Douaumont.[118]

To manage the affairs of every commune of the French Republic there exists an executive mayor *(maire)* and a municipal council *(conseil municipal)*. The two (mayor and municipal council) enjoy identical powers in all the communes despite great

---

113 *Ibid*, p. 103.
114 *Ibid*, p. 103-104.
115 *Ibid*
116 *Ibid*
117 *Ibid*
118 *Ibid*

variations in their size and population. The only exception to this arrangement is the city of Paris, where the city police is in the hands of the Central government rather than in the hands of the mayor of Paris. This uniformity of status is in fact, a legacy of the French Revolution.[119] Hence, the organizational structure of a commune consists of two organs: the mayor and the municipal council.

The Mayor acts as chief executive of the commune. He is elected by the municipal councillors from amongst themselves for a term of 6 years. The mayor can also be re-elected. The role of mayor of a commune is analogous to that of the Prefect. Thus, like the Prefect, the mayor also operates in dual capacity - as the commune's elected authority and as the state's representative. As the chief executive of the commune, he presides over the municipal council and carries out the decisions of the municipal council. He is the municipality's legal representative and is personally responsible for ensuring the public security, morality and hygiene of the commune. He ensures the conservation and management of the commune's natural environment and build heritage and issue building permits.[120] For smooth governance of the communal administration, he appoints a number of communal employees. He proposes and implements the budget of the commune. Summarizing his role, Robert Neumann has observed, the mayor "... prepares and executes the budget, is responsible for public safety and order, administers local licensing and inspection of regulations, and maintains house keeping functions."[121]

As the state's representative, he follows the directions issued by the Prefect or Sub-Prefects. At the commune level, he ensures the execution of parliamentary acts and laws and decisions of the Central government. He is also responsible for publicizing laws .and regulations and drawing up the electoral register. As a judicial officer, he ensures peace in the commune and maintains law and order. He is entitled to exercise special powers in connection with the repression of crime under the authority of the public prosecutor. His police powers are enormous. Besides, he maintains the records of births, death and marriages. He also maintains land records. He is liable to be suspended if he fails to carry out the directions of higher authorities. It is because the acts of the mayor are "...unilateral administrative acts, generally orders, whose legality is subject to a posteriori control by the courts when they are issued by the mayor as the commune's chief executive and to the approval of the prefect to whom the mayor is subordinate when acting in the capacity of the state's representative."[122]

The council also elects deputy mayors who assist the mayor in discharging his responsibilities. At the apex of the administrative hierarchy of the commune is a secretary, who is a close confidant of the mayor. He is responsible for the management of day-to-day administrative affairs of the commune. He co-ordinates a series of services at the commune level. Under him, there operates a staff belonging to 4 cadres, viz. the administrative cadre, the technical cadre, miscellaneous or special cadre and the manual workers.[123] The number of these officials differ from commune to commune.

---

119 *Ibid*
120 http://www.ambafrance-au.org/article. Php3? Id article=445
121 Neumann, G. Robert, *op. cit.*, p. 352-353
122 http.//www.ambafrance-au.org/article. Php3? Id article=445
123 S.R. Nigam, *op. cit.*, p. 142.

The deliberative wing of the commune is the municipal council. Its members, known as councillors, are directly elected by the inhabitants of the commune for a term of 6 years through direct universal suffrage. The number of councillors in a commune is proportional to its population and, therefore, their number varies from commune to commune. Except the three largest communes viz. Paris, Marseille & Lyon, the number of councillors in communes varies from 9 to 69.[124] The council may be dissolved earlier through a decree of the central government in case of abuse of powers or breach of laws. The sittings of the municipal councils are held in public to promote transparency in communal affairs.

Four regular sessions (in February, May, August and September), each lasting for 2 to 6 weeks, of the municipal council are held every year. Its special session can be called by the Mayor, the Prefect and the Sub-Prefect or at the request of 1/3 of its councillors. Mayor presides over its sessions and in his absence the senior-most Deputy Mayor presides over it.[125]

The municipal council plays an important role in the management of the affairs of the commune. It has enormous responsibilities particularly in the fields of primary schools, public health, town planning, construction and maintenance of roads and streets, highways, housing, environment, culture social welfare and even the police. The "... municipal councillors lay down guidelines for municipal policy, adopt the budget, manage municipal assets, notably primary school buildings and equipment, and decide how the municipal administration is to operate."[126] The council also takes decisions in different respects and thus manages the affairs of the commune. "It passes the budget, approves the annual accounts, sets up municipal services, manages what belongs to the commune and gives opinions on the contracts awarded by the commune."[127]

Most of the work of the council is discharged through a number of adhoc and standing committees constituted by it for discharging specific tasks. The number of such committees varies from commune to commune. They are constituted in almost every commune. The municipal council is free to set any number of committees. The municipal council defines and specifies their powers.

(D) CONTROL MACHINERY

In France, the external control over administration is exercised by the French Parliament and judiciary whereas the internal control is fitted within the administrative system itself. However, the internal control is more effective in comparison to the external control. This is because unlike the UK and India, the legislative control in France is relatively less effective and unlike the US, the judiciary in France lacks the power of judicial review. However, the weakness of the judicial courts has been counterbalanced by the creation of another system of courts viz. the administrative courts.

Along with the ordinary courts, there exists a parallel system of administrative courts. These courts play a dominant role in exercising their control over administration. In France, a small group of public servants enjoying both legislative and judicial

---

124 *Ibid*
125 *Ibid*
126 http://www.ambafrance-au.org/article. Php3? Id article=445
127 Agarwal, R. C, IJPA, *op. cit.*, p. 235.

powers and holding high positions exercise control over the whole administrative-machinery. A brief picture of the control machinery in France can be discussed as under:

A. Executive Control: In France, the executive has a number of ways of "...keeping itself informed and of ensuring that the administration properly executes its decisions while respecting the laws and rules in force." [128] Following are the main techniques utilized by the executive in France to exercise control over the administrative machinery.

1. **Ministerial Control:** Functions of the French ministries are divided in the same manner as those of the government departments in other countries. These ministries are organized on a uniform pattern and every ministry is headed by a minister, who is the chief executive of his department. All the administrative functionaries working at various levels of the department are responsible to him for their acts of omission and commission. The minister can take punitive actions against the wrongful deeds of the administrative functionaries.

   One of the peculiar features of a ministry in France is the existence of a 'Cabinet' (in each ministry) to assist the minister. "It is headed by a chief (Chief de cabinet) and is composed of an assistant chief, a secretary, and several attaches."[129] This cabinet helps the minister in discharging his duties. Its members are not part of civil service but are political colleagues or personal appointees of the minister. This cabinet renders advice to the minister to discharge his parliamentary duties and to exercise a check over the working of his department. However, the advice so rendered is not binding. "The institution of ministerial cabinet strengthens the political direction and control of the ministry and acts as the staff of the minister, meaning multiple heads, eyes and hands."[130]

2. **Inspectorates System:** French administration is fitted with a system of special inspectorates. The officers of the respective inspectorate visit the different branches of the administration for which they are competent. These officers prepare reports about the mal-administrative working particularly in case of any misconduct, irregularity or abuse of powers. In this way, the special inspectorates keep a vigil on the administration. Howard Machin has observed that, if any allegation of misconduct is raised against an administrative officer, special investigations may be carried out by "...a number of the relevant inspectorates or, in certain cases, by members of the intelligence service *(Service des renseignements generaux)*. All this information may be used for disciplinary proceedings or simply, in most cases for deciding promotions between different ranks within a class and corps."[131] The reports prepared by these inspectors serve as an effective measure of control over the administration.

3. **Prefectorial Reports:** France is a unitary State and all the authority is constitutionally conferred on the Central government. But for administrative convenience, the French government has divided the whole country into

---

128 Meny, Yves, "France" in Rowat, Donald C, *op. cit.*, p. 287.
129 Neumann, G. Robert, *op.cit.*, p. 304.
130 Maheshwari, *op. cit.*, p. 97.
131 Machin, Howard, "France" in Ridley, F.F., *op. cit.*, p. 98.

Regions which are further divided into Departments.[132] In this regard, it is noteworthy that neither the region nor the department is a political entity; both are creations of the Central government for administrative purposes. Each department is headed by a Prefect who acts in dual capacity - firstly as the head of the department and secondly as the agent of the Central government. Though he is appointed by the President of the Republic, but for all practical purposes he is an appointee of the Minister of Interior, who is his immediate boss. The Prefect possesses wide powers and actually has become the pivot of French administration

Each Prefect is required to send a detailed and comprehensive report of his department to the Central government. These prefectorial reports help the Central government in examining the law and order situation, in evaluating the governmental policies/programmes and in getting the feedback from the public about the governmental policies. Resultantly, these reports are vital in having an overview of the entire field administration. In this way, the prefectorial system leads to controlling the administration in two ways. First, the Prefect maintains his own control over department administration. Second, he helps the Central government in maintaining control over it (department administration).

4. **Expenditure Regulations:** Expenditure regulation is also an effective weapon in the hands of the executive to control the administration. In France, such regulations are exercised at two levels: before/at the time of spending the moneys *(a priori)* and after the moneys are spent *(a posteriori)*. Each financial regulation is two-fold. The two stages of *a priori* financial control are: control through financial controllers and control through the treasurer. An official of the Ministry of Budget called the financial controller is attached to each ministry "... to check the regularity of all spending plans and his approval is needed before the ministry can commit itself to any action that will involve expenditure."[133] The second *priori* control is conducted at the time of making payments and is conducted by the treasurer and his accountants. "All actual payments are made by the treasurer-paymaster general of the department on warrants issued by the local officer of the ministry concerned. The treasurer and his accountants make a full check of the regularity of each payment."[134]

The *posteriori* expenditure regulation is conducted by the finance inspectorate and the Court of Accounts. The former supervises "...all financial services of the state, of local councils and of semi-public bodies... It operates by sending (theoretically without prior notice) a team of inspectors to carry out a full audit. The inspectors investigate not only the accuracy of the accounts but also the efficiency of the administration under examination."[135] Further, the Court of Accounts also conducts an annual audit of the public accounts. It examines not only "...the regularity of accounts and also the efficiency of the administrative services. Its lengthy reports may criticize not only abuses and inefficiency but

---

132 The Regions and the Departments in France are comparable to the states and districts in India.
133 Machin, Howard, *"France"* in Ridley, F.F., *op. cit.*, p. 99.
134 *Ibid*
135 *Ibid*

also defects in governmental policy, and proposals for reform may be made."[136]

From the above it is obvious that the regulation of expenditure in France is conducted in a comprehensive and organized manner. This regulation enables the executive to control the administration effectively.

5. **Executive Orders:** The executive in almost every country is constitutionally authorized to issue executive orders. The French Constitution (Article 34) also empowers the executive to issue decrees (executive orders) that have almost equal force as that of laws enacted by the Parliament. Through these decrees the government directs and controls the behaviour of the administrative functionaries. Article 34 also pertains to subordinate legislation and authorizes the executive to fill in the details of the laws framed by the Parliament. In this article, "…there is a category of subjects where the law decides the rules in detail and there is another category where the law determines only the general principle. In the latter sphere, the government can act by decrees and administrative regulation." [137] Besides, Parliament enjoys the right to delegate the power to legislate even in those matters that are normally in the field of parliamentary legislation. This provides as opportunity to the executive to exercise control over the administration and to motivate the administrative functionaries to act in desired direction.

B. Legislative Control: Though the Prime Minister and the Council of Ministers are not the part of French Parliament; they are merely appointees of the President. However, the Prime Minister and the Council of Ministers (who are in charge of various administrative departments in France) are required to participate in the meetings of the Parliament and to answer the parliamentary questions. They are accountable to the Parliament and can even be removed by it. Thus, the Parliament is an agency of exercising external control over administration through the Prime Minister and the Council of Ministers. Various mechanisms adopted by the Parliament to exercise external control over the administration in France are detailed below.

1. **Legislation and Policies:** Being the legislature, the French Parliament enjoys the power of enacting the laws and framing the policies. The policies determine the sphere of activity of the administration and the laws provide the procedural guidelines of administrative activity. In other words, the Parliament sets the tone for the administration i.e., it decides what the administration has to do and how to do that. In this regard though it is true that most of the policy and legislative proposals emanate in the executive but they have to be debated, discussed and enacted by the Parliament. The Parliament enjoys every right to amend or disapprove any policy or legislative proposals initiated by the executive. This is an effective mechanism in the hands of Parliament in France and for that matter the legislature in every democratic country.

But it is noteworthy that under the Fifth Republic, the length of the parliamentary sessions has been restricted. "While in the Fourth Republic, the Assembly could meet for eight months, in the Fifth Republic it can meet for 5/4 to six months every year."[138] Resultantly, ordinary sessions of French Parliament

---

136 *Ibid*
137 Gupta, Madan Gopal, *op. cit.*, p. 110.
138 Gupta, Madan Gopal, *op.cit.*, p. 101.

are much shorter than the British Parliament. This inhibits detailed debate and discussion on policies and legislative proposals as well as on various aspects of administration and hence the control of the Parliament has not been much effective. The law making power of the Parliament is "...further restricted by the possibility of a veto by the Constitutional Council... even Parliament's abilities to amend laws and to defeat governments are strictly limited."[139]

2. **Parliamentary Questions:** Like the Parliament in England and India, the French Parliament also enjoys the power to ask questions from the Prime Minister and the Council of Ministers in regard to the administration. The questions may be written or oral and the Members of Parliament may also ask supplementary questions in case they are not satisfied with the responses. The parliamentary questions are a potent weapon in the hands of Parliament to exercise control over the administration and keep the administration on its toes.

   After 1958, this power of the Parliament has also considerably declined. It is mainly because the previous republics had the institution of "interpellation," whereby a deputy "...could use an inquiry as peg for an attack on some government action. This has been eliminated. Written questions may be submitted, but answers may come late or never. Friday afternoon was set-aside for the question period because deputies are usually on their way home for the weekend."[140]

3. **Censure Motion:** Censure motion is a very powerful method of exercising control over the executive and the administration in a country having parliamentary form of government. Thus, for instance, in India and Great Britain, if the Parliament is not satisfied with the working of the government, it may move the censure motion and if it is adopted, the government is obliged to resign. This is also true in the case of France also. Thus, the Parliament in France can censure the government and take up the motion. The grounds for taking up the motion may be numerous, for instance, it may highlight the failure to implement the policy in the desired manner. To bring this motion in the House, the signatures of at least one tenth (10%) of the deputies are needed. It may be noted that they cannot sign more than one such motion per session if it is defeated in Assembly. It is deemed to be adopted if majority of the total membership votes fall in its favour. Proxy voting is not allowed. In France, this motion was carried out first time in October 1962, against Pompidou in protest against the proposed unconstitutional referendum for the popular election of the President.[141] Along with this, the National Assembly has a right to disapprove the policies of the government and thus force it to resign. "The legislature can reject a statement of policy of the government by a simple majority, but such occasions will be rare in practice."[142]

   Though the power of the Parliament to remove the government through the adoption of this motion is real and substantial, yet it is also true that the

---

139 Machin, Howard, "France" in Ridley, F.F., *op. cit.*, p. 110.
140 Wesson G. Robert, *Modern Government: Three worlds of politics*, U.S.A: NJ Englewood Cliffs, Inc. Prentice Hall, 1981, p. 105.
141 *Ibid*, p. 105.
142 Madan Gopal Gupta, *op. cit.*, p. 111.

passage of such a motion to overthrow the governments is made very difficult under the Fifth Republic (after 1958).

4. **Budgetary Control:** Like the Parliaments of India, the US and the Great Britain, the French Parliament also has the power to approve the budget. However, the financial powers of the French Parliament are far too few in comparison to those of the Indian and British Parliaments, let alone the US Congress. The French Parliament can not reduce revenues or raise expenditures. The time period to consider the budget is too inadequate with the French Parliament. If there is no consensus between the two Houses of Parliament on the budget and if it is not passed by it within 70 days, the government can enact it by decree.[143] Moreover, "the financial powers of Parliament are greatly reduced (the government may veto private bills which increase spending or reduce taxes and, in certain circumstances, could introduce its budget by ordinance)..."[144]

5. **Parliamentary Committees:** In France, there exists permanent general committees and special committees. The permanent committees are appointed at the beginning of each legislative term for the following two years. Each committee has a bureau composed of the president, two vice-presidents, and two secretaries. Theoretically, the basic purpose of these committees is to discuss legislation and to prepare bills for final submission to the full House. The permanent committees keep a close watch over the government departments which correspond to their field of specialization.[145] The Parliament can also appoint special committees to conduct some specific purpose. All committees, whether permanent or special, can conduct investigations. Any committee can call a minister and ask him to provide information needed by it or to clarify a point under discussion.

However, the elaborate committee structure of the French Parliaments of the Third and Fourth Republics, (having 19 permanent committees in watch houses of Parliament), is reemphasized under the Fifth Republic. The number of committees has been reduced to six in each house in order to prevent specialization and close oversight of ministries. Resultantly, the parliamentary committees under the Fifth Republic share the general decline of parliamentary power.

C. **Judicial Control:** The French judicial system is divisible into two types of courts - ordinary courts and administrative courts. In case a conflict arises between two or more private citizens, it is taken to the ordinary courts and dealt with under ordinary law of the land while if there arises a conflict between a citizen and an administrative official in his official capacity, it is dealt with by the administrative courts. While dealing such disputes, the administrative courts apply a separate set of laws and procedure which in France is known as *Droit Administratif* (Administrative Law). The administrative courts hear complaints made by the citizens who have suffered as a result of official acts of civil servants. The complaint may be regarding an individual administrative-decision, a local by-law of a prefect, or even a decree issued by the government. These courts investigate the full details of the complaints made by a citizen and give their advice to the government.[146] Furthermore, they

---
143 *Ibid*
144 Machin, Howard, "France" in Ridley, F.F., *op. cit.*, p. 101.
145 Neumann G. Robert *op.cit.*, p. 319-320.
146 Machin, Howard, "France" in Ridley, F.F., *op. cit.*, pp. 99-100.

may "... declare an administrative action invalid not only because the legal powers of the administration have been exceeded (ultra vires) or correct procedure has not been respected, but also on the grounds that administrative powers have been used for purposes for which they were not intended."[147]

In France the judicial courts are relatively weak as they do not enjoy the power of judicial review. Further, their procedure is formalistic and expensive thereby making the judicial control less effective in comparison to that in Great Britain and the US. However, the system of administrative courts in France is less expensive and less formalistic and hence more effective. Commenting on administrative courts, Naumann has observed, "The French system of administrative-justice affords an easy and generally inexpensive way of keeping the administrative machine in line."[148]

D. Role of Pressure Groups

In France, the pressure groups are comparatively more strong and active and thus exert significant influence on the working of administration. It is mainly because the French people are relatively more politically conscious. Thus they are mostly organized in the form of pressure groups and thus take keen interest in the activities of administration to get their interests fulfilled. Some prominent interest groups are - National council of French Employers, National Federation of farm Syndicate National Teachers Federation, National Union of French Students etc.[149] These pressure groups operate at both national as well as local level in France. They keep a constant vigil on the activities of the administrative functionaries through a vast network of their committees and commissions. They conduct a constant scrutiny of actions of administrative officials and thus contribute significantly in regulating their behaviour. The volatile activities of these pressure groups keep the administration cautious and alert. It is mainly because there remains a fear that any irregularity in the administration will become a subject of massive (popular) criticism.

---

147 *Ibid*, p. 100.
148 Naumann G. Robert, *op. cit.*, p. 344.
149 *Ibid*, p. 284-85.

9
ADMINISTRATIVE SYSTEM IN INDIA

*I*ndia is a parliamentary democratic republic with federal features. Constitutionally, all the executive powers are vested in the President yet he acts as *de jure* (nominal) head of the state, whereas the council of ministers headed by the prime minister enjoys the real executive powers. The Council of ministers is collectively as well as individually responsible to Parliament. The Indian Parliament is bicameral consisting of two houses – Lok Sabha and Rajya Sabha. The former house consists of directly elected people's representatives whereas the latter consists of representatives of states and union territories. Lok Sabha comparatively enjoys more powers than the members of Rajya Sabha specifically in financial matters. Like USA, no organ of the state is supreme but a system of checks and balances exists in the form of judicial review, constitutional amendment by Parliament and the existence of the process of impeachment.

The administrative system at both at the Union and state's level is divided into certain ministries/ departments. Being political heads of the respective ministry/ department, ministers are accountable to Parliament for the acts of administrative officials of their respective departments. Every ministry/ department is administratively headed by a secretary who is a senior civil servant. The civil servants are recruited through competitive examination on merit basis. They are career civil servants holding their position by virtue of their professional and educational expertise. Like Britain, the system of rank classification prevails in India. The civil servants in India are expected to be politically neutral and do not enjoy any political rights except the right to vote in general elections. Adequate arrangements have been made to democratize the local government system at the grassroots level by setting up Panchayati Raj Institutions in rural areas and municipalities in urban areas. The rural and urban local institutions are constitutional entities under the 73rd and 74th Constitutional Amendments, respectively.

In the present chapter, *salient features of administration, political executive, local government, and control machinery* of India have been discussed.

(A) Administrative Features

Following are the prominent characteristics of India administration

1. Legacy of the British Rule

An important feature of the Indian administration is that it is a legacy of the British administration. It is mainly because after independence, almost the same administrative machinery that was developed during British Raj was adopted with minor modifications. Consequently, the Indian administration has deep imprints of British rule on various aspects like form of government, structure of the administration, rule of law, appointment of governors, civil services, district administration, judicial administration, local government etc. These aspects continued to be the prominent ingredients of the Indian administration. A brief description of some of these legacies is as under:

i) Parliamentary Form of Government

One of the prominent legacies of British rule is the adoption of the parliamentary form of government in India after independence. In fact the British had rich experience in the institutions and processes of Parliament. The origin and growth of parliamentary institutions and processes in India has a direct connotation from the British rule as they established parliamentary democracy in India. Further India's British connection for almost two centuries led to train Indians in parliamentarism.

ii) Rule of Law

Another important legacy of the British administration is the Rule of Law. In England, it implies the supremacy of law. It is defined by an English jurist, as "the supremacy or dominance of law, as distinguished from mere arbitrariness, or from some alternative mode, which is not law, of determining or disposing of the rights of individuals."[1] Rule of Law essentially means that no one is above the law and all are treated at par without discrimination. No one can be punished except as provided by the law. This doctrine does not permit discriminatory behaviour on the part of the administration and all are treated at par. "This doctrine which binds the government as much as the subjects to justify its action in the courts was a typically British contribution to the Indian polity. In general, the British administration left a strong legal tradition whose aim was to guard against the abuse of power."[2]

iii) Institution of District Collector

Another important legacy of the British administration is the institution of the district magistrate or collector. For administrative convenience, the provinces during British India were divided into division, districts and *tehsils* and district was the most important unit of administration. It was headed by the District Magistrate (officer-in-charge) who belonged to the Indian Civil Services and was the kingpin of the whole local and district administration. In essence he was the physical embodiment of the British Raj. In the post-independence era, the structure of the district administration remained relatively unaltered and even today the district magistrate who belonged to the Indian Administrative Services still operates almost in the same capacity.

iv) Civil Services

The Indian Civil Services, the "steel frame' of administration in India is perhaps the most important legacy of British Raj in India. After independence, the Indian

---

1 Lord Hewart as quoted in Bhagwan, Vishnu and Vidya Bhushan, New Delhi, *World Constitution*, Sterling Publishers Pvt. Ltd., 1991, p. 24.
2 Fadia, B.L. , kuldeep Fadia, *Indian Administration*, Agra: Sahity Bhawan Publication, 2012, p. 52.

government retained the basic structure, functions and overall ethos of the then Indian Civil Services (ICS) *in toto*. The present Indian administrative service is the offshoot of the Indian Civil Services during the British rule whose officers hold the key administrative positions in India like their counterparts during British rule. These services carry great respect and responsibilities even today. "Indian Civil Services popularly known by its acronym ICS, originated as the elite civil services of the Indian government under the British colonial rule in India and continues in the contemporary civil services of India, though these are now organized differently."[3]

2. Federal Structure with Unitary Bias

One of the important features of the Indian administration is that it has a federal structure with unitary bias. In fact, the word 'federation' has been mentioned nowhere in the constitution; rather India has been described as the 'Union of States'. Unlike the US, the Indian states are not 'inviolable' or indestructible units as they enjoy no sovereign status and no state has the right to secede. Moreover, the Indian Parliament enjoys the right not only to alter their names but also their area and boundaries. But India has dual government system functioning at national and state levels having division of powers. There is a written constitution and both governments draw their powers directly from the constitution. In case of conflict, there exists an independent judiciary to interpret the constitution. But unlike the US Constitution, the Indian Constitution does not provide any safeguard for the protection of the rights of states. In the US the consent of states is vital to the amendment of the Constitution but this consent in India is restricted only to a few specific matters.

Further, not only the division of subjects is in favour of the centre but unlike the US the residuary powers also rests with the centre. During Emergency, the Indian Constitution enables the federal government to acquire the strength of unitary system. Even in normal times the Union executive enjoys the right to give direction to the State governments, but this power relates only to specific matter. But after the proclamation of Emergency, this power extends to all matters and the legislative power of the centre extends to state subjects. The constitutional provision with regard to the creation of All India Services is further a part of unitary bias. The members of the All India Services are appointed by the Centre but are transferable in both centre and states. They have to administer both the laws of the centre and state governments as applicable to the matter in question. But a member of the All India Service can only be dismissed or removed by the Union government and states can only initiate disciplinary proceeding against them.

The existence of the system of unified judiciary headed by the Supreme Court at its apex is further a case of unitary bias. As a result the Supreme Court administers both the Union and state laws as are applicable to the cases coming up for adjudication. On the same pattern, the election machinery, accounts and audit are also similarly integrated. Moreover there exists the concept of single citizenship which means unlike the US, an Indian citizen need not take the separate citizenship of the state in which he is living. All theses aspects are again going to reflect the unitary bias of the Indian administration.

---

3   Chattopadhyay, H.P., Indu Baghel, *Indian Administration* Vol II, New Delhi: Global Vision Publishing House, New Delhi, 2009, p. 323.

3. Accountable Administration

Another important feature of the Indian administration is that it is an 'accountable administration'. Public accountability is exerted through a number of channels. The most significant among these is the ministerial accountability. The administration is hierarchical in structure and public servants in all the departments are bound by senior-subordinate relations. All the administrative functionaries are responsible through their seniors to the administrative head who is the secretary of the department, and to the political head of the department who is its minister-in-charge. It being a parliamentary form of government, the ministers are part of the Parliament and are responsible to it for all acts of omission and commission of the officers under them.

Any Member of Parliament can ask any question to the minister concerned, who is supposed to provide a satisfactory answer failing which he has no option but to resign. However, the minister, in turn, can take disciplinary action against the guilty officials for their acts of omission and commission. Besides, the cabinet is also collectively responsible to Parliament. Being sailors on the same boat, the cabinet members sink and swim together. Thus, cabinet ministers share collective responsibility for the general policies and record of the government and bear individual responsibility for the actions and record of that portion of the administrative-machine placed directly in their charge.[4] In addition to the individual and collective responsibility of the ministers to Parliament, they also face a substantial influence from other social forces such as the political parties, pressure groups etc. Civil society and the media also act as deterrents to administrative malfunctioning.

4. High Profile of Civil Services

Another important feature of the Indian administration is that the civil services enjoy a high profile as they constitute the backbone of the Indian administration. The civil servants enjoy a respectable place in society. The civil service in India is a career service that attracts the talented and brightest youth of the nation. They are generally chosen in an early part of their life. India's best brains make serious and sincere efforts to enter into these services. It is despite the fact that "... corporate jobs may offer the best of salaries and perks, a majority of the youngsters and their parents still crave entry to the prestigious Indian Civil Services held by the Union Public Service Commission."[5]

Unlike the US, the civil servants in India are classified on the basis of traditional ranks and perhaps still the most common principle of classification known as rank classification. This doctrine of classification is common in military organizations. As per this doctrine, "...the rank or title of the individual gives him a right to the pay, prestige and prerequisites of the rank or title; and he carries with him the title and its right whatever role in the organization he may play at a particular time."[6] Contrary to position classification that emphasizes on the particular job performed/ position held (Position is considered as a structure of duties and responsibilities) here the emphasis is on the rank or title of the performer. Under this system, "...

---
4 Moodie, Grame C, *The government of Great Britain (3rd ed)*, London: Methuen and Co. Ltd., 1971, p. 102.
5 Chattopadhyay, H.P., Indu Baghel, *op. cit.*, p. 323.
6 Fadia, B.L., kuldeep Fadia, *op. cit.*, p. 761.

civil service posts are grouped into distinct homogenous cadres under a common service named on the basis of specific function attached to the posts in question."[7]

The civil services in India are career civil services and thus the officers enjoy security of tenure. They draw handsome salaries that are intended to maintain their status. Other fringe benefits like promotions, family allowances, various social security arrangements, gratuity, and retirement benefits in the form of pension are lucrative. "The very fact that a major share of every year's top posts in the civil services exams is bogged by professionals from various streams shows that IAS is still the dream job for many."[8] Unlike the French Civil Servants, the political rights of civil servants in India are very restricted.

The Indian civil servants being the inevitable ingredients of the government apparatus discharge multifarious administrative activities under the direction and control of the elected representatives of the people in strict accordance with rules and regulation. The most important task of civil servants is relating to the formulation and implementation of public policy. To this end, they remain engaged in the collection of relevant data in order to find out the crux of the problem. In essence they are known as the 'think-tanks' of the government. However, recent decades have experienced a trend towards rolling back of the state at the global level and India is no exception. "Thatcherism in UK and Reaganomics in USA tried to pull out the state from the morass of over involvement. The decline of communism in Eastern Europe has furthered the trend towards economic liberalization and disinvestment in public sector. India could not have remained unaffected by these global trends."[9]

5. Emphasis on Good Governance

There has been growing realization about the prevailing inefficiency, non-responsiveness, lack of accountability in the Indian administrative system. Efforts have, therefore, been made to promote good governance during the last about two decades. Some of the more important initiatives in this direction are discussed below.

i) *Transparency*

To protect its imperial interests, the British government in India enacted the Official Secrets Act, 1923. The Act restricted public insight into the official machinery and its functioning. The provisions of the Act, however, were incompatible with the democratic governance since undue secrecy and lack of openness in the operations of government promote inefficiency, non-responsiveness, lack of accountability, and corruption. Therefore, there has been a demand since long to promote transparency in the functioning of the government. The need of openness in government was mainly realized during the National Emergency imposed under Article 352 of the Constitution during the mid-seventies.

Some initiatives were made to curtail the sway of Official Secrecy Act by providing access to the people to 'information' and the most prominent among these was by the National Democratic Alliance government which in 2002, enacted the Freedom of Information Act, which however was never notified. The United Progressive

---

7 Ibid, p. 763.
8 Chattopadhyay, H.P., Indu Baghel, *op. cit.*, p. 323.
9 Fadia, B.L., kuldeep Fadia, *op. cit.*, p. 750.

Alliance government in 2005 enacted the Right to Information Act which allows every citizen of this country to ask for any information from any public authority. "The Act has thrown open the system of governance to total transparency and therefore inescapable accountability."[10]

Under the Act, all the public authorities are required to provide most of the information *suo moto* and to designate a Public Information Officer (PIO) who is responsible for providing the information asked for. The citizens are not even required to disclose the purpose for seeking the information. The PIO is obliged to provide the information within 30 days of filing of an application. If the requisite information pertains to one's life or freedom it needs to be made available within 48 hours. Delay beyond 30 days in dispensing information would invite a fine of Rs. 250 per day which may extend to a maximum of Rs. 25000 from the public official responsible for delay. Further, in case a public authority fails to provide the information sought within the stipulated period or if the information provided is inadequate or inappropriate, the applicant may contact the appellate authority of the respective public authority and later on the state and central information commission which have been provided under the Act.

ii) E-Governance

E-governance denotes governance through electronic means. It implies the use of information and communication technologies (ICT) towards effective governance. It promotes transparency and openness in government working. It considers a paperless government and gets rid of the system from the dusty files. It has emerged as an important 'digital revolution' and transformed the citizen -administration interface. "At the most fundamental level e-governance would mean facilitating government citizen interface by making it not just efficient but transparent too.[11]" Thus e-governance is the mode of generating openness in the governmental working as well as empowering the citizens to enable them to interact with the government. While commenting on the motive of e-governance, the chairman of the second Administrative Reform Commission, has expressed that the very purpose of ensuring e-governance is "... to achieve better delivery to citizens, ushering in transparency and accountability, empowering people through information, improved efficiency within governments and improved interface with business and industry."[12]

In India, the first step towards e-governance was taken when efforts were initiated to connect all the district headquarters with the efforts of the National Informatics Center (NIC) that was created in 1975 for the purpose. Visualizing the importance of this concept Rajiv Gandhi, the then Prime Minister advocated its application in the governmental organizations. But it got prominence only in the 1990s with the onset of the IT revolution in the country. "From the early nineties, e-governance has seen the use of IT for wider sectoral applications with policy emphasis on reaching out to rural areas and taking in greater inputs from NGOs and private sector as well."[13]

---

10 P.M. Manmohansingh's address, *op. cit.,* p. 267.
11 Verma, S.P., ed., *Information Technology and Indian Administration*, Kanishka Publishers and Distributers, 2004, p. 13.
12 http://www.hindu.com/2009/01/25/stories/2009012556000900.htm
13 http://dqindia.ciol.com/content/top_stories/203101501.asp

E-governance is now increasingly used to facilitate the service delivery mechanism particularly in areas involving citizen-government interface, both at the Centre as also in the states.

The second Administrative Reforms Commission felt that a legal framework is necessary in view of the mammoth dimension of the task and the levels of co-ordination between the Centre and the States. It has asked the Centre to prepare a clear road map with a set of milestones to transform the citizen-government interaction at all levels to the e-governance mode by 2020. It has asked all organizations and departments of the Union and State governments to identify e-governance initiatives which could be undertaken within their functional area, keeping the needs of citizens in view. The Commission also suggested that governmental forms, processes and structures should be re-designed to make them adaptable to e-Governance, backed by procedural, institutional and legal changes.[14]

iii) Citizen Charter

A wider consensus was evolved to make the administration more accountable and responsive in the Conference of Chief Ministers of various States and Union Territories which was presided over by the Prime Minister, held in 1997. The Conference broadly deliberated on the introduction of citizens' charters specifically with those sectors having a large public interface. The task of formulation, implementation and co-ordination of these Citizens' Charters was entrusted to the Department of Administrative Reforms and Public Grievances (DARPG) at Centre. To this end, a core group was constituted by DARPG.[15]

Citizen's Charter (CC) is a document of commitments made by an organization to the citizens/ client groups in respect of the services being provided to them. In general terms a "Citizens Charter represents the commitment of the organization towards standard, quality and time frame of service delivery, grievance redressal mechanism, and transparency and accountability."[16] The underlying purpose of the Citizens' Charter is to empower citizens by persuading a public organization to improve the quality of public services.

A number of citizens' charters have been adopted by the centre and state government organisations. "Till April, 2006, 111 Citizens' Charters had been formulated by the Central Government Ministries, Departments and Organisations and 668 Charters by various agencies of State Governments & Administrations of Union Territories"[17]. Majority of these charters are available on websites and are open to public scrutiny.

6. Public-Private Partnership (PPP)

Before the structural adjustment programmes (SAP) of the early 1990s in India, there was limited intervention of the third party especially in the delivery of public services. The World Bank Report advocated the engagement of multiple actors in the

---

14 11th Report of 2nd ARC entitled "Promoting e-governance: The smart way forward"
15 Kaur, Inderjeet, *Public Grievance System In India*, Bava,Noorjahan, ed.,(2004), *'Public Administration In 21st Century'*, New Delhi: Kaniska Publishers, Distributers, p. 362.
16 *Ibid*
17 *http://goicharters.nic.in/ccinitiative.htm 27/02/09*

process of governance so that the standard and quality of public services could be improved; it rejected exclusive dependence on the state. Consequently, the concept of Public-Private Partnership (PPP) became prominent and was introduced across the world and India has been no exception in this regard. PPP was an answer to bureaucratic non-responsiveness and fund crunch with the government. It was also advocated that PPP would facilitate the public sector to manage rather than operate thereby ensuring specialization in service delivery, and letting the public concentrate only on policy-making and planning.

The Scheme for support to PPP in infrastructure and the procedure for approval of PPP projects at central sector projects have been approved by the Cabinet Committee on Economic Affairs in India.[18] A Public Private Partnership Approval Committee[19] (PPPAC) has been set up for approval of projects under PPP initiatives in infrastructure. The committee would be serviced by the Department of Economic Affairs, who will set up a special cell for servicing such proposals. The Committee may co-opt experts as necessary.

There can be a wide spectrum of PPP arrangements under which public and private sector jointly contribute to public good. 'Joint ventures, private finance initiative, partial privatization through partnering with strategic investor, Build-Own and Operate (BOO), Build-Operate and Transfer (BOT) and Build-Own-Operate and Transfer (BOOT) are some of the PPP arrangements'.[20] Many private institutions like Infrastructure Development Finance Company (IDFC), a Special Purpose Vehicle (SPVs) company IIFCL and private sector banks and financial institutions like State Bank of India, ICICI bank, and HDFC bank etc. are funding various PPP projects in India.[21]

7. Democratic Decentralization

The issue of local self government has become prominent in India since the enactment of the 73rd and 74th Constitutional (Amendment) Acts. The two Acts respectively provide for the establishment of Panchayati Raj Institutions (PRIs) in rural areas and the establishment of local bodies in urban areas. These Acts not only imparted constitutional status to these bodies and hence the respectability but also made them third tier next to the centre and states, of the governing structure. 1/3rd reservation both in urban and rural local bodies has been provided to women representatives and to people belonging to SC/ST category on the basis of their population. Various functions have been entrusted to these bodies by 11th and 12th schedules of the constitution. To ensure the people's participation in local affairs these Acts provide

---

18 Cabinet Committee on Economic Affairs approved the Scheme for support to Public Private Partnerships in infrastructure and the procedure for approval of PPP projects at central sector projects in its meeting of 25th July and 27th October 2005, respectively. http://www.pppinindia.com/approval-committees.asp, retrieved on Feb 24, 2009.
19 The committee comprised the secretary of Department of Economic Affairs as chairman and secretaries of Planning Commission Department of Expenditure, Department of Legal Affairs; and Department sponsoring a project as members., . http://www.pppinindia.com/approval-committees.asp ,retrieved on 2402/2009.
20 Gupta, M.P.,Kumar , Praphat (ed, al.), *Government Online: Opportunities and Challenges*, New Delhi: TMH Publishing Company Ltd, p. 214.
21 http://www.pppinindia.com/financing.asp, retrieved, 24/02/09.

legal status to Gram Sabha and Ward committees. In addition to this, the provision of constituting District Planning Committees (DPCs) proved significant in ensuring the involvement of common people in the task of planning at the local level. "In the comparatively newer bottom – up approach, District Planning Committees have been entrusted to consolidate micro plans to be finally accommodated in the plan proposals of the respective state and ultimately the National Plan."[22] Besides, these Acts provide for a Local List and constitutionally allotted 29 subjects to rural local bodies and 18 subjects to urban local bodies.

8. Politic-Administrative Corruption

Indian administration is further marked by the problem of continuously growing corruption.[23] Corruption has become a serious malady of our politico-administrative system and is prevalent at all levels of our administration. It is one of the fundamental hurdles obstructing the path of development. Mention may be made of the recent glaring examples of the 2-G spectrum scam, Commonwealth Games scam, Adarsh housing society scam, coal scam in which the high profile politico-administrative leadership has been stated to be involved.

Corruption, in India, is mainly because of two defects of 'our culture of governance'. The first defect pertains to the lack of transparency in the administration. The emergence of the problem of nepotism is an outcome of this defect. It means showing special favour on the basis of family, kinship relations, caste, creed etc. particularly in matters of appointment. Thus the officials while discharging their administrative obligations extend as much help to their kin as possible. Though such behaviour is theoretically proscribed yet it is effectively practised in administrative working. Still the kinship bonds are so strong in the society that the administrative officials can not come out of the clutches of these ties. Merit is often sacrificed at the altar of nepotism and consequently even inefficient persons enter the administration thereby destroying the efficiency of the administration.

The second defect pertains to delay and red tapism. It is an outcome of the complicated administrative procedures. The procedures usually involve much paper work moving through many levels of organizational hierarchy thereby causing inordinate delay and frustration. This problem is further aggravated by too much adherence of the administrative officials to the administrative procedures. In addition to this, the delay in administrative working is also because of the tendency of our public servants not to take decisions. "While the corrupt are prepared to take even the most brazenly illegal decisions propelled by the Viagra of the right amount of

---

22 Mishra, Sweta, "Decentralisation: Concept, Characteristics and constraints," in *Contemporary Debates in Public Administration (ed)* by AlkaDhameja, New Delhi: Prentice-Hall of India, 2003, p. 178.
23 Corruption is a deviation from established norms or from what is prescribed. It includes material as well as non-material gains. It has been defined as "deliberate and intentional exploitation of one's position, status, or resources directly or indirectly for personal aggrandizement whether it to be in terms of material gains or enhancement of power, prestige or influence beyond what is legitimate or sanctioned by commonly accepted norms to be detriment of the interests of other persons or the community as a whole." (Avasthi, A. and Maheshwari, S.R., *Public Administration*, Agra: Lakshmi Publications, 1971, p. 342)

bribe, many honest public servants contribute only delay by not taking decisions at all."[24]

(B) POLITICAL EXECUTIVE

India is a parliamentary democracy in which there exists two types of executives – nominal and real. The President of India belongs to the first category and the Cabinet headed by the Prime Minister falls in the latter. A brief discussion of the two is as under:

PRESIDENT

The Indian President is the counterpart of the British Monarch and the two play almost an identical role in their respective spheres but unlike the later (who is hereditary), the former is elected. Constitutionally, all the executive powers are vested in the President under Article 53 who exercises them on the 'aid and advice' of the Cabinet as provided in Article 74(i). Being the head of the State, the government is run in his name. The framers of the Constitution preferred indirect election for the Indian President. He is elected by an electoral college which consists of all the elected members of both Houses of Parliament (Lok Sabha and Rajya Sabha) and the elected members of the Legislative Assemblies of states.

Qualifications

According to Article 58 of the Indian Constitution, for being eligible to hold the office of the President a person must:
i) be an Indian citizen;
ii) have attained 35 years of age
iii) fulfill all the qualifications as are required for being elected as a member of Lok Sabha.
iv) not hold any office of profit under central, state or local government.

Tenure

The Indian President enjoys a fixed tenure of 5 years from the date of joining. He can be re-elected and unlike in the case of America, the Indian Constitution limits neither any time period nor the number of terms for his re-election. However, he may be removed from his office before the expiry of his term through the process of impeachment as provided under Article 61 of the Constitution. The incumbent may even tender his resignation to the Vice-President before the expiry of this term.

The process of impeachment can be initiated against the President in case he violates the Constitution. The process of impeachment is a quasi-judicial process brought in Parliament after considering the charges of violation of the Constitution leveled against the President. Either House of Parliament 'can prefer the charge of violation of the Constitution'. However, such a resolution can be moved only after a 14-days' notice in writing signed by not less than one-fourth of the total number of members of that House. If the resolution is passed by two-thirds majority of

---

24 Vittal, N., "Effective Management in Government System," in *Public Administration: Fresh Perspectives* (ed.) by R.K.Arora, *op. cit.*, p. 218.

the total membership of that House, then the resolution will be sent to the second House, which will investigate the charge itself or cause it to be investigated through a committee. The President enjoys the right to appear or to be represented at such investigations. If the second House also passes the resolution by the same majority after investigating the charges, the resolution will have the effect of removing the President from his office from the date of passage of this resolution.

Remuneration

Initially, his remuneration was fixed Rs. 10,000 by the Constitution (second schedule). However, it has been revised by the Parliament from time to time. At present, the President is given a salary of Rs. 1.5 lakh per month. It was fixed by Parliament through the legislation passed in 2008. Besides, he is entitled to certain allowances as are fixed by Parliament. Also, he is provided a rent-free accommodation called the *Rashtrapati Bhavan*. After retirement, he is entitled to a decent pension, a free house and some secretarial assistance.

Immunities

The Indian President enjoys complete immunity from any court procedure. He cannot be arrested for any sort of offence. No court of law can issue orders against him for the duties discharged by him in his official capacity.

Succession

Constitutionally, the Vice-President succeeds if the office of President falls vacant either due to his death, resignation or removal through impeachment. There may also arise the possibility of temporary vacancy to this office either due to the absence of the President from India, his long illness or due to some other reason. In that case the Vice-President shall discharge his duties till the date on which the President resumes his duties.

Powers of President

Constitutionally, the Indian President enjoys a vast array of powers which include executive, legislative, financial, judicial and even emergency powers. Being the head of the State, all powers have been formally assigned to him. A brief view of these powers is as under:

Legislative Powers

Like the British Crown, the President of India is a constituent part of the legislature. Being a part and parcel of the Indian Parliament, he exercises a number of legislative powers that are discussed as under

Summoning, Prorogation, Dissolution

Constitutionally, there are four sessions of Parliament in a year. It is the President who summons these sessions. The President can also summon some special session of the Parliament. He also prorogues the sessions of the Parliament. In case of some deadlock between the two Houses of Parliament, the President summons a joint sitting of the both the Houses. In addition to this, the President also enjoys the power to dissolve the Lower House of Parliament.

Nomination of Members

Though majority of the members of both the Houses of Parliament are elected either by direct or indirect election yet the President enjoys the power to nominate certain members to both the Houses of Parliament. He nominates twelve such members to the Council of States (Rajya Sabha) who have 'special knowledge or practical experience of literature, science, art and social service' and two members belonging to the Anglo-Indian community to the House of the People (Lok Sabha), if he feels that they are inadequately represented in the House.

Addressing the Sessions of Parliament

After every general election to the Lower House, the President addresses the joint session of the Parliament. He also addresses a joint sitting of both Houses at the beginning of the first session every year in which he spells out the broad policies of the government to be under taken during the ensuing year. He also enjoys the right to address the Houses of Parliament separately or jointly, at any time.

Right to Send Message

The Indian President like his US counterpart also enjoys the right to send a message to either House of Parliament in regard to any pending Bill or to any other matter. The concerned House is obliged to consider such a message. However, it is not obligatory for the House to follow the message while framing the law.

Previous Sanctions to Legislations

Constitutionally, the prior approval of the President is required on a number of issues before being introduced into the Parliament. Such matters prominently involve the money bills, the bills regarding formation of new states, the bills regarding alteration of the boundaries of the existing states, the bills drawing expenditure from Consolidated Fund of India, state bills imposing restrictions on the freedom of trade, the bills affecting taxation in which states are interested etc.

Approval to Legislations and Veto Power

For being enacted as laws, all bills passed by the Parliament need presidential approval. In case the President does not wish to give his assent to the bill submitted for his approval, he may either return the bill to the Parliament for reconsideration, or withhold assent to the bill. In the first instance, i.e., when the bill is returned for reconsideration, it is mandatory for the Parliament to reconsider the bill. However, in case, if the Parliament again passes the bill, with or without amendments, even by a simple majority, the President has no option but to approve it. Unlike the United States, no special majority of the Parliament is required for passing such bills.

But the Constitution does not prescribe any time-limit for the President to give assent to a bill; this provides a certain amount of discretion to the President who may withhold his assent to a bill especially under certain special circumstances. He may simply let the bill lie on his table for an indefinite time especially when the ministry is unstable or when it has tendered resignation. This discretion can also be exercised in case of private members' bills.

Ordinance Making Power

The President even enjoys the power to issue ordinances if the circumstances so require. Such ordinances are usually issued when either of the two Houses of Parliament has been prorogued or is otherwise not in session. The President shall not have the power to issue ordinance when both the Houses of Parliament are in session. These ordinances have equal force as any law enacted by Parliament does have.

However, any such ordinance shall cease to have effect after six months from the date of its issue. Further, such ordinances must be laid before Parliament after it reassembles and to remain in force, such ordinances require the approval of Parliament within a period of six weeks from the date of its reassembly.

Executive Powers

Constitutionally, the President enjoys all the 'executive powers' of the Union. Article 53 of the Constitution states that the "executive powers of the Union shall be vested in the President." Being the chief executive of the government, he is concerned with the management of national affairs. He is also responsible for the smooth working of the government. His executive powers can be discussed under following heads:

Power of Appointment and Removal

The President enjoys the power to appoint a number of high dignitaries under the government of India. He formally designates the Prime Minister and the other Ministers of the Union on the advice of the later. He appoints the Comptroller General of India (CAG), the Attorney General of India, the Judges of the Supreme Court and the High Courts of the states, the Governors of the states and the Lieutenant-Governor of the Union Territories, the Chairman and the members of various commissions like Election Commission, Finance Commission, Union Public Service Commission, Commissions for the SCs & STs, BCs, Minorities etc. Most of these appointments are made by him on the advice of Cabinet. However, in case of some appointments like the appointment of the Judges of the Supreme Court, the President is required to consult the Chief Justice of India and the other judges of Supreme Court or High Courts as he deems fit.

The President even enjoys the power to remove these functionaries. Except a few officials like the judges of the Supreme Court and the High Courts, Chairman and the members of the Union Public Service commission, etc., who can be removed through the process of impeachment, the other functionaries may be removed by the President.

Military Powers

The President also acts as the supreme commander or the commander-in-chief of the Armed Forces. In this capacity he enjoys the power to appoint the military officials at higher levels. He acts as the Chairman of the National Defense Committee. He can give orders for the reorganization and experimentation of military forces but such orders are usually issued with the prior consultation and advice of the higher military officials. He may declare war or peace in the country. However, his military powers are far less in comparison to those of either the U.S. President or the English Crown.

Diplomatic Powers

Being the head of the State, the President enjoys a lot of powers with regard to foreign affairs. He represents India at the international level. He also enjoys the power to appoint Indian diplomats to other nations and to receive foreign diplomats to India. In addition to this, he is empowered to negotiate treaties and agreements with foreign nations. However, such treaties and agreements require the ratification of Parliament before coming into force.

Power to Seek Information

The President further enjoys the right to seek any sort of information from the prime minister with regard to any matter. The prime minister, being the chief adviser to the President, keeps him informed on all important issues pertaining to the council of ministers and Parliament.

Administration of Union Territories and Directions to State Governments

In India, the administration of Union Territories is run in the name of the President. So, he is responsible for conducting the administration of these territories smoothly. He appoints the Lieutent-Governors or the Chief Commissioners, as the case may be, in these territories. He can appoint a joint administrator for more than one Union Territory.

The President also enjoys the power to issue directions to state governments for the strict observance of some Union laws. He also enjoys the right to constitute Inter-State-Councils to resolve the disputes and to promote co-operation among various states.

Judicial Powers

Almost all the constitutions equip their executive with some judicial powers and the Indian President in this regard is no exception. Thus, like the US President and the British Crown, the President in India is constitutionally empowered to grant pardon to those who have been tried and convicted of some offence. These pardoning powers of the executive include pardon, reprieve, respite, remission, suspension, commutation. *Pardon* generally provides immunity to the convict from all charges levelled against him for the breach of laws. The scope of his pardoning power is quite extensive as he can pardon any convict except one convicted by impeachment. *Reprieve* simply means the suspension or postponement of penalties awarded to a person e.g., pending a proceeding for pardon or commutation. The President grants it usually on humanitarian grounds. *Respite* refers to reducing the sentence than the prescribed penalty by keeping in view some specific facts like pregnancy in case of a woman offender. Through *Remission*, the President may reduce the amount of sentence without changing its nature, e.g., a sentence of life imprisonment may be remitted to one year. On the other hand, *commutation* means changing one form of punishment by another and also that of lighter character, e.g., death sentence may be commuted into life imprisonment.[25]

---

25 D.D., Basu, *Introduction to the Constitution of India*, (12th Edition), New Delhi: Prentice Hall of India Private Ltd., 1989, p. 176.

Emergency Powers

The Indian Constitution provides several emergency powers to the President to meet any sort of exigency in abnormal circumstances. These powers of the President have been mentioned in the 18th Part of the Constitution (Articles 352–360). However, these emergency provisions have been at length amended by the 42nd and 44th Constitutional (Amendment) Acts in 1976 and 1978, respectively. The Indian President enjoys emergency powers under three different situations.[26] The circumstances, the provisions and the impacts thereof are briefly discussed below in brief.

(A) Emergency due to War, External Aggression or Armed Rebellion or the Threat thereof

Under Article 352, the President of India is empowered to proclaim national emergency if he is satisfied that the security of India or any part thereof has been threatened due to war, external aggression or armed rebellion. This emergency can even be declared in case of the imminent threat of external aggression or armed rebellion. Such declarations of the emergency situations under Article 352 fall within the purview of judicial review. This proclamation shall cease to have effect unless approved by both the Houses of Parliament by two-thirds majority within one month from the date of declaration. Such declaration, if approved by the Parliament, will remain in force for a period of six months from the date of its approval. This means, the declaration shall cease to have effect unless it is again approved by a fresh resolution of both the Houses of Parliament within that period for another six months. It has also been provided under the Constitution that if the Lok Sabha by majority passes a resolution against the continuity of the national emergency under Article 352, the President has to issue a proclamation of revocation of the emergency. The President is even obliged to convene a special session for the consideration of the resolution regarding revocation of the emergency in case not less than one-tenths of the members of Lok Sabha give in writing to the Speaker or to the President a notice in writing to convene a session.

The effects of the declaration of emergency under Article 352 can be discussed under the following heads:

- *Effect on Executive:* Such a proclamation result into enhancing the powers of the executive exorbitantly because it leads to disturb the federal system of the country, which acquires a unitary character. Thus, during such a proclamation, all the executive powers are vested into the hands of the Central government. Though the state governments remain in operation, the Central government may give directions for the management of their affairs.
- *Effect on Legislature:* During the proclamation of the national emergency the Parliament enjoys extraordinary powers. Firstly, it can extend the normal life of the Lok Sabha by Law for a period of one year at a time. However, such extension of life of the House can not extend beyond a period of 6 months after such proclamation cease to operate. Secondly, it enhances the power of Parliament to legislate even on subjects falling under the State List. Such Proclamation, however, does not lead to the suspension of the state legislature;

---

26 *Ibid*, pp. 315-28.

it merely disturbs the division of legislative powers between Centre and states.
- *Effect on the Financial Relations between the Centre and States:* During national emergency the President is constitutionally empowered to alter the constitutional provisions with regard to the distribution of financial resources between the Centre and the states.
- *Effect on Fundamental Rights:* The proclamation of emergency under Article 352 curtails the Fundamental Rights of the citizens. As soon as the national emergency is declared by the President, Article 358 automatically comes in operation and it suspends Article 19 i.e., Right to Freedom and as a result all the six freedoms available to the citizens under this Article stand suspended. If the President also applies Article 359 by an Order, the right of the citizens to move to the courts for enforcement of their Fundamental Rights (Article 32) is suspended. It leads to the suspension of all the Fundamental Rights of the citizens except those mentioned under Articles 20 and 21, i.e., 'Right to Life and Liberty'.

(B) Emergency in States due to Constitutional Breakdown

The President is also empowered to proclaim emergency in any state under Article 356, in case the Governor of that state sends a report stating that there is a breakdown of the constitutional machinery in the state or the administration of the state is not being carried out in accordance with the constitutional provisions or he himself is satisfied about the failure of such constitutional machinery in that state. If the President is satisfied with the report of the Governor or otherwise, he may proclaim the state of emergency under Article 356 in that state.

This kind of emergency may further be proclaimed by the President if the state failed to comply with the directions and orders of the Union government (Article 365). After the proclamation of such emergency, the approval of both the Houses of Parliament needs to be sought within two months; otherwise the proclamation ceases to have effect. Such parliamentary approval will remain in force for a period of six months after which it will have to be approved by Parliament again. However, such a proclamation will cease to have effect on the expiry of one year except when national emergency under article 352 is declared in whole of the country, or that part of the country in which the state falls, or the Election Commission feels that it is difficult to conduct elections in that state within one year. In this context the Election Commission is required to produce a certificate to that effect.

The following would be the effects of this kind of proclamation:
- The President becomes empowered to suspend or dissolve the state legislature.
- The Governor of the state, being the representative of the President, becomes the real chief executive of that state.
- The President can issue direction for the smooth governance of such state.
- The President may assign special duties on the state functionaries. However, the President can't diminish the powers of the state High Court.
- The Parliament enjoys the right to frame laws for such states on the subjects falling under State List.
- The President can give orders to spend money from the Consolidated and Contingency Funds of that state.

(C) Emergency due to Financial Crisis

This kind of emergency is proclaimed by the President under Article 360. If the President is satisfied that the financial stability or credit of India or any part of its territory is under crisis or faces threat thereof, he may declare financial emergency in whole of the country or any (affected) part thereof. The proclamation regarding financial emergency will have to be approved by Parliament as in the case of other two types of emergencies.

The proclamation of financial emergency has following effects:
- The President can bring necessary changes in the existing pattern of revenue distribution between the Centre and the states.
- The Union executive can give necessary directions to any state to observe some canons of financial propriety as the Centre may consider fit.
- The Centre can give direction to the states to reserve their all Money Bills or other financial Bills passed by their legislatures for the consideration of the President.
- The Centre is empowered to reduce the salaries and allowances of all or any class of functionaries including the judges of the Supreme and High Courts.

Position

From the above discourse, it would appear that the President in India possesses vast powers and may be one of the most powerful chief executives in the world. However, the actual position is immensely different from this and the President, in effect, possesses far too few powers. In fact, the very fact that India is a parliamentary democracy makes the position of the President weak. This is because such a system of government is characterized by the existence of two types of executive viz. the nominal and the real – the former formally possessing all the powers while the latter actually exercising all the powers formally held by the former. This is also explicitly explained in the Constitution of India. Thus, according to Article 74(i), all the powers of the President listed above are to be exercised by him according to the 'aid and advice' of the council of ministers. Article 74(i) reads "there shall be a Council of Ministers with the Prime Minister at the head to aid and advice the President who shall, in the exercise of his functions, act in accordance with such advice." It is noteworthy, however, that the President may return the 'advice' tendered by the council of ministers for their reconsideration but in case it again sends the 'advice' with or without modifications, as desired by the President, the latter has no option but to give assent to it.

There are only a few occasions when there does not exist the council of ministers and the prime minister to 'aid and advice' the President and there arises the possibility of exercise of discretion by the President. One such occasion is the appointment of prime minister. However, in normal circumstances, the President cannot exercise his discretion even in this case because by convention he has to invite the leader of the majority party in the Lok Sabha to form the government. In case, no single party has been able to secure majority of seats in the House, the President has to take his own decision. But even in that case, the President has to call the leader of some pre or post election alliance to form the government. Further, before calling any such claimant to form the government, the President has to ensure about the stability of such a government. Moreover, the President is also obliged to consider the decisions taken by his predecessors in such situations. Again, the President also has to seek the opinion of the constitutional experts in such cases, though he is not bound by their advice. However, despite all these limitations, it cannot be denied that there remains room for presidential discretion in such a situation.

When the council of ministers loses the confidence vote on the floor of the House and the prime minister advises the President to dissolve the House, there arises another situation of vacuum in which President has to use his discretion before taking a final decision. This is because the current council of ministers has lost its right to 'aid and advice' the President while the new council of ministers is yet to be constituted.

Further, under Article 61 of the Constitution, the President has to 'preserve, protect and defend the Constitution and the law.' As a natural corollary to this, in case, the council of ministers and the prime minister advises him to do anything which is against the Constitution or advises him not to do something which is obligatory for him to do, he can exercise his discretion and, in that case, is not bound by such advice. For instance, if the council of ministers advises him "…to call the next session of Parliament after a year … it is the duty of the President … to disregard such advice and call a session of the two Houses as required by Article 85(I) of the Constitution."[27] Thus "the President is not bound by the advice of the council of ministers if such advice compels him to violate the Constitution or where the competence of Parliament to pass such a Bill is itself in doubt."[28]

The question of discretion of the President is a very complicated issue and its complexity is growing with the passage of time as more and more such situations are arising and more such questions are being asked to which neither the Constitution nor the conventions has any answer.

VICE-PRESIDENT

The Constitution of India also provides for a Vice-President under Article 63. Like the President, he is also elected by an electoral college which consists only of both the Houses of Parliament by means of single transferable vote and secret ballot. Unlike the presidential election, the nominated members of both the Houses of Parliament also exercise their franchise in the election of the Vice-President. On the other hand, however, the members of the state legislative assemblies do not participate in this election.

Qualifications

The necessary qualifications for the office of the Vice-President are mentioned under Article 66 (4) of the Constitution. Thus, he must:

    i) be a citizen of India;

    ii) have completed 35 years of age;

    iii) qualify for election as a member of the Rajya Sabha;

---

27 *The Tribune*, New Delhi, August 16, 2006, p. 11.
28 *Ibid*

iv) not hold any office of profit under the Union or state government or local authority;

v) not be a member of Parliament or a state legislature.

Tenure

The term of the Vice-President is 5 years. But he may resign from his post prior to the completion of his term. He may send his resignation to the President. He can even be removed from this post and the provision in this regard is mentioned under Article 67(b). Constitutionally, he can be removed from his office, "… by a resolution of the Rajya Sabha passed by a majority of all the existing members of the House and agreed to by the Lok Sabha."[29] However, a prior notice of 14 days needs to be served on him before passing a resolution to this effect. It needs to be mentioned here that in case of his appointment, both the Houses of Parliament take part while in case of his removal; it is only the Rajya Sabha that takes part.[30]

Role

The post of the Vice-President though is one of great dignity and prestige, yet his office is based on the political expediency alone. His role is clearly that of a "political Standby" as he is remembered only when there arises a vacancy to the office of the President due to his removal, resignation, illness, death or inability to discharge his duties. Article 65(1) states, if there is a vacancy to the office of the President, the Vice-President shall act in his capacity till the date a new incumbent is elected to this office. As per Clause 2 of the same Article, if the President fails to discharge his duties either because of his long illness or any sort of disability, the Vice-President shall discharge those functions and responsibilities.

Secondly, as per the provisions of Article 64, The Vice-President shall be the ex-officio Chairman of the Rajya Sabha. In this capacity, he presides over the meetings of this House.

PRIME MINISTER

India is a parliamentary democracy and, therefore, like UK, has a council of ministers headed by the prime minister which acts as the real chief executive. The position of the prime minister acquires special significance and enjoys immense powers in India. In fact, all those powers which have been constitutionally vested in the President are actually exercised by the prime minister. He is the chief adviser of the President, the leader of the Lower House and the head of the government. It would not, therefore, be erroneous to say that, like in the case of his British counterpart, the entire administrative machinery in India revolves around him. His position is also comparable to that of the President in the US.

Appointment and Removal

According to Article 75 of the Constitution, the Prime Minister in India is appointed by the President. However, the Constitution is silent as to whom the President will

---

29 Arora, R.K, & Rajani Goyal, *Indian Public Administration: Institutions and Issues,* New Delhi: Wishwa Prakashan, 1995, p. 97.

30 *Ibid*

appoint as prime minister. But this does not mean that the President is free to appoint anyone as the prime minister. India is a parliamentary democracy and usually follows the practices, especially where the Constitution and the Law are silent, as adopted in the UK. Therefore, conventionally, he appoints the leader of the majority party in the Lok Sabha as prime minister. Usually, the President has to appoint a person who is a member of the Parliament but there is no bar on appointing a person as prime minister who is not a member of either House. In that case, however, the incumbent will have to become a member of either House within a period of six months from the date of appointment as the prime minister. This has been rendered essential by the doctrine of ministerial responsibility. If the prime minister is not a member of the Parliament, he/she would not be able to attend the sessions of Parliament and will, in turn, not be able to respond to the queries of the members thereby diluting the principle of ministerial responsibility.

Further, usually, the prime minister is a member of the Lower House and when Indira Gandhi, who was a member of the Council of States, was appointed as the prime minister in 1967, she preferred to resign from the Upper House and became a member of the Lower House within the stipulated period of six months. However, this is not a mandatory provision and the present incumbent, Manmohan Singh, is a member of the Upper House.

As regards the removal of the prime minister, Article 75(2) states that he holds the office 'during the pleasure of the President'. However, in practice, the President, being the nominal head, has no power to remove the prime minister till he enjoys majority support in the Lower House. Thus, in effect, the power of the President as regards to removal of the prime minister takes shape only when the prime minister loses majority support in the Lower House.

Functions

As discussed earlier, Prime Minister is the chief executive in India. Therefore, he holds a position of pre-eminence and wields great authority. He plays a significant role in the management of governmental affairs. There is barely any affair of the Union government where the prime ministerial authority does not extend. In fact, even the affairs of the state administration are not beyond the purview of his authority. Needless to say, he performs a wide variety of functions. A brief view of the powers wielded and functions discharged by the prime minister is listed below.

Formation of the Council of Ministers

The prime minister starts performing his functions immediately after taking oath, rather even before that. As soon as he is appointed and sworn in by the President as prime minister, he submits a list of the persons to be appointed as ministers and the President is obliged to sworn in those persons as ministers. Theoretically, the prime minister enjoys full freedom regarding the formation of council of ministers. However, in effect, there are several compulsions and constraints which limit his authority in performance of this function. The authority regarding the choice of the ministers is further limited in the case of a coalition government. In modern times coalition governments have become an order of the day. Resultantly, the complicacy of the task of formation of council of ministers has become multifold. While selecting his council of ministers the prime minister has to bow to a number of pulls and pressures of the coalition partners. The inclusion of certain tainted persons such as Shibu Soren, Anirudh "Sabhu" Yadav, Prabhunath Singh etc. in the council of ministers by Prime Minister Manmohan Singh may be cited as an example in this regard. The compulsions of the prime minister regarding their induction and keeping them in the council of minister were so grave that he could not drop them despite a lot of uproar both in and out of Parliament.

Allocation of Portfolios

The next important function of the prime minister after the formation of council of ministers is the allocation of portfolios. As was the case with the formation of council of minister, formally, allocation of portfolios amongst his colleagues is the prerogative of the prime minister, but factually he enjoys limited freedom in this regard. He virtually cannot disregard the wishes of the prominent and senior party leaders and in case he does so, he has problems in store for him in future. These constraints are more at work during a coalition regime when not merely the interests of the different factions within the party but those of the coalition partners have also to be taken into consideration. There always remains a strong competition for some of the important portfolios such as the home affairs, finance, defence, railways etc. The quantum of constraints imposed on the prime minister in the discharge of this function posed due to the interplay of different rival forces/contenders can be gauged by the fact that sometimes the task of allocation of portfolios is delayed for days together only because there is more than one relentless aspirant for a particular portfolio.

Shuffling of Portfolios and Dismissal of Ministers

Article 74(i) provides that there shall be a council of ministers with the *prime minister at the head* to aid and advise the President. From this provision, there flows a natural corollary that the prime minister should enjoy the authority to analyze and evaluate the performance of his ministerial colleagues and, if upon such analysis and evaluation, finds some minister inconvenient or less capable of conducting the affairs of one department, he enjoys the power to transfer him to some other. In other words, the prime minister reserves the right to shuffle and reshuffle the portfolios among the different ministers. Though practically, it is not always easy for the prime minister to reshuffle the portfolios of his ministerial colleagues at his will or convenience. By dint of the same corollary, the prime minister also possesses the right to drop any minister, if in his view, the latter has not been able to discharge his functions or if some of his action brought embarrassment to the government or if there is some fundamental disagreement on some policy matter. However, in such a situation it has been more usual to demand the resignation from the minister concerned instead of resorting to dismissal.

Head of the Council of Ministers

The prime minister enjoys a pivotal position in the council of ministers. The prime minister acts as the guide of the council of ministers and acts as the chief co-ordinator of the policies of different ministers. He not only convenes and presides over the meetings of the council of ministers but also decides the agenda for these meetings. In other words, it is he who not only decides when the council of ministers shall meet but also what it shall discuss. His role is crucial in setting the agenda of the cabinet meetings and he can accept or reject the proposals of the ministers. Although the views of all the members matter, yet the prime minister's decision is final. Therefore, it becomes clear that the prime minister is the undisputed leader or chairman of the council of ministers.

Leader of the Lower House

Like the UK, the prime minister is the leader of the Lower House in India. However, in case, he belongs to the Upper House, he is the leader of that House. In consultation with the Presiding Officer of the House, he decides the general business to be transacted in the sessions of the House. In that capacity, he has to spell out the policies of his government, defends his ministerial colleagues and intervenes in debates and reply to points of criticism leveled against his government. He is also supposed to remain in constant touch with the leader of the opposition party to resolve the controversial issues and to understand their viewpoint on such issues.

Channel of Communication

The Prime minister is the vital link between Parliament and the President and as the sole communicator between the council of ministers and the President. He keeps the President informed about the wishes of the council of ministers and those of Parliament. He also conveys the messages of the President to the council of ministers and to Parliament. The individual ministers are not permitted to see or communicate with the President unless they are authorized by the prime minister to do so and any violation in this regard is considered as a conspiracy against the prime minister and is treated accordingly.

Chief Adviser to the President

The prime minister is the chief adviser of the President. The former advises the latter on all matters pertaining to the discharge of his functions. Further, the President reserves the right to be kept informed about certain matters such as foreign affairs, defence, finance etc. and the prime minister is legally bound to furnish all such information to him.

Power of Dissolution

The prime minister being the leader of the Lower House enjoys the power to recommend to the President its dissolution and the latter is bound to dissolve the House provided the former possesses majority support in the House. What is important is that he can render this advice to the President even without any consultation with the council of ministers. This power of dissolution in the hands of the prime minister puts the members of the House, his party colleagues and even his cabinet colleagues on his mercy as dissolution means new elections without the certainty of returning to the House, or the Government or the Cabinet as the case may be.

Representative of the Nation

The prime minister also acts as the representative of the nation. He represents the nation at the national and international levels. The prime minister participates in the "… international conferences, pays official visits to foreign countries, maintains relations with the UN and other international organizations, negotiates with the heads of states, signs treaties and agreements, advises the President to declare war and conclude peace and advises the President to grant or withhold recognition to nations."[31] In these conferences and meetings he presents his views as the leader of the nation, and his views are regarded to be the views of the nation.

Position

Several scholars have used colourful phrases to explain the position of the prime minister in Britain. Lord Morley has described the position of the prime minister among his Cabinet colleagues as *primus inter pares* i.e., 'first among equals' while Harcourt has described him as *inter stellas lunaninores* i.e., 'the moon among lesser stars.' Similarly, Jennings has held that the prime minister is the 'sun around which planets revolve.' Munro equates his position with the 'captain of the ship of the state' and Laski has called him as the 'pivot around which the entire government machinery revolves.' These phrases hold equally good in the Indian context. The prime minister enjoys a prominent position in Indian administration. He is the leader of the council of ministers along with which he constitutes the real chief executive of the country. He is the repository of actual powers. This places him at a very powerful position and the above mention of his powers is merely 'a modest appreciation of his position.' His position is comparable to any other head of the government in the world and, according to Arora, he possesses "… such a plentitude of power as no other constitutional ruler in the world possesses."[32]

The prime minister manages the President, Parliament and the council of ministers. Besides, he even manages the electorates. He is the leader of the majority party and the Lower House of Parliament and leads the government in internal as well as external policy matters. He maintains the party solidarity and keeps it united. Not merely in the administration of the Union affairs, his authority pervades even over the affairs of the state governments.

It should, however, not be forgotten that the position of the prime minister largely depends upon the prevailing circumstances and the numerical strength of his party in the House. In case of a coalition government, usually, the position of the prime minister remains quite weak. Thus, for instance, the position of V.P. Singh, Chander Shekher, I.K. Gujral and Deve Gowda proved to be weak prime ministers because they headed fluid coalitions. But simultaneously, the personality and capability of the incumbent is still another aspect which determines his position. Thus, P.V. Narshima Rao and Atal Behari Vajpayee proved relatively strong prime ministers even though they headed minority and coalition governments, respectively. Power equations inside the party is still another important factor that determines the position of any

---

31 Arora, Ramesh K., and Rajni Goyal, *Indian Public Administration: Institutions and Issues* (2nd Revised edn.), New Delhi: Wishwa Prakashan, 2004, p. 107.
32 *Ibid*, p. 112.

prime minister. For instance, even though the present incumbent Manmohan Singh is also heading a coalition government like his predecessor Atal Behari Vajpayee, but due to internal party politics he is alleged to be less effective in comparison to his predecessor.

COUNCIL OF MINISTERS

Like Britain, India has a parliamentary form of government in which the council of ministers headed by the prime minister acts as the real executive whereas the President works as the nominal head. Thus, it is the council of ministers that lies at the heart of the Indian administrative system. Being the real executive, it is responsible for discharging the executive function of policy-making and co-ordination. It acts as the supreme directing authority of government. Every administrative department/ministry is headed by a minister who is responsible for all acts of omission and commission of the administrative functionaries working in that department. Besides, the council of ministers is also responsible for co-ordinating the activities of more than one administrative department. Thus, the ministers are both individually and collectively responsible for all administrative actions.

Organization of the Council of Ministers

The process of formation of council of ministers in India starts with the formal selection of the prime minister by the President. The President usually invites the leader of the majority party in Lok Sabha to form the government and sworn him in as the prime minister. Thereafter, the prime minister prepares a list of persons to be sworn in as 'ministers.' These ministers are usually selected from both the Houses of Parliament. A minister can even be selected from outside the Parliament but in that case, he has to become the member of the Parliament within a period of six months from the date of his being sworn in.

The council of ministers in India consists of four different categories of ministers viz., the cabinet ministers, ministers of state, deputy ministers and parliamentary secretaries. However, it is only the first category of ministers – the cabinet ministers – who constitute the core part of the administrative machinery. They are in charge of important portfolios of the Union government.

Salient Features

From the operational working of the council of ministers in India over the years, certain characteristic features of the council of ministers have evolved. These features are summarized below.

The President is Not Part of the Council of Ministers

On the British pattern, the President of India is not the part of the council of ministers. He neither attends its meetings nor chairs them. It is the Prime Minister who chairs the meetings of the council of ministers and conveys its decisions to the President. Being the formal head, he has to either approve the decisions made by the council of ministers or send them to the council of ministers for its reconsideration.

Close Affinity with the Parliament

After election, the President invites the leader of the majority party in the Lok Sabha to form the government. With the advice of the prime minister, the President then constitutes the council of ministers. There is no qualification for becoming a minister except that the person should be a member of the Parliament or should become so within a period of six months, in case he is an outsider. Further, it is obligatory for the ministers to attend the parliamentary sessions and to answer the questions raised by the members of Parliament. In fact, the ministers are responsible for all the deeds of the administrative functionaries of their respective departments. Again, the very survival of the council of ministers depends upon the majority support enjoyed by it in the Lok Sabha. If it looses confidence in the House, it has to resign. From the above, it is discernible that there exists a close affinity between the council of ministers and the Parliament.

Ministerial Responsibility

The ministers are directly responsible to the Parliament for all acts of omission and commission for their own acts as well as those of the officials of their respective departments. The ministerial responsibility is two-fold – individual as well as collective. In the earlier case, the ministers are responsible to the Parliament for the acts of the officials of their respective department while in the latter case, ministers collectively share and own the policy and actions of the government.

Individual responsibility connotes that the minister has to own individual responsibility of all the decisions pertaining to the management of his departmental affairs either taken by himself or by subordinates to him. He will be personally held liable on the floor of the House for all such actions. Further, if his department is involved in a scandal or in case he proves to be incompetent, he has to resign.

On the other hand, the minister is collectively responsible for the decisions taken by the council of ministers collectively. In case, he does not agree with the decisions taken by the council of ministers, he has to submit his papers. This is because the council of ministers is highly cohesive and works like a well-knit unit and the ministers sink and swim together.

Leadership of the Prime Minister

The council of ministers is headed by the prime minister under whose guidance and leadership it operates. Though all the ministers including the prime ministers are equal in status yet the prime minister is first among equals and, therefore, the decisions of the prime minister are final. He co-ordinates the activities of different departments and is responsible to remove any conflict between more than one ministry. He is responsible for maintaining harmony and acts like an umpire. In the meetings of the council of ministers, though the views and opinions of different ministers are given due weight but in case of difference of opinion his decision prevails.

Secrecy

Council of ministers operates on the doctrine of secrecy. The ministers are not supposed to reveal what transpires in the meetings of the council of ministers. They are required to maintain utter secrecy of the proceedings of these meetings.

Nothing is made open to public or press. Only the prime minister or the authorized spokesman is entitled to reveal what has been decided to be revealed.

Political Homogeneity

The council of ministers further operates on the principle of political homogeneity. This means that all the members of council of ministers belong to the same political party or to the same group which have come together to form the government, in case of coalition government. Consequently, the views of all the ministers are usually identical in nature and in case any dissension arises, it is resolved before taking a final decision. The formation of council of ministers on party line helps the ministers to work like a team and thus ensures the unity of purpose.

Functions

As mentioned earlier, the council of ministers headed by the prime minister is the real chief executive in India and, in that capacity, discharges a plethora of functions. In fact, all those powers that are constitutionally vested in the President are exercised by the council of minister. Following are the main functions that are discharged by it:

Policy Making Function

The council of ministers being a deliberative organ, acts as the chief policy making body of the government. It plays a vital role in identifying the areas that needs policy framing. The initiative, however, usually comes from the side of the minister in-charge of specific ministry. Any minister can express his desire/idea for formulating or reformulating policies concerning his portfolio. Various policy alternatives are scrutinized by the concerned ministry and, if need be, the help of outside experts or agencies, is also taken. After a thorough debate at the level of the ministry, a final shape in the form of a proposal is given to the policy and is submitted to the council of ministers for approval. The policy proposal is then thoroughly probed and examined at the level of council of ministers before providing final approval to it. Thus, the role of the council of ministers is pivotal in framing and/or reframing of policies. Once the council of ministers takes such decisions, they become binding on all the ministers irrespective of their personal likes or dislikes.[33]

Chief Co-ordinator

The council of ministers in India works as the chief co-ordinator. It co-ordinates the work of different government departments/ministries. For the effective management of the affairs, the administration is segregated into several ministries/departments. The intra-departmental co-ordination is secured by the minister concerned whereas the inter-departmental co-ordination is the responsibility of the entire council of ministers. It decides broader issues that affect different departments. It tries to iron out the vital differences that might be prevailing among them, removes all possible overlapping and so that they might not work at cross-purposes. However, in recent times, the problem of co-ordination has complicated multifold particularly due to consistently increasing complexities in the governmental working. Besides, the consistent increase in the number of departments of the government further

---

33 Arora, Ramesh K. and Rajni Goyal, *op. cit.*, p. 122.

aggravated this problem substantially. Resultantly, the task of co-ordination has emerged as a most challenging one in recent times.[34]

Legislative Functions

Being an integral part of the Parliament and enjoying its majority support, the council of ministers plays a vital role in guiding, managing and controlling the legislative business of Parliament. It is the initiator of most of the legislative bills in the Parliament. "Although Parliament is the supreme law making body of the nation, legislation is essentially the handiwork of the council of ministers. It is the council of ministers that all the important government bills are drafted."[35] Thus, the Indian council of ministers enjoys enormous powers with regard to the legislative business of the nation. When the necessity of a new law is felt, "…the council of ministers approves its broad framework and the concerned minister asks the secretary of his department to fill in the bill with the relevant details. Such important bills are initiated and piloted through the legislatures by the council of ministers."[36] Due to the majority support in the Parliament, most of these bills are approved by the Parliament and thus takes the shape of a law. The council of ministers is further responsible for drafting all the ordinances (order-in- council) proclaimed by the President, when the Parliament is not in session. In addition to this, council of ministers is the originator of most of the amendments to the Constitution which after being passed by the Parliament take the shape of Constitutional Amendment Acts.

Executive/Administrative Functions

The council of ministers in India operates as the real chief executive. It is because each government department/ministry works under the charge of a minister, who acts as its political head. The minister is responsible for the smooth management of the entire business of his department. As a result, the minister exercises necessary supervision and control over the departmental machinery and its operations. To assist him, there exists a secretary in every ministry to manage the affairs of the department/ministry and thus, he operates as the administrative head of the department. He keeps the minister informed about all major developments of the department. In this way, the respective ministers are responsible for the management and administration of the entire business of the government. Thus, it maintains an effective supervision and control over the entire governmental machinery.

Besides, the council of ministers plays a crucial role in matters of appointment of all high dignitaries. The President appoints most of the prominent administrative functionaries like the Comptroller General of India (CAG), the Attorney General of India, the Judges of the Supreme Court and the High Courts of the states, the Governors of the states and the Lieutenant-Governor of the Union Territories, the Chairman and the members of various commissions like Election Commission, Finance Commission, Union Public Service Commission, Commissions for the SCs & STs, BCs, Minorities etc. on the aid and advice of Council of ministers. In addition to this, the President appoints the key officials to the Army, Military, and Air Forces in consultation with the council of ministers. He can give orders for the reorganization

34 Ibid, pp. 123-24.
35 Ibid, p. 122.
36 Ibid

and experimentation of military forces but such orders are usually issued with the prior consultation and advice of the council of ministers. He can not declare war or peace in the country without its prior approval. "The conduct of foreign relations, reception and dispatch of diplomatic agents and recognition or non-recognition of new states are done after the approval of the council of ministers."[37] He further negotiates treaties and agreements with foreign nations after the approval of the council of ministers.

Chief Controller of the Finance

Finance is the life blood of administration and its management is an important function of the council of ministers. It is mainly because the determination of the fiscal and monetary policies of the nation is its exclusive privilege. The finance minister every year prepares the budget in accordance with financial policy laid down by the council of ministers. The annual budget of the Union government prepared by the finance minister comes up for discussion before the council of ministers before being presented in the Parliament. The council of ministers considers the budget proposals and brings about necessary alterations in the budget in the light of the socio-political compulsions and circumstances. Again, the council of ministers defends the budgetary provisions, answers the questions of the members relating to the budget and ultimately gets it passed through the Parliament.

The council of ministers also determines the tax structure of the government and thus, takes decisions with regard to the imposition and collection of various direct and indirect taxes. In other words, it is the council of ministers that decides which fresh taxes are to be imposed, which are to be increased, which are to be reduced and which are to be abolished.

Miscellaneous Functions

In addition to its routine working, the council of ministers in India is responsible for discharging miscellaneous nature of function also. It is required to take a number of emergent decisions particularly when the security of the nation is in danger. Further, a number of unforeseen problems and situations that may arise both at home and abroad also need sudden and quick decisions of the council of ministers. Besides, the council of ministers is required to take frequent decisions to bring changes in the national economy in consonance with the global changes. Various problems concerning environment protection also need urgent attention of the council of ministers. Besides, the situations created due to the natural calamities may even require decisions of the council of ministers. Thus, the council of ministers also acts as the 'crisis manager.'

(C) LOCAL GOVERNMENT

The roots of local government institutions in India can be traced since the Rig Veda period. Evidences suggest that self-governing village bodies called 'sabhas' were even in existence during the Rig Veda period which later on acquired the shape of panchayats. They were the functional bodies at the bottom tier. These bodies were organized with vast powers both executive and judicial in almost every village. The

---
37 *Ibid*

villages and towns had been managing their own affairs in an effective way. The villages exhibited a well-developed system of local government. However the powers of these bodies were restricted during Mughal rule mainly because of the emergence of feudalistic system of governance in the medieval period. "A new class of feudal chiefs and revenue collectors (zamindars) emerged between the ruler and the people. And, so began the stagnation and decline of self-government in villages."[38] During the British rule, the earlier institutions of local government found a great set back due to the "…establishment of local civil and criminal courts, revenue and police organisations, the increase in communications, the growth of individualism and the operation of the individual Ryotwari '(landholder-wise) system as against the Mahalwari or village tenure system."[39] The British smashed the autonomous character of the panchayats and put in place their own system which helped in perpetuating their colonial interests. Therefore, they introduced "… their own brand of local government, first in urban areas and later in the countryside."[40] They established Municipal Corporations in Madras in 1687 and in Calcutta and Bombay in 1726 to serve their own interests. Lord Ripon's resolution of local self-government laid the democratic fabric of municipal governance in India in 1882. As a result most of the towns in India had laid down the structure of municipal governance till the early part of 19th century. However, the British had least interest in raising the democratic character of local bodies as they showed no respect to the suggestions and findings of the commissions constituted by them in this connection.[41]

In 1919, dyarchy was introduced at provincial level by the Montague-Chelmsford Reforms under which the subject of local government was transferred to the popular control under the charge of a minister. As a result village panchayats were set up in a number of provinces. Further apart from extending the taxation powers of these bodies, these reforms proved significant in enhancing their representative element. However, these reforms failed to transform these bodies into truly democratic and vibrant bodies due to organizational and fiscal constraints.

The introduction of provincial autonomy under the Government of India Act, 1935 led to the emergence of popularly elected governments in provinces. These government enacted legislations to further democratize the local government institutions. This Act marked the evolution of panchayats in India. However, these reforms failed to get materialized due to the eruption of World War II.

The development of local government, however, remained staggered even in the post independence era but the growth of these bodies was comparatively faster than

---

38 http://en.wikipedia.org/wiki/History_of_panchayatiraj_in_India
39 *Ibid*
40 Sharma, M.P. and B.L. Sadana, *op. cit.*, p. 749.
41 Lord Mayo's resolution of 1870 attempted to strengthen the municipal institutions by providing increasing association of Indians in administration. Thereafter, Lord Ripon's resolution of 1882 advocated the establishment of a network of local self-governing institutions, financial decentralization, the adoption of election as a means of constituting local bodies and the reduction of the official element to not more than a third of the total membership. Similarly, the Royal Commission on Decentralization (1907) suggested that the chairman of the urban local bodies should be elected non-officials and that they should be given sufficient financial powers and the elected non-official members should comprise a majority in these bodies.

the colonial and pre-colonial period. For its revival, local government was placed under Article 40 dealing with Directive Principles of State Policy which states: "the state shall take steps to organize village panchayats and endow them with such powers and authority as may be necessary to enable them to function as units of self government." Consequently, 'local government', was placed in the State List and the State legislatures were authorized under Article 264 to enact any law with regard to the local bodies. However, no worthwhile legislation was enacted either at state or national level to implement it and it took them almost four complete decades to attain a constitutional status in the early 1990s. During the intervening period, there has been several developments given below which helped these institutions to be transformed into the units of self -governance at grass roots level.

Failure of community development programmes[42] and National Extension Services[43] due to excessive bureaucratic control and limited involvement of panchayats in implementation process underlined the dearth of a more extensive system of local government in India. Hence B.R Mehta Committee[44] recommended the establishment of elected local bodies and devolution of necessary resources, power and authority to them. A three-tier structure of PRIs[45] was recommended so that the path of a genuine democratic decentralization could be ensured. The recommendations were accepted in the National Development Council in 1958 and it was left to the states to evolve their own pattern as per their requirements. Resultantly by the mid-1960s legislations were enacted in almost all the states.[46] However, different states lack uniformity in terms of structure, electoral procedure and functions of the PRIs. Even these efforts could not succeed in generating requisite democratic momentum due to political and bureaucratic unwillingness to share power and resources with local level institutions. Lamentably, these institutions remained at the mercy of the state governments rather than becoming institutions of decentralized governance. In some of the states, these bodies were frequently superseded and elections were not held for long and these bodies remained most of the time redundant. However, by the mid-1970s the central and state governments had appointed many committees and commissions to examine the various aspects relating to both rural and urban local bodies. The prominent aspects were related to the elections, auditing, accounting and augmentation of their financial resources (taxation), training and service conditions of their personnel, rural-urban relationship, role of these bodies in development administration etc. Despite the important recommendations of the various committees, these institutions failed to emerge as the real entities of grass roots democracy.

42 Launched in 1952 to ensure people's participation in development process.
43 Launched in 1953 to promote decentralization under which the entire country was covered with National Extensive Service Blocks through the institutions of Block Development Officers, Assistant Development Officers, Village Level Workers, in addition to nominated representatives of village panchayats of that area and some other popular organisations like co-operative societies.
44 It was set up in 1956 to review and examine the working of CDPs) found that these programmes could not evoke enthusiasm among local bodies higher than the panchayats and the people. Even the panchayats did not come within the fold of community development moreover; both programmes were trapped within the control of the bureaucracy.
45 Gram Panchayats at village level, Panchayats Samiti at block level and Zila parishad at district level.
46 Except the states of Meghalaya, Mizoram, Nagaland and Union Territory of Lakshadweep.

Given the situation, The Ashok Mehta Committee was appointed on PRIs for their revival. The Committee inter alia recommended a two-tier structure of panchayati raj institutions and compulsory powers of taxation to mobilize the necessary resources on their own thereby reducing their dependence on devolution of funds from the government.[47] The Committee submitted its report in 1978, which, however, could not be implemented. In the decade of the 1980s two prominent committees - G.V.K. Rao Committee[48] and L.M. Singhvi Committee[49] were appointed to revitalize the PRIs. The Rao Committee came out with a blue print of a decentralized system of field administration and recommended a pivotal role of PRIs in local planning and development. It further recommended that the zila parishad should be given central importance in terms of planning and management of rural development programs and the lower order of these bodies should be entrusted with the task of monitoring and implementation of such programmes. The Singhvi Committee inter alia recommended for awarding the constitutional status to these bodies to protect them from state hegemony and the setting up of judicial tribunals in states to adjudicate controversies about election and dissolution of these bodies. It also emphasized the "...importance of the *gram sabha* with the reorganization of villages and suggested the creation of *Nyaya Panchayats*..."[50]. All these efforts resulted in shaping the 64th Amendment Bill.

Since there was no specific mention of the urban local bodies in the Indian constitution, so during first four decades after independence, suggestions were forwarded to extend the scope of Article 40 for incorporating the municipal governments and also to provide a constitutional status to them. Several commissions and committees like Administrative Reform Commission (ARC), Committee on Centre-State Relations and National Commission on Urbanization have examined this issue and recommended constitutional status to these bodies. In 1988, the National Commission on Urbanization[51] recommended restructuring of the Ministries of Urban Development at the central and state levels to articulate urban policy. It also recommended the creation of councils for citizens' action both at national and state levels to encourage citizens' interaction through organized voluntary efforts. It recommended the creation of a two-tier structure at the municipal level. To alleviate poverty in urban areas it recommended universalisation of basic services programmes emphasizing on participatory approach. These efforts led to the framing of the 65th Constitutional Amendment Bill.

---

47 Maheshwari, S.R., *Local Government in India (6th ed.)*, Agra: Lakshmi NarainAgarwal Publishers, 1992-93, p. 10.
48 Popularly known as Committee on Administrative Arrangements for Rural Development (CARD Committee) was constituted in 1985 to review the administrative arrangements for rural development and poverty alleviation.
49 Constituted in 1986 on revitalization of panchayati raj institutions.
50 Arora, R.K, &RajaniGoyal, *Indian Public Administration*, New Delhi: Wishwa Prakashan, 1996 (reprinted in 2004), p. 288.
51 Constituted by Central government to strengthen and revitalize the functioning of urban local bodies, under the chairmanship of Sh.Charles Correa to examine and revive various aspects of urbanization and urban development and to recommend policy measures and institutional changes.

The Central government in 1989, introduced the 64th[52] and 65th[53] Constitutional Amendment Bills regarding rural and urban local bodies respectively to ensure maximum decentralization and devolution of powers. These were passed by the Lower House, but rejected in the Upper House. However, most of the provisions of these Bills later on were incorporated in the 73rd and 74th Amendment Acts enacted in 1992 and 1993, respectively. These Acts mandated all the state legislatures to enact or amend their respective (rural and urban local government) legislations to conform to the Constitutional Amendments within one year. These Acts have been hailed as revolutionary in two sense; firstly, for providing constitutional status to the local bodies and secondly for political empowerment of SCs/STs and women through reservation. The 73rd Amendment Act provides for a three-tier[54] structural arrangement for PRIs and the statutory recognition to the Gram Sabha consisting of all registered voters of the village. The Act assigned 29 subjects to the PRIs contained in 11th schedule of the constitution for the preparation and implementation of economic development and social justice. Like wise, 74th Amendment Act provides for three types of municipalities[55], obligatory constitution of wards committees within the territorial area of a municipality having a population of 3 lakhs or more. The Act assigned 18 subjects contained in 12th schedule of the constitution for the preparation and implementation of plans for economic and social development. However the rest of the provisions of both these Acts are to a large extent identical in nature as both provides for reservation to the SCs/STs in proportion to their population and not less than one third reservation to women, direct election of the members of these bodies, a fixed tenure of five years to these bodies and the provision of holding fresh elections within six months in case of dissolution, establishment of finance and election commission at state level, constitution of district planning committees to consolidate the plans of panchayats and municipalities to prepare a development plan for the district as a whole. It is to mention here that five states[56] have provided 50 percent reservation which is sufficiently higher in comparison to that stipulated

---

52 The Bill, *inter alia*, proposed the establishment of a three-tier structure of Panchayats based on direct election for a fixed period of five years in all states, reservation to SCs/STs and women, devolution of powers and responsibilities to the Panchayats by the State legislatures, sufficient financial resources through grants-in-aid and authority to levy taxes, duties, tolls and fees, constitution of state finance and election commission after every five year etc.

53 The Bill, *inter alia*, proposed a three type structures of urban local bodies—municipal corporation, municipal council and nagarpanchayats according to the population by direct election for a fixed period of five years, reservation to SCs/STs and women, devolution of powers and responsibilities to the municipal bodies by the State legislatures, sufficient financial resources through grants-in-aid and authority to levy taxes, duties, tolls and fees, constitution of state finance and election commission after every five year, constitution of elected wards committees, creation of district level committee for co-ordinating the plans of Nagar Palikas and Panchayats etc.

54 Zila Parishad at the district level, Panchayat Samiti at the block level and Gram Panchayat at the village level.

55 Nagar Panchayats, for transitional areas (that has been transformed from a rural to urban areas, municipal council for a smaller urban areas, and Municipal Corporation for a large urban area.

56 Bihar, Madhya Pradesh, Uttrakhanda, Chattisgarh, Himachal Pradesh. See, Chhibber Bharti, *Empowerment of women: Fifty percent reservation in panchayats a major step*, The Tribune, New Delhi, 2/10/2009 p. 13.

in the Act. More over, the state of Rajasthan and Kerala and the central government are also planning in the same direction.

As an outcome of these Acts most of the states passed their respective legislations in consonance with their provisions and established a three-tier structure of rural and urban local governments. The number of village panchayats in the country as on 1st December, 2006 was 2, 32,913; of the intermediate panchayats 6,094 and of the district panchayats 537. The total number of representatives elected to these bodies is 28, 28,779 – out of which 10, 38,989 (36.7%) are women.[57] Likewise almost 3300 urban local bodies including municipal corporations, municipal councils and nagar panchayats are operational across the country.

PRESENT STRUCTURE: For the sake of convenience the present structure of the local bodies can be discussed separately under two heads - Rural Local Bodies (RLBs) and Urban Local Bodies (ULBs) A brief discussion of the two is given below:

I. RURAL LOCAL BODIES: The three tier structure of the rural local bodies at the grass roots level is given below:

Gram Panchayat: Gram panchayat is the bottom tier of local government. Its members are elected directly by the registered voters constituting the gram sabha of the village. The gram sabha acts as a village assembly for deliberative purpose while gram panchayat acts as an executive body for implementation of such deliberations. Any member of the village, who has attained the age of 21, is eligible to contest the election of gram panchayat. The number of members of village panchayat may vary from 7 to 15 depending upon the population of the village. The gram panchayat is headed by a chairman who is usually designated as the sarpanch. The chairman/sarpanch of panchayat may be elected directly or by the elected representatives of the panchayat amongst them as decided by the state legislature. He convenes and presides the meetings of the gram panchayat and gram sabha. It is mandatory for the gram panchayat to hold at least two meetings of gram sabha in a year. In the meetings of gram sabha a quorum[58] is required which may differ from State to State. The gram panchayat is required to place various issues like, "…budget proposals, reports of the previous year, annual statements of audit and accounts, proposals of fresh taxes or enhancing the existing taxes, launching of various schemes and the selection of beneficiaries etc before the meetings of gram sabha."[59] While deliberating on vital issues, gram sabha comes out with certain recommendations which are given due weight by the gram panchayats. The gram panchayat is responsible for the management of the affairs at the village level and maintains the relevant records. Besides, it is also responsible for the implementation of all sorts of development programmes sponsored by central or state governments at the village. In discharging these functions it is assisted by the panchayat secretary in each village.

Panchayat Samiti: It is the intermediate unit of the three tier structure of PRIs; it lies between gram panchayat and zila parishad. It is designated by different names in different states. The constitution of panchayat samiti at intermediate level is

---

57 Sixth Report of 2nd ARC on local governance, p. 8.
58 In most of the states one-tenth of the members present constitute the quorum.
59 Sharma, M.P. and B.L. Sadana, *op. cit.*, pp. 772-73.

mandatory in all the states except a few[60] or states having a population not exceeding twenty lakhs. The members from territorial constituencies of the panchayat samiti are directly elected while the chairman is elected indirectly from amongst, the elected members. Apart from the elected members the state may provide for the representation of chairpersons of village level panchayats, MPs, MLAs and MLCs representing constituencies which comprise wholly or partly a panchayat area, at intermediate level as ex-officio. Both the elected and ex-officio members have the right to vote in the meetings of the panchayat samiti. The number of members of the panchayat samiti is decided by the state legislature and thus differs from state to state.[61] The chairman of the panchayat samiti is responsible for managing the affairs of this body. He invites its meetings at least once in 2 or 3 months as per the legislation of the state and chairs them. He not only directs its workings but also maintains an effective supervision and control over the employees of the samiti. He is further responsible for up keeping and maintaining the records of the samiti. The vice chairman assists the chairman of the samiti in discharging his responsibilities. Besides, there exists the post of block development officer (BDO) who plays a significant role in carrying out the functions of the samiti. In this connection, he operates with the assistance of several extension officers.[62]

The functions performed by the panchayat samities differ from state to state. Usually they "...supervise the working of village panchayats falling within their territorial jurisdictions, approve their budgets, co-ordinate the development plans prepared by them and submit them to zila/district parishad so as to be incorporated in the district development plan."[63] However the state governments and the zila parishads are authorized to assign additional functions to these bodies in addition to their routine functions. They prepare their own annual budget and submit it to zila parishad for approval. These bodies operate through committees[64] the appointment of which is almost mandatory in every state. In most of the states the number of these committees is three while in some other states like West Bengal, Rajasthan and Tripura their number may vary from four to seven.[65]

Zila Parishad: It is constituted at district level and is the apex body of the three-tier structure of PRIs in India. The members of zila parishad are directly elected by the registered voters of the district. Like the panchayats samities, the state may provide for the ex-officio members[66] i.e. chairpersons of panchayat samities, MPs, MLAs and MLCs of the district who have mandatory right to vote in the meetings of the zila parishad along with elected representatives. The meetings of the zila parishad are usually convened quarterly in most of the states. However in some states like Haryana, Karnataka and Goa, their meetings are convened bi-monthly.[67]

---

60 Goa, Manipur, Mizoram, Meghalaya, Nagaland, Sikkim and Jammu and Kashmir, *Ibid*, p. 774.
61 Usually their membership ranges from 15-20.
62 Arora, R.K, &Rajani Goyal, *op. cit.*, p. 296.
63 Sharma, M.P. & B.L. Sadana, *op. cit.*, p. 780.
64 These committees usually involve General Standing Committee, Finance, Audit and Planning Committee, and Social Justice Committee.
65 Sharma, M.P. & B.L. Sadana, *op. cit.*, p. 781.
66 Members representing constituencies which comprise wholly or partly a panchayat area at district level.
67 Sharma, M.P. & B.L. Sadana, *op. cit.*, p. 783.

The zila parishad is presided over by the chairman also known as zila parmukh or zila pradhan in some states. The chairman is elected by the elected members from amongst them. He presides and convenes the meetings of the zila parishad. He scrutinizes the business of the lower tiers of PRIs and presents his report to the zila parishad. The members of the zila parishad can remove him through a vote of no-confidence.[68]

The functions of zila parishad are not uniform in all the states through out the country. Usually the zila parishad scrutinize and approve the budget of the panchayat samities, issue directions to the panchayat samities for discharging their duties effectively, co-ordinates the developmental plans of various panchayat samities at the district level, distributes financial resources to various panchayats samities in accordance with the state allocations, informing the district authorities about the irregularities if any, in the PRIs, advising the state governments regarding the development works going on at the district level etc.[69] To discharge these functions smoothly, like the panchayats samiti, the zila parishad also operates through some standing committees.[70] However, the number of such committees differs from state to state.

II URBAN LOCAL BODIES: The structure of urban local bodies is simplified and rationalized with the passage of the 74th Amendment Act through out the nation. Prior to the passage of this Act a number of bodies like town area committees and notified area committees were prevailing for the management of urban affairs of smaller towns. Now basically a three tier set up of urban local bodies is mandated under this Act – municipal corporations, municipal councils and nagar panchayats along with some other small bodies. However a municipality may not be constituted in such urban area or part thereof in which municipal services are being provided by an industrial establishment notified as *Industrial Township* by Governor. A brief mention of these bodies is given as under:

Municipal Corporation

Municipal Corporation is the biggest urban local body in term of size and is created for the administration of cities having large urban area.[71] The municipal corporation is established by state legislature in states and by Parliament in case of union territories. It may be created under general Act[72] or under separate Acts.[73] Among all urban local government units, it enjoys a greater degree of administrative and

---

68 Arora, R.K, & Rajani Goyal, *op. cit.*, p. 295.
69 Ibid, p. 296.
70 General Standing Committee, Finance, Audit and Planning Committee, Social Justice Committee, Education and Health Committee, Agriculture and Industries Committees.
71 It refers to the area as specified by the Governor of the state, taking into account the population, density of the population therein, revenue generated by the population, density of the population in non-agricultural activities, and other factors.
72 For instance Municipal Corporations in Kanpur, Allahabad ,Varansi, Agra and Lucknow have been constituted under Mahanagarpalika Adhiniyam,1959 and Municipal Corporation in Jalandher, Amritsar and Ludhiana cities under the Punjab Municipal Act,1956 .
73 For instance the Municipal Corporations of Delhi, Madras and Bombay have been set up under the Delhi Municipal Corporation Act 1957, Madras City Corporation Act 1951 and the Mumbai Municipal Act 1888 respectively.

fiscal autonomy and thus are free from the state control as they operate strictly in accordance with the provisions of the Act under which they have been established. A municipal corporation consists of two wings - executive and legislative and there remains a statutory separation between the two. The legislative wing incorporates the council headed by the mayor and its standing committees which deliberates on various issues whereas the executive wing involves the municipal commissioner who is responsible for the implementation of these deliberations. The council of the corporation constitutes the deliberative and legislative wing of the municipal corporation which generally consists of elected members, ex-officio members and nominated members. The directly elected members[74] designated as councillors are elected for a period of 5 years by the registered voters of that municipal area divided into wards. MPs, MLAs and MLCs representing that constituency act as the ex-officio members of the corporation council. Moreover the state may also nominate persons having special knowledge or experience in municipal administration. Along with elected members, the ex-officio members also enjoy the right to vote in the meetings of the council but nominated member don't have this right. The number of members of the corporation council differs from city to city and is decided by the respective state legislature. A number of standing/permanent committees are established to deal with specific issues of municipal governance. These committees are very helpful in taking decisions on various matters. The corporation council is headed by a mayor who may be elected directly or indirectly as the state may decide but in most of the states in India, the mayor is indirectly elected from amongst the members of the council for a renewal term of one year. He is even removable from his office by a no-confidence motion. He acts as the ceremonial head and not the real executive of the council though he is considered as the "First Citizen" of the city. The Mayor convenes/presides the meetings of the council. He may be assisted by the deputy mayor.

The Municipal Commissioner, an apex dignitary in the municipal hierarchy of the corporation plays a pivotal role in execution of the decisions either taken by the council or its standing committees. He is appointed by the state government. He acts as the chief executive of the corporation and is usually a member of Indian Administrative Services or the state services as the case may be. He..."prepares the budget estimates, makes appointments to certain categories of post and can enter into contracts not exceeding 25,000 on behalf of the corporation and keeps all municipal records."[75]

For the effective management of the affairs of the municipal corporation, it is mandatory for the corporation to constitute wards committees.[76] The wards committee operates for a single or group of wards. The state may also provide for constitution of other committees like standing committees which are created to facilitate the working of the municipal corporation too large in size. These committees deal with public works, education, health, taxation, finance and so on. They enjoy a lot of freedom

---

74 Any member of the ward who has attained the age of 21 is entitled to contest election.
75 Arora, R.K, &Rajani Goyal, *op. cit.*, pp. 265-66.
76 Created within the territorial area of a municipality having a population of three lakhs or more and a member of a municipality representing a ward within the territorial area of the wards committee shall be a member of that committee.

in taking decisions in their fields. They are generally constituted from amongst the members of the corporation council in majority of states. Moreover, constitution of a *Metropolitan Planning Committee* for preparation of a draft development plan for the metropolitan area as a whole has been provided under the 74th Amendment Act. The state may provide for the composition of such committees but two thirds of the members of such committee shall be elected by, and from amongst the elected members of the municipalities and chairpersons of the panchayats in the metropolitan area.

A municipal corporation has to discharge a number of functions. The 74th Amendment Act incorporated an illustrative list of 18 functions mentioned in the 12th Schedule of the Constitution which may be assigned to them by state legislature. Some broad functions discharged by them in most of the states incorporates — construction of roads and bridges, planning for economic and social development, water supply, sanitation, public health, protection of environment, urban forestry, slum improvement and up gradation, conservancy and solid waste management, construction and maintenance of burials and burial grounds, promotion of cultural, educational and aesthetic aspects, prevention of cruelty against animals, improvement of public amenities and facilities like street lightening, maintenance of public parks, playgrounds, libraries etc.[77]

Municipal Council:

The Municipal Council is created by the government for managing the affairs of the town and comparatively small cities or smaller urban areas as the Governor may specify in view of the same factors/criteria as are mentioned above in case of municipal corporation. The adoption of criteria in this respect differs from state to state.

A municipal council consists of three authorities— Council, Standing Committees and the Chief Executive Officer (CEO). The Council constitutes the deliberative and legislative wing of the municipal council. Its members are designated as councillors who are directly elected by the registered voters of that municipal area on the basis of adult suffrage and secret ballot for a period of five years. For the election purpose the whole council is divisible into wards. The size of each municipal council and the number of its members is determined by the state government. Resultantly, the numbers of councillors differ from council to council. In addition to the elected members the municipal council also have nominated as well as the ex-officio members on the pattern of the municipal corporation. The number of nominated members in a council ranges from 1 to 5.[78]

The municipal council is headed by a president/chairman. In most of the states he is elected by the councillors from amongst them for a term of 5 years and can be removed by the council through a no-confidence motion. The council also elects a vice-president to assist him. He convenes the meetings of the council and presides over them. He enjoys deliberative as well as executive powers to guide the deliberations and implementation of decisions. " He is the administrative head of all the officers of the municipality, is the custodian of the municipal records, approves all financial

---

77 Sharma, M.P. & B.L. Sadana, *op. cit.*, p. 804.
78 *Ibid*, p. 795-96.

matters before they are placed in the council and represents the council on national and social occasions"[79].

Like the corporation, the council also operates through standing committees which deal with public works, education, health, taxation, finance and so on. The number of such committees differs from state to state. These committees discharge the assigned functions in their respective ward.[80]

For the management of the day to day affairs of the municipal council, the state government appoints an Executive Officer in the council. He is the pivotal functionary of the council and keeps a general supervision over the administrative work. "He exercises general control and supervision over the municipal office, can transfer clerical employees, prepares the municipal budget, keeps an eye on expenditure, is responsible for the collection of taxes and fees and takes measures for recovering municipal arrears and dues."[81]

The states may assign 18 functions contained in 12th schedule of the constitution to the municipal councils. Moreover; states may assign additional functions thus there lacks a uniformity with regard to the functions discharged by the councils. In nutshell, the functions generally discharged by the municipal councils incorporates-- drainage, water supply, public health and child welfare, fire- fighting, regulating markets and dangerous trades, managing crematorium and slaughter houses, street lighting, maintenance of public streets and parks, construction of shelter for the destitute, registration of births and deaths, allotment of numbers to the houses, sweeping and scavenging etc[82].

Municipal Committees/Nagar Panchayat:

The 74th Amendment Act also provides for the establishment of municipal committees/ nagar panchayat for management of the affairs of smaller towns which are notified as *transitional areas*[83] having blending of the characteristics of both urban and rural areas. It is going to replace the earlier two categories of bodies viz., Town Area Committees and Notified Area Committees. For setting up a municipal committee/ nagar panchayat in a transitional area, the population required differs from state to state. Usually in different states it ranges from 10,000 to 25,000. On the basis of its population, the number of members of a municipal Committee/nagar panchayat finds variation. Like the corporation as well as the municipal councils, there exist three categories of members: elected members, nominated members and ex-officio members in the municipal committee/ nagar panchayat. The members of the earlier category are directly elected by the registered voters of that area for a fixed period of five years. For this purpose the whole municipal committee/nagar panchayat is divisible into single member wards. In the 2nd category the state may nominate 1or 2 members who have expertise knowledge in municipal administration. Thus the number of members of a municipal committee/nagar panchayat directly corresponds to the number of wards in that area. The last category of ex-officio members

---

79 Arora, R.K, & Rajani Goyal, *op. cit.,* p. 267.
80 Sharma, M.P. &B.L. Sadana, *op. cit.,* p. 796.
81 Arora, R.K, & Rajani Goyal, *op. cit.,* p. 267.
82 Sharma, M.P. & B.L. Sadana, *op. cit.,* p. 7967.
83 An area in transition from a rural area to an urban area.

incorporates the M.Ps, M.L.As. (or M.L.Cs. if any) representing that area. Though the tenure of the municipal committee/nagar panchayat is fixed for 5 years but it may be dissolved earlier on certain ground like incompetence, negligence, default, and abuse of authority etc. In case of dissolution fresh election are inevitable before the expiry of 6 months.[84]

The head of the municipal committee/nagar panchayat is known as the President who is assisted by vice- president. They are elected by the members from amongst them. The president is responsible for managing the affairs of the municipal committee/nagar panchayat. The functions of the municipal committee/nagar panchayat may fall under two categories: discretionary and obligatory. The earlier category incorporates urban poverty alleviation, urban forestry, social and economic development planning, organization and management of fairs, primary education etc whereas the later category involves street lightning, drainage, sanitation and health, water supply etc.[85]

In addition to these bodies, a number of other bodies exist in the urban areas which incorporate the following:

Cantonment Board*

The body was established particularly by the British to serve the civilian population in the cantonment areas[86]. Such boards were established under the provisions of a legislation passed by the Central Government in 1924 viz., The Cantonments Act. These bodies function under the direction and control of the Defense Ministry rather than under state government. The number of Cantonment Boards in India today is 63.[87]

The members of the Cantonment Board are both elected as well as nominated. The members of the earlier category are directly elected by the registered voters of that cantonment for a period of three years whereas the nominated members hold their office as long as they stay at that station.[88] "The military officer commanding the station is the ex-officio president of the board and presides over its meetings."[89] The elected members elect one person from amongst themselves as the vice president of the Board after their election. Like a municipality, the cantonment board also performs obligatory as well as discretionary functions. An Executive Officer is appointed by the Indian President[90] to manage the administrative affairs of the cantonment board.

Improvement Trusts

An improvement trust is usually created by a state government for a specific purpose of developing the *newer areas* in a city. Such areas fall outside the jurisdiction of a

---

84 Ibid, p. 793.
85 Ibid, p. 794.
  * They are grouped into following three classes: Class I (having civilian population more than 10,000), Class II (having civilian population between 2500 and 10,000), and Class III (having population less than 2500. Arora, R.K, & Rajani Goyal, *op. cit.*, p. 270.
86 The areas where military forces are permanently stationed.
87 Laxmikanth, M. *Indian Polity*, New Delhi: Tata McGraw-Hill Publishing Company Limited, 2004, p. 293.
88 Ibid
89 Ibid
90 Ibid

municipal council. They are created by the State Legislature by a special Act which mentioned their powers and functions. Resultantly, there is wide variation in their composition and functions from state to state. Usually it is headed by a chairman who is an appointee of the state government. The state government also nominates certain representatives of the municipal body, with in whose jurisdiction it functions. In addition to them, the state government also nominates the other members of the Trust like the Chief Town Planner, Engineer and heads of departments.[91] In brief, "an improvement Trust is a multi-development agency, which performs an important co-ordinative role by bringing the representatives of a large number of government agencies engaged in the process of urban development under one roof."[92]

Port Trust

The port trust as its name applies is created in the port areas. It is the Parliament that creates such bodies under a special Act. The purpose behind their creation is twofold—management and protection of the ports as well as extending civic amenities to the common people in that area. It consists of elected as well as nominated members. Its chairman is usually an official. Its functions are almost akin to those of a municipality.[93]

Industrial Township

This kind of urban local bodies are created by several large-sized public enterprises. The purpose behind their creation is to provide civic amenities to its staff and workers residing in housing colonies that evolve near and around the plant. To manage the administrative affairs of the township, the enterprise appoints a town administrator who is further assisted by the technical and non-technical staff in discharging his duties.

PROBLEMS AND PROSPECTS: Now almost more than one and half decades have passed since the passage of these Acts and three successive elections have been held in almost all the states. Panchayati Raj Institutions (PRIs) in India have, over the years, developed certain critical strengths, although they are characterized by several systemic weaknesses and constraints as well. The success of the Acts lies in the fact that these Acts have provided opportunities to women and weaker sections of the society to participate in the institutions of local self governance. Recently the UPA government at centre in September, 2009, has cleared a constitutional amendment to enhance women reservation to 50% in PRIs at all levels[94]; this would further pave the way of women empowerment in India. Moreover a uniform structure backed by mandatory regular elections has accorded enhanced stability to these institutions. However, unluckily the conferment of the subjects allotted to the respective local government and the genuine devolution of powers still remain a distant dream. As a result, hardly any change is perceptible in their actual working even after such a long time since the passage of these revolutionary Acts.

---

91 Arora, R.K, & Rajani Goyal, *op. cit.*, p. 271.
92 *Ibid*
93 Laxmikanth, M., *op. cit.*, p. 293.
94 Chhibber Bharti, *Empowerment of women: Fifty percent reservation in panchayats a major step*, The Tribune, New Delhi, 2/10/2009, p. 13.

(D) CONTROL MACHINERY

In a democratic state, the accountability of the holders of public offices is inevitable towards the common masses for the authority exercised by them. It is because the democracy is an affair of the governed and the people have a live interest in seeing that administration should be both responsible and efficient. Thus, the public officials in a democratic country are liable to give a satisfactory account of the powers, they exercise. In order to check the abuse of public authority, the Indian administration has devised various forms of safeguards to hold the administration responsible for the deeds they discharged. In India, control over the administration is exercised broadly in two ways i.e. external as well as internal. The former type of control over administration is exercised from outside while the latter is fitted within the administrative machinery itself and work automatically as the machinery operates. Like Britain, the Parliament and the judiciary exercises the external control whereas the executive exercises its control internally in India. These two forms of control over the administration are in essence supplementary as well as complimentary in nature and play a significant role in ensuring efficiency and accountability in the administrative system. A brief picture of the control machinery in India is as under:

I. **Legislative Control:** The Indian Parliament acts as an important instrument of control over administration. It is mainly because all state activities emanate from the legislature. In a parliamentary system the executive is directly responsible to the legislature and cannot afford to be irresponsible. It is answerable to the Parliament for the deeds of the administrative officials. The minister of the concerned department is supposed to shoulder the responsibility of each and every act of the civil servants of his department. Thus, the civil servants remain in the background and are indirectly responsible to the Parliament for their acts of omission and commission through the minister. In other words, the minister is individually responsible to the Parliament and has to quit office if he fails to satisfy the Parliament. Besides this, the executive is also collectively responsible to the Parliament and has to quit office if it loses the confidence of the legislature. Thus, it is obvious that the Parliament exercises its control over administration indirectly through the executive.

Means of Parliamentary Control: The Parliament in India utilized following means to exercise its control over administration:

1. **Determination of Policies and Laws:** Since the Parliament enjoys the power to legislate so the basic structure of administration including the organizational-structure, powers, functions and procedures etc. is determined by the legislature. The creation/abolition of a particular ministry falls clearly within the ambit of Parliament. Further all the policies framed by the government require parliamentary approval. Though the policy initiation comes from the executive yet on every policy proposal, the assent of the Parliament is inevitable. In fact, it is the Parliament that provides the final shape to these policies. However, the legislature's control through the law-making process is very general.

2. **Parliamentary Questions:** In a parliamentary system, the parliamentary questions act as a potent tool to exercise control over the administration. In a democratic country, the role of parliamentary questions is significant in making the government accountable directly to the Parliament and through the Parliament to the people for its acts of omission and commission. In India, the right to ask

questions by the legislators, for the first time, was introduced in 1892. First hour of every parliamentary sitting is reserved for Question Hour. During this hour, any member of Parliament can ask any question from the ministers relating to the matters of public interests. "A question is a request made by a member for an oral explanation from the concerned minister. However, a notice of 10 days has to be given to the concerned minister before a question can be asked."[95] These questions are of three kinds–starred, unstarred and short notice. The starred questions are marked by an asterisk and require an oral answer. They may even invite supplementary questions[96] if the Member of Parliament is not satisfied with the answer given by the minister concerned. On the other hand, the unstarred questions are not marked with an asterisk and require a written reply. These questions are not followed by supplementary questions. The short notice questions are those which asked at a notice of less than ten days and are answered orally. The questions may either be concerned with limited interests or may involve issues of national importance. The minister concerned collects the material for answering these questions with the help of officials and secretaries of his department. Thus the parliamentary questions play a crucial role in keeping the administration at its toes. The underlying purpose behind asking questions formally is to elicit information but in actual terms, "…it is a potent weapon to focus attention on the failures and abuses of authority or on the grievances of the people."[97] The parliamentary questions keep the administration in India under a constant vigil and public scrutiny and thus serve the purpose of asserting the supremacy of Parliament.

Immediately after the Question Hour, the Zero Hour starts in the Parliament and it lasts till the start of the regular business of the House. In fact, Zero Hour is the time gap between Question Hour and the agenda. It is an Indian innovation and finds no place in the rules of procedure unlike the Question Hour. First time it was introduced in the field of parliamentary procedures in 1962. It is an informal device used by MPs to raise issues without any prior notice.

3. **Adjournment Motion:** It is an extra-ordinary device of exercising a check on administrative system as it interrupts the normal business of the Parliament for discussing the definite issue of public importance. It is introduced in the Lok Sabha to attract the attention of the house towards a matter of urgent nature and of public importance. The proposing member has to give a notice to the speaker for its introduction in the House. This motion needs the support of 50 members to be admitted. In that situation, the ordinary business of the house is suspended and an immediate debate takes place on the matter for which this motion is moved. A debate on an adjournment motion may last for three hours. At the end of the allotted time, "…the Speaker closes the debate and puts the motion to vote. In case such a motion is passed by a majority, it amounts to a censure against the government."[98] Since this motion involves the element of censure against the government, so Rajya Sabha is not permitted to make use of this device.

---

95 Arora, R.K. & Rajani Goyal (2010), *op. cit.*, p. 496.
96 The practice of asking supplementary questions was introduced in India in 1909.
97 Arora, K, Ramesh, *op. cit.* p. 496.
98 *Ibid*, p. 498.

4. **Non-Confidence Motion:** No-confidence motion is further an important weapon in the hands of opposition to exercise an effective check over the working of government. As per article 75 of the Indian constitution, the council of minister will remain in power as long as it enjoys the confidence of the Lok Sabha. If the House expresses a lack of confidence in the council of ministers, the government has no option but to resign. This motion can be brought in the house either due to the general poor performance of the government or when the whole policy of the government or a part of it, comes under fire. If this motion is passed in the House of the people, the government has no alternative but to resign.

5. **Calling Attention Motion:** It is another popular device which is purely an Indian innovation in the parliamentary procedures. It came into existence in 1954. It has resemblance with Zero Hour in the sense it is an Indian innovation but differs in the sense that it finds place in the rules of procedure. By this motion any member of the Parliament can ask a minister or call his attention towards a matter of urgent public importance and to seek an authoritative statement from him relating to that matter at a short notice. However, the speaker enjoys the freedom to allow or disallow the request. If the request is granted, the matter is presented before the House at once and the minister is expected to make a statement as soon as possible.

6. **Budgetary Control:** Budget is an important instrument in the hands of legislature to exercise its control over administration. It is mainly because in a parliamentary system, the executive can't spend even a single penny without the prior approval of the Parliament. It enjoys the ultimate authority to sanction the raising and spending of government funds. The Parliament controls the revenue and expenditure of the government through the enactment of the budget. During the enactment process of budget, the members specifically that of opposition get an opportunity to criticize the policies and actions of the government and point out the lapses and failures of administration. Hence the Indian Parliament regulates the activities of the government by controlling the purse string of the nation.

7. **Debate and Discussion:** Debate and discussions constitute the significant part of parliamentary proceedings. The members of Parliament utilize this tool to exercise their control over the council of ministers at various occasions. "Discussion takes place over the various clauses of a bill and over every demand in the budget; the purpose of every motion is to hold debates and discussion. Debates can be arranged on the government's own initiative or at the request of the opposition. " [99] The various readings of a bill provide opportunity to the House to criticize the entire policy of the government underlying the bill. "The value of debate lies in the fact that they compel the government to explain and defend particular issues of their policy at length and enable it to gauge the strength of various shades of opinion there on."[100]

8. **Control through Committees:** Since the realm of administration is extremely large, so certain committees are constituted by Parliament to control the functioning of administration. These committees are the ears and eyes of the Parliament and they operate on behalf of the Parliament. To exercise an effective control

---
99 *Ibid*
100 *Ibid*

over administration, the Parliament appoints these committees from amongst its members both belonging to ruling as well as opposition parties. These committees are required to examine certain subjects that the House assigned to them. "These committees exercise control through research and investigation of the varied activities of the spending departments and submit their reports to the Parliament."[101] However, recommendations mentioned by these committees may or may not be accepted by the later. Some of the prominent committees include Public Accounts Committee (PAC) and the Estimates Committee (EC), Committee on Public Undertakings (PUC) etc. The work of PAC is more precisely related to the routine administration in comparison to the other committees. This committee acts as a traditional watchdog over the governmental expenditure. This committee considers and examines the report of the Comptroller and Auditor General. The EC is supposed to suggest economy in the governmental expenditure. The Public Undertaking Committee is focused on the broader policy and operational issues of public enterprises. Besides, there exist almost seventeen standing committees having 45 members -30 from Lok Sabha and 15 from Rajya Sabha.The system of standing committees was introduced in Indian Parliament in 1893. The meetings of these committees are held in camera and they enjoy vast powers summon the bureaucrats for seeking information.

9. **Audit:** This is an important instrument of parliamentary control over public expenditure. The Comptroller and Auditor General (CAG) of India is an extended arm of the Parliament and helps the Parliament in ensuring that money spent by the executive matches with the money granted by the Parliament. CAG audits all the government accounts and submits an annual report to the Parliament regarding the financial transactions of the government. The CAG report highlights the improper, irregular, illegal and unwise expenditures of the government. This report is ultimately submitted to the Parliament as the CAG is responsible to the Parliament only. This report further helps the Parliament in securing financial accountability of the government. Thus, the role of audit in India is quite significant in tightening the bridle of the executive.

II. **Executive Control:** Executive control over administration is the control exercised by the chief executive and it is another potent instrument in keeping a constant vigil on administration. In the USA, this control is exercised by the President and his secretaries whereas in Britain and India it is exercised by the cabinet headed by the prime minister. Being a parliamentary democracy, cabinet in India is collectively responsible to the Parliament for its functioning and its ministers, who are in charge of respective governmental departments, are individually responsible for the acts of omission and commission in their respective ministries. Thus the chief executive has a direct control over administration. The executive exercises its control over administration through following means:

1. **Political Direction**: In India, the cabinet headed by the prime minister plays a crucial role in providing direction to the administration through the formulation of administrative policies. It decides all the policies, rules, regulations and procedures with regard to the working of administration. The ministers being the heads of their respective departments not only contribute in laying down their departmental policies but also play a crucial role in their implementation

---

101 *Ibid*, p. 503.

by providing necessary direction to administrators. Thus the officials of the respective departments operate directly under the control of the minister and look towards him for necessary direction. In all respects, they are responsible to ministers for their acts of omissions and commissions.

2. **Power of Appointment and Removal**: It is an important power in the hands of executive to exercise control over administration. The cabinet enjoys a lot of power in management of personnel through its power of appointment and removal of apex level administrative functionaries. These appointees help the ministers of respective departments in exercising full control over the various departments under their charge within these ministries. However, these appointments and removal of administrative functionaries are done by the President, but he does so only on the advice of the cabinet.

3. **Hierarchical Control**: Further, the structure of administration in India is hierarchical in nature. Thus every department operates under the guidance and supervision of a political head i.e. a minister and an administrative head i.e. a secretary. All the functionaries of the ministry work under the close supervision and subordination of the secretary and are arranged in a chained and hierarchical fashion right from top to the bottom in a senior-subordinate relationship. They are guided and directed by the in-build control mechanism fitted within the administrative hierarchy.

4. **Delegated Legislation:** The executive further exercises its control through the practice of 'delegated legislation'. It is also known as executive legislation. Due to the paucity of time with the Parliament, it passes laws in a skeleton form and authorizes the executive to fill in the minor details. Thus, under the practice of delegated legislation the executive is empowered to make rules, regulations and bye-laws to guide and direct the operational working of the administration. These rules have almost equal force as that of a law and could help in specifying some administrative procedures and determining the authority of different functionaries in a department.

5. **Control through Budget**: Budget is an important tool in the hands of the executive in India to exercise its effective control over the administration. The executive plays a crucial role during the budget process. During the preparation of budget, it issues broad guidelines to the respective ministries to prepare and submit their annual financial proposals in the form of demands. These financial proposals before being submitted to the Cabinet, are scrutinized by the respective heads of the ministries and then by the Finance Ministry. After the preparation of the budget, it is submitted to the Parliament for its enactment. During its enactment, the executive clarifies the queries raised by the members of the Parliament. Once the budget is approved by the Parliament, the Ministry of Finance (which is the central financial agency of the Government of India) bears its overall responsibility with regards to its execution. It allocates necessary funds to the administrative agencies to meet their expenditure.

6. **Control through Staff Agencies**: These agencies also exercise their influence and control over the administrative agencies indirectly and play an important role in co-ordinating their policies and programmes. The prominent staff agencies in India includes Cabinet Secretariat, Prime Minister's Office, Planning Commission and Department of Administrative Reforms. These agencies act as eyes, ears

and hands of the executive to aid and advice him to formulate and implement various plans

III. Judicial Control: Judiciary in India is an important means of external control over administration. There exists an Independent unified system of judiciary established by law having the Supreme Court at the apex. To deliver impartial justice, the Indian constitution has ensured the independence of judges through various ways. In India, judiciary is considered as the custodian of the civil rights and liberties of the common people. Thus, it implies the rights of aggrieved citizens to challenge the wrongful administrative acts in a court of law and protects them from all sorts of administrative excesses and the bureaucratic tyranny. Courts in India exercise control over the unlawful acts of the administration and ensure their legality. They enjoy the autonomy and freedom to determine the constitutionality of unlawful administrative actions and the executive orders and declare them ultra *vires* if they are not in consonance with law.

Scope of Judicial Intervention: The courts in India intervene in administrative matters on following grounds: -

1. *Lack of Jurisdiction:* In technical terms it is known as 'overfeasance' which means beyond the scope of one's authority. In general, an administrative officer is required to operate within the specified geographical limits of his authority. Sometimes the administrator acts without authority or crosses the limits of his authority, his deeds will be declared null and void by the court.

2. *Error of Law:* Technically it is known as 'misfeasance' which means misinterpretation of law. Statutory laws prescribe the extent and limits of powers of different public functionaries. But there is a possibility that an administrator misinterprets the law and thus imposes some conditions on the citizens that are not required by the content of law which is challengeable in any court of law. Then the court on behalf of these citizens' intervenes into the matter not only to provide a correct explanation of law but also to declare the actions of the administrative officials ultra-vires.

3. *Error in fact-finding:* If an administrative officer makes an error in the discovery of facts and acts on faulty presumptions, then his acts are challengeable in the courts of law. In such cases, the courts intervene in the administrative matters and try to rectify the error in discovering the actual facts.

4. *Abuse of Authority:* In technical terms, it is known as malfesance which means use of one's authority either vindictively to harm some another or to gain some personal end. If there is an abuse of authority on the part of any administrative functionary, his acts are challengeable in the court of law and the latter can intervene and punish the official if he is found guilty.

5. *Error of Procedure:* An administrative official *is* required to operate in accordance with the laid down procedures. But if he fails to follow them, his acts can be challenged. In such cases the courts get an opportunity to intervene into administrative matters to question the legality of such administrative actions.

Methods of Control: Following methods of control are utilized by judiciary to exercise control over the administration:

1. *Judicial Review:* Like US, the courts in India enjoy the power of judicial review. They can examine the legality and constitutionality of administrative acts, if

challenged by an aggrieved citizen. On examination, if they are found to breach the constitutional laws, they can be declared illegal by the court. In Britain, the scope of judicial review is limited due to the unwritten constitution and supremacy of Parliament but it is much wider in US. However, India falls in between the two because of certain constitutional and statutory limitations.

2. *Statutory Appeal:* The parliamentary statue/law may itself provide that an aggrieved citizen in India will have the right to appeal to the courts in a specific type of administrative acts. In such situations, the statutory appeal is possible.

3. *Suits against the Government:* The provision of suitability of the state finds mentioned under article 300 of the India constitution. As per this provision the union and state Governments can be sued, subject to the provisions of the law made by the Parliament and State Legislature respectively. In matters of contracts, the Union and State Governments have the same liability as that of an individual under the ordinary law of contract. However, in matters of torts, the position is different and here a distinction is made between the sovereign and non-sovereign functions of the state. In matters of tortuous liability of its servants, the state is liable to be sued only in case of its non-sovereign functions and not that of its sovereign functions.

4. *Suits against Public officials:* In India, the formal head of the state i.e. the President and the state governors enjoy legal immunity and are not liable for their official acts in any court of law. During their tenure, they are completely immune from all sorts of criminal proceedings in respect of their acts either done in personal or public capacity and they cannot be arrested or imprisoned during this period. However, in respect of their personal acts, civil proceedings can be instituted against them by giving a prior notice of two months. However, this immunity is not available to the ministers of the government and they can be sued like any citizen in ordinary courts for crimes. The judicial officers, in their judicial capacity are also immune from legal proceedings with regard to their acts of commissions as guides of courts under the Judicial Officer's Protection Act of 1850.

   As far as civil servants are concerned, they enjoy personal immunity under article 299 of the Indian Constitution from legal liability for official contracts. However, in other cases, they can be held liable for their deeds as that of an ordinary citizen. After a prior notice of two months, civil proceedings can be instituted against them for any action done in official capacity. In criminal cases, prior permission of the government is inevitable to institute criminal proceedings against them for the acts done by them in their official capacity.

5. *Extra-ordinary Remedies:* Like Britain, it is a general kind of supervision and control over all administrative acts in India which is exercised through a number of prerogative orders. These remedies are issued by the Supreme Court under article 32 and by High Courts under article 226 and are available to the citizen in extra ordinary circumstances. The extra ordinary remedies are designed to ensure that public functionaries do not misuse their authority, make errors of law or refuse to exercise their powers. In this regard some extra ordinary remedies viz. *Habeas corpus, Mandamus, Certiorari, Prohibition,* and *Quo-waranto* are available. A brief discussion of all these writs has already been made in the control machinery of the UK.

10
ADMINISTRATIVE SYSTEM OF JAPAN

The modern state of Japan came into existence with the Meiji Restoration in 1868 which remained in force till the end of World War II. After the War, Japan was placed under allied occupation headed by MacArthur and adopted a written constitution in 1946 that came into force in 1947. The new constitution provides for the constitutional monarchy. The position of Emperor is now that of *de jure* head of the state having nominal executive powers. The Constitution further establishes the principle of constitutional supremacy having a parliamentary form of government. The Diet is bi-cameral in nature having a House of Representatives (512 members) and a House of Councillors (252 members). The members of the House of Representatives are elected for a term of 4 years whereas those of the House of Councillors are elected for a term of 6 years. The Diet is the supreme legislative authority in Japan.

Executive powers are vested in the cabinet headed by the prime minister. The prime minister must be a member of the Diet and is designated by his colleagues. The prime minister has the power to appoint and remove ministers, a majority of whom must be Diet members. Japan's judicial system has been drawn from the customary law, civil law, and Anglo-American common law. It consists of several levels of courts, with the Supreme Court as the final judicial authority. The system of administrative courts does not exist in Japan. The Supreme Court in Japan is endowed with the power of judicial review.

The civil servants in Japan are recruited by the National Personnel Agency (NPA) on the basis of merit. Unlike UK and France Japan has adopted positional classification which favours for specialization and professional expertise by demarcating the requisite skills to discharge particular job responsibilities attached with the post. The political rights of the civil servants are restricted and their right to strike is legally denied. The civil servants in Japan have to remain within the same ministry for whole period of their service. There exists a system of *Amakudari* in Japan which enables the retired civil servants to work in private sector.

Though Japan retains the unitary system yet the principle of local autonomy grants extensive rights of self-government to the local institutions. Unlike the US, Japanese local government is structurally uniform to a great extent except the local government in Tokyo and a few designated cities. For administrative convenience Japan is divided into 47 prefectures and each prefecture is further divided into cities, town and villages.

In the present chapter an endeavour has been made to discuss *the salient features of administration, political executive, local government,* and *control machinery* of Japan in detail.

(A) Administrative Features

Following are some important characteristics of the administration in Japan:

1. Unitary and Centralized Administration

Unlike the USA and India, the Japanese administration is unitary in character. It is because the entire executive authority is vested in the government at Tokyo. The devolution of authority to the provinces has been merely a matter of administrative convenience and not for any federative principle. These powers can be varied at any time by the centre. The unitary character of the Japanese government highlights a general view of its being centralized. It is mainly because there is no separate division of power at the lower levels and the whole of Japan is governed from the centre. The central government is entirely responsible for managing the overall affairs of the nation. All the national laws and policies for the whole nation are framed at the central level and are implemented by the different functionaries of the respective operative departments/ministries. Each ministry is formally headed by a minister, who is the head of ministerial career service.[1] Most of the central departments and other national organizations operate through a well-developed network of regional and local offices. The former are the largest jurisdictional areas of the central government whereas the "prefectural" and "municipal" offices roughly correspond to the local government's jurisdiction. Consequently, local authorities are the principal operating agencies of the government in Japan.

Apart from being unitary in nature, the Japanese administration is characterized by centralization of authority as the decision making power of the government rests with the chief executive who acts as the main source of entire gamut of policies and programs. Irrespective of the fact that local governments are conferred considerable autonomy under the constitution of Japan and successive legislations, it has yet to become a reality. At the local level, both the Governor (at the prefecture level) and the Mayor (at the municipality level) act as the agents of the central government and are responsible for implementing the central laws and policies apart from the directions issued to them by the central government. "Model bills are prepared at Tokyo and passed on to the local units all over Japan. The local units have no option but to follow these bills."[2] The central government also maintains hegemony over the local governments through its power of purse as "twenty percent or more of the revenues of the local units are in the nature of grants-in-aid from the central government."[3] In fact, the local units have to look towards the central grants to meet out their expenditures. "In Japan tradition is also in favour of central control."[4]

2. Powerful Bureaucracy

The bureaucracy in Japan is quite influential and powerful since its very inception. The growth and reform of bureaucracy actually took place under the Meiji

---

1 Rowat, Donald, C, *Public Administration in Developed Democracies: A Comparative Study*, (ed), New York: Marcel, Dekker, Inc. 1988, p. 376.
2 Goyal, O.P., *Comparative Government: UK, USA, USSR, Japan, Switzerland*, New Delhi: Macmillan India, Ltd., 1985, p. 334.
3 *Ibid*, p. 334.
4 *Ibid*, p. 334.

Constitution and the recruitment of the bureaucrats started on the basis of merit due to the introduction of examination system in 1880s. Till the end of the Second World War, the bureaucracy in Japan had to function under imperial ordinances and regulations and thus the bureaucrats were designated not as 'public servant' rather the 'servants of the emperor'.[5] In the post World War scenario, Japan came under occupation of Allied forces which established "... new patterns in Japanese politics and administration."[6] The pre-war bureaucracy was transformed from the 'servants of the emperor' to the 'servants of the public as a whole'. To counter the devastating effects of World War II, the role of government expanded enormously in context of reconstruction, industrial and infra-structural development of the nation. In such a situation Japanese bureaucracy got an opportunity to play a central role in economic and infra-structural development of the country which is not only limited to the execution but had a strong influence on the formulation of policies.[7] Thus its role was proliferated and expanded to a great extent as the bureaucrats in Japan have traditionally been viewed as more capable than politicians. The politicians including the prime minister are considered as part timers "...who have little power and have to be taught how to make the 'right decisions'."[8] The role of bureaucracy is crucial in drafting new budgets and writing legislations. In an interview given to the New York Times magazine, the US Ambassador to Japan, Walter Mondale holds that, "In the Diet, when you see bureaucrats also participating in the debates, answering questions, preparing amendments, preparing the budget, you realize that this is a society in which the publicly elected side is very limited."[9] Commenting on the Japanese Bureaucracy, Williams holds that "Since the war," "the bureaucracy has normally dominated the legislative process, and in this narrow sense can be said to have ruled with the Diet reigned."[10] It is further substantiated from the observations of Pemple that "approximately 90 percent of all legislation passed since 1955 was drafted within a government Agency..."[11]

The position of bureaucratic dominance in Japan was not questioned till 1980s but the "... failure of the bureaucrats to deal with Japan's economic problems in the 1990s and 2000s has led some Japanese to look more to politicians and political parties for policy solutions to Japan's problems."[12] Resultantly in recent years specifically after the August 2009 elections, the emerging political leadership is inclined to "... take power out of the hands of the bureaucrats and put it in the hands of the politicians."[13]

---

5   Heady, Ferrel, *Public Administration: A Comparative Perspective*, 6th Edition, New York: Marcel Dekker, Inc. 2001, p. 239.
6   *Ibid*, p. 239.
7   Rowat, Donald, C, *op cit.*, p. 380.
8   http;//factssanddetails.com/japan.php?itemid=800&catid=22&sucatid=146 retrieved on 18.8 2011.
9   http;//factssanddetails.com/japan.php?itemid=800&catid=22&sucatid=146 retrieved on 18.8 2011.
10 Williams, *Japan: Beyond the End of History*, as quoted in Ferrel heady, *Ibid*, p. 248.
11 Pempel, *The higher Civil Service in Japan*, as quoted in Ferrel Heady, *Ibid*, p. 243.
12 http;//factssanddetails.com/japan.php?itemid=800&catid=22&sucatid=146 retrieved on 18.8 2011.
13 *Ibid*

3. Trend towards Administrative Reforms

Right from the middle of the last century, Japan made several efforts to compete with the developed world. To compete with the western developed world, the importance of administrative reforms as a continuous process was recognised especially in the wake of slow economic growth since 1973 triggered by the unexpected oil crisis. The administrative reforms carried out before the establishment of the Second Reform Commission in 1981 mainly aimed at improving administrative efficiency while the prime objective of the second reform commission was financial reforms which were aimed at reconstruction of public finance.

Prominent reforms since the establishment of second Administrative Reform Commission till 1997 include: privatization of three major public corporations, downsizing bureaucracy by eliminating 45,388 positions at national level and setting up of the Management and Co-ordination Agency for overall co-ordination in 1984, reforming the public pension system, reducing fiscal deficit and lastly enactment and implementation of Administrative Procedures Law.[14] In 1996, the newly formed Cabinet further strengthened the process of administrative reforms and the Administrative Reform Council was established to examine reorganization of central ministries and agencies, review of public corporations and deregulation. Besides, the extremely difficult financial situation in 1996 forced the government to chalk out and implement fiscal structural reforms for which a conference was called to prepare a set of guidelines for the said structural reform in June 1997.[15]

4. Trend towards Transparency and Accountability

The content of secrecy in the decisions made by bureaucracy was all pervasive due to the bureaucratic dominance in execution and framing of policies. Consequently, the necessity of more open and transparent government was realized by late 1970s and the Japan Civil Liberties Union (a non-governmental organization) published a draft of Information Disclosure Law. This was followed by intense campaigning, efforts and persuasion during the next more than two decades in support of the law. Finally, Diet adopted the first national information disclosure law in May, 1999 which ultimately took the shape of law in April, 2001. The Act confers the right to demand information with some exceptions to all Japanese citizens to secure information from the national agencies as well as the government owned agencies who are required to supply that information within thirty days of the request. In case of information denial, the applicant can appeal to the Information Disclosure and Personal Information Board established under a separate law. Appeals in these boards are made free of cost. Moreover, these boards conduct their own investigations including review of documents and other information at issue.

This Act is considered as a revolutionary step in the direction of promoting transparency and accountability on the part of administration which is reflected from the fact that "requests filed by journalists, lawyers, activists and ordinary citizens have uncovered a wide range of information concerning public health, government expenditures, international relations and other issues of broad public interest."[16]

---

14 http://www.unpani.un.org/intradoc/groups/public/documents/un/unpan 000230.pdf. retrieved on 18.8.2011
15 Ibid
16 Ibid

5. Trend towards Decentralization

The new constitution introduces the doctrine of local autonomy. To ensure local autonomy, Diet passed the Local Autonomy Law of 1947 which is oriented towards 'decentralization and direct democracy'. "In addition to this law, a series of related laws like the Public office election law, Local Public Service Law, and Local Finance Law were enacted in order to strengthening local autonomous entities."[17] The local government units have two main organizations - the assembly as the legislative wing and the chief executive officer as the executive. The units include prefectures, cities, towns and village municipalities; have been provided with extensive rights of self government by this Local Autonomy Law. It is quite comprehensive and regulates all issues concerning local public entities. It succeeded in replacing the previously existing several laws which emphasized on 'centralized local government system'. Thus like the other developed democracies, the local government in Japan enjoys considerable autonomy but the continuously increasing national financial pressure demands more accountability.

The momentum of economic growth was slowed down by the Oil Crisis in 1973, specifically in the late 1970s, which ultimately affected the health of public finance at both national and local level. Efforts were made to reduce the financial dependence of the local government on national subsidies. "Supported by the economic boom of the late 80s, the local governments shifted their uniformed policies to various policies cheering up and creating regional diversity. The recession after the collapse of the "economic bubble" in the 1990s exposed all the structural problems accumulated since the end of the WWII, and the local government system was not the exception."[18] The emergence of 'structural reform for decentralization' as a major issue in 1993 at the level of political coalition of various parties, ultimately led to the enactment of Decentralization Promotion Law in 1995. "The aim was to set forth the principles of decentralization and to clarify the procedures to realize it by setting up the Decentralization Promotion Committee... [which] recommended five prominent recommendations on the basis of which the government drafted a Decentralization Promotion Plan and submitted it to the Diet.[19] Further, in January 1999, 'reform package containing more than 500 related legal amendments' was also submitted before the Diet and after being passed, it was implemented from April 2000.

Meanwhile, the move towards 'more mergers' of local authorities and the heavy reliance on private sector and the reinforcement of municipal co-operation led to the introduction of the revisions of the Municipal Merger Special Measures Law in 1995 and 1999 and 'fortified initiatives for assembling a joint council for mergers and fiscal assistance for mergers'. Consequently it was decided to merge 581 joint councils by March 2005. Later on this Law was replaced by new Municipal Merger

---

17 *Ibid*, p. 380.
18 http: www.soum.go.jp/pdf/lgsij.pdf retrieved on 28.3.09
19 The biggest feature was the abolition of the "agency-delegated tasks", which started from the pre-war era when the state delegated tasks to the appointed prefectural governors, and the comprehensive "directive and supervisory power" of the government related to these tasks. The plan also called for the reduction and reorganization of subsidies appropriated to local governments for specific purposes, which were other tools that the state used to intervene in local government. See website http: www.soum.go.jp/pdf/lgsij.pdf retrieved on 28.3.09

Special Measures Law in April 2005 and under the new law the government will keep 'promoting municipal merger for 5 years more[20].

6. Growing Influence of Information and Technology in Governance

Since the very beginning Japanese administration has a great influence of technology and thus succeeds in making a remarkable progress in all spheres of life. This impact of technology is quite visible from the excellence it has attained in exporting technology intensive products in the international market. The influence of the technical growth is also visible on its administration which not only helped in promoting the capability and efficiency of administration but proved significant in developing new methods of management and organization.

With the changing needs of time, administrative needs got diversified in view of the steadily rising demands for better public services, responsiveness and transparency. Also, the rising fiscal deficit made it imperative for the government to reduce and rationalize public spending. These factors ultimately pressed the government to become more responsive, open, rational and efficient. The necessity of introducing information and communication technologies (ICTs) in the administrative system was advocated in the final report of Provisional Council on the Promotion of Administrative Reforms (PCPAR) in October, 1993 for efficient delivery of public utilities, increasing administrative responsiveness, reducing administrative delays caused by red-tapism, enhancing public accountability and promoting public participation in governance process. Keeping the recommendations in view, the cabinet adopted a five year plan called 'The *Basic Plan for Computerization of the Government*' in December 1994.[21]

Under the plan, a joint action programme was established with the approval of every ministry and agency under which they were required to design their own programmes. This plan can be designated as a conscious effort in the direction of e-governance in Japan where the comprehensive use of computers was started. Resultantly, by the end of fiscal year 1996, various ministries and agencies were equipped with around 30 thousand computers. Moreover, the head offices of almost all the ministries and agencies established local area networks (LANs). Likewise a wide area net work (WAN) for connecting ministries and agencies to facilitate information exchange became functional in 1997.[22]

7. Trend towards Public Private Partnership (PPP)

In response to the influence of good governance new public management (NPM) and public choice approach which favours market liberalism provide impetus to the role of multiple actors in governance in realizing public goods. This tendency led to the popularization of the concept of Public-Private Partnership (PPP) across the world including Japan[23]. Thus, a close interaction between the government and the private sector was openly accepted. Moreover, inefficiency due to bureaucratic clutches on the part of government, availability of better technical skill with the private sector

---

20 *Ibid*
21 http://www.unpani.un.org/intradoc/groups/public/documents/un/unpan 000230.pdf. retrieved on 18.8.2011
22 The Inter-Ministerial Council on Government Information Systems composed of heads of the secretariats of ministries and agencies, approved this development plan in June 1996.
23 http://www.meti.go.jp/english/report/downloadfiles/AsianPPP.pdf

and the problem of fund crunch with the government led to commence such kind of initiatives in Japan.

In Japan, an effort in the direction of PPP originated with the enactment of the Private Finance Initiative in 1999. The Law aimed at "...promoting the introduction of management skills in the private sector for public services." Later in 2001, an independent administrative institution (IAI) system was introduced. IAIs utilize management methods of private-sector corporations and are given considerable autonomy in their operations and how to use their budgets. Further, Local Autonomy Law was amended to introduce the 'designated manager system' to allow the management and operation of public facilities by private entities in 2003. In 2005, model projects for market testing were adopted by the cabinet on the recommendations of the Council for Regulatory Reforms and Public-Private Partnership given in 2004.[24]

(B) POLITICAL EXECUTIVE

Being a parliamentary form of government, Japan like India and England has the Emperor as a formal head and the Prime Minister and his cabinet as a real executive. A brief description of the Japanese Emperor, Prime Minister and the Cabinet is as under:

EMPEROR

Like Great Britain, Japan has had a sufficiently long experience of Monarchy. Under the Meiji Constitution, he was the main source of authority, as most of the legislative and executive powers were concentrated in him. He was conferred the sovereign authority by this constitution. He was assigned the responsibility of running the government smoothly and the Diet was made a subordinate agency to him. "The Meiji Constitution had bestowed divinity on him and he was made to look as a divine person".[25] Under the Meiji Constitution, the Emperor was thought the real head of the Empire yet most of his powers were exercised by his ministers or the Supreme War Council. It is mainly because, prior to 1945, the military leadership dominated the overall scene. Like the British Monarch, he reigns but does not rule.

The constitution (1947) imposed in the post war scenario, though retained the monarchy in Japan but brought significant changes to the position of the Emperor. It conferred the sovereign power to the people and thus reduced the Emperor to a constitutional head. It led to a great transition from imperial sovereignty to popular sovereignty or a cipher. The new constitution made him the ceremonial head of the state. The emperor "... is not even the head of the state. He is merely a symbol for the nation, something like a national flag or a national song. Therefore the cabinet is the sole and exclusive executive authority under the new Japanese constitution".[26] In accordance with Article 1 of 1947 Constitution "...the emperor shall be the symbol of the state and shall derive his powers from the people because sovereignty resides with them".[27]

---

24 http://www.meti.go.jp/english/report/downloadfiles/AsianPPP.pdf
25 Bhagwan, Vishnoo and Vidya Bhushan, *World Constitutions*, New Delhi: Sterling Publishers Private Limited, Reprinted in 1991, p. 27.
26 Goyal, O.P. *op. cit.*, p. 357.
27 Bhagwan, Vishnoo and Vidya Bhushan, *op. cit.*, p. 25.

Succession- The succession to the Imperial Throne is dynastic. It takes place strictly in accordance with the Imperial House Law passed by the Diet. Under the Meiji Constitution the Diet was not empowered to amend this law but the 1947 constitution made such provisions. Accordingly the Diet amended this law in 1947 and now "... Imperial throne will be succeeded by a male offspring in the main line belonging to the Imperial lineage... No adoption is permitted. Regency is established in case the Emperor has not come of the age (18 years)".[28]

Powers- The powers of the Emperor in Japan can be discussed as under-

1. *Executive Power*: The Japanese Emperor is authorized to appoint a person (who is designated by the Diet) as the Prime Minister. In accordance with law, he attests the appointment and removal of the Ministers of State and other officials. In foreign matters he receives foreign ambassadors and ministers accredited to Japan. He also attests the full power and credentials of ambassadors and minister. He appoints the chief justice of the Supreme Court as designated by the Cabinet.[29]

2. *Legislative Power*: He promulgates all the national laws and constitutional amendments made by the Diet. He also promulgates the Cabinet Orders and the treaties. He summons the sessions of the Diet. He is empowered to dissolve the lower House (House of Representatives) on the completion of its term or on the recommendation of the Prime Minister. He proclaims the general election of the members of the Diet.[30]

3. *Judicial Power*: The emperor enjoys some judicial powers also. He attests the general pardon or special amnesty to political offenders, commutation of punishment, reprieve and restoration of rights.

4. *Fountain of Honour* – He participates in ceremonial functions and as a symbol of the state, awards honours to the persons who have done their best in different fields.

Position: After a careful perusal of the powers of the Emperor in Japan, it is obvious that he is merely a titular, constitutional or formal head of the nation. He enjoys least or almost no power or influence in governmental affairs. He is simply required to act upon the advice of the Cabinet. For instance, in the appointment of the Prime Minister he has no say as he simply appoints the person as Prime Minister who is designated by the Diet. In foreign matters, his powers are sufficiently restricted.

Further the laws passed by the Diet and the treatise made by the Cabinet do not need his assent rather he simply promulgates them. His role is insignificant in the dissolution of the House of Representatives as it is an exclusive privilege of the Cabinet in Japan. In the field of judiciary, his powers are sufficiently restricted. He enjoys no pardoning powers. He simply attests them. The new constitution has further weakened his position as, "...without the assent of the Diet he cannot give away any property, nor receive it, nor can accept any gifts. The imperial expenditure also is to be approved by the Diet".[31] He is neither the sovereign nor the source of sovereign authority. "However, one thing is quite clear that he does

---

28 Ibid
29 Ibid, p. 25.
30 Ibid
31 Ibid, p. 29.

not have any specific political or executive function to perform. His functions in the new constitution are purely ceremonial or ritual. He is not an inch more than a symbol of a Japanese political system. Politically, he has been reduced to a cipher and no political role has been assigned for him in the constitution".[32] The position of the Emperor in Japan is too weak to be compared with the Indian President or the British King. In the appointment of the Prime Minister, the latter enjoys at least some discretion but the former is deficient on this part. It is because in Japan, it is the Diet and not the Emperor who nominate the Prime Minister. He is only required to formally appoint him. Even his assent is not needed on the bills passed by the Diet. He only promulgates these laws. Unlike the Indian President, he neither vetos the bills passed by the Diet nor can return them.

Unlike the British King, who enjoys three important rights - right to be consulted, right to encourage and right to warn, the Emperor of Japan has no rights. He is not the commander-in-chief of the military as militarism was abolished in Japan. Unlike the British King who influences the manifold decisions of the cabinet, he enjoys least influence. He has almost no say in foreign matters. "In fact, he has been reduced to a position which at least in theory, is inferior to that of the British Monarch. The British Monarch is still the head of the state. On the other hand, the emperor in Japan is not even the head of the state. He is merely a symbol. He is something like a national flag or a national song".[33]

PRIME MINISTER

In Japan, the Prime Minister is the actual head of the Government. His office is a creation of the Japanese Constitution. It is the Prime Minister in Japan who wields the actual political power as the Emperor is merely a symbol of the nation and no longer acts either as head of the state or the head of the Government. The Prime Minister, being the real executive, exercises enormous executive authority in close co-operation with the members of his Cabinet.

Appointment: The Prime Minister of Japan is formally appointed by the Emperor but the latter enjoy no discretion in his appointment. It is because in Japan, it is not the Emperor but the Diet who elects the Prime Minister. Both houses of the Diet elect a person to this post amongst the members of the Diet and that too from the House of Representative. If there is no consensus between the two houses in this regard, a joint committee of both the houses is appointed. "If the Joint committee fails to reach an agreement, the decision of the House of Representatives finally prevails after ten days. The Emperor issues a formal appointment letter to the person so elected." [34] Hence the Japanese Prime Minister is elected by the whole House and is not merely a choice of the majority party.

Powers and Functions: The Prime Minister of Japan, being the pivot of the government enjoys enormous powers and discharges the following functions –

1. *Selection of the Ministers* - One of the most important function to be discharged by the Prime Minister right after being appointed is the selection of the ministers or the formation of his cabinet. In Japan, theoretically the ministers need not

---

32 Goyal, *op. cit.*, p. 366.
33 *Ibid*
34 Bhagwan, Vishuoo, Vidya Bhusan, *op. cit.*, p. 35.

necessarily be the members of the Diet. They may be civilians. However in practice majority of these ministers are selected from the House of Representatives. In the selection of his ministers, the Prime Minister is guided and directed by several considerations and then he prepares the list of ministers and presents it to the Emperor for his attestation. In the selection of ministers his authority is in no way limited. The Emperor's attestation is only a formality.

2. *Allocation of Portfolio, their reshuffling and Removal of Ministers-* After selection of the ministers, the next important task of the Prime Minister is to allocate portfolios among his team members. All the cabinet members are of equal rank. Twelve of them preside over the twelve ministries while the rest of the members are known as Minister of State. [35] In the allocation of portfolio, his decision is final. He is further empowered to reshuffle their portfolio and can ever remove them. "Article 68 states that the Prime Minister can remove the ministers. He can reshuffle his cabinet, wherever he likes. He has full control over his cabinet."[36]

3. *Chairman of the Cabinet-* The Prime Minister is the boss of the cabinet. His power to select the cabinet ministers (after his appointment as prime minister), to allocate portfolios to them and the power of dismissal of minister, makes him the master of the cabinet and far superior to his ministerial colleagues. As such he is definitely *primus inter pares*. He convenes and presides over the meetings of the cabinet. It is he who decides not only when the cabinet shall meet but also what it shall discuss. His role is crucial in setting the agenda of the cabinet meetings and can accept or reject the proposals made by its members for discussion. He acts as a guide of the cabinet and is responsible for maintaining co-ordination among the policies of different ministries. He settles the disputes that arise among different ministries. He also maintains effective supervision over the work of different ministries. The meetings of the cabinet are held in camera and its proceedings are kept secret. Without his approval, no legal actions can be taken against a minister. His resignation is considered as the resignation of the whole cabinet. Therefore, it becomes obvious that the prime minister is the undisputed leader or chairman of the cabinet.

4. *Representative of the Nation-* The prime minister as a leader of the nation represents Japan at the national and international levels. He participates as a representative of the whole nation in international conferences and his views expressed in such conferences are considered as the views of the nation. He makes all commitment on behalf of the nation. In this capacity, he concludes a number of treatise and agreements with different nations. "He holds the reins of the administration of the country. He acts as a link between the Emperor and the people. He holds the most powerful office in the government. The people look to him for the redressal of their grievances."[37]

5. *Leader of the House of Representatives* – The Prime Minister is the leader of the House of Representatives in particular and that of the Diet in general. In that capacity, he takes decisions regarding the general business of the House during the session. He further guides and directs the proceedings of the House and

---

35 Goyal, *op. cit.*, p. 359.
36 Bhagwan, Vishnoo, Vidya Bhusan, *op. cit.*, p. 36.
37 *Ibid*, p. 38.

makes all important policy announcements. He also safeguards his ministers, intervening in the debates of general importance.[38] Here it needs to be mentioned that though he is elected by both the houses of the Diet but the lower House (House of Representatives) primarily dominates. Thus, he holds his offices as long as he enjoys its confidence. However, being the leader of the majority party in the House, he also enjoys its support.

6. *Power of Dissolution* - The prime minister enjoys the power to dissolve the House of Representatives and by this power, he regulates the business of the House. This power of the prime minister brings the members of the House, his party colleagues and even his cabinet colleagues at his mercy as, dissolution means new election without the certainty of being returned to the House. If the members of the House of Representative operate contrary to his wishes, he may simply advise the Emperor to dissolve the House. For instance "in 1953, when the House of Representatives passed a no-confidence motion against Prime Minister Yoshida, he at once got the House dissolved. After the general election, he was again elected as the Prime Minister."[39]

Position- The position of the Japanese Prime Minister is a formidable one which is clearly visualized from his functions and powers discussed above. He is the pivot of the Japanese government and administration and the entire governmental machinery revolves around him. He manages the sovereign, the cabinet and the House of Representatives. He is the actual wielder of the political power and has a central place in Japanese politics. He holds a position of unmistakable supremacy and thus specifically dominates in the decision making process.

In Japan it is not the Emperor (who is merely symbol of state), rather it is the prime minister who acts as the real head of the government. He is the actual wielder of the authority of the Emperor. Besides, he enjoys a special position in comparison to the other executive officials. The new constitution further contributed significantly in enhancing his powers manifold primarily by abolishing the Privy Council and the Supreme War Council. "In fact he is the executive authority of the state and his powers are so vast that any other constitutional ruler can hardly compete with him. Even the President of the United States is not so powerful."[40]

Unlike Britain, the office of the prime minister in Japan is not an outcome of conventions but a creation of the constitution. He is the nerve centre or boss of the cabinet. He not only enjoys the power to appoint its members but he can even remove them. "No wonder, therefore, that the Prime Ministers in Japan have enjoyed greater stability than the members of their cabinets. This in itself is an indication of the fact that the position of the Prime Minister in relation with his colleagues in the cabinet has been more than that of a first among equals".[41] Hence in his cabinet, the prime minister of Japan enjoys a position that is *'Supra intra pares'* (superior among equals) instead of *Primus inter Pares.'*[42] He is the undisputed leader of the cabinet. Moreover he is the leader of the majority party in power and the leader of the House

---

38   *Ibid*, p. 36.
39   *Ibid*, p. 37-38.
40   *Ibid*, p. 36.
41   Goyal, *op. cit.*, p. 363.
42   Vishnoo Bhagwan and Vidya Bhusan, *op. cit.*, p. 36.

of Representatives. His power to dissolve the lower house brings the members of the house and his cabinet colleagues on his mercy.

The importance of Japanese Prime Minister has enhanced further in view of the recent developments and the progress registered by Japan in the field of science and technology both at the national and international. The personality and character of the persons holding this office, in Japan has further made this office strong. It high lights how they carried out the challenging tasks of this office. "Most of the Prime Ministers in Japan have been highly skilled people. Most of them had been in the civil service before they became Prime Ministers. Shidehara, Yoshida, Ashida, Kishi and Ikeda were all career bureaucrats before they became prime ministers. They were skilled bureaucrats."[43]

CABINET

Today Japan has a parliamentary form of government. The new constitution, though maintained the institution of the Emperor, yet it has undermined his position. Under the new Japanese Constitution, he is even not the head of the state rather a symbol of state somewhat like a national flag or a national song. It added a complete chapter on the cabinet and equipped the cabinet with all the executive powers. In other words, the new Japanese constitution vested the sole and exclusive executive authority in the cabinet, which consists of the prime minister (who is its head) and the other ministers of state.

Evolution: The evolution of Japanese Cabinet can be traced from 1855 when it came into existence for the first time by an Imperial Ordinance. It consisted of nine departments.[44] Under the Meiji Constitution in 1989, the word 'cabinet' found no mention. Instead of the word 'Cabinet', it mentioned the word 'Ministers of State.' "Article 55 stated that there would be "Minister of State" who was "to give advice to the Emperor and be responsible for it." But since this constitution did mention the Ministers who were also responsible, so it may be said that the constitution established a sort of cabinet though it did not expressly mention it."[45] Thus the members of the pre-war cabinet were the sole appointees of the Emperor and were exclusively responsible to him. They were not responsible to the Diet. Moreover the sense of collective responsibility was also found lacking among its members and it was primarily dominated by military people.[46] "The Cabinets of pre-war years were more like the president's cabinets in the United States and had no resemblance with the cabinet system as it operated in Great Britain and now operated in India. What the Japanese had in pre-war years was a cabinet but not a cabinet system."[47] It is quite obvious that the pre-war cabinets were primarily dominated by the militarists instead of civilians. During this period it evolved as an extra-constitutional institution. A significant turn took place in the history of Japanese cabinet with the promulgation of the New Japanese Constitution in 1947. Apart from providing a due place to the cabinet system, it invested all the executive powers in it (which were previously

---

43 Goyal, *op. cit.*, p. 363
44 Bhagwan, Vishnoo and Vidya Bhusan, *op. cit.*, p. 31.
45 *Ibid*, p. 31.
46 Goyal, *op. cit.*, p. 357.
47 *Ibid*, p. 357.

vested in the Emperor). This Constitution significantly curtailed the powers of the Emperor and reduced him to a position of symbol of nation or big cipher. Now the members of the cabinet are no more responsible to the Emperor but to the Diet or to the people. "Article 66 of the constitution says that the cabinet shall consist of the Prime Minister, who shall be its head, and other Ministers of State, as provided for by law."[48] The new law broke down the hegemony of the military people in the cabinet by providing that "...Prime Minister and other Minister of state must be civilians."[49]

Organization – The process of cabinet formation in Japan starts with the appointment of the prime minister after he has been selected by both the houses of the Diet. In the selection of the prime minister, the Emperor has no discretion. After the general election, both the houses of the Diet (in its first session) vote separately and usually select the leader of the majority party in the House of Representative, as the prime minister. In case of dissension, between the two houses, the matter is referred to a joint committee. If the joint committee even failed to reach a decision within 10 days, the will of the House of Representative prevails.[50] Now, the prime minister prepares a list of persons to be designated as 'minister' by keeping in view a number of considerations. This list bearing the names of the ministers and the portfolios assigned against their names is presented to the Emperor at an attestation ceremony in the Imperial Palace.[51] Constitutionally, the members of the cabinet need not to be necessarily from the Diet but usually the prime minister selects most of them from the lower House. "The cabinet consists of two types of ministers- those holding the portfolios and those who do not hold any portfolio... The ministers without portfolios are allotted some important administrative functions. Every minister is assisted by three vice ministers."[52] According to Prof. Goyal, "Recent cabinets have consisted of twenty members, including eighteen ministers, a chief cabinet secretary and a director of the cabinet legislation bureau."[53]

Salient Characteristics – From the evolution of the Japanese Cabinet, it is obvious that its functions and role underwent tremendous change over the years. From merely an advisory body, it emerged as a real executive. Over the years it has developed following characteristics:-

1. *The Emperor is not a part of the Cabinet-* In the pre-war Japan; the ministers of state (or the cabinet) were the appointees of the Emperor, to assist him. They were not responsible to the Diet or to the people but only to the Emperor. But the New Japanese Constitution curtailed the powers of the Emperor significantly by reducing him to a cipher. It endowed all the executive authority in the cabinet and now the Emperor is no more a part of it. The cabinet is even not responsible to the Emperor but to the Diet or the people.

2. *Leadership of the Prime Minister-* The cabinet operates under the leadership of the prime minister. He is recognized as the nerve centre of the cabinet arch.

---

48 *Ibid*, p. 357.
49 *Ibid*
50 Bhanwan, Vishnoo and Vidya Bhusan, *op. cit.*, p. 32.
51 *Ibid*, p. 33.
52 *Ibid*, p. 34.
53 Goyal, *op. cit.*, p. 358.

He presides over the cabinet meetings. He provides general direction and kind supervision to it. He resolves all sorts of conflicts at the level of cabinet. There is no problem of quorum and voting. Consensus is taken and all decision are supposed to be unanimous decision. "If a minister does not sign the decision, he must resign otherwise the Prime Minister will remove him."[54]

3. *Secrecy-* The cabinet operates on the doctrine of secrecy. Utter secrecy is maintained regarding the cabinet proceedings and they are not made open to the public. The record of the proceedings of the cabinet is usually not maintained. The ministers can not reveal to the press any thing that transpired in these meeting. All the ministers are required to maintain the complete secrecy in this regard. Non-observance of secrecy by the ministers can invite risk to them. Thus, all support and co-operate each other.

4. *Affinity with the Diet-* Like Britain, in Japan also, the Cabinet has a close affinity with the Diet. In theory the cabinet is a creation of the Diet and is accountable to it. The prime minister in Japan is selected by the House of Representatives, the lower house of the Diet. Then the prime minister selects his team of ministers i.e. Cabinet from the same house. Unlike the UK, however, it is not necessary in Japan that the cabinet ministers must belong to the Diet. So the Japanese Prime Minister is even free to select the outsiders even to the cabinet. Usually all the cabinet ministers are taken from the Diet. The cabinet ministers further attend the sessions of the Diet and provide satisfactory answers to the questions raised by the members of the Diet. Again the Diet enjoys the power to accept, amend or reject the bills presented by the cabinet. Even the Diet can impeach the members of the cabinet. Moreover the Diet can pass a no confidence motion against the whole cabinet.[55] However in practice, the cabinet enjoys legislative supremacy in the Diet and acts as the legislative leader in Japan. It is because only one single political party has an overwhelming number of members in the lower house "The relationship between the Diet and the cabinet is exactly like the one that exists in Great Britain or in India."[56]

Functions- In Japan, the cabinet is vested with all the executive powers of state at the national level. Besides in the legislative sphere even, it has emerged as the legislative leader. Thus it has to perform a multiple number of functions. Its important functions can be discussed under following heads-

1. *Determination of Policies and Issues-* The cabinet being the legislative leader of the Diet plays a significant role in determining the major policies and issues of the government both at home and abroad. It takes all important policy decisions regarding various policy issues in order to generate or frame the requisite policy. It concludes treatises and does negotiations to manage foreign affairs. Once the decisions are taken, they became binding on all the ministers irrespective of their personal likes or dislikes.

2. *Chief Co-ordinator-* For the smooth and effective implementation of the government policy, adequate co-ordination is inevitable among the affected departments. It

---

54 Bhagwan, Vishnoo and Vidya Bhusan, *op. cit.*, p. 34.
55 Goyal, *op. cit.*, p. 362.
56 *Ibid*, p. 361.

is because the government works like a well co-ordinating unit. The Japanese Cabinet plays an important role in co-ordinating the policies of various governmental departments. These departments can not be separated into water tight compartments and thus a constant liaison among their operations is essential. It not only ensures that the work of different departments does not overlap but also ensures that they do not adopt contradictory policies. In other words, it tries to iron out all the differences among them. In this regard the cabinet is assisted by the cabinet secretariat. The Cabinet Secretariat co-ordinates the work of the cabinet, it's administrative affairs and looks after the implementation of the policies laid down by the cabinet and approved by the Diet.[57]

3. *Legislative Function-* The role of Japanese cabinet is further important in guiding, managing and controlling the legislative business of the Diet. It initiates most of the legislative bills and submits them to the Diet. It affixes signatures on all laws and cabinet orders. It also issues cabinet orders to execute the provisions of the constitution of law.[58] It further regulates the business of the House of Representatives. It even advises its dissolution.

4. *Exercise Effective Control and Supervision over Governmental Working-* The cabinet ministers, being the heads of their respective departments are responsible for effectively managing their respective affairs. As a result, they exercise tight control and supervision over the business of their respective department. They try to ensure that the respective policies of the government formed by the cabinet be implemented in letter and spirit. In this way, the cabinet exercises its control and supervision over the different branches of administration. It ensures that the law is administered faithfully and thus the affairs of the state are conducted properly. It presents reports on general national affairs and foreign relations to the Diet.[59]

5. *Controller of Finance-* The cabinet also exercises its tight control over the purse string of the nation. It prepares the outlines of budget in association with other departments and ultimately finalizes it. It further decides with regard to the imposition of new taxes, enhancement of existing taxes and their collection. It submits the budget to the Diet and gets it passed. Its role is significant in the execution of the budget. It conducts both pre and post budget scrutiny and tries to remove the irregularities. It further submits the final accounts of expenditure and revenue to the Diet along with the statement of audit prepared by the Board of Audit.[60]

6. *Take Decisions on major unforeseen Situations-* In addition to the management of routine affairs, the cabinet had to take decisions with regard to unforeseen situations also. These situations may be generated due to natural calamities like flood, earthquake, draught etc and require immediate cabinet decisions. Besides, the problems with regard to environment protection may further need urgent cabinet decisions. To combat such unforeseen situations the cabinet makes

---

57 *Ibid*, p. 361
58 Bhagwan, Vishnoo and Vidya Bhusan, *op. cit.*, p. 33.
59 *Ibid*, p. 33.
60 *Ibid*

payments for them from the reserve fund in the budget and gets the subsequent Diet's approval.[61]

(C) LOCAL GOVERNMENT

Prior to the Meiji Restoration (1867), the Japanese governmental system had been characterized by the modernized feudal system. There existed more than 300 feudal lords who maintained their own military to rule and govern their respective territories and thus collect rent from the villages encompassing their territory. These lords ultimately had to operate under the overall control of Tokugawa Shogunate. To stabilize the feudal system, the lords organized the local system further. In this system the villages are entitled as "factual entities". The head of the village was responsible for the collection of rent and thus acted as mediator between the people and the lord.[62]

The Meiji Restoration in 1867, led to dramatic change of the entire feudal system into the Imperial system that compelled the feudal lords to return their territories to the central government which smoothened the path of the establishment of the prefectures as administrative districts through out the country in 1871. Resultantly, the "factual entities" began to metamorphose into modern administrative local authorities and with the enactment of Imperial Constitution; the local autonomous system was set up. In 1878, *San-shinpo*, (Three New Ordinances)[63] marked the first step in the history of modern local government system in Japan.

In 1888, the Municipal Government Act, mainly drafted and modelled on the Prussian local system, was promulgated. This Act led to the introduction of a system of municipalities (cities, towns and villages) and provided for the publicly elected municipal assemblies along with a Mayor as the executive head. "Mayors of *Cho* (towns) and *Son* (villages) were to be elected among the members of the assembly, while those of *Shi* (cities) were appointed by the Minister of Interior from the list of candidates made by the assemblies themselves."[64] The promulgation of the Prefectural Government Act in 1890 provided for the publicly elected prfectural assemblies along with a governor as the executive head nominated by the Minister of Interior.[65]

Further to promote rationalization of local administrative areas and to remove the social influence of the feudal lords, the Meiji Government, proceeded with the consolidation of prefectures and municipalities in order to implement the local autonomous system effectively. As a result, 309 territories which belonged to the feudal lords were consolidated into 47 prefectures and 19 cities and 71,478 towns

---

61 Ibid, p. 34.
62 http: www.soum.go.jp/pdf/lgsij.pdf dated 28.3.09
63 The Municipal Formation Ordinance divided prefectures into counties (*Gun*) and cities (*Ku*), and subdivided counties into towns and villages (*Cho and Son*). Three of these divisions, *Ku*, *Cho and Son*, had the dual character of local public entities and of national administrative constituencies. The Prefectural Assembly Ordinance, which introduced prefectural assemblies composed of elected members, and the Local Tax Ordinance, which provided procedures for collecting local taxes, and gave prefectures the characteristics of local authorities, to some extent. These ordinances show some of the basic elements of the Japanese local government system which remains today. (See http: www.soum.go.jp/pdf/lgsij.pdf retrieved on 28.3.09.
64 Ibid
65 Ibid

and villages which were again consolidated into 39 cities and 15, 820 towns and villages by 1889. The number of municipalities was, thus, reduced to one fifth.[66]

However, the central government's extensive control over these bodies led to shrink their powers. It was mainly because the governors in the prefectures being nominated by the central government had to operate under the direct supervision and control of the Minister of Interior. Moreover most of them happened to be the bureaucrats. The position was also similar at the municipality level. However, after 1911, trivial changes were made at this level. The mayors were selected by the municipal assemblies but they had to operate under the strong general control of the Minister of Interior and the governors of the respective prefectures.

The trend towards more democratization of local government continued and "the wave of "Taisho Democracy" pushed the government to extend suffrage and eligibility for election to all men over 20 years of age (by the revision of election system in 1921 and 1926): the prefectures were permitted to enact regulations in 1929..." [67] Thus the period from the 1890s to the 1920s can be marked as the evolutionary stage of the local government system under the Imperial Constitution. However, the adoption of emergency measures and the increased centralization in the wake of preoccupation of Japan with the war after 1929, the powers of the local authorities were curtailed and this situation became grimmer in 1943.[68]

After the defeat of Japan in World War II, a complete revival of the national and local government took place. The tendency towards democratization of local government was so extensive that it led to the promulgation of Local Autonomy Law in 1947. "The principles of this law involved a respect for local self-government, the separation of the executive and legislative branches and the definition of local councils and their status in relation to central government."[69] Under the new system, more powers were assigned to councils and their sphere of responsibility was widened. The control, earlier maintained by the central government over these bodies, was abolished and now its control is restricted only to render advice and recommendations. Both municipalities and prefectures were made autonomous entities. The powers of local assemblies have been reinforced by extending the scope of the matters on which it can vote. In the elections of governors, mayors and members of assemblies, a system of direct citizens involvement (including women) has been introduced where the citizens elect them by direct voting. The formerly supervisory body (the Ministry of Interior) was abolished.[70]

In the post war scenario, a two tier system of local government much influenced from the American model was created in Japan. In fact, the core legislation divided the local public entities into two major categories – the municipalities, which were further broken down into cities, towns, and villages and the prefectures. The prefectures are comparable to the counties and the municipalities are comparable to the cities and towns of the U.S. Further, there exists many special local authorities

---

66 Toshiyuhi Masujima and Minoru Ouchi, *The Management and Reform of Japanese Government* (ed), Tokyo: The Institute of Administrative Management, 1993, p. 56.
67 http: www.soum.go.jp/pdf/lgsij.pdf retrieved 28.3.09
68 Ibid
69 http://www.citymayors.com/government/jap_locgov.html retrieved on 30 May 2007.
70 Toshiyuki Masujima and Minoru O'uchi, *op. cit.*, p. 56-57.

within the prefectures and municipalities which have equivalence with the special districts in the United States.

Unlike the US, the Japanese local government, to a great extent is structurally uniform except the local government in Tokyo and a few designated cities.[71] Further it needs to be pointed out that the local government in Japan has been assigned with such responsibilities and functions like social insurance, healthcare, strategic planning, disaster management, police and fire fighting services that usually falls within the realm of central government in most of the countries.[72] Consequently, in the administrative sphere, budgetary matters and local legislations/bylaws, the prefectures and municipalities enjoy considerable autonomy. To impart local services to the citizens, the Japanese local government imposes a variety of taxes. Average Japanese citizen has a considerable tax burden for the services he enjoys. "For instance, the prefectures are empowered to levy taxes on tobacco consumption, fuel, car purchases and a general sales tax, while the municipalities can levy property, residency and city planning taxes."[73]

In the post-war scenario the demand of ensuring rationality and efficiency at local level got impetus. This resulted in the insertion of organizational as well as fiscal reforms at local level. In this regard, a mention of the Shoup Report of 1949 can be made which provided a theoretical base to the Japanese local government system. Apart from emphasizing on the 'adequate redistribution of tasks to each level of local governments' it also stressed on the 'reinforcement of financial resources for local authorities.' The large scale reforms pertaining to the local tax system in the 1950s is an outcome of the influence of this report. Further the passage of the Local Public Service Law (1950) and the Local Public Enterprise Law (1952) by the Diet led to the establishment of the local civil service system and the local public enterprise system respectively. In 1953, the Municipal Merger Promotion Law was introduced which proved significant in a sweeping reorganization of municipalities and reducing their number to a sufficient extent. To boost up the general deterioration of local public finance in 1954, Special Measures Law on Local Public Finance Restructuring was enacted in 1955[74]. In 1960, the cabinet established the Home Affairs Ministry (having the charge of planning and co-ordinating administrative and financial systems in the local governments) as the liaison office between the central and local governments. As an outcome, "... the reinforcement of relations between central and local governments and between prefectures and municipalities can be observed largely by way of non-authoritative action."[75]

In Japan, the decade of the 1960s can be marked as an era of economic growth which led to concentration of industry and population in large cities and the neglect

---

71 The only exceptions to this are the 13 designated cities, which enjoy more autonomy than basic municipalities and Tokyo, being the nation's capital has the special arrangements of having an elected Metropolitan Government headed by a Governor and 23 Wards as sub-councils for the central Tokyo area. Under this arrangement, the division of responsibilities that usually takes place between prefectures and municipalities is different. See web. http://www.citymayors.com/government/jap_locgov.html visited on 30 may 2007.
72 Ibid
73 Ibid
74 http: www.soum.go.jp/pdf/lgsij.pdf retrieved on 28.3.09
75 Ibid

of the countryside. This growth of Japan not only promoted the 'excessive influx of the population to urban areas' but also led to generate the problem of noise and pollution during this period. Visualizing such tendencies and to ensure an overall development of the nation the necessity of 'enactment of legislation for new industrial cities promoting rural development with the initiative of local authorities'[76] was made. This problem required "...a shift from development to environmental protection and social welfare for residents. Local authorities showed sensitivity to this problem which directly affected the lives of residents. They enacted bylaws for the regulation of pollution ahead of national legislation."[77]

The momentum of economic growth was slow down by the Oil Crisis in 1973 specifically in the late 1970s which ultimately affected the health of public finance at both national and local level. To overcome the problem of fiscal deficit, the governments took financial and administrative reforms in the 1980s. A Special Advisory Council on Administrative Reform was convened thrice by the Cabinet for suggesting rationalization of central and local administration. Efforts were made to reduce the financial dependence of the local government on national subsidies. "Supported by the economic boom of the late 80s, the local governments shifted their uniformed policies to various policies cheering up and creating regional diversity. The recession after the collapse of the "economic bubble" in the 1990s exposed all the structural problems accumulated since the end of the WWII, and the local government system was not the exception."[78] The emergence of 'structural reform for decentralization' as a major issue in 1993 at the level of political coalition of various parties, ultimately led to the enactment of Decentralization Promotion Law in 1995. "The aim was to set forth the principles of decentralization and to clarify the procedures to realize it by setting up the Decentralization Promotion Committee". In 1998, the committee recommended five prominent recommendations on the basis of which the government drafted a Decentralization Promotion Plan and submitted it to the Diet.[79] Further, in January 1999, 'a reform package containing more than 500 related legal amendments was also submitted before the Diet and after being passed, it was implemented from April 2000.

Meanwhile, the move towards 'more mergers' of local authorities and the heavy reliance on the private sector and the reinforcement of municipal co-operation led to the introduction of the revisions of the Municipal Merger Special Measures Law in 1995 and 1999 and 'fortified initiatives for assembling a joint council for mergers and fiscal assistance for mergers'. Consequently it was decided to merge 581 joint councils by March 2005, Later on this Law was replaced by new Municipal Merger Special Measures Law in April, 2005, and under the new law the government will

---

76 Ibid
77 Ibid
78 Ibid
79 The biggest feature was the abolition of the "agency-delegated tasks", which started from the pre-war era when the state delegated tasks to the appointed prefectural governors, and the comprehensive "directive and supervisory power" of the government related to these tasks. The plan also called for the reduction and reorganization of subsidies appropriated to local governments for specific purposes, which were other tools that the state used to intervene in local government. See website http: www.soum.go.jp/pdf/lgsij.pdf retrieved on 28.3.09

keep 'promoting municipal merger for 5 years more[80]. The government is aimed at reforming the existing number of municipalities into just 1,000.[81]

LOCAL GOVERNMENT STRUCTURE:

In Japan the local public entities can broadly be categorized into two categories- ordinary local public entities – prefectures and municipalities and special local public entities-special wards, co-operatives etc. Though most of the local public services are discharged by the former, yet the latter are institutionalized for discharging some specific function. In comparison to the ordinary local public entities the organization and functions of the special local public entities are limited. A brief description of both kinds of local public entities is as under:

I. **Ordinary Local Public Entities**: In this category a two tier structure of local government units is included which has been in existence since 1921, despite many arguments for reforms. The upper tier is called prefecture and the bottom tier is called municipality. Originally, the prefecture system was introduced by the Meiji government by abolishing the han system in July, 1871.[82] Initially there were "... over 300 prefectures, many of them being former han territories, this number was reduced to 72 in the latter part of 1871, and 47 in 1888."[83] However, the prefecture system got more political powers and importance only after the passage of the Local Autonomy Law. Even today the number of prefectures in Japan is same. These includes – one "metropolis"(Tokyo), one "circuit"(Hokkaido), two urban (Osaka and Kyoto) and 43 other prefectures popularly called To, Do, Fu and Ken respectively in Japan.[84] The territory of each prefecture is divided into cities, towns and villages which are governed through municipalities. The term municipality is further divisible into three categories: *Shi* (cities), *Cho* (towns) and *Son* (villages). Structurally, the institutional characteristics of cities differ from town as well as villages i.e. 'larger number of council members and the establishment of social welfare offices' etc. To obtain a title of 'city', a population of more than 50,000 is necessary.[85] The present Special City system in Japan is broadly classified into three categories: Designated Cities (*Shitei Toshi*)[86], Core Cities (*Chukaku-Shi*)[87] and exceptional cities (*Tokurei-Shi*)[88]. The more concentration of population in cities requires special measures to assign

---

80   Ibid
81   http://www.citymayors.html com/government/japlocgov.
82   http://en.wikipedia.org/wiki/prefectures_of_Japan last visited on 30 May, 2007.
83   Ibid
84   http: www.soum.go.jp/pdf/lgsij.pdf retrieved on 28.3.09
85   It is reduced to 30,000 for merged municipalities by March 31, 2010. In addition to this, more than 60% of the total number of residences is located within the central urban area and almost same percentage is engaged in commercial, industrial or other urban activities and other conditions introduced by prefectural byelaws. See web. http: www.soum.go.jp/pdf/lgsij.pdf retrieved on 28.3.09
86   A city with a population of more than 500,000 designated by Cabinet order is known as a designated city.
87   This categorization is introduced in 1994 and such cities are smaller than the designated cities and are allowed to share limited prefectural responsibilities. The criteria for being designated a "core city" are that the city has a population of more than 300,000 and an area of more than 100 km.
88   They are introduced in late 2000, and these are smaller than "core cities" and are allowed to share some prefectural responsibilities to an even more limited extent. The criterion for the designation is that the city has a population of more than 200,000.

some of the powers usually reserved for the prefectures. Since April 2007, there are 1,804 municipalities – [*Shi* (cities) 782, designated cities 17, core cities 35, exceptional cities 44, ordinary cities 686, *Cho* (towns) 827, *Son* (villages) 195] in Japan.[89] A brief description of the ordinary local public entities is as under.

A. Prefecture – Prefecture is the most important unit of the ordinary local public entities. The whole country is divisible into 47 prefectures. It is the upper-level local public entity that comprises municipalities. The composition of almost each prefecture is same except the special ward system in Tokyo. In Japan the names of the prefectures differ from each other and this distinction instead of indicating any substantive difference, is merely for historical reasons. Though in the hierarchical order, the prefecture stands above the municipalities of which it is comprised, however it cannot exercise hierarchical or authoritarian power over them. The tasks of both are separate and are specifically mentioned by the Local Autonomy Law. Thus they co-operate on an equal standing as local entities with each other. As per this Law, the arena of prefecture includes three broad tasks - tasks covering a broader area than municipal territory; tasks requiring the co-operation and co-ordination of multiple municipalities; tasks exceeding the capacity of municipalities for efficient implementation.[90] The composition of each prefecture includes prefectural assembly and chief executive, a brief discussion of which is as under:

Prefectural Assembly - A single chamber assembly constitutes the legislative wing in a prefecture. Its members known as councillors are elected for a term of four years. During this term, the councillors are prohibited from simultaneously holding any other public office[91] or working as local civil servants. All these restrictions are imposed to root out the possibility of any sort of unfairness and to ensure that the councillors may act in a moral and ethical way. They are elected directly by adult suffrage.[92] For candidature eligibility, a councillor must have attained an age of 25 and must be a resident of that prefecture for more than 3 months prior to election. The number of councillors in a prefectural assembly depends upon the population of the prefecture and thus varies from 40 to 120 in different prefectures[93].

The councillors of each assembly elect a chairman and a vice chairman amongst them. The chairman of the assembly is entrusted with the task of managing the business of the assembly sessions. He presides over the sessions of the assembly and maintains necessary decorum. He also represents the assembly in external matters. In the absence of the chairman, the vice-chairman discharges his functions. The assembly meets at its regular sessions as determined by byelaws. However, special sessions can be convened if needed by the governor or on the demand of at least one fourth of the total councillors. The bills in the assembly may be submitted by the governor or with the consent of one twelfth of the total councillors. But bills on some issues fall within the privilege of the executive only. For instance, the

---

89 http://www.soum.go.jp/pdf/lgsij.pdf retrieved as on 28.3.09
90 *Ibid*
91 They are prohibited from simultaneously being a member of the National Diet (the House of Representatives or the House of Councillors), or a councillor in any other local authority.
92 For the voting right a person must have attained an age of 20 years and must have resided in the concerned prefecture for a period of more than three months.
93 Tokyo Metropolis is an exception with 130 members.

original budget plan can be submitted to the assembly only by the governor. The assembly can be dissolved by the governor of the prefecture before the completion of its term. The members of an assembly may even be recalled by the electorate. Generally all the decisions are made through deliberations in the plenary sessions of the assembly. But due to the increase in volume and complexity of issues and problems, a network of committees has been instituted to facilitate deliberations. Three types of committees - standing committees[94], steering committee[95] and special committees[96] have been constituted by the respective assembly for this purpose.

For the management of the prefectural affairs, the assembly performs diverse nature of functions. It enacts bye laws having the same force as that of national laws, provided these are not in contradiction with the national legislation. It passes the annual budget, discusses the audit report, imposes taxes and fixes the fees for public services. It can even enter into contracts and manage public property under its control. It also enjoys the power to authorize the filling of law suits/administrative appeals.[97] Besides, it directs and supervises the activities of the respective municipality and co-ordinates its activities. It can inspect any document or book related to affairs of the local authority and demand an administrative or financial report from the executive officer.

Governor - The head of the prefecture is called governor who is elected by direct election by the electorates of the prefecture. This procedure of electing the chief executive, make him independent from the council. The tenure of the governor is four years which is co-terminus to that of the councillors. Any Japanese citizen[98] who has attained the age of 30 is qualified to this office. After being elected to the office, the governor has to shed the membership of the Diet or the prefectural assembly if he happened to be their member.

The governor in a prefecture discharges a variety of functions. He enacts regulations; submits bills to the council and gives assent to the bills passed by the latter. He is further responsible for preparing and executing the prefectural budget. He also submits reports on accounts; levies and collects local taxes and fees; and manages public properties.[99]

Since both the prefectural assembly and the governor are elected by direct election, so they remain independent but due to sharing of tasks, a possibility of conflict arises. To maintain harmony, a system of checks and balances has been introduced in Japan. The Governor can veto the resolution of the assembly and enjoys the power to dissolve it before the expiry of its term. Every bill passed by the assembly needs the approval of the Governor and when the bill is sent to the Governor for his approval, he may pass it or veto it. In the latter case, if the assembly passed

---

94 These committees are created to deliberate, investigate and examine bills and petitions related to their specialty on various domains of administration.
95 It is engaged in the management of sessions, i.e. acceptance of bills, investigation of petitions.
96 Such committees are created to deliberate either on issues concerning several standing committees or on some specific important themes.
97 http: www.soum.go.jp/pdf/lgsij.pdf retrieved on 28.3.09
98 In case of governor it is not necessary that he should be a resident of the concerned Prefecture.
99 http: www.soum.go.jp/pdf/lgsij.pdf retrieved on 28.3.09

that bill again by a 2/3 majority, the bill is deemed to be passed[100]. Alternatively, the prefectural assembly is empowered to pass a no confidence motion supported by a 2/3 majority against him. In such circumstances, the governor will have two options – either to resign or to dissolve the assembly and call for a fresh election. In the latter case, if the newly elected assembly also passes a vote of no confidence motion, he has to vacate his office. The governor may even be removed by means of a recall i.e. if 1/3 of the electorate in the prefecture file a petition for his removal and the petition is approved by majority of voters in a recall election.[101]

The governor of a prefecture operates in several capacities and thus performs multifarious functions. Apart from the chief executive of the prefecture, he also acts as the agent of the centre and supervisor of the municipalities. A brief description of his role is as under:

(i) *As Chief Executive* – In the prefecture, the governor is responsible for the effective management of the prefectural affairs. If necessary he may appoint an assistant governor and other prefectural officials to assist him. These functionaries operate at his disposal. He promulgates the regulations and ordinances and imposes fines up to a certain extent for their violation. In this context, his role is crucial in the management of financial and administrative affairs of the prefecture.

(ii) *As an Agent of the Centre* – Being the agent of the centre, he ensures the smooth and efficient execution of the laws and policies passed by the Diet, decisions given by the Supreme Court and the direction issued by the central government from time to time. Moreover, he plays a significant role in managing the other national affairs within the prefecture and exercises general supervision and control. He is also responsible for the effective execution of all the programes framed by the central government in the prefecture.

(iii) *As supervisor of the Municipalities:* The Governor's power of co-ordination also authorizes him to supervise and direct the working of municipalities. He exercises control over the mayors in his prefecture and can direct them to perform their responsibilities by obtaining writ of mandamus against them.

B. Municipality: Municipalities are primary level local entities which take charge of all local administration other than those tasks attributed to prefectures. Like the prefectures every municipality is also designed in a uniform way in Japan. They consist of a municipal assembly and a directly elected Mayor. A brief description of which is as under:

Municipal Assembly: It is the legislative wing of the municipality. The councillors of the assembly are elected directly for a term of four years by the residents who have attained the age of twenty. For candidature eligibility, a councillor must have attained an age of 25 and must be a resident of that municipality for more than 3 months prior to election. Having been elected to the assembly, a councillor is not allowed to hold other public offices or work as a local civil servant simultaneously. The number of councillors in an assembly depends upon the population of a locality

---

100 The Local Autonomy Law also provides for another procedure to review illegal decisions via which the council and the governor may appeal to the Minister for Internal Affairs and Communications or to the court.

101 N. Jayapalan, *Modern Governments*, New Delhi: Atlantic Publishers and Distributors, 1999, p. 155.

and thus the size of the municipal assemblies of various local authorities[102] varies from each other.

Councillors of each municipality elect a chairman and a vice chairman amongst them. The chairman is responsible for the management of the affairs of the assembly. He presides over the assembly sessions and smoothly runs the business of these sessions and in his absence, the vice chairman assumes the duties of the chairman.

The assembly meets at its regular sessions as determined by byelaws. However, special sessions can be convened if needed, by the mayor or on the demand of at least one fourth of the total councillors of the municipal assembly. The bills in the assembly may be submitted by the mayor or with the consent of one twelfth of the total councillors of the municipal assembly. The assembly can be dissolved by the mayor of the municipality before the expiry of its tenure. The members of an assembly may even be recalled by the electorate of the concerned municipality.

Being the legislative wing, the assembly at the municipal level discharges a multiple number of functions. It enacts bye laws in tune with the prefectural and national laws. It passes the annual budget, imposes taxes and fixes the fees for public services. It also determines the matters relating to levy and collection of taxes. It further, investigates into local affairs and imposition of penalties for violation of its by-laws. Specific concern of the municipal assembly includes - the fire services; the maintenance and construction of municipal roads and small rivers; provision of kindergartens, establishment of libraries, museums and civic halls and other cultural facilities, ensuring environmental sanitation, extending various health care services and undertaking agricultural, fishery, forestry, industrial and commercial services.[103]

Mayor - The mayor is the chief executive of the municipality and is elected directly for a period of 4 years by the residents of that municipality. His election is separate from that of the councillors which provide him legitimacy independent of the municipal assembly. Any Japanese citizen[104] who has attained the age of 25 is eligible to this post. Like the councillors, the mayor once elected to this office can not hold any other public office simultaneously.

As both the municipal assembly and the mayor are elected by direct election, hence they remain independent, which may result into conflict due to sharing of tasks. To overcome such conflicts, there exists a system of checks and balances. The mayor may send back a resolution passed by the assembly for review but if the assembly passed that resolution again by a 2/3 majority, the resolution is deemed to be passed. Alternatively, the municipal assembly may pass a no-confidence motion against him by two-thirds majority. He may even be removed from his office on losing the requisite eligibility for election, or a recall by the electorates.

The functions of the mayor in a municipality are almost analogous to that of the governor in a prefecture. The Mayor in a municipality operates in twin capacities as under:

---

[102] Cities have 26 -96 councillors whereas towns and villages have 12 - 26 councillors. Local authorities set the number through bylaws in the range of these maximums. See http: www.soum.go.jp/pdf/lgsij.pdf retrieved on 28.3.09
[103] Samuel Humes and others, *op.cit.*, p. 451.
[104] In case of mayor it is not necessary that he should be a resident of the concerned municipality.

i) *As Chief Executive Officer* – He is responsible for the effective management of the municipal affairs. He is empowered to appoint and remove supervisors and other municipal officials to assist him. He provides for budget allocations at the municipality level and submits the same to the assembly. The bills passed by the assembly needs his assent to become laws. He enjoys limited veto which can be overridden by a special (2/3) majority of the assembly. He can issue regulations which have the same force as that of bye-laws during emergency. Besides, he is also responsible for the collection of local taxes and auditing of local accounts.[105] In brief, he is the manager of the financial and administrative affairs of the municipality.

ii) *As an Agent of the Centre* – At the municipality level, the mayor operates as the agent of the central government. So, he is entrusted with all those matters that are of national importance. He ensures the smooth enforcement of central laws and the judgments of the Supreme Court at the municipality level. Besides, he carries out the directions of the central ministers as well as the governor of the respective prefecture. He is further, responsible for the promotion of child welfare services, prevention of epidemics; maintenance of national roads; city planning tasks; and census registration. To discharge his duties effectively in this respect he is assisted by an assistant mayor(s), a treasurer, and directors of a number of bureaus or departments, and other staff as needed.[106]

II **Special Local Entities**: Like the USA, in Japan also, there exits special purpose local bodies along with above discussed ordinary local bodies. They comprise special wards, co-operatives of local authorities and other special entities. These bodies have been institutionalized to attain a specific purpose A. brief description of these bodies is as under:

1) *Special Wards*

   Like any other country, the Tokyo Metropolis, being the capital of Japan has a different pattern of managing its local affairs. Unlike the composition of almost each prefecture there exists the special ward system. It may be mainly because it has a population of more than ten million. There exists 23 special wards in the capital to discharge some functions such as sewerage or garbage disposal etc. These functions have been transferred from the Tokyo Metropolitan Government to these wards by amending the Local Autonomy Law, recently in April, 1998. Some of the special provisions applicable exclusively to special wards were either revised or repealed by this amendment and they were explicitly given the legal status.[107]

2) *Co-operatives of Local Authorities*

   Due to the increasing complexities in the tasks of local bodies over the years, sometimes, these tasks are beyond the capacity of a local body. Consequently, to overcome this handicap, prefectures and municipalities may create co-operatives of local authorities (*Kumiai*) for the sake of efficiency. The Local Autonomy Law provides four categories of co-operatives as per

---

105 Bombwall, K.R., *op.cit.*, p. 543.
106 Samuel Humes and others, *op. cit.*, p. 451.
107 http: www.soum.go.jp/pdf/lgsij.pdf retrieved on 28.3.09

their functions. This includes full co-operatives[108], joint-office co-operatives[109], partial co-operatives[110] and wide-area union[111].

3) **Other Special Entities**

In addition to these special wards and co-operatives, there exists other special entities viz., property wards[112], local development corporations[113] and special districts in merged municipalities.

(D) CONTROL MACHINERY

Like Britain, the Shova Constitution in Japan establishes a parliamentary democracy where sovereignty lies with the people. So the holders of public offices derive their authority from the Constitution and are responsible to the common people for the authority exercised by them. To safeguard the public interest, sufficient accountability measures have been devised by the Japanese Administration. To keep an effective control over the working of administrative machinery in Japan, both internal as well as external checks have been introduced. The control exercised by the executive falls in the former category where as the control exercised by the Diet and the Judiciary falls in the latter category. A brief description of control machinery in Japan is as under:

I. Legislative Control: The legislative control in Japan is exercised by the Diet which is the highest law-making body of the State. It not only plays a crucial role in law making process but also interferes in the operational working of administration. However, in comparison with the British Parliament, the position of the Diet is quite weak in Japan. It approves all the administrative policies and frame certain laws required to regulate and control the administrative system. It also gives legal form to the decrees issued by the Emperor. The Diet in Japan exercises control over the administration in the following manner:

1. *Determination of Policies and Laws*: The Diet, being the legislative body, is responsible for framing laws and policies which, thus, regulates the working of administration. The laws and policies before being passed, undergo a lot of debates and discussion in both the Houses of Diet. During the course of such debate and discussion, the members of the Diet may, apart from criticizing the proposed legislations, also point out the failures of the government in general. Besides, the Diet in Japan also approves all the decrees issued by the executive.

---

108 In such co-operatives member authorities delegate all their affairs to them. Such co-operatives have not yet been set up.

109 Here the member authorities unify their executive offices. Unlike the full co-operatives, these are also not been set up till date.

110 These are the most popular co-operatives in which member authorities delegates some specific areas of service to them, such as garbage disposal, fire, defense or compulsory education.

111 These co-operatives are instituted in 1994. This co-operative not only takes charge of what is accorded to it in the 'wide-area plan' by the member authorities but undertakes tasks delegated by the central government or the non-participant prefecture. The wide-area union also has the characteristics of a stronger and more participatory liaison with residents in regard to the stipulation of initiatives to the union.

112 The local Autonomy Law provides for the existence of 'property wards' owned by a municipality for the management of forests, marshlands, irrigation canals, cemeteries, etc.

113 They are created jointly by several local authorities to develop a specified domain of public service. However; recently the use of this institution is very rare.

2. *Question-Hour:* In a parliamentary system, parliamentary questions act as a potent instrument in exercising control over the administrative system. Like Britain, in Japan, also any member of the Diet can ask questions or seek information from the ministers on matters of public interest. They may seek information both through oral and written question as per Article 63 of the Constitution. The urgent questions are usually answered orally whereas for asking written questions, a prior notice of 7 days is required. It is an important means to highlight the shortcomings of the executive and ventilating the grievances of the people.[114] However the control through question-hour is not effective as much as in Britain. It is because the questions are asked on the last day of the week in the afternoon when most of the ministers are in a hurry to leave for their respective homes. Some of the questions are rarely answered in the House.

3. *No-Confidence Motion:* No-confidence motion is still another crucial tool to exercise an effective control over the working of executive. The Cabinet in Japan will remain in office as long as it enjoys the confidence of the House of Representatives. If the House passes a no confidence motion against the cabinet, the government has no option but to resign. This motion can be brought in the House either due to the general poor performance of the government or its failure on some particular front. If the House does not approve either the whole policy or a part of it, it would also be equivalent to that of no confidence.

4. *Budgetary Control:* Budget is an important instrument in the hands of the Diet to exercises its control over administration. Through budget the Diet in Japan exercise a full control over the purse string of the nation. Being a parliamentary form of government, the executive in Japan has to seek the prior approval of the Diet before appropriating public money. In fact, without its prior sanctions, the executive can't spend even a single penny. It also streamlines the taxation proposals. No fresh taxes can be levied nor can any sort of alteration be affected without its consent. When the budget is presented before the Diet, its members get an opportunity to review and criticize the operational working of government. Thus the debate on the annual budget is an important instrument in the hands of Diet as it provides an opportunity to the opposition to reveal deficiencies in the overall working of the government.

5. *Control through Committees:* Like the other modern democracies, the Diet in Japan also operates through committees and thus forms the core of the legislative process. The committee system in Japan resembles more like that of the US. The Meiji Constitution could not attach more importance to these committees. However, under the Showa Constitution, they have been assigned vital role in the legislative process. In general the Diet has two main types of committees -- standing committees and special committees. The former are permanent in nature and are appointed for the whole duration of Diet while the latter are temporary in nature and came to an end with the completion of the assigned work. In 1955, the number of standing committees has been reduced from 22 to 16 in each House.[115] The number of members of these standing committees

---

114 Bhagwan, Vishnoo and Vidya Bhusan, *World Constitution*, Sterling publishers Pvt Ltd, 8th revised edition, reprented in 2006, p. 472.

115 *Ibid*, p. 478.

may range from 20 to 50. In the process of law–making, the standing committees play a vital role. "All the bills introduced in the Diet are referred to the Standing Committee concerned. The committee examines the bill thoroughly. It may hold public meetings and invite persons to give their public opinion."[116] After a lot of deliberations on the proposed bill, it prepares a report which is presented to the House by its Chairman. Besides, each House may appoint a special committee to study a particular problem. "Such a committee may be appointed to investigate into any particular problem like a disaster, an administrative scandal, repatriation, trade etc. In February 1960, the Diet appointed a special committee of forty-five members to reconsider the proposal of the Americo-Japanese peace treaty." [117]

II. Executive Control: The executive in any democratic country exercises an effective control over administration. Sitting at the apex of the administration, it keeps a constant surveillance over its operational activities. Like India and the UK, the Japanese Cabinet headed by the prime minister constitutes the executive which plays a significant role not only in streamlining the working of administration but also regulating and controlling its business. The executive adopts the following ways to exercise its control over the administration:

1. *Control through Appointment and Removal:* The executive in Japan exercises its control over the administration through his power of appointment and removal. After the selection of the Prime Minister by the Diet, he appoints his team of ministers who need not necessarily be the members of the Diet. These ministers, who head the various departments of administration, work at his disposal. They can be removed by him at any time. Thus he has full control over his cabinet. In addition to this, he makes appointments to all the important offices viz., ambassadors, the chief justice of the Supreme Court, other judges, members of various boards and commissions etc. However these appointments are made by him in prior consultation with his cabinet, yet his choice is final. Through his power of appointment, the executive command and direct a large number of apex administrative officers and keep a close vigil over their activities. Besides, the executive is empowered to remove these functionaries in case there is any charge of mis-behaviour, misdeeds, bribery or any other corrupt practices on their part.

2. *Control through Budget:* The executive in Japan exercises its control over the administration through the budget. The executive plays a crucial role during the budget process. It conducts a detailed pre-budget and post-budget control. It issues broad guidelines to the respective ministries to prepare and submit their annual financial proposals in the form of demands. These financial proposals before being submitted to the cabinet, are scrutinized by the respective heads of the ministries and then by the Finance Ministry. After the preparation of the budget, it is submitted to the Diet for its enactment. During its enactment within the Diet, it clarifies the queries raised by the member of the Diet. Once the budget is approved by the Diet, the Ministry of Finance bears its overall responsibility with regards to its execution. It allocates funds to the respective spending ministries. By keeping in view the allotted budget "… the head of each

---

116 *Ibid*, p. 479.
117 *Ibid*

spending ministry must draft payment plans for each quarter of the year which explains the required expenditures for each disbursing officer, and must acquire approval of the Ministry of Finance."[118] Moreover, each spending ministry is further required to maintain the detailed accounts of the money spent which are to be audited by the Board of Audit.

3. *Control through Administrative Hierarchy*: The Japanese administration being unitary is hierarchical in structure. The whole of Japan operates under the central government at Tokyo as there is no division of power between the Centre and the Prefectures. Japan is divisible into 47 Prefectures which are equivalent to the states in India. The Prefectures in Japan are somewhat like the geographical units which operate under the direct supervision and control of the centre. Each prefecture is headed by a Governor who operates in dual capacities- as the chief executive of the prefecture and as the agent of the centre. The total territory of prefecture is divided into cities, towns and villages which are governed by a municipality. In Japan there exists more than 3300 municipalities. Each municipality is headed by a Mayor. Like the Governor of the Prefecture the Mayor also operates in dual capacities - as the chief executive of the municipality and as the agent of the centre. In hierarchical terms the Mayor is responsible to the Governor of the prefecture for the management of its affairs and likewise the latter is responsible to the government at Tokyo.

4. *Control through Administrative Inspection:* The executive further maintains its control over the administrative machinery through the system of administrative inspection that was created in 1948. Administrative inspection is an evaluative function of the government that is created within the administrative machinery to ameliorate the situation. Through this system, the operation of government programmes are scrutinized and evaluated on the basis of facts or evidences gained through the investigations. This task is discharged by the Management and Co-ordination Agency (MCA). This agency was established in 1984 for strengthening central management and overall co-ordination capabilities of the national government by clubbing the functions of the Administrative Management Agency and the Prime Minister's Office. The agency institutionalizes a nation-wide inspection network. There are seven Regional Administrative Inspection Bureaux and 43 Prefectural Administrative Inspection Offices – to investigate operations and problems in the nation's overall administration. During the administrative inspections, the MCA is entitled by law to all documents and other materials as well as testimony by ministries, agencies and other organizations subject to inspection or investigation.[119]

The objective of administrative inspection is to maintain the effectiveness of government operations, to prevent unlawful or improper practices and damages to the national treasury, and to maintain official discipline. It ensures that administrative operations in different areas of the government are justly,

---

118 Tsukamoto, Hisao, *The budgetary Process, in The management and Reform of Japanese Government* (ed) by Toshiyuki Masujima and Minoru O'uchi, Tokyo: The Institute of Administrative Management, June 1993, p92.

119 http://unpan1.un.org/intradoc/groups/public/documents/UN/UNPAN000230.pdf visited on October 20, 2008.

economically, efficiently and effectively carried out. It is further concerned with suggesting improvement and thus makes recommendations on the basis of its findings to the various ministries and agencies.

5. *Control through Administrative Evaluation*: Internally Administrative Evaluation Bureau (AEB) and its field offices enjoy the authority to conduct administrative evaluation of the programmes launched by the respective governmental departments. Thus they play a crucial role in conducting the performance appraisal of the various programmes of different governmental agencies. After completing an analysis and evaluation of a programme based on the results of surveys/investigations, the Head of the MCA (the Minister of State) recommends areas for improvement to the relevant ministries or agencies. The MCA holds press conferences to explain the results of administrative evaluations and the nature of the recommendations. Mass media helps the public to generate awareness about the problems of these programmes. In addition, they can access information through personal computer networks via the Internet. The MCA has set up an Internet Home Page to improve public access to government information.[120] In this manner, administrative evaluation ensures administrative accountability to the public. Apart from administrative evaluation, there also exists a mechanism of administrative counselling, fitted with in the executive branch to hear the complaints of the common citizens against administrative excesses. Through this system AEB field offices and the administrative counsellors receive citizen's complaints across the country regarding the harassment, misuse of authority and mal-functioning of the governmental agencies and act to bring the matters to a satisfactory conclusion through mediation.

6. *Control through Administrative Reports*: The executive in Japan i.e. the cabinet headed by the prime minister, further exercise their control over the administrative system through the periodic reports sent by the Governors of the prefectures and the Mayors of the municipalities. These administrative reports contain the minute details about the operational working of the prefectures and the municipalities. The central executive conducts a scrutiny of these reports and came to know about the problems and prospects of the administrative working at the subordinate levels.

III Control by Board of Audit:

In order to ensure the fair and proper execution of public finance, every country has its own supreme audit institution with differing name, status and type of organization. In Japan, this institution is popularly known as Board of Audit. Unlike India and the U.K., the Board of Audit is not an extended arm of the Parliament rather it has an independent status. In fact, it is an external means of control over administration and it neither belongs to the legislature nor to the judiciary. Moreover, it is separate from the cabinet also.

To audit the final accounts of expenditure and revenues of State, the Board of Audit in Japan came into existence in 1880. However, the constitutional status was awarded to this Board only after the promulgation of the Meiji Constitution in 1889.

---

120 http://unpan1.un.org/intradoc/groups/public/documents/UN/UNPAN000230.pdf visited on October 20, 2008.

In Japan, this Board supervised the public finances as an independent organ directly subordinate to the Emperor till the enactment of the new Constitution of Japan in 1947. In the new Constitution, Board of Audit Law came into effect under article 90, which made it independent from the cabinet. Moreover, the coverage of audit was also expanded.[121]

Composition: The Board of Audit comprises the Audit Commission and the General Executive Bureau. The earlier is a decision-making organ, whereas the latter is an executive organ. The audit commission consists of three commissioners who are appointed by the cabinet with the consent of both the houses of the Diet. Their appointments are attested by the Emperor of Japan. They hold office for a term of 7 years which is much longer than the term of the executive, to ensure their independence from the executive. The cabinet further appoints the president of the Board which is based on the mutual election among the three commissioners. The president represents the Board and presides over it.[122]

On all crucial matters the audit commission acts as a collegiate decision-making body of the Board. The adoption of the collegiate system of decision making with in the audit commission is to ensure fairness and propriety in its judgments as an evaluating authority. The audit commission directs and supervises the activities carried out by the General Executive Bureau.[123]

The General Executive Bureau comprises of a Secretariat and five Bureaus, under which many divisions are set up to perform auditing and administrative work. The five Bureaus perform audit activities with respect to different ministries, public corporations and other state bodies. They conduct the audit of all government accounts and ensure that money spent by the executive has compliance with the money sanctioned by the Diet.[124]

Status: As has already been discussed the Board of Audit is an independent organ of the government. It has been kept independent from the other organs of the government i.e. the Diet, Cabinet and Courts as a government auditing institution. Article 1 of Board of Audit Law provides that it shall have an independent status of the Cabinet. Consequently, the Board of Audit in Japan enjoys the opportunity to perform its functions without any sort of interference. It is neither appointed by the Diet nor responsible to it. Though it is appointed by the cabinet but its tenure is 7 years which is much longer than the term of the cabinet. This arrangement is made to keep it independent from the executive. Moreover it is also kept independent from the judiciary.

Role: This Board of Audit audits all government accounts and ensures that money spent by the executive has compliance with the money sanctioned by the Diet. Article 20 of *Board of Audit Law* provides that Board of Audit shall

- audit the final accounts of revenues and expenditures of the State.
- constantly audit and review the public accounts to secure their adequacy and to rectify their defects.

---

121 http://www.jbaudit.go.jp/engl/engl2/contents/frame22.htm
122 http://www.jbaudit.go.jp/engl/engl2/contents/body01.htm
123 *Ibid*
124 *Ibid*

- conduct its audit from the viewpoints of accuracy, regularity, economy, efficiency and effectiveness, and from other necessary viewpoints of auditing.[125]

Thus, the Board of Audit annually audits the final accounts of the expenditure and revenue of the State and prepares its audit report. It tries to reveal all sorts of irregularities and misappropriations made by the executive in its report. The report is then sent to the cabinet which is ultimately submitted to the Diet by the cabinet. This report is then used for deliberation of the state's final accounts and for future administration by the financial authorities in the Diet session. This report is further useful in imparting general information to the common people about the results of the state budget execution. The press and the media try to attract the attention of the public with regard to the submission of the Audit Report in the cabinet by presenting their detailed reports.[126] Thus it plays a crucial role in exercising its control over public expenditure

IV. Judicial Control: Under the Showa Constitution the position of the judiciary has been ameliorated to a greater extent in Japan. It has established a unified system of judiciary like India having the Supreme Court at the apex. The Constitution also ensured the independence of the judges through various ways so that impartial judgment may be delivered. "No judge has ever been impeached or removed. Their appointment is enthusiastically approved by the people."[127] The Supreme Court has been equipped with the power of judicial review and as a result it has emerged as the custodian of the citizens rights in Japan. It has been assigned the responsibility of safeguarding the interests of the common people. It protects them from all sorts of administrative excesses and the bureaucratic tyranny. Unlike in the Imperial system, the judiciary now-a-days is free from the executive control in Japan. Today it enjoys the autonomy and freedom to determine the constitutionality of the laws and the executive orders in case they violate the Constitution. Thus, the courts can declare the administrative actions *ultra vires* if they are not in consonance with law. Further, to establish the Rule of Law, the administrative tribunals have been abolished. Thus, the judiciary in Japan is an important means of external control over administration.

Grounds of Judicial Intervention: To safeguard public interest the judiciary in Japan intervenes in the administrative working on a number of grounds. However, these grounds are not hard and fast. In a number of occasions the judiciary in Japan restricts the scope of mal-administration to a great extent and imposes several restrictions on the administration. Following are some such grounds of judicial intervention in Japanese administration:

1. *Lack of Jurisdiction:* Lack of jurisdiction is a prominent ground of judicial intervention in the administrative matters. All the administrative officials have been entrusted with a specified authority and also they are supposed to operate with in a specific area. In case of violation either of the authority or the geographical limit, the judiciary can declare their actions ultra-vires.
2. *Error of Law:* There may be the possibility of wrong interpretation of law by the administrative officials. If a public servant misconstrues the law and imposes

---

125 http://www.jbaudit.go.jp/engl/engl2/contents/frame22.htm
126 *Ibid*
127 Bhagwan, Vishnoo and Vidya Bhusan, *op. cit.*, p. 491.

some obligations on the citizens that are not required by law, then his actions can be challenged in the court of law. The court intervenes in such matters not only to provide a correct explanation of law but also to declare the actions of the administrative official *ultra vires*.

3. *Misuse of Authority:* To attain some personal interest or to harm some people, the administrative officer may utilize his authority in a vindictive manner. In that case the courts can intervene and punish the official if he is found guilty of abusing his authority.

4. *Error in fact-finding:* Some times the administrative officers may take decisions by avoiding the actual facts which may jeopardize the interest of some common citizens. In such cases, the courts intervene in the administrative matters and try to rectify the error in discovering the actual facts.

5. *Error of Procedure:* At some occasions, the administrative officials may side track the officially prescribed procedures which may cause harm to some citizens. In such cases the courts get an opportunity to intervene into administrative matters to question the legality of the actions of such officials.